BONG JOON HO

BONG JOON HO

DIRECTOR'S INSPIRATION
Edited by Michelle Puetz

ACADEMY MUSEUM OF MOTION PICTURES
LOS ANGELES

DELMONICO BOOKS · D.A.P.
NEW YORK

DIRECTOR'S FOREWORD
6

ACKNOWLEDGMENTS
8

INTRODUCTION
10

BONG JOON HO: THE ART OF GENRE
Amy Taubin
16

DIRECTOR'S INSPIRATION: BONG JOON HO
25

Guillermo del Toro
60

Lee Isaac Chung
77

Hong Kyung Pyo
82

Seo Woo-Sik
87

Dooho Choi
95

Catherine George
99

Jung Jaeil
113

Steven Yeun
114

Dede Gardner and Jeremy Kleiner
122

Miky Lee
128

Lee Hajun
132

Choi Woo-shik
135

Robert Pattinson
147

Darius Khondji
150

Dan Glass
155

Toni Collette
160

INTERVIEW: BONG JOON HO
Nam Lee
164

CONTRIBUTORS
186

CREDITS
189

DIRECTOR'S FOREWORD

Director Bong Joon Ho's *Parasite* (2019) made history as the first non-English-language film to win an Academy Award for Best Picture. It was a landmark achievement for Korean cinema and a moment of international recognition for this visionary filmmaker whose stories span many cultures, countries, and languages while retaining an unmistakable creative fingerprint: innovative storytelling, bold themes, and a genre-blending style born from his lived experience and unique way of seeing the world. Bong emphasizes and embodies the universal language and love of cinema—something that, as he has famously said, should not be held back by "the one-inch barrier of subtitles."

It is all of these qualities that make Bong Joon Ho a perfect subject for Director's Inspiration—the Academy Museum's unique exhibition series highlighting preeminent directors and the influences that most shape their work—and it is our honor to be the first museum to deeply explore his filmography and creative process. First and foremost, I'd like to thank Director Bong for generously providing us access to his personal archives, including never-before-seen production materials, without which we could not have had the same insight into his development as an artist. My sincere thanks also to his longtime producer Dooho Choi, whose guidance throughout this process has been truly instrumental.

I would like to express my gratitude to Exhibitions Curator Michelle Puetz and her team, including Assistant Curator Nicholas Barlow and Research Assistants Josue Lopez and Jeongsil Yoon, for creating such an engaging exhibition. At the Academy of Motion Picture Arts and Sciences, I am deeply grateful to CEO Bill Kramer, Chief Operating Officer and Academy Foundation General Counsel Brendan Connell, Jr., Chief Marketing and Communications Officer Jennifer Davidson, and Chief Revenue Officer Jenny Galante, as well as Academy Foundation President Janet Yang, for their unwavering support throughout the planning and organization of this show. I would also like to extend my thanks to Executive Vice President of Exhibitions Shraddha Aryal and Vice President of Curatorial Affairs Doris Berger for making this exhibition a reality, and to Director of Publications Stacey Allan for leading the development of this accompanying book with such care.

Academy Museum Board Trustee Miky Lee, vice-chairwoman of CJ Group, has been a driving force behind the international ascent of Korean cinema. I'm deeply grateful for her support of this project and her enduring commitment to the cinema of Bong Joon Ho. Netflix CEO Ted Sarandos, who also serves on the museum's board, is another longtime champion of Bong's work. I thank them and the entire Academy Museum Board of Trustees, chaired by Olivier de Givenchy, for playing such a vital role in the museum's work through their governance and guidance.

This exhibition was made possible in part by leadership support from CJ ENM, Korea Foundation, and Netflix, with additional support provided by Sara Risher and Yeardley Smith. I extend my thanks to Gerald Schwartz and Heather Reisman, Barbara Roisman Cooper and Martin M. Cooper, Jocelyn R. Katz, John Ptak and Margaret Black, Lauren Shuler Donner, Randy E. Haberkamp, Kevin McCormick and A. Scott Berg, and John and Lacey Williams for their ongoing support of *Stories of Cinema*, which includes the Director's Inspiration exhibitions. Thanks also to our corporate and foundation partners, including PwC, Amazon MGM Studios, Ruderman Family Foundation, FotoKem, Panasonic, Dolby Laboratories, Sony Electronics, and Bloomberg Philanthropies.

Amy Homma
Director and President

ACKNOWLEDGMENTS

One of the great joys of curatorial work is being able to collaborate with living artists. Each opportunity to do so shapes my approach and perspective, but none has affected me as deeply, both professionally and personally, as this one. Organizing this first-ever exhibition on Bong Joon Ho has not only changed the way I see his filmography—both its global importance and its artistry—but it has also changed me. Being able to study how Director Bong works and immerse myself in his personal archive has enriched my understanding of what it truly means to be an artist. My most heartfelt gratitude goes to him for entrusting me with this great honor and for giving us all a glimpse into his creative spirit.

At the Academy Museum, the intellectual rigor, sensitivity, and keen eye of Assistant Curator Nicholas Barlow came at a critical point in the exhibition's development. I am deeply indebted to him, as well as Research Assistants Josue Lopez and Jeongsil Yoon, and to Getty Marrow Curatorial Intern Janice Kim, for their invaluable contributions. Associate Director of Film Programs Hyesung ii joined me in Seoul and offered steady support throughout; her insights and thoughtful contributions touched nearly every part of this project, and her friendship has been a true gift.

This exploration of Bong Joon Ho's work would not have been possible without the guidance, expertise, and unwavering enthusiasm of producer Dooho Choi, an essential partner to me on this journey. Deepest thanks to Joonhee Kim for his critical support and kind hospitality during my trips to Seoul. Jaehyuk Lee and Lee Hajun were extraordinarily generous in sharing their work and offering insights into their creative processes.

The Korean Film Archive provided beautiful preservation files of Bong Joon Ho's films for the exhibition, in addition to scans of posters from their collection. I am grateful to Director Hong-Joon Kim, whose knowledge of and passion for Korean cinema greatly shaped the scope and breadth of this project. Thanks also to Eric Choi, Yeo Eun Jeong, Min Byunghyun, Chonghwa Chung, and Shin Jae-young for their assistance.

Academy Museum board member Miky Lee has long been, and continues to be, a champion of Korean cinema on the global stage. I'm grateful for her early commitment to this project and her ongoing dedication to Bong Joon Ho's work. Thank you to Khan Kwon, Victoria Chon, and Hannah Chun for their assistance throughout. My immense gratitude to all of the exhibition lenders, including CJ ENM, Dooho Choi, Chungeorahm Film, Jaehyuk Lee, Netflix, and ZiBEZI.

Director's Inspiration: Bong Joon Ho would not have been possible without the vision, dedication, and steadfast leadership of the museum's director and president, Amy Homma. Her support and enthusiasm were instrumental in bringing this project to life. Thank you to Academy of Motion Picture Arts and Sciences Chief Executive Officer Bill Kramer and his entire leadership team. Special thanks to Vice President of Advancement Matt Youngner and his team, especially Dawn Mori and Sabira Parajuli. I'm endlessly thankful for Vice President of Curatorial Affairs Doris Berger and my colleagues in the curatorial department for their encouragement and camaraderie throughout.

Exhibitions are collective endeavors made possible by the creativity and skill of many. I am deeply grateful to Executive Vice President of Exhibitions Shraddha Aryal, whose vision and tireless problem-solving were instrumental at every stage of this project. Sincere thanks to her team, especially Phy Cottrell, Greg Eberhardt, Christopher Garcia, Melissa Garza, Kelly Howland, Audra Jacot, Stephen Morrissey, Trevor Myers, Christopher Richmond, Sabrina Sharifi, Will Slade, and Bert Thomas. The steady guidance of Daqian Cao kept us moving forward with unfailing humor and clarity. The exhibition came to life through the thoughtful and elegant work of former exhibition designer Kalani Mah. Chelsea Bingham's sharp intellect brought editorial clarity and nuance to the in-gallery texts. Special thanks to Tempe Hale and Josh Porro, who created impactful original media pieces for the exhibition.

I'd like to thank Director of Registration and Collection Management Renée Kiefer and her team, including Celina Candrella, Jillian Griffith, Veronica Rascona, and Celeste Voce. Very special thanks are due to Bernie Sale, whose expertise and calm perseverance were crucial to the successful realization of the exhibition. The outstanding conservation work of Sophie Hunter, Rio Lopez, Sara Bisi, Dawn Jaros, and Yoojung Hong is visible throughout the galleries. There are many Academy and Academy Museum team members, current and former, who contributed their expertise to this project and have my enduring thanks. Among them I would especially like to acknowledge Jacqueline Stewart; Anne Coco; Sonja Wong Leaon; Lena Wong, Bria Grant, and McKell Forbes; Daniel Gomez, Ananya Iyer, and Michelle Briand; Agnes Stauber and Sarin Cemcem; Drayton Benedict and Emily Tobias; Christina Ybarra, Stephanie Samera, Tuni Chatterji, and Monay Brown; and Erin Golightly.

The realization of this book was only possible through the leadership of Director of Publications Stacey Allan, whose generosity and dedication cannot be overstated. Thank you to her remarkable team, especially Chelsea Bingham and Lars Eckstrom. Writer Darcy Paquet brought skill and sensitivity to his work with our Korean contributors. For their thoughtful book design, I thank Carina Huynh and Adam Michaels of IN-FO.CO. My additional thanks to editor Deirdre O'Dwyer, proofreader Dianne Woo, Mary DelMonico and Karen Farquhar of DelMonico Books, and Tony Manzella of Echelon.

My heartfelt thanks to Amy Taubin for lending her critical voice to this publication. Director Bong has long admired her writing, and her essay frames his work with insight and passion. It has been an honor to work with scholar Nam Lee, whose interview with Bong adds another vital and richly personal dimension to this project. Finally, my deepest gratitude to Dooho Choi, Choi Woo-shik, Lee Isaac Chung, Toni Collette, Guillermo del Toro, Dede Gardner, Catherine George, Dan Glass, Hong Kyung Pyo, Jung Jaeil, Darius Khondji, Jeremy Kleiner, Lee Hajun, Miky Lee, Robert Pattinson, Seo Woo-Sik, and Steven Yeun for sharing their insightful, nuanced, and illuminating perspectives on Bong Joon Ho for this volume.

Michelle Puetz
Exhibitions Curator

INTRODUCTION

The depth and breadth of Bong Joon Ho's love for and knowledge of cinema is seemingly boundless. It is also inseparable from his own visionary and groundbreaking form of story-telling. Set in disparate times and places, featuring monsters both real and imagined, his films blend his unique narrative style with incisive and complex social commentary in such a way that the pleasure of viewing is never compromised. They embed the anxieties and pressures of contemporary life within captivating stories that mix humor, suspense, and emotional depth. He challenges the boundaries between "art house" and "mainstream," proving that socially conscious films can also be entertaining and commercially successful.

Bong is a master of craft: His meticulous attention to structure, pacing, and visual composition results in films that are rich with meaning and endlessly rewatchable. His distinctive voice, tone, and perspective have resonated with global audiences, and the historic wins for *Parasite* (2019) at the 92nd Academy Awards—Directing, Original Screenplay, Best International Film, and Best Picture—symbolized not just personal achievement but a breakthrough moment for non-English-language cinema in the global film industry.

This book and the accompanying exhibition are the third iteration of the Academy Museum's Director's Inspiration series, which takes as its premise the idea that a filmmaker like Bong Joon Ho has established a unique narrative and visual style that can be traced through his body of work and has, in turn, become a touchstone for other filmmakers. By uncovering key aspects of Bong's process and approach, I hope that readers of this book will gain new insights into his films.

Equal parts cinephile and filmmaker, Bong's belief in cinema's power as an international visual language is evident in his own work, as well as in the films he admires. As Guillermo del Toro writes in his contribution

to this book, Bong is "profoundly enamored of cinema. … He doesn't exist high above the material or the medium; he swims in it." Bong's deep love and appreciation for cinema of all kinds—ranging from films like Henri-Georges Clouzot's *The Wages of Fear* (1953) to Joel and Ethan Coen's *Fargo* (1996), Shohei Imamura's *Intentions of Murder* (1964) to John Carpenter's *The Thing* (1982), Steven Spielberg's *Jaws* (1975) to Jane Campion's *An Angel at My Table* (1990)—is so much a part of him that it is inseparable from the films he makes.

At the heart of Bong's filmmaking is a profound mistrust of authority mixed with a deep love and respect for humanity in all its contradictions, complexities, and failings. His films interweave stories of complex yet relatable characters—flawed and compromised reflections of their environment, shaped in response to the systems that surround them. They deny our desire for tidy narrative resolution in favor of exposing the underpinnings of the structures that govern

Installation view of *Director's Inspiration: Bong Joon Ho*, March 23, 2025–January 10, 2027, at the Academy Museum of Motion Pictures, Los Angeles

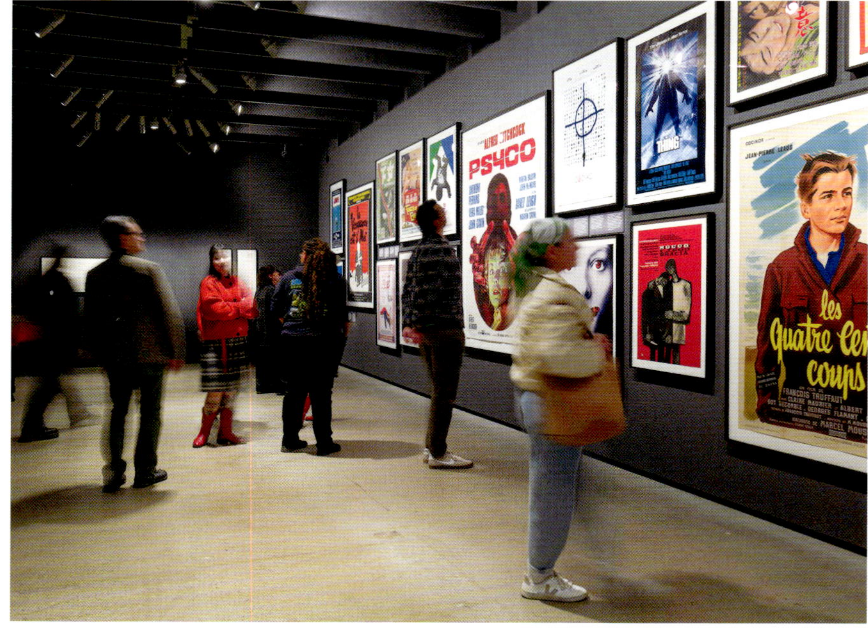

our lives. In his interview for this volume, Bong speaks with film scholar Nam Lee about the dark shadow left by the military dictatorship in 1980s Korea and how his films carry the residue of that history.

Memories of Murder (2003) examines this period through the dramatization of the real-life serial murders that took place in and around Hwaseong, Gyeonggi Province. The film subverts the police procedural genre by embracing the moral ambiguity and emotional complexity of its characters, who are depicted as violent, corrupt, and arrogant yet wholly obsessed with solving the crimes. Films like *Barking Dogs Never Bite* (2000), *The Host* (2006), and *Mother* (2009) expose, with subtlety and sensitivity, various ways in which Korea's postwar economic development pushed society's most vulnerable individuals into desperate, compromised situations. These are films that are infused with specifics of the sociopolitical climate that Bong grew up in yet also transnational. They ask us to carefully observe the nuances and idiosyncrasies of their characters in lieu of passing judgment. From Bong's first films, made with the Yellow Door film club—which he helped found with friends in the early 1990s while he was an undergraduate student at Yonsei University—through his first Hollywood studio film, *Mickey 17* (2025), his films do, as he described to Nam Lee, the "same things he's always done." They carry hallmark traces of him—his kindness, irreverent sense of humor, antiauthoritarianism, attention to human contradictions, and ability to find great beauty and grace in the most unexpected situations.

I traveled to Korea in February 2024 to meet Director Bong for the first time and view his personal archive. In what I now see as a misguided and insensitive attempt to be efficient with my limited research time, I asked if the materials I was there to see could be made available before our meeting. I was told this wouldn't be possible because

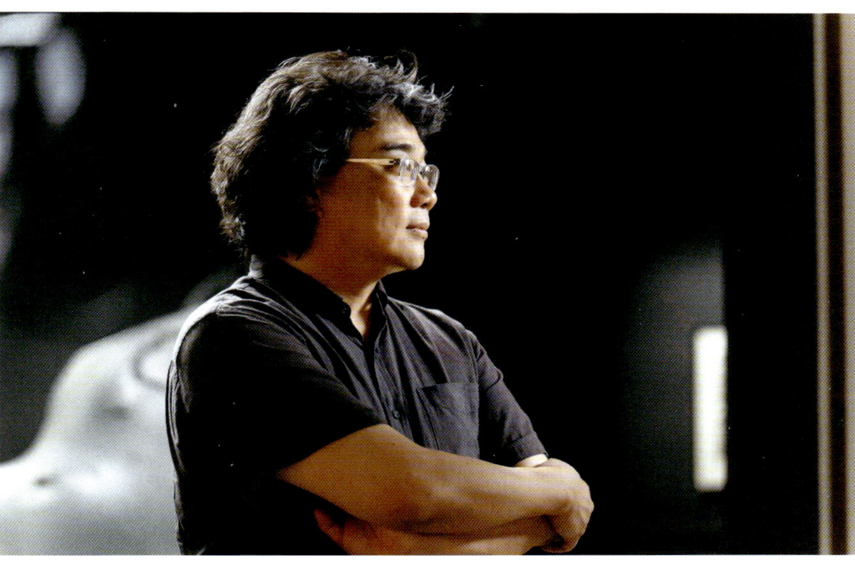

Bong Joon Ho visiting the Director's Inspiration gallery, March 20, 2025

Bong wanted to share the collection with me himself. What I didn't realize fully in the moment was that he knew, with much more clarity than I did, that building a successful exhibition through the lens of a filmmaker's inspirations—past and present—starts with a genuine connection between the objects and the person who made them.

When the day came to meet Bong in his office in Seoul, I was nervous and intimidated, but from the moment he greeted me and we entered his workspace, all apprehension and stress dissolved. Classical music filled the space, giving it an atmosphere of being deeply lived-in, almost domestic. Neat rows of books, CDs, DVDs, Blu-rays, and the occasional VHS tape filled the bookshelves lining the room. Stacks of papers and books were on a long table that, it quickly became clear, was his desk. There was a peaceful, quiet chaos to it all—the kind of feeling you find only in a space that is actually used and loved, not one that is carefully curated.

Bong was disarmingly nice—gracious, warm, and instantly comfortable to be around. This impression echoes how he is described in nearly all the texts his closest collaborators have written for this book. It sounds cliché to say that he is lovely and kind, self-deprecating and funny, but he is. As we sat together and started to talk about the exhibition, he began pulling notebooks, binders, sketchbooks, photo albums, and folders from the shelves. He would describe each item and tell a short story about it while quickly flipping through the pages, often laughing at things he had written or drawings and photographs from the past. As these mementos began to pile up on the table, I realized why it had been so important for us to meet and review his archive together. An exhibition is not just a collection of materials related to a person or a body of work; each item is a reflection, in some small way, of an artist's process, creativity, and spirit. My aim for the exhibition, and this accompanying book, was to highlight not only Bong's films but also the person behind them—his curiosity, passion, discipline, irreverence, and quiet confidence.

Both the exhibition and book are structured chronologically, not with the intention to survey Bong's career to date but rather to examine how different aspects of his creative process have developed over time. Drawing is a thread that runs throughout and begins with the comics Bong created while he was an undergraduate student at Yonsei University. Published in the school's newspaper, *Yonsei Chunchu*, they show his expressive, self-taught illustration style and the interweaving of art with social and political critique that would later define his films. A self-described otaku who was inspired by manga as well as the illustrated books in his father's library, Bong began drawing at an early age. Comics were his first passion, and his ability to communicate movement, emotion, and action can be seen in these early illustrations and in the storyboards he famously draws for all of his films.

Early continuity drawings for his short film *White Man* (1993) and storyboards for his

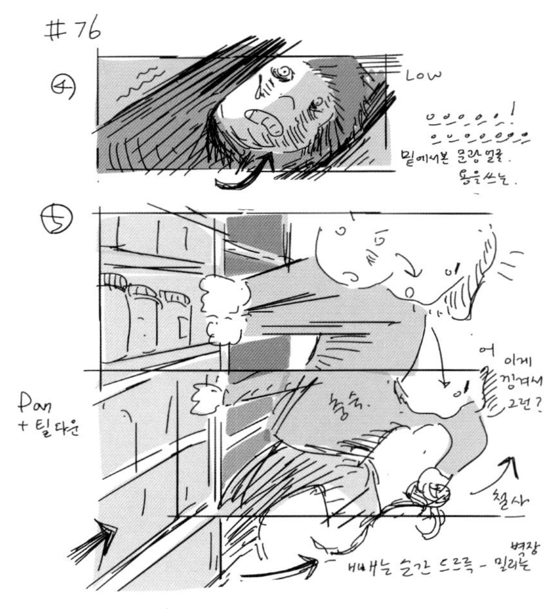

Storyboard for *Parasite* (2019), drawn by Bong

feature films, including *Memories of Murder*, *Mother*, *Parasite*, and *Mickey 17*, illustrate the way in which Bong visually constructs not just shot composition but the flow of one shot into the next. As cinematographer Hong Kyung Pyo writes in this volume, "You can look at the storyboard and see his cinematic style. The rhythm of the film is already there in the images." Bong's storyboards are filled with dynamic lines that frequently disregard the boundaries of the individual shot frames on each page. They illustrate not only shot composition and camera movements but also how the light will fall and how actors will gaze and gesture—seemingly small details that contribute to a tonality specific to Bong. Cinematographer Darius Khondji further describes the storyboards as "complex opera scores made up of shots," likening Bong to a composer carefully arranging notes to create layers of action, rhythm, and meaning.

The drawings Bong made as an undergraduate student were not just for publication in *Yonsei Chunchu*; they also found their way into his work with the Yellow Door film club. Bong illustrated the poster for the club's first seminar, at which he presented scene analyses from Francis Ford Coppola's *The Godfather* (1972) and *The Godfather Part II* (1974), Ermanno Olmi's *The Tree of Wooden Clogs* (1978), Alfred Hitchcock's *Psycho* (1960), and Jean Renoir's *The Grand Illusion* (1938). He also drew a detailed shot analysis to accompany a comparative breakdown of two murder sequences for the first edition of the club's journal: the calculated death of Luca Brasi in *The Godfather* and the impulsive shooting of a motorcycle cop at the beginning of Jean-Luc Godard's *Breathless* (1960). Bong's careful linework and expressive style are evident even in these precise explorations of other directors' work.

During our first meeting in Seoul, I saw drawings and storyboards for his current project were hung on large sliding panels that stretched the length of one side of his office. I was so moved by the experience of being in this space—surrounded by music, books, and films; storyboards and illustrations detailing scenes and characters from the film he was working on then; and posters and mementos from his past films—that capturing something of its essence became crucial for the exhibition. An inner gallery presents museum visitors with a creative reimagining of his workspace and showcases select objects I saw that first day: clapperboards and books, a locket created for *Snowpiercer* (2013) but never seen on screen, the prop suseok (scholar's stone) from *Parasite*, a small model of Okja, the acupuncture kit from *Mother*, and a haunting photograph by actor Ko Asung—a thank-you gift to Bong for encouraging her interest in photography as a form of creative expression.

My immersion in his creative environment that day, for reasons I still cannot fully put into words, completely transformed the way I thought about both the exhibition and Bong Joon Ho. There was no pretense in that space, no ego. Bong was generous with his time and reflections, curious about my intentions for the show, and incredibly thoughtful about the materials he made available. The experience shaped not only what I decided to include in the exhibition but also how I would present it. Bong joked that if I was going to borrow all these precious things, I might as well take his massive worktable too—which, to his amusement, I did. Inlaid with the Wilford Industries logo, it was originally used as a prop in *Snowpiercer*. Occupying a central position in the exhibition's inner gallery, it represents a living and ever-evolving creative process: That long table, surrounded by books, papers, posters, and storyboards, is where his films take shape. It's a practical space and an imaginative one, a zone for both mundane tasks and conceptual leaps.

Seeing an artist in their studio reveals something deeper than a conversation ever

Installation view of *Director's Inspiration: Bong Joon Ho*, March 23, 2025–January 10, 2027, at the Academy Museum of Motion Pictures, Los Angeles

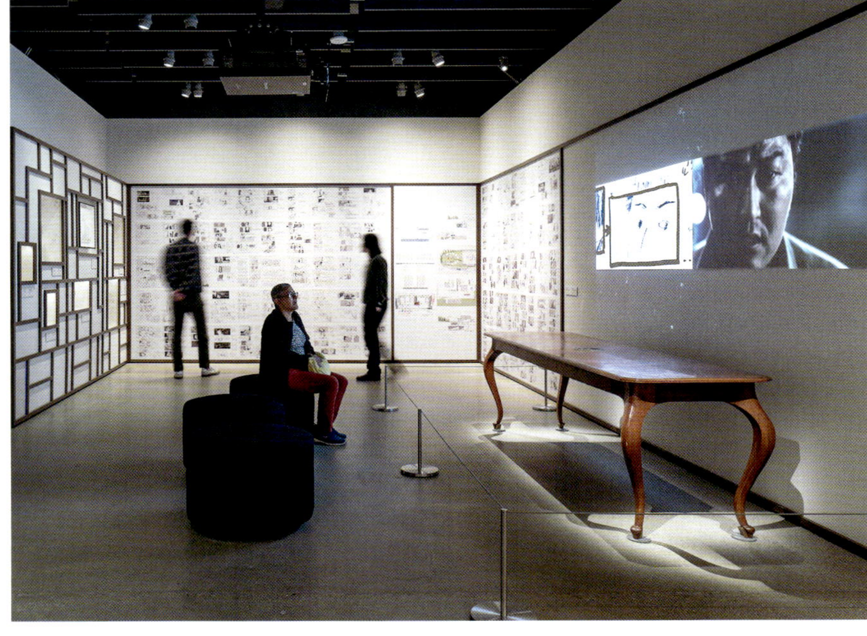

could. It shows you what they love, how they think, what they return to. Bong's workspace reminded me that creativity is something artists cultivate every day, in hours spent listening, reading, thinking, watching, and drawing. What I tried to capture in this exhibition is a particular kind of tension between precision and artistic imagination. Bong is an artist who works with incredible rigor, yet he is also a deeply instinctual thinker—someone who makes space for the unexpected, for the messy, for the human. That duality is a part of what makes his films feel so taut with energy and emotion, so alive and so meaningful.

Working with Bong on the exhibition in the months leading up to the release of his latest film, *Mickey 17*, felt a bit like peering backward into the past while also looking expectantly forward at a vibrant imagination still unfolding. I kept returning to the idea of his workspace as a site of both memory and possibility. As much as this book and exhibition are a celebration of Bong's unique artistry and vision, they are also an attempt to bring us closer to him. The objects and artworks in the exhibition, and the texts in this book, contain fragmented traces of his history, personal ethos, and evolution. Each tells a story and, seen together, can start to tell his.

Michelle Puetz
Exhibitions Curator

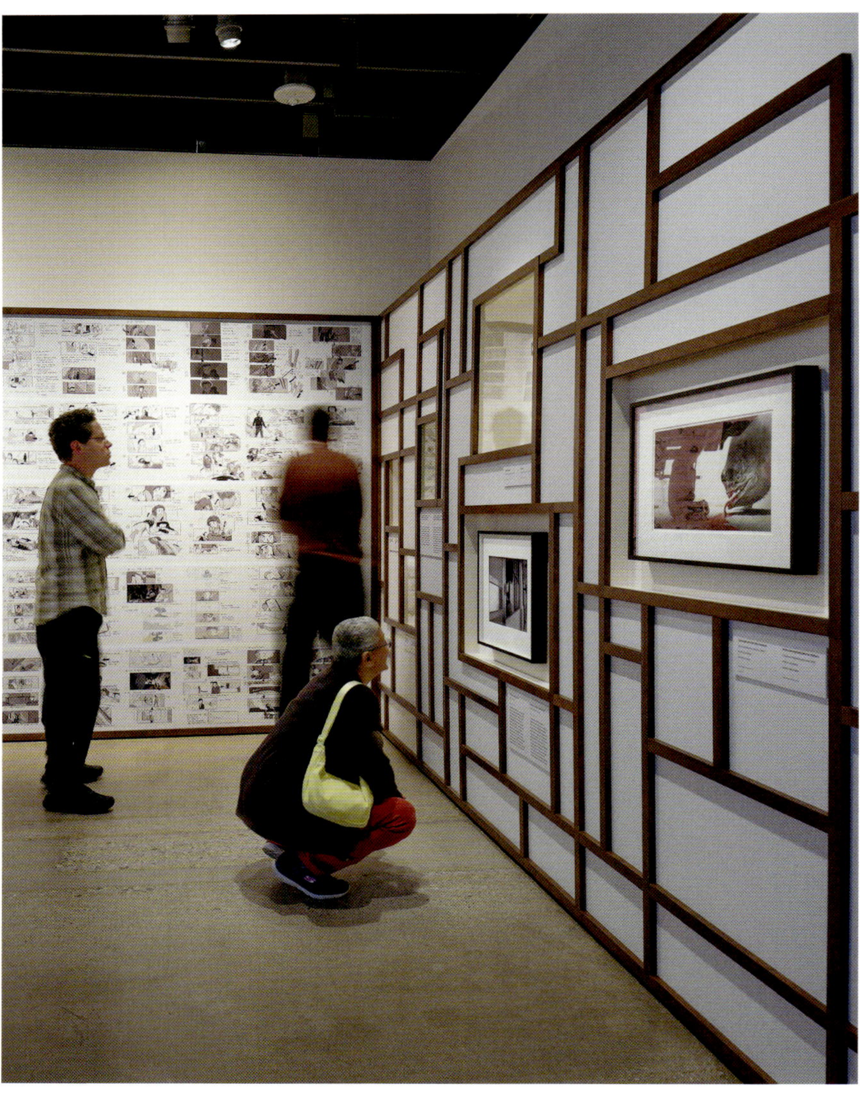

Above and opposite: Installation views of *Director's Inspiration: Bong Joon Ho*, March 23, 2025–January 10, 2027, at the Academy Museum of Motion Pictures, Los Angeles

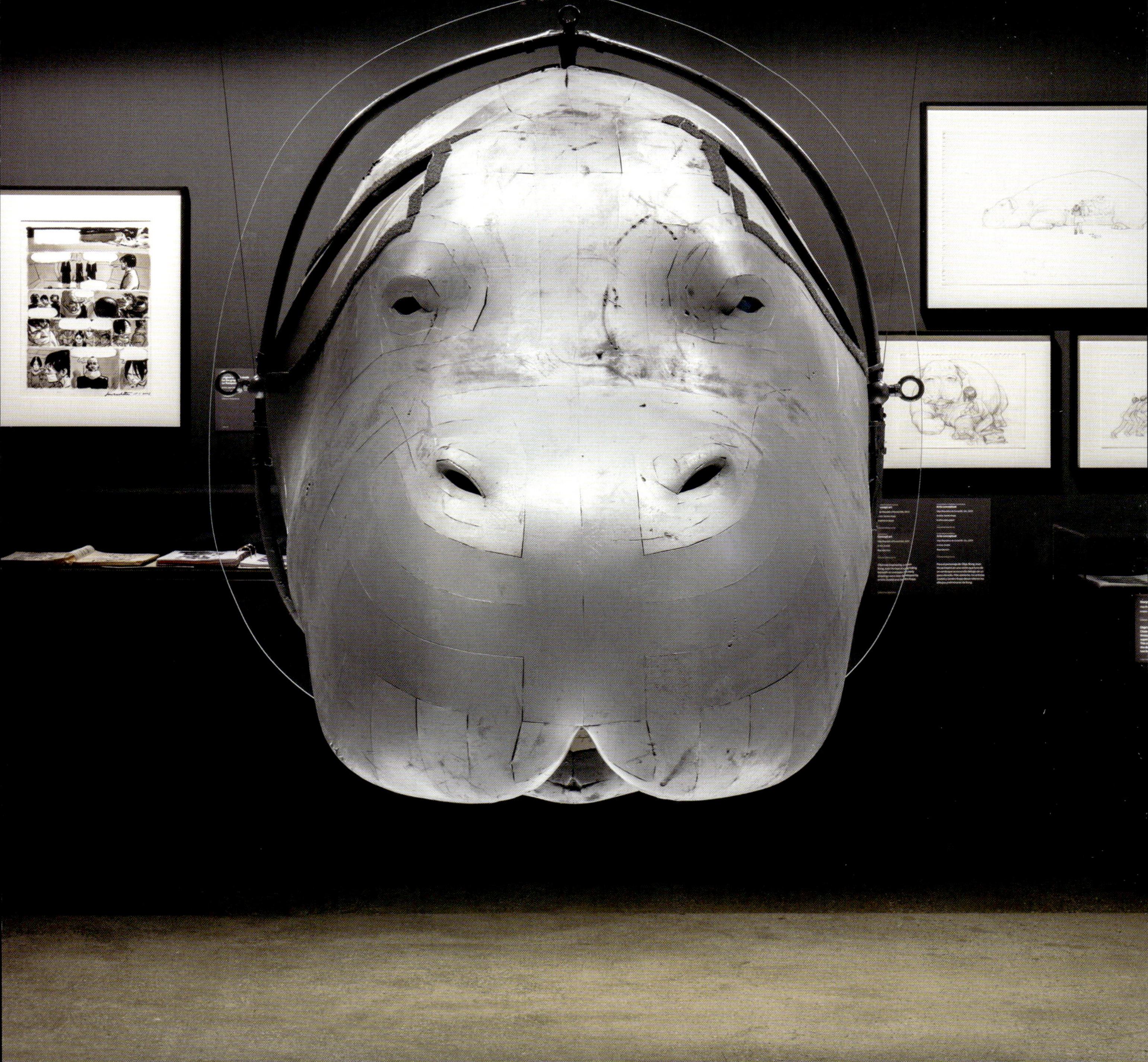

BONG JOON HO:
THE ART OF GENRE

Amy Taubin

I love the films of Bong Joon Ho because they prompt me to laugh, cry, and think while I watch them, and to continue thinking after the screen goes dark. Bong infuses genre movie forms with a realism drawn from his personal experience of bruising, often absurd social institutions. His eight features are all shape-shifters—they move from raucous comedy to heartbreaking pathos in the blink of an eye. "We often chuckle at the funerals of people we love," he told me once, when I asked about his mash-ups of tragedy and comedy.[1]

Parasite (2019), his masterpiece, easily measures up to Jean Renoir's sublime *The Rules of the Game* (1939). Both are tragicomedies of manners and misrecognitions, played out by characters in denial of the looming catastrophe that will end their way of life. Renoir's film concludes just before the Nazi invasion of Western Europe, foreshadowed in the well-regulated savagery of its hunting scene. In *Parasite*, the bloodbath takes place on screen—the revenge of the poor against the rich, and even against each other, in a society where the hope of upward mobility has been destroyed. *Parasite* won awards and audiences worldwide because, as Bong once said in an interview, "Essentially, we all live in the same country, called Capitalism."[2]

In 2003, I wandered into a New York City theater to watch *Memories of Murder*, by a Korean director I'd never heard of. Some years before, I had written several essays on serial killer films, among them Jonathan Demme's *The Silence of the Lambs* (1991), David Fincher's *Se7en* (1995), and the progenitor of American film serial horror, Alfred Hitchcock's *Psycho* (1960). Although Bong has often expressed admiration for these movies—he has mentioned the ending of *Psycho*, mud-caked ropes pulling Marion Crane's car from the swamp, as an image that terrified him as a child—*Memories of Murder* differs notably from these, and

indeed from most serial killer movies.[3] In Bong's hybrid horror-police procedural, the killer appears only as a shadowy figure, and his victims are nearly anonymous: women and girls walking alone at night, to or from jobs or school. The central characters are the police, who are incompetent but also underfunded and unsupported by the military government. And in the end, although they fail to identify the perpetrator, they've brutalized suspects and stupidly caused the death of their best witness.

Bong based the film on an actual series of rapes and murders that took place between 1986 and 1991 in a group of small farming and newly industrialized villages about 20 miles from Seoul. There was ample material for him to research, including newspaper coverage and a true-crime television documentary. He also discovered a trove of images that had been deemed too graphic for TV and says these haunted him throughout the writing and shooting of his film.[4] Bong projected his—and perhaps

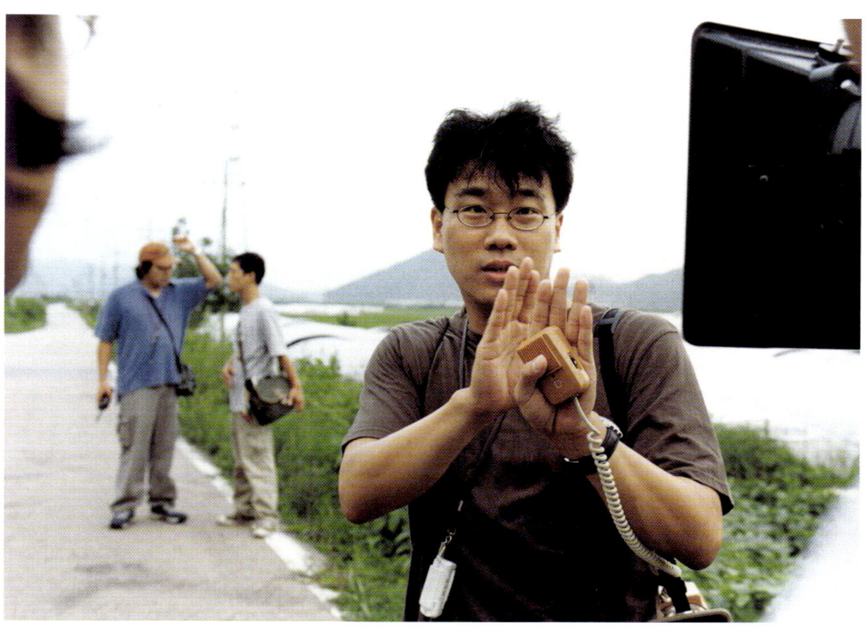

Bong Joon Ho during production of *Memories of Murder* (2003)

his entire country's—obsession with solving these psychosexual murders onto the film's protagonist, Detective Park Doo-man, played by Song Kang-ho. In that respect, the filmmaker and the central character are doppelgängers. *Memories of Murder*, like all of Bong's movies, can be classified as a genre picture, and yet it is as profoundly personal as any art film. The same is true of every film he has made.

Marvelously inclusive of their audiences, Bong's films do not position us simply as spectators. They lure us into their frightening worlds and disarm us with humor that ranges from understated irony to carnivalesque slapstick to cartoonish farce. They put us in the grip of an anxiety that runs beneath their narratives and resonates with our own in this volatile era of planetary degradation, technology run amok, and grotesque inequality. And they offer no solutions. For this profoundly humanist moviemaker, the happiest ending is a withdrawal, to a life of watchful waiting with those you love.

Instability is Bong's beat. But paradoxically, he achieves the chaotic worlds of his films through a Hitchcockian control of the timing of every edit and the framing of every image. What makes Bong's films different from the vast majority of genre movies is that they pivot on moments that we never expect to occur at all, or at least not in the way they do. They take us by surprise, lifting our blinders and disavowals of what we should have realized was inevitable, or at least had a pretty good chance of happening.

In the opening scene of *Memories of Murder*, a man we don't yet realize is Detective Park squats at the opening of a narrow vault that is no more than a roof over a section of an irrigation ditch alongside a vast rice paddy. He finds a piece of broken glass and uses it to reflect sunlight into the dark space. But rather than seeing the interior from his point of view, the camera angle changes 180 degrees, and we are looking into the darkness from the opposite end of the vault. As the camera racks focus, we see the man's face superimposed with the date 10.23.1986 and then, with just the slightest shift of angle, a girl's crumpled body in which insects are nesting. With that utterly unexpected countershot, Bong puts us inside the darkness and decay of this open grave and a crime that coincides, historically, with a particularly violent period in South Korea's struggle against the military dictatorship. He makes us Park's partner—his opposite number—in what will be a failed investigation. In his gut, Park believes he will identify the sexual predator, but his gut fails him, and so does his belief in his masculinity. ("I think it fell out," he says to his girlfriend as they are having sex. I can't recall ever having heard such a straightforward admission of sexual failure by a male protagonist, and certainly not when the character stands in for law and order. Hitchcock's approach in *Vertigo* is more oblique.)

Memories of Murder ends in the same place it began, but 17 years have passed. No longer a detective, Park is a traveling salesman for a dubious green-juice company. His route takes him past the scene of the first

Song Kang-ho in
Memories of Murder

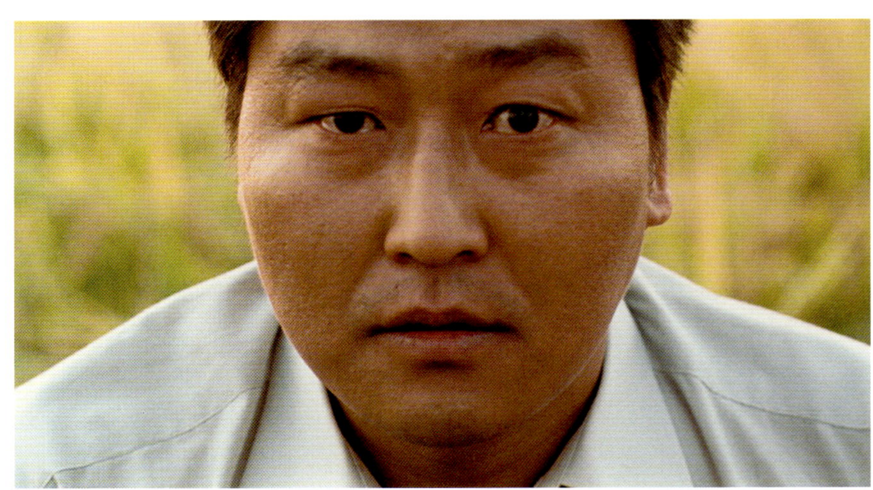

murder. Once again, he gets out of a vehicle to crouch at the vault opening. A teenage girl, the only other person in the now empty rice paddy, tells him that a short while ago she saw another man looking into the vault. When Park asks her what he looked like, she replies, "Ordinary." We see Park in close-up, his gaze turned inward. Then suddenly he turns his head and looks straight into the camera lens, just as he did in that opening sequence. We are ordinary-looking people, and so is the killer, who might be sitting next to us. One person who claimed that the movie had no effect on him, although he said that he saw it three times, was the actual serial killer; he was finally identified via DNA evidence in 2019, a few months before *Parasite* won four Academy Awards, including Best Picture and Directing.[5]

Bong followed *Memories of Murder* with a monster-horror movie, which gave Song the greatest role of his career. At the climax of *The Host* (2006), Song's Park Gang-du runs frantically along the bank of the Han River, carrying the body of his dead daughter in his arms. Song is the only actor I've seen on stage or screen who could play King Lear and his Fool in the same production, breaking your heart twice over by conveying the tragedy of both. Monster movies are seldom heart-breaking character studies—unless, as in *Frankenstein* (1931), it's the monster with whom we empathize. But in Gang-du, Bong and Song together create an unforgettable character, one whose terrible failures cause the deaths of the two people he most cares about, and who yet survives and even transforms to become a hope for the future.

The Host opens with a monster movie cliché, here based on an actual incident: An American military morgue director orders a Korean subordinate to dump leftover formaldehyde down the drain, into Seoul's Han River. In the movie, the pollutants create a mutant, *Alien*-sized tadpole with a talent for parkour and a hunger for anything that

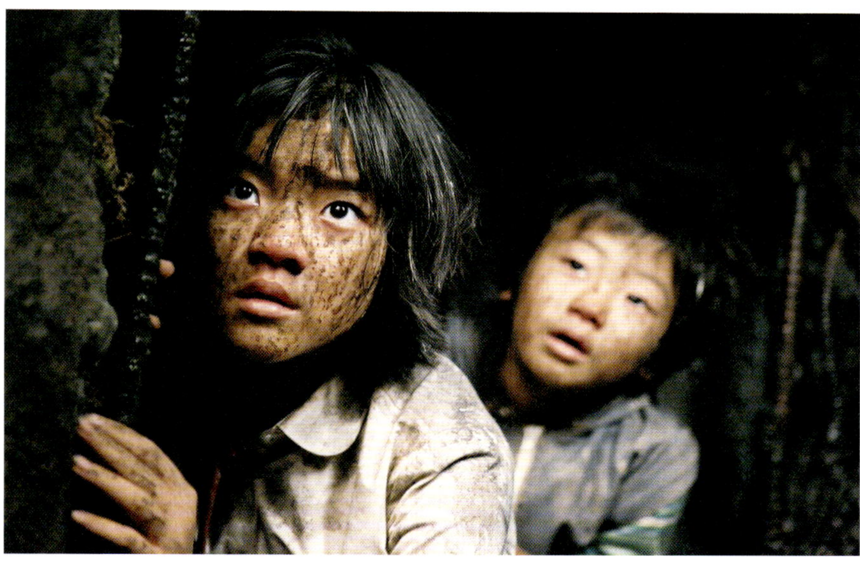

Ko Asung (left) in
The Host (2006)

moves. Gimbling across a popular beach, it tramples dozens and carries Gang-du's teenage daughter, Hyun-seo (Ko Asung), back to its lair in a bone-strewn sewer beneath the river. A communal funeral is held, but Gang-du refuses to believe his daughter is dead, claiming that she has been calling him on her failing cell phone. Mentally disabled and sleepwalking through life, Gang-du had lost his grip on Hyun-seo's hand as they fled the monster. Empowered by his need to rescue her, he breaks his entire family out of the phony quarantine the government has placed them in, and together they search for Hyun-seo.

When I interviewed Bong in 2017, he was adamant that the most courageous character is Hyun-seo, who risks her life to rescue the five-year-old boy imprisoned with her. The scene where she attempts to use the sleeping monster's back as a springboard to reach the top of the sewer is terrifying from beginning to end. At one point, Hyun-seo freezes in place when she sees a yellow-bodied spider crawling up her skirt. Extreme differences in scale figure in some of Bong's most powerful compositions. The monster is huge, the spider is small, but as Bong explained, "Sometimes the smallest things are the most frightening." Whether the spider throws off her timing or the desperate plan was never in the realm of possibility for a starving girl to execute, Hyun-seo does not escape and the monster eats her alive.

I've watched *The Host* a half dozen times, and I'm always shocked when Hyun-seo is caught, even though Bong barely shows what physically happens. It is such a violation of the codes of the genre, although perfectly logical if this were real life. At that point of ultimate horror, *The Host* is no longer a genre movie; it is, indeed, about real life, where children die because governments put no value on their lives. The death of Hyun-seo, for me, called up the famous 1972 photograph of the girl who had been napalmed during the war in Vietnam, an association underscored by the scenes in which the military gases protesters with Agent Yellow. When Gang-du and his family finally kill the monster with bullets, flaming arrows, and a Molotov cocktail, Gang-du pulls Hyun-seo's corpse from its throat, her arms wrapped around the boy she succeeded in protecting even as she died. He is alive. Like almost all of Bong's films, *The Host* ends in the physical space where it began, but the character who lives there has changed. We are again in the shack on the beach where we first saw Gang-du as he slept on the job, his bleached blond hair covering the snacks he was meant to sell. Now he is setting out a meal for the little boy, whom he will protect as Hyun-seo would have wanted. When there is a sound outside, Gang-du looks out the window, panic in his eyes. He'll never sleep soundly again.

Though Hyun-seo is, for Bong, the most heroic character in *The Host*, the narrative is dominated by Gang-du. Of Bong's eight features, only two focus on a female character: *Mother* (2009) and *Okja* (2017). In *Mother*, Kim Hye-ja, a television and film star who had

been the emblem of the good Korean woman throughout her career, plays a character so attached to her son that she kills to protect him and frames another boy for the crime her son committed. A single mother, her meager income is derived from her unlicensed acupuncture practice and the sale of herbal remedies. When her son was only a few years old, she tried to poison him so that he wouldn't die slowly of hunger. Although she saved him at the last moment, he grows up mentally disabled; her guilt, combined with the fear of losing him, drives her mad. A straightforward melodrama, *Mother* is built around Kim's performance, and she is extraordinary. When I asked Bong about his frequent use of close-ups, particularly of Song, he answered that the most drastic close-up he ever made was of Kim. He said that he chose her for *Mother* because he was drawn to her eyes and wanted the camera to move in and film them as closely as possible.

Okja's titular character is a giant, genetically modified pig. She is a computer-generated creature, but Bong and his visual effects supervisor knew it was crucial for

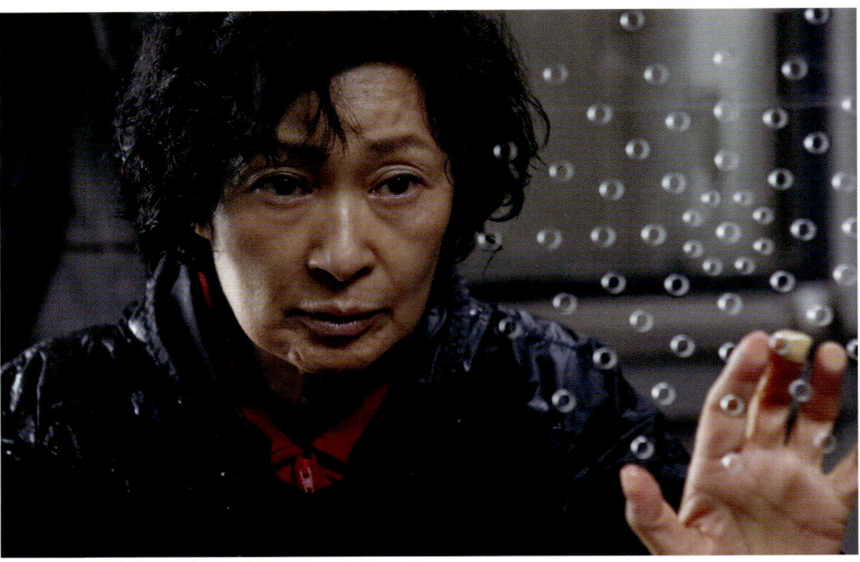

Kim Hye-ja in *Mother* (2009)

her eye movements to be so lifelike that they could be shown in close-up. The film is about the bond between Okja and Mija (Ahn Seo-hyun), the 14-year-old girl who has cared for Okja since the creature was a piglet. For Bong, the way to show their friendship was by framing Mija's face in close-up nestled under Okja's eye, which is as large as Mija's entire face. For 10 years, Mija nurtures Okja on her grandfather's farm in the mountains, believing that Okja will be with her forever. But the bioengineered "super pig" is only a foster. One day, Okja is claimed by her real owner, a multinational factory-farming corporation that intends to ship her to New York, show her off as their prize-winning super pig, and send her to the slaughterhouse.

Okja begins as a kind of pastoral children's movie, turns into cartoonlike farce as Okja attempts to escape from her captors and Mija pursues her across half the world, and finally transforms into an exposé of the horror of factory farming. Mija is unaware of what is in store for her best friend until her pursuit takes her into an abattoir. Looking down, she sees her shoes submerged in a river of blood. For a moment, she freezes. But unlike *The Host*'s Hyun-seo, who was paralyzed by the sight of the yellow spider, Mija has a coming to consciousness, the kind of awakening young girls sometimes have in children's fairy tales. She cuts a deal to buy Okja's freedom in exchange for the chunk of gold she was awarded for raising her. As Mija and Okja walk out of the slaughterhouse, the corralled super pigs who are about to die salute them, and one of them manages to push her newborn out of the pen so that Mija can rescue it too.

At the Cannes Film Festival press screening, many critics, myself included, were in tears during that scene. Just as many angrily walked out of the screening. Perhaps they were annoyed at being reminded about how their ham sandwich got to their lunch table. "It is not easy to be a vegetarian in Korea, but I eat less red meat than I did before," Bong explained. "At the end of *Okja*, Mija and her grandfather have a meal of free-range eggs and chicken," he says, and these are probably the very chickens we see them feeding just after the film opens. While not promoting veganism, *Okja* exposes factory farming as an economic engine of capitalism, a super polluter of the environment, and a blight on the possibility of a humane social order.

As audacious, assured, and intelligent as Bong's films had been up to this point, nothing prepared me or the global audience for the dazzling cinematic production, and dire analysis of inequitable economic conditions, that is *Parasite*. Here, Bong fuses scathing social satire with a despair that is much more profound than anything in his previous work. While *Parasite* is an upstairs-downstairs narrative—and staircases, both interior and exterior, figure prominently—the focus is on the lower-class Kim family. Father Ki-taek (Song Kang-ho), mother Chung-sook (Chang Hyae-jin), son Ki-woo (Choi Woo-shik), and daughter Ki-jung (Park So-dam) live in a cluttered, moldy semi-basement apartment.

Choi Woo-shik and crew during production of *Parasite* (2019)

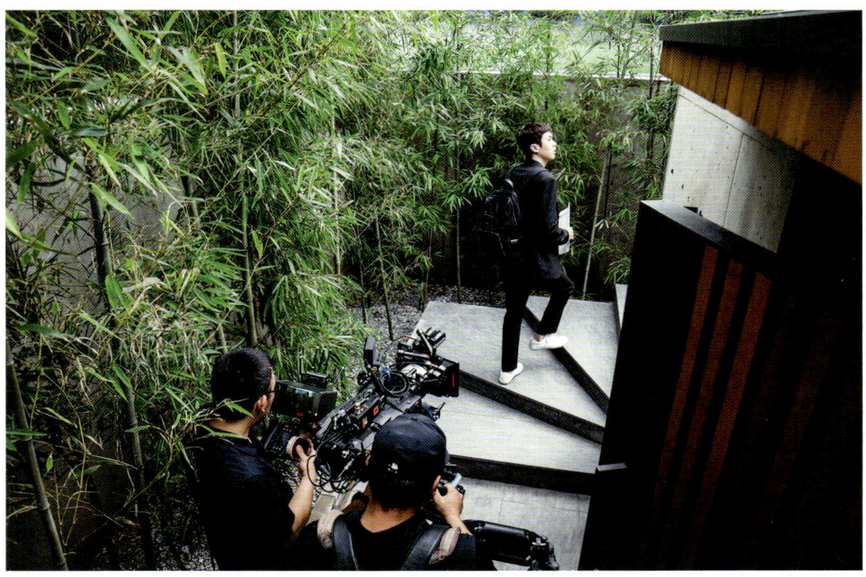

Ki-woo and Ki-jung have both failed their college entrance exams; Ki-taek has been involved in a succession of failed businesses; and Chung-sook, a track-and-field silver medalist in her youth, now uses her competitive drive to motivate the family in the scams they pursue.

The Kims catch a break when Ki-woo's closest friend, who is going to a university abroad, asks him to take over his job as English tutor to the daughter of a very rich family, the Parks. Ki-woo is momentarily intimidated when he climbs the hill to the Park family's home; the sun-drenched, minimalist McMansion in a new-money Seoul neighborhood is the polar opposite of his family's digs in the city's lower depths. But Mrs. Park (Cho Yeo-jeong) unquestioningly accepts Ki-woo on the basis of the former tutor's recommendation and the college diploma his sister has forged for him. It's then ridiculously easy for Ki-woo to create a job for his sister as an art therapist for the Parks' spoiled seven-year-old son, and together they defame Mr. Park's chauffeur, bringing in Ki-taek as his replacement.

The Kims' pièce de résistance is to convince Mrs. Park that her longtime housekeeper, Moon-gwang (Lee Jung-eun), has tuberculosis. Set to composer Jung Jaeil's "The Belt of Faith," a slow-building and ultimately jubilant facsimile of a baroque orchestral piece, Moon-gwang's destruction is accomplished in a seven-minute montage of more than 50 shots ending with Mrs. Park, frozen in horror as Ki-taek brandishes what she believes is Moon-gwang's blood-soaked tissue, but which we've just seen him stain with hot sauce. The contemporary equivalent of the "Odessa Steps" sequence in Sergei Eisenstein's *Battleship Potemkin* (1925), it is thrilling to behold; it is also the moment where we might become somewhat queasy about cheering for the Kim family to succeed in their employment strategy. The breezy, comedic tone of the Kims' ingenious home

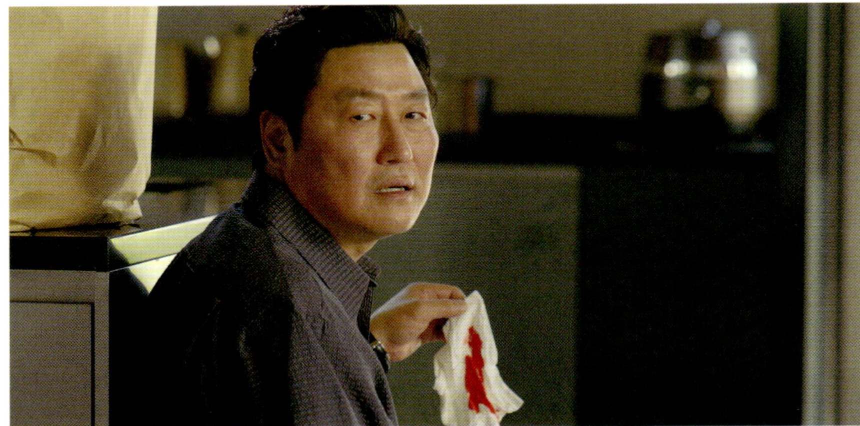

Song Kang-ho in *Parasite*

invasion gradually darkens from there, and finally real blood is shed.

By the end of *Parasite*, four people are dead. Among them is Moon-gwang, who is sent tumbling down a secret stairway by a kick delivered by Chung-sook, a sight gag so precisely timed that we laugh even if it makes us complicit in the horror now unfolding. The narrow stairway leads to a secret basement where Moon-gwang's husband has been hiding from loan sharks for years. Perhaps constructed as a bomb shelter in the event of a North Korean attack, it is the most elaborate of the nightmare spaces in Bong's films, more terrifying than the basement in his 2000 debut feature, *Barking Dogs Never Bite*; the irrigation vault in *Memories of Murder*; the sewer in *The Host*; or the abattoir in *Okja*. Though Moon-gwang tried to protect her spouse, the prolonged isolation has destroyed his mind and drained his body. He is the ghost in the machine of the parasitic body formed by the enmeshed Kim and Park families, and he will soon emerge into the sunlit house and its verdant garden to kill and be killed. It is then, finally, Ki-taek who takes his place in the underground hideout after killing Mr. Park.

Parasite, like Bong's previous films, ends where it began, in the Kims' semi-basement apartment, with Ki-woo again standing in front of an utterly non-picturesque picture window. When we first met him, he was attempting to hack into a neighbor's Wi-Fi. Now he is writing a letter to his father, whom he hopes to rescue from his hiding place beneath what was the Parks' home. However impossible, it is a plan, and plans are what gave his father hope until everything fell apart. Bong told me that he depended on close-ups of Song's eyes at the turning points in the film, particularly in the massacre scene when Ki-taek no longer has a plan with which to contain his rage. "Is this a cautionary tale about the future?" I asked. "No," he said. "In Korea, there are already families whose situation is much worse than that of the Kim family. I actually softened it a bit for the film."

Bong found a way out of depicting an increasingly dire 21st century through science fiction. *Mickey 17* (2025), adapted from Edward Ashton's novel *Mickey7*, is set in a future where corrupt politicians lead expeditions to colonize outer space, recruiting desperately poor people as labor. Robert Pattinson's Mickey, fleeing loan sharks and careless about reading the fine print in contracts, signs on to perform the most dangerous jobs as an "expendable"—he agrees to be scanned and stored as a digital file so that he can be reprinted every time he dies. When the film begins, Mickey has been cloned 17 times. Like *Snowpiercer* (2013), Bong's first foray into science fiction, *Mickey 17* is an English-language film, and it is dominated by Pattinson's remarkable voice-over, as expressive as Song's eyes in Bong's previous films.

The big idea in *Mickey 17* is that our humanity is founded on our awareness of mortality. It is Mickey's desire to break the cycle and become mortal again (and, paradoxically, his openness to new experiences) that allows him to bond with the huge, supremely intelligent, roly-poly creatures that are indigenous to the new world the

Americans have invaded. Love and respect across species, a central theme here as in *Okja*, is essential for human life to continue. *Mickey 17* "portrays a cruel world," Bong says in his interview with Nam Lee in this volume, "but it's very hopeful." He has the same view of *Snowpiercer*, in which the only survivors of a new ice age, caused by a failed experiment to counter global warming, have lived for years on a train circling the planet. The upstairs-downstairs division in this film is lateral—the rich live in the front cars and the enslaved lower class live in the back—and Song plays the small but crucial role of Nam, a worker who guards the dividing line between the two sections. Nam has observed that the ice outside is slowly melting, and he has a plan to derail the train and escape with his daughter. Though he does not survive the melee that ensues, his daughter does, along with a five-year-old boy. *Snowpiercer* "has violent energy and destruction on the train," Bong says in the interview, "but I've always insisted that it has a happy ending—there's hope at the very end." As the children emerge from the wreckage and survey the vast tundra, they see on an icy cliff a polar bear. Its eyes are pools of black, so we cannot tell if it is looking at the girl and boy or at us. No matter, it is the bear's world forever.

Notes

1. All quotations from Bong Joon Ho are from conversations with the author conducted on June 9, 2017, and May 23, 2019, unless otherwise noted.

2. Bong Joon Ho, "Bong Joon-ho Discusses *Parasite*, Genre Filmmaking and the Greatness of *Zodiac*," Birth Movies Death, October 16, 2019, https://birthmoviesdeath.com.

3. Jung Ji-youn, *Korean Film Directors: Bong Joon-ho* (Seoul Selection USA, 2009), 186.

4. Jung, 99–100.

5. Ed Park, "*Memories of Murder*: In the Killing Jar," Criterion Collection, April 20, 2021, https://www.criterion.com.

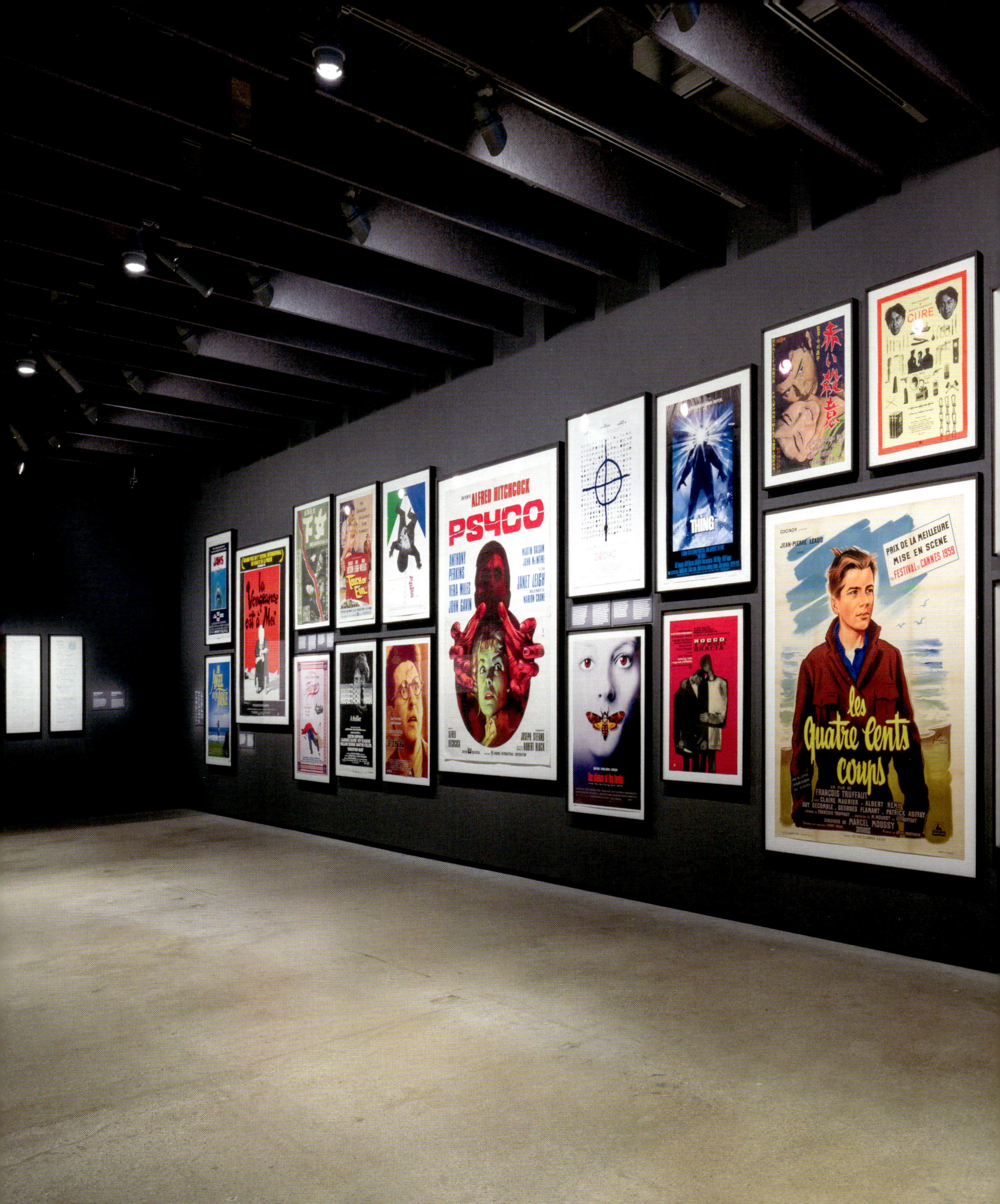

DIRECTOR'S INSPIRATION: BONG JOON HO

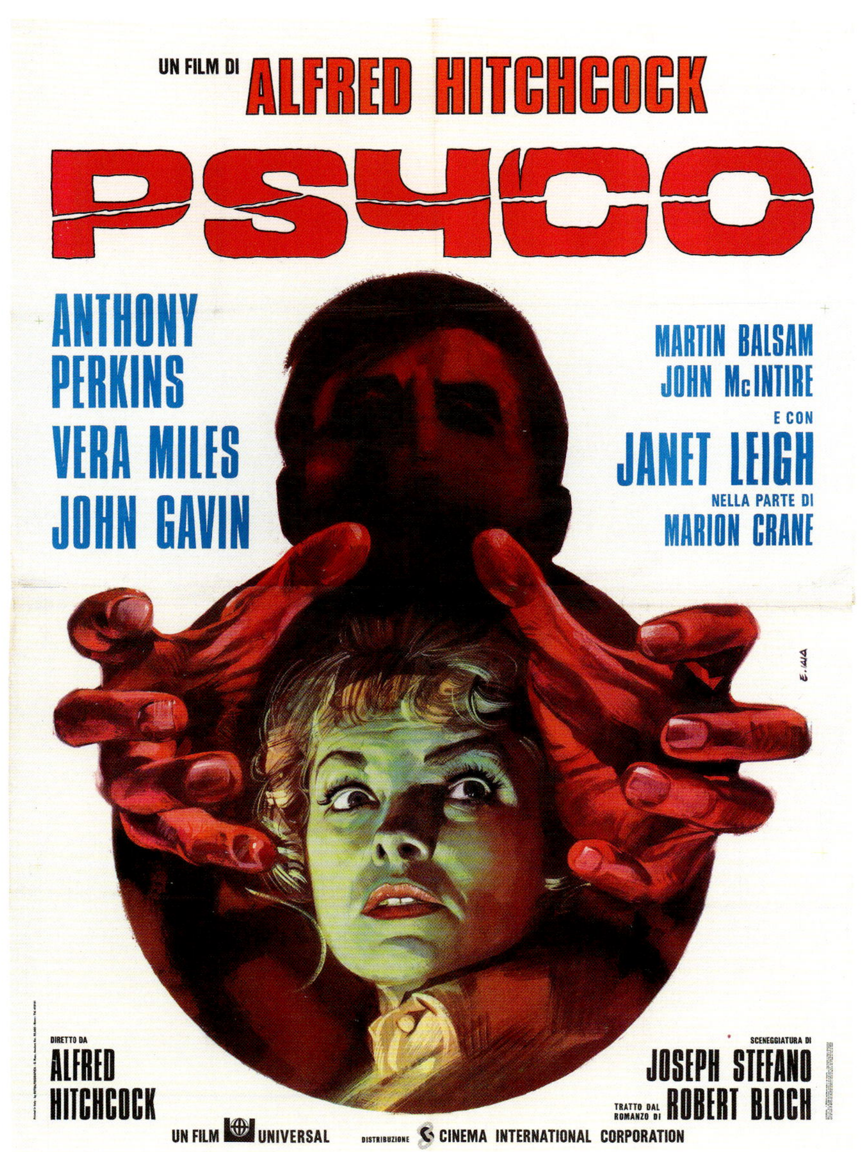

When I was a kid, I watched so many Alfred Hitchcock movies on Korean television. Hitchcock is still one of my biggest inspirations. I've seen *Psycho* more than 50 times.

Bong's love for cinema began on a small television set in his childhood bedroom. He watched international films broadcast on Korean public television and the American Forces Korea Network, a channel for US troops stationed in Korea. "TV was my cinematheque," he says.

Left: Italian poster for Alfred Hitchcock's *Psycho* (1960), from Bong's personal collection

Opposite: French poster for Henri-Georges Clouzot's *The Wages of Fear* (1953)

The French movie *Wages of Fear* by Henri-Georges Clouzot is a very suspenseful movie that was shocking to me when I was eight or nine years old. I was overwhelmed by that film.

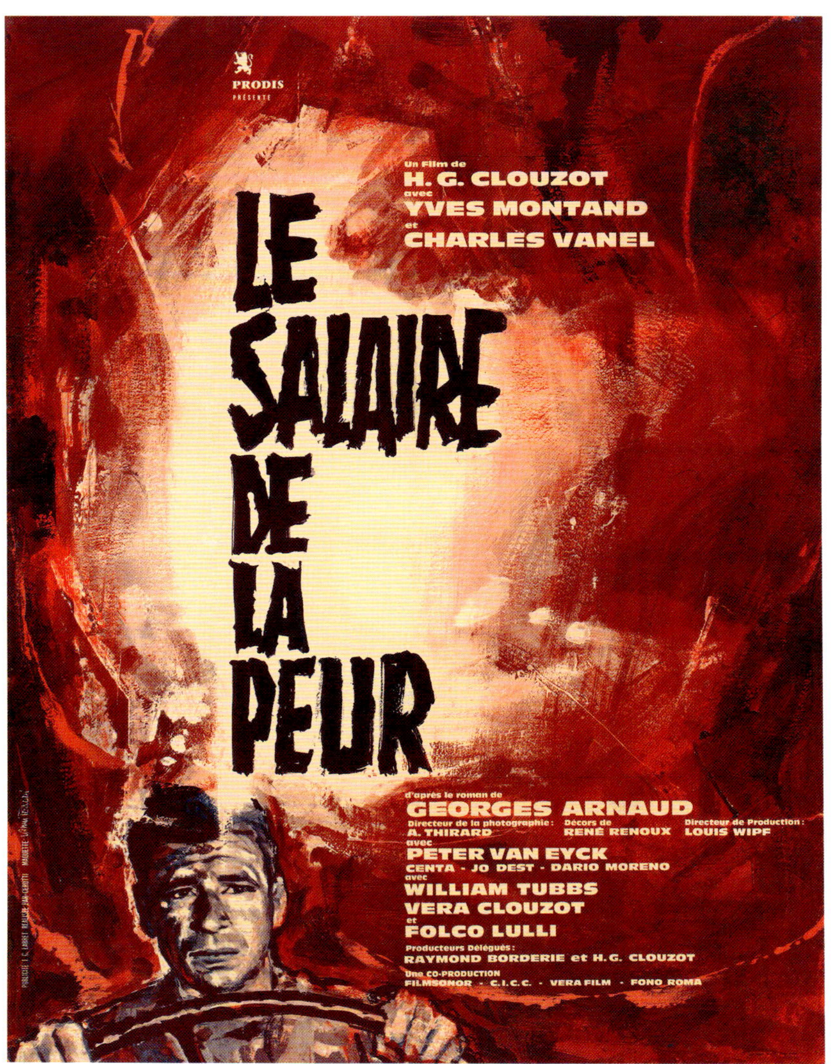

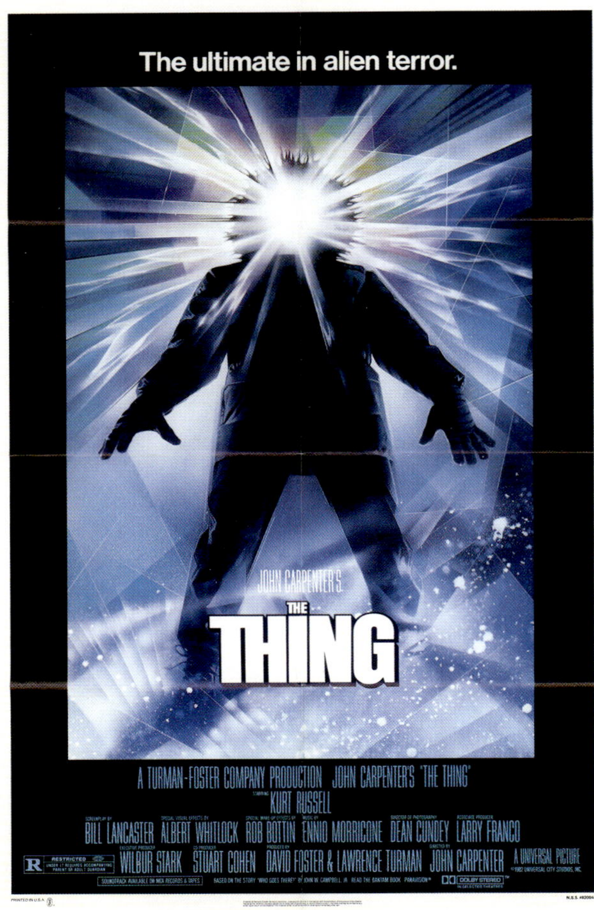

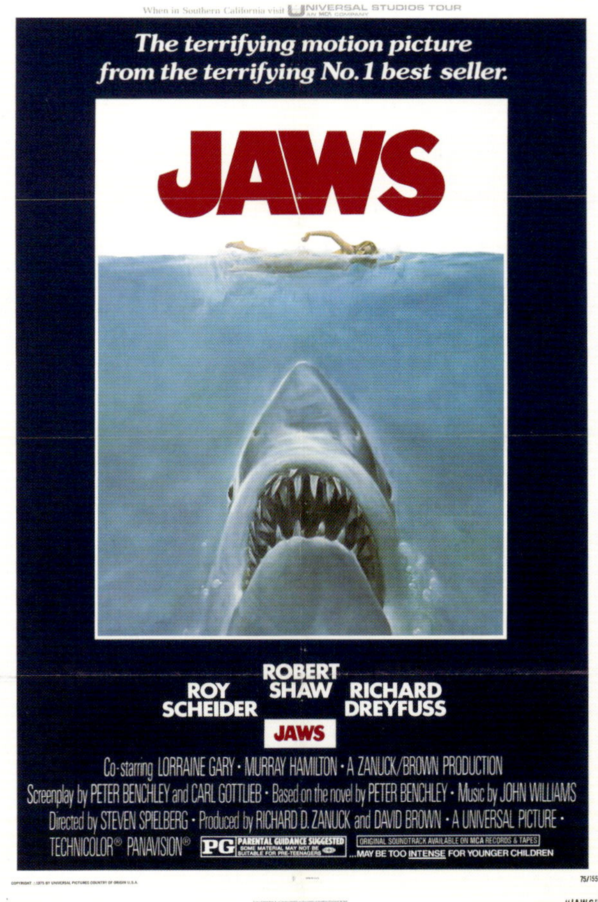

I grew up watching American genre films. It's like the blood flowing through my veins. It's not like I'm conscious of the blood in my veins. I just know that it's there and always flowing.

Within Korean cinema history, I strongly recommend *The Housemaid* by Kim Ki-young, one of my great mentors. I also love Japanese director Shohei Imamura's *Vengeance Is Mine*.

Opposite, left: US poster for *The Thing* (1982)

Opposite, right: US poster for *Jaws* (1975)

Below, left: Korean poster for *The Housemaid* (1960)

Below, right: French poster for *Vengeance Is Mine* (1979)

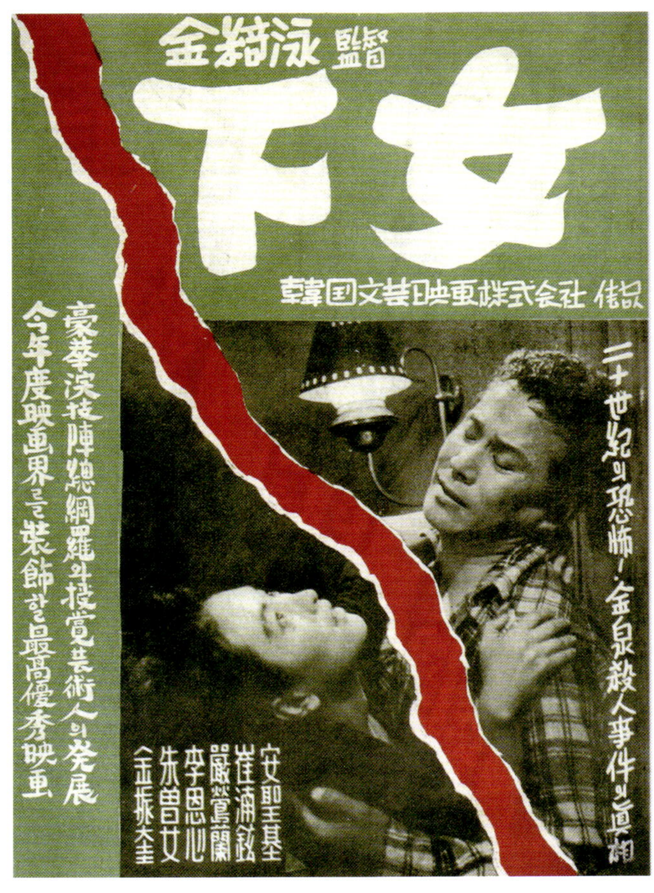

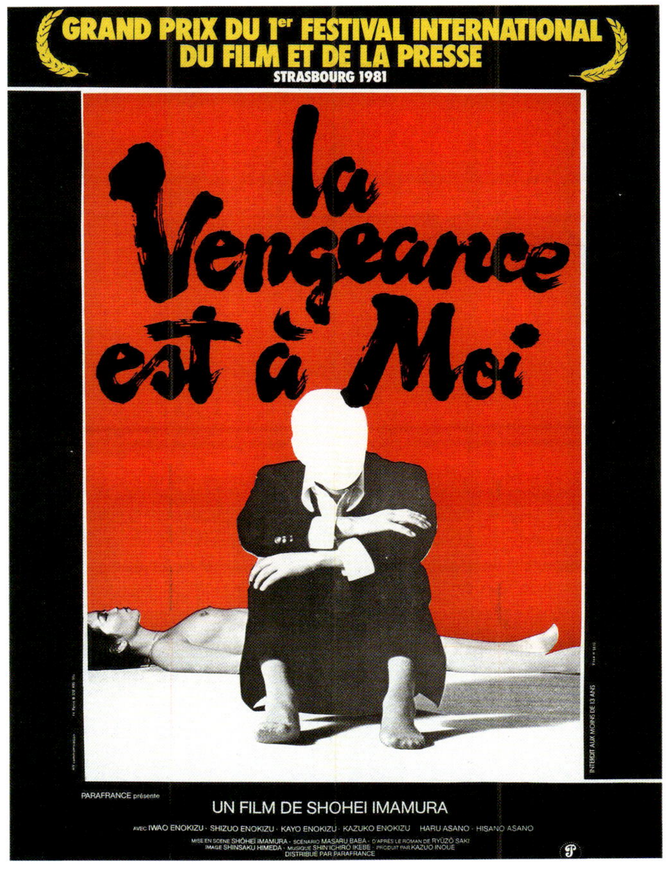

The most significant turning point in my college life—and perhaps in my entire life—was my involvement with the film club Yellow Door.

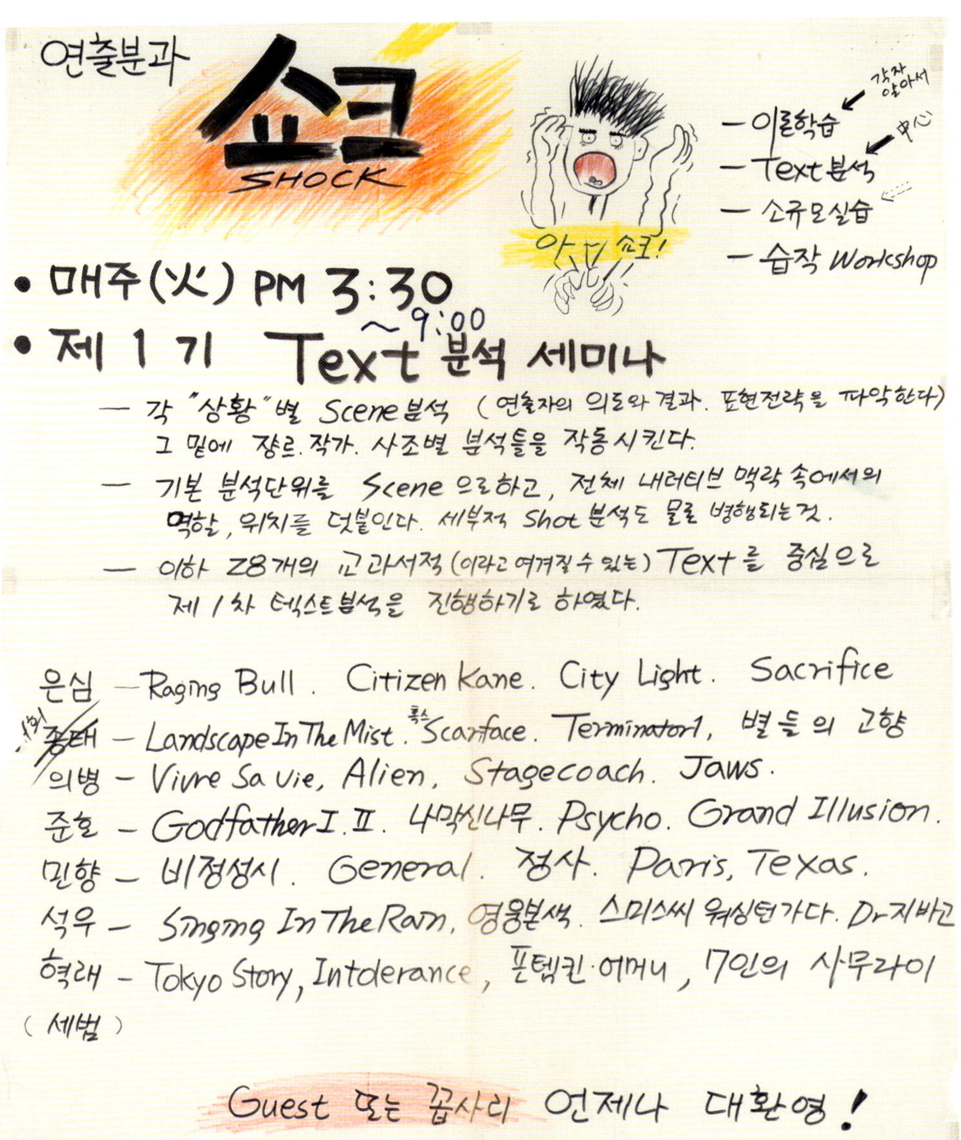

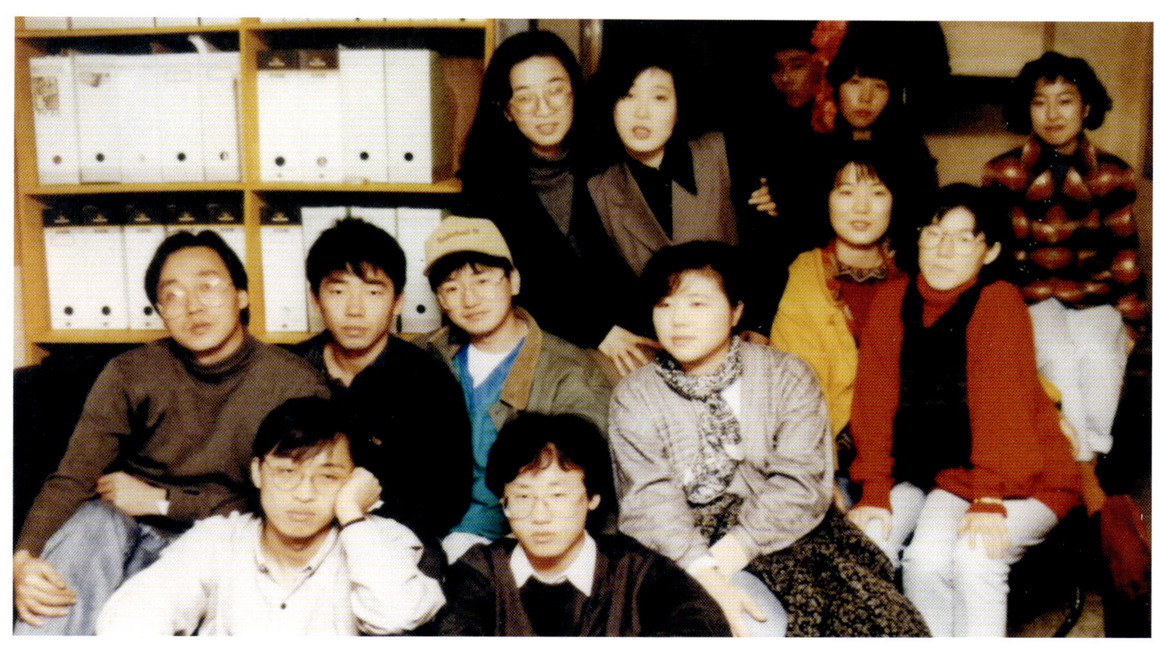

We didn't just watch the movies, we held workshops and made movies ourselves. We collected cameras on our own. Nothing was structured for us in the early '90s, so we had to figure everything out on our own.

As a student at Yonsei University in Seoul in the early 1990s, Bong helped formed the Yellow Door film club. "We would study these clips, then spend our evenings drinking and passionately discussing movies. It was an incredibly energetic time in our lives."

Opposite: Poster for Yellow Door film club's first analytical seminar, ca. 1993, drawn by Bong

Above: Yellow Door film club members, ca. 1993. Bong can be seen in shadow in the back row, third from right.

It was my chance, for the first time ever, to properly discuss and study film as much as I wanted and watch them over and over.

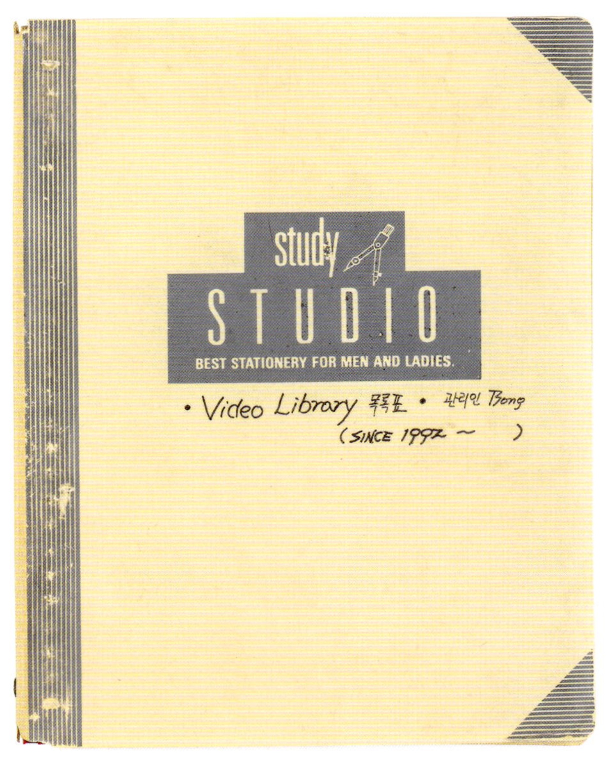

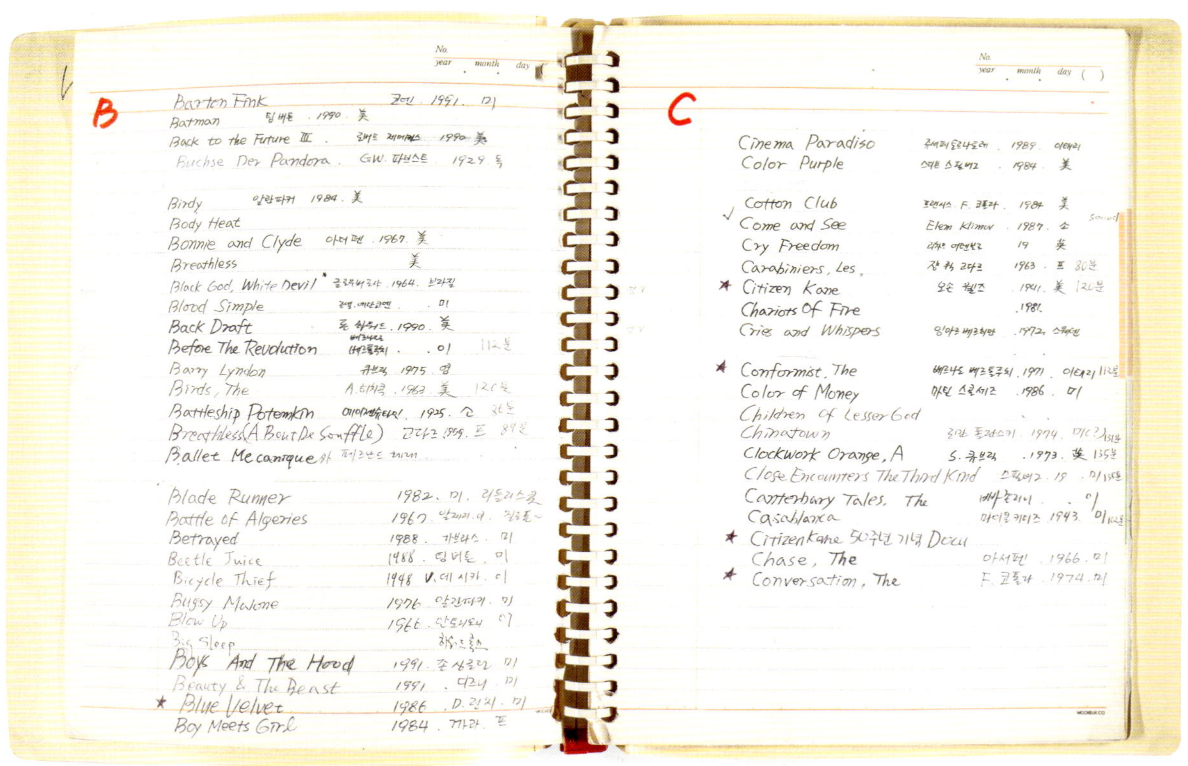

With few opportunities to see international films in theaters, Yellow Door film club members traded bootleg VHS tapes they could watch repeatedly and pause for close analysis. Bong maintained a handwritten logbook of the club's lending library of over 300 tapes.

Opposite: Cover and pages of video library logbook kept by Bong

Right: Bootleg VHS tapes collected by Yellow Door film club

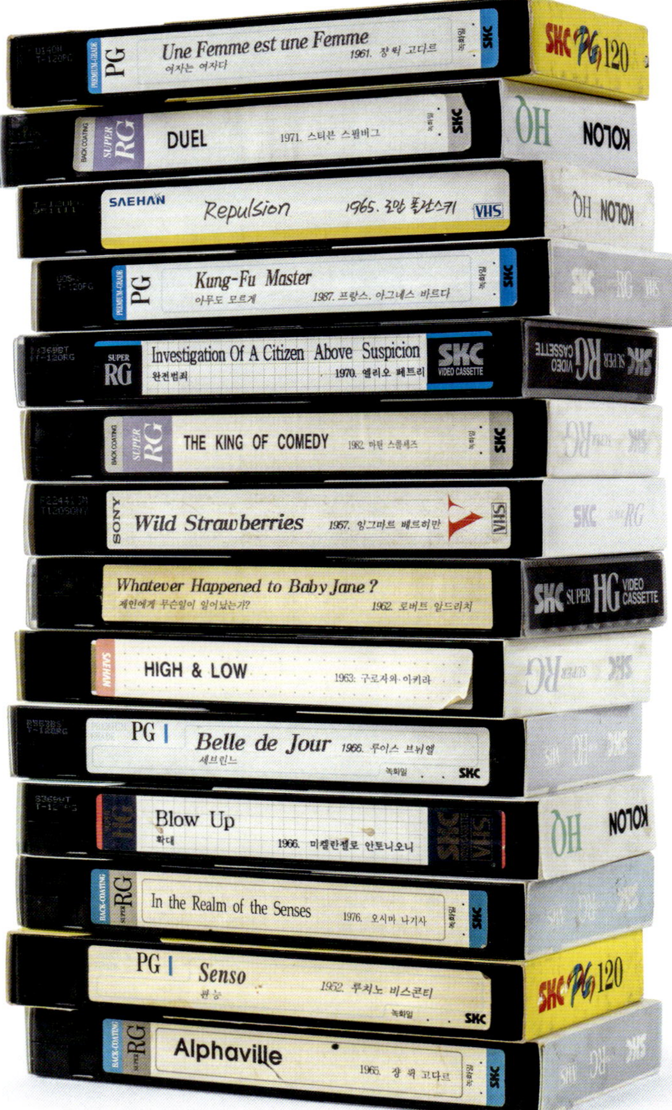

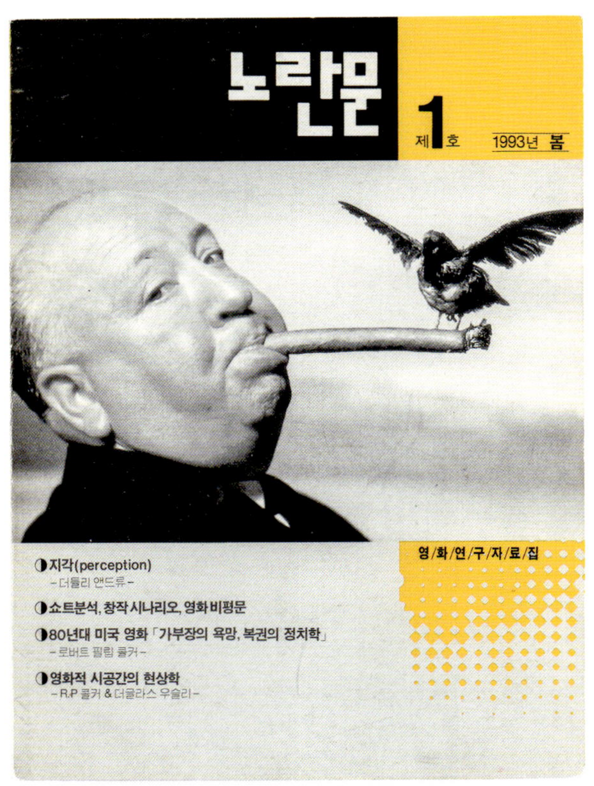

This page: Cover of Yellow Door Film Club journal, vol. 1, 1993, and scene analysis of *The Godfather* (1972) illustrated by Bong.

Opposite: Scenes from Bong's first live-action short, *White Man* (1994)

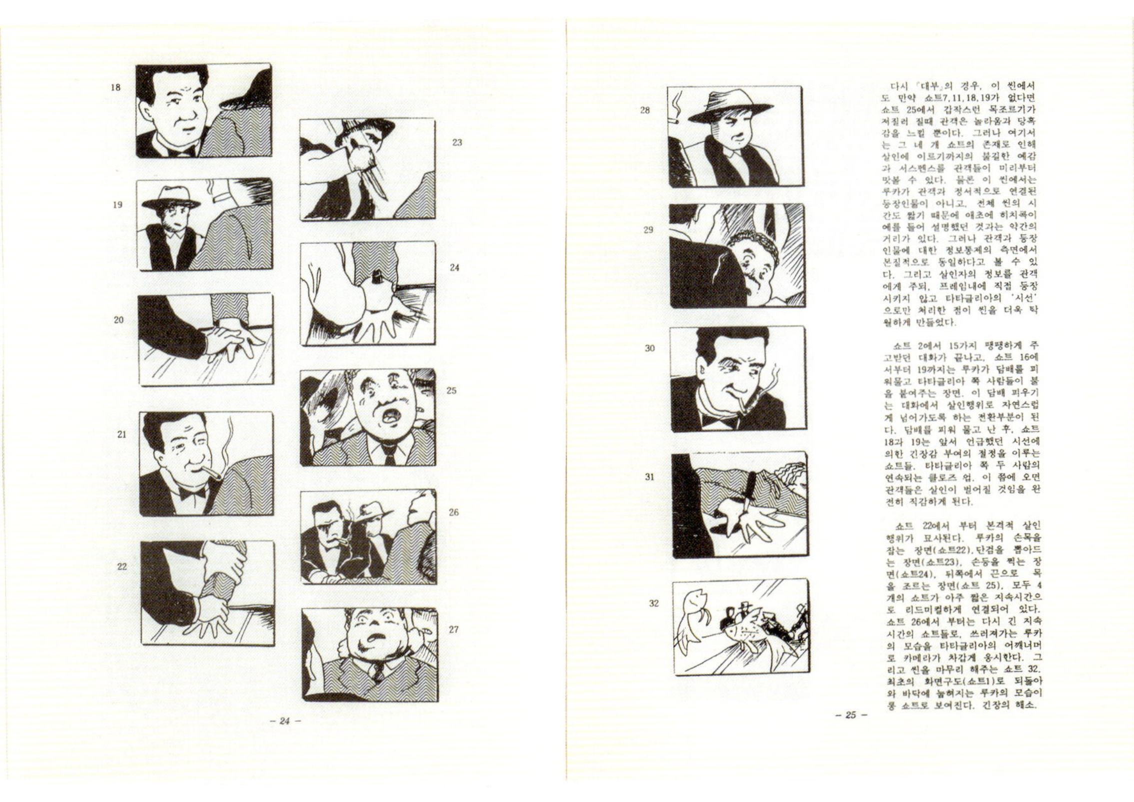

다시 「대부」의 경우, 이 씬에서도 만약 쇼트7, 11, 18, 19가 없다면 쇼트 25에서 갑작스런 목조르기가 저질러 질때 관객은 놀라움과 당혹감을 느낄 뿐이다. 그러나 여기서는 그 네 개 쇼트의 존재로 인해 살인에 이르기까지의 불길한 예감과 서스펜스를 관객들이 미리부터 맛볼 수 있다. 물론 이 씬에서는 루카가 관객과 정서적으로 연결된 등장인물이 아니고, 전체 씬의 시간도 짧기 때문에 애초에 히치콕이 예를 들어 설명했던 것과는 약간의 거리가 있다. 그러나 관객과 등장인물에 대한 정보통제의 측면에서 본질적으로 동일하다고 볼 수 있다. 그리고 살인자의 정보를 관객에게 주되, 프레임내에 직접 등장시키지 않고 타타글리아의 '시선'으로만 처리한 점이 씬을 더욱 탁월하게 만들었다.

쇼트 2에서 15가지 팽팽하게 주고받던 대화가 끝나고, 쇼트 16에서부터 19까지는 루카가 담배를 피워물고 타타글리아 쪽 사람들이 불을 붙여주는 장면. 이 담배 피우기는 대화에서 살인행위로 자연스럽게 넘어가도록 하는 전환부분이 된다. 담배를 피워 물고 난 후, 쇼트 18과 19는 앞서 언급했던 시선에 의한 긴장감 부여의 절정을 이루는 쇼트들. 타타글리아 쪽 두 사람의 연속되는 클로즈 업. 이 쯤에 오면 관객들은 살인이 벌어질 것임을 완전히 직감하게 된다.

쇼트 22에서 부터 본격적 살인행위가 묘사된다. 루카의 손목을 잡는 장면(쇼트22), 단검을 뽑아드는 장면(쇼트23), 손등을 찍는 장면(쇼트24), 뒤쪽에서 끈으로 목을 조르는 장면(쇼트 25), 모두 4개의 쇼트가 아주 짧은 지속시간으로 리드미컬하게 연결되어 있다. 쇼트 26에서 부터는 다시 긴 지속시간의 쇼트들로, 쓰러져가는 루카의 모습을 타타글리아의 어깨너머로 카메라가 차갑게 응시한다. 그리고 씬을 마무리 해주는 쇼트 32. 최초의 화면구도(쇼트1)로 되돌아와 바닥에 눕혀지는 루카의 모습이 롱 쇼트로 보여진다. 긴장의 해소.

白色人
White Man
화이트 맨

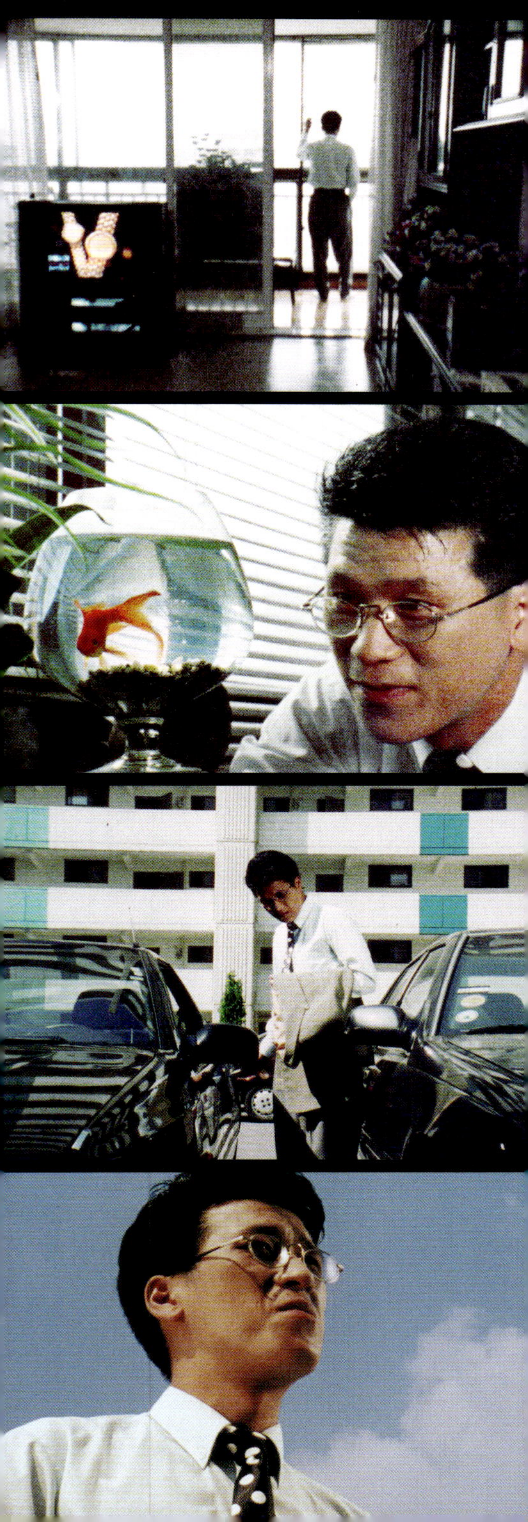

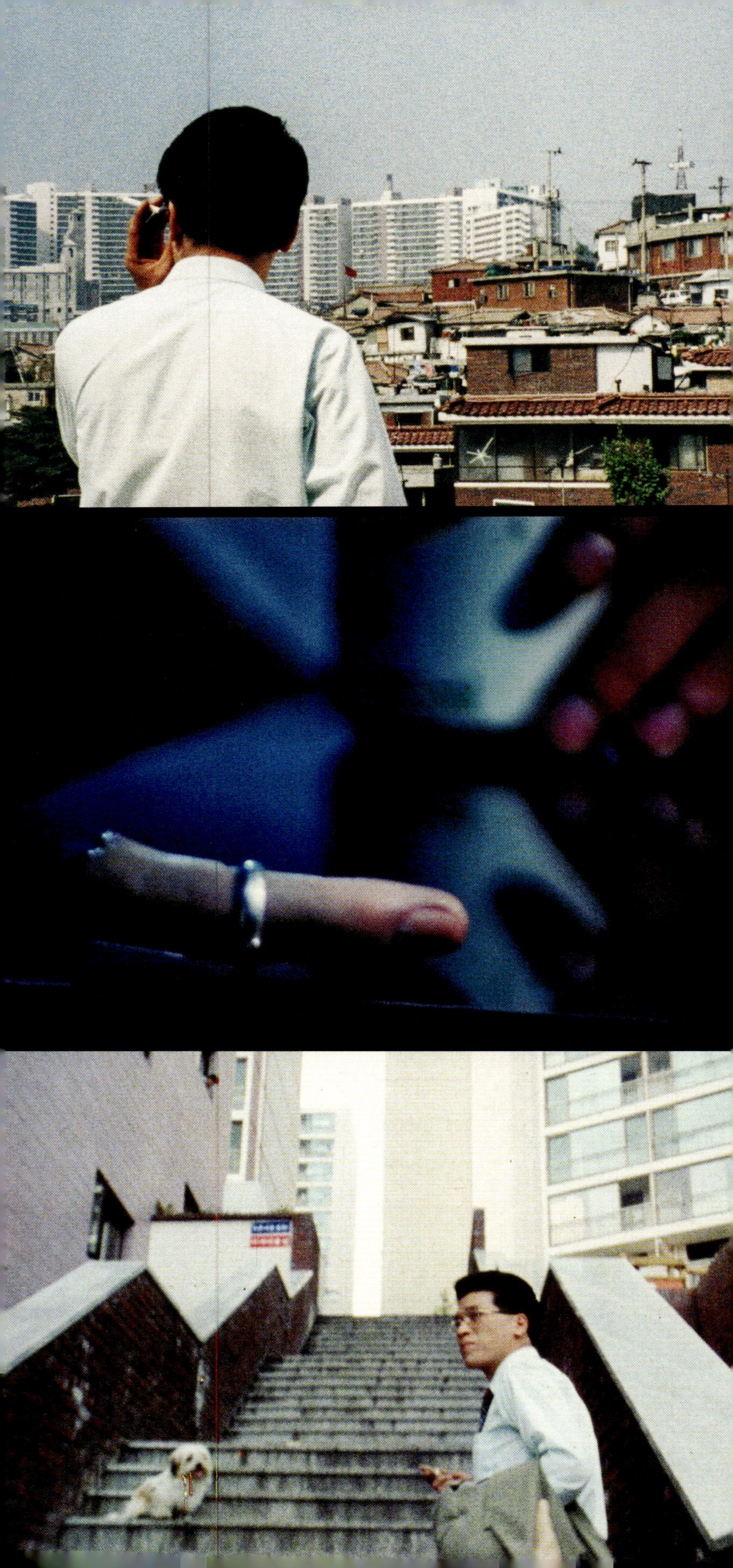

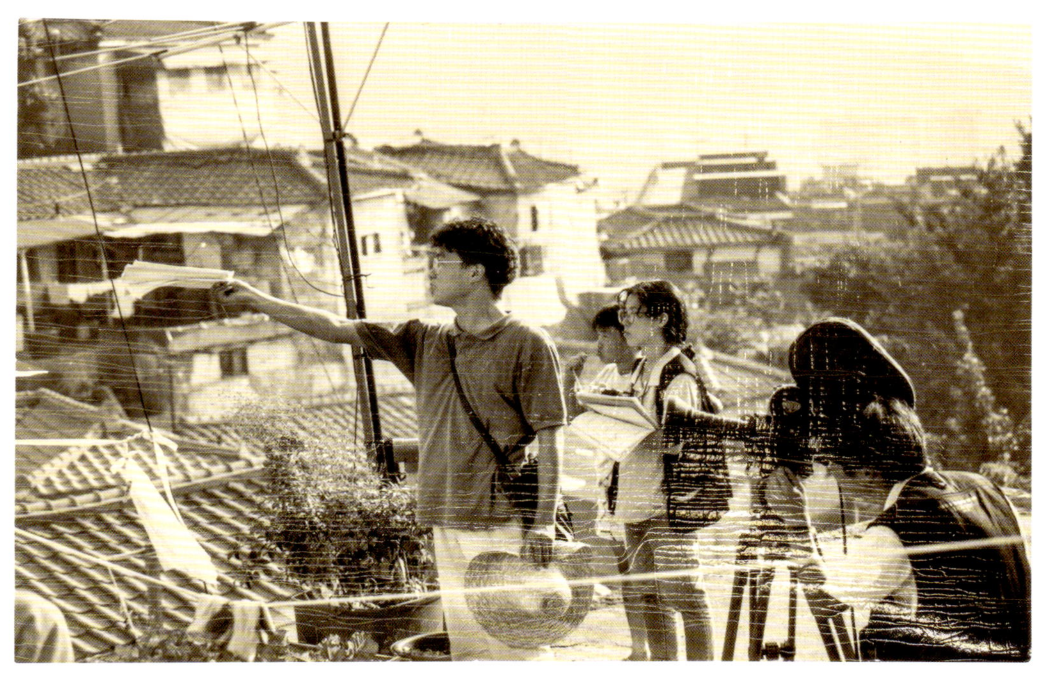

I didn't major in film studies. I had never worked on a film set before. But for the first time, I was able to do something with films. Yellow Door is where I made my dream of becoming a director come true.

Bong's 16mm short *White Man* was the first film made by Yellow Door's production team. It helped secure his admission to the Korean Academy of Film Arts (KAFA), a one-year program that gave him hands-on training with professional film equipment.

Opposite: Scenes from *White Man*

Above: Bong (center) and crew during production of *White Man*

支離滅裂 /지 /리 /멸 /렬

INCOHERENCE

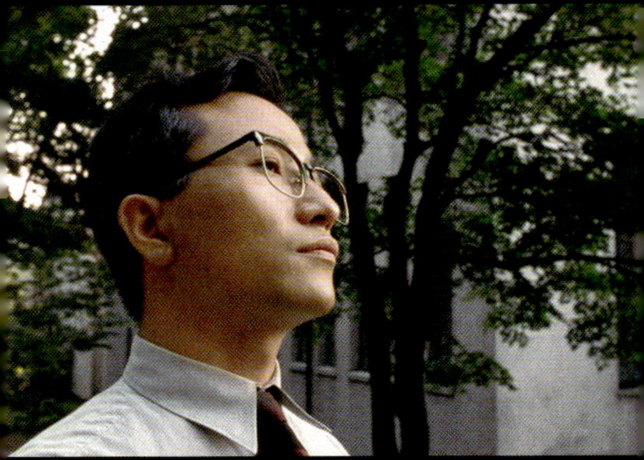

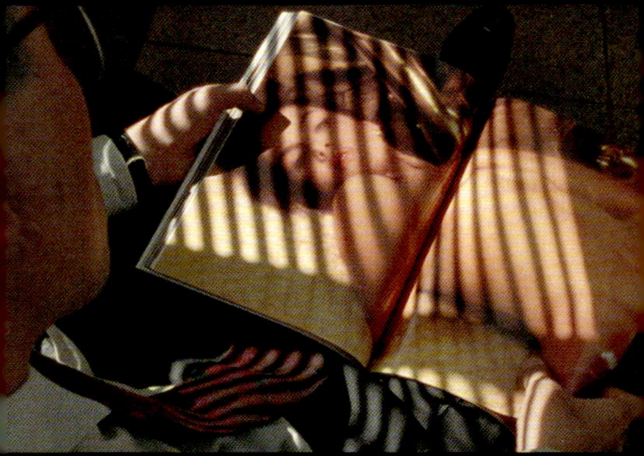

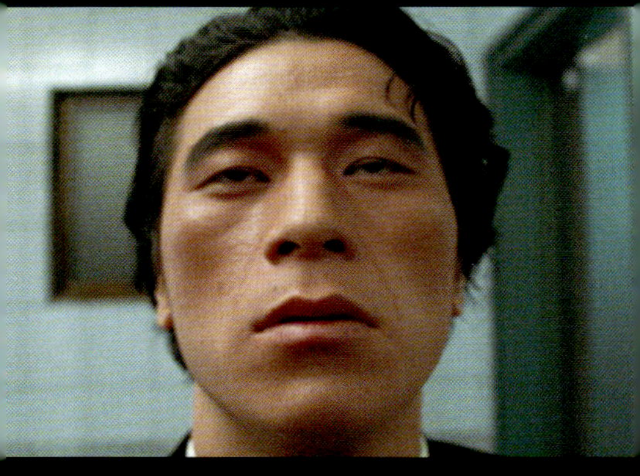

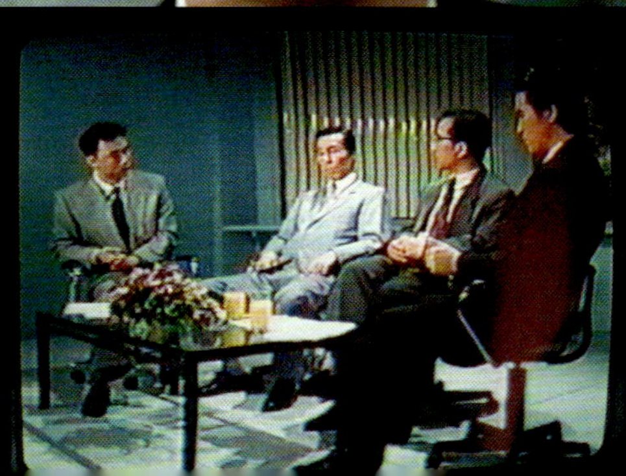

The absurdity of Korean society in itself excites me cinematically. It's bewildering. When you depict it cinematically, it may look like comedy at first, but it's actually the most realistic portrayal.

Incoherence (1994), Bong's **KAFA** graduation film, follows three respectable men—a professor, a newspaper editor, and a lawyer— engaging in misconduct and petty crimes. An epilogue brings them together as participants in a televised panel discussion on "the moral crisis in our society."

Opposite and this page: Scenes from *Incoherence*

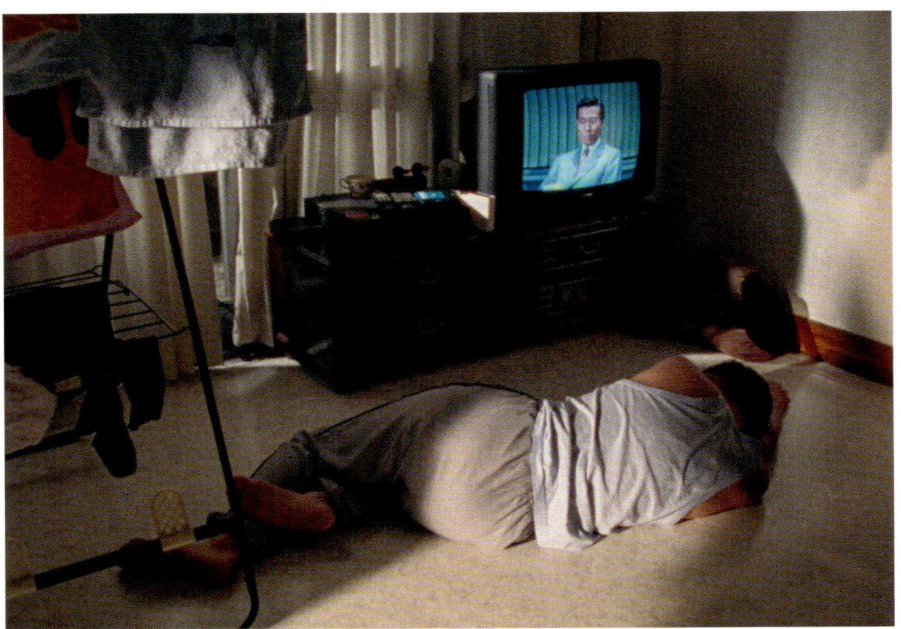

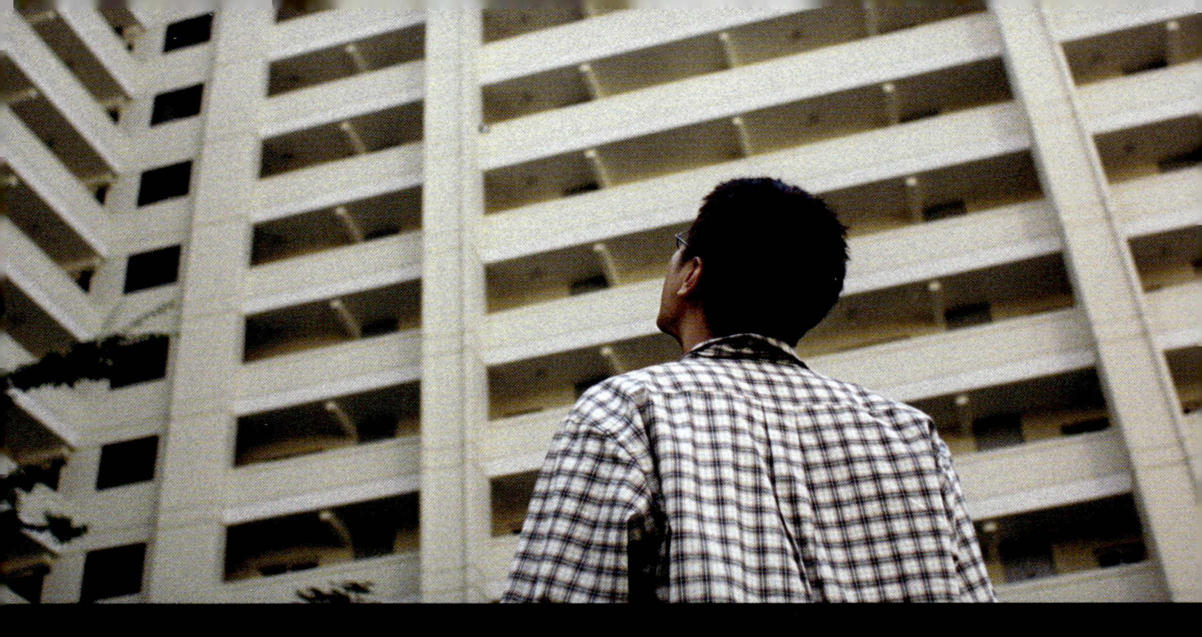

플란다스의 개

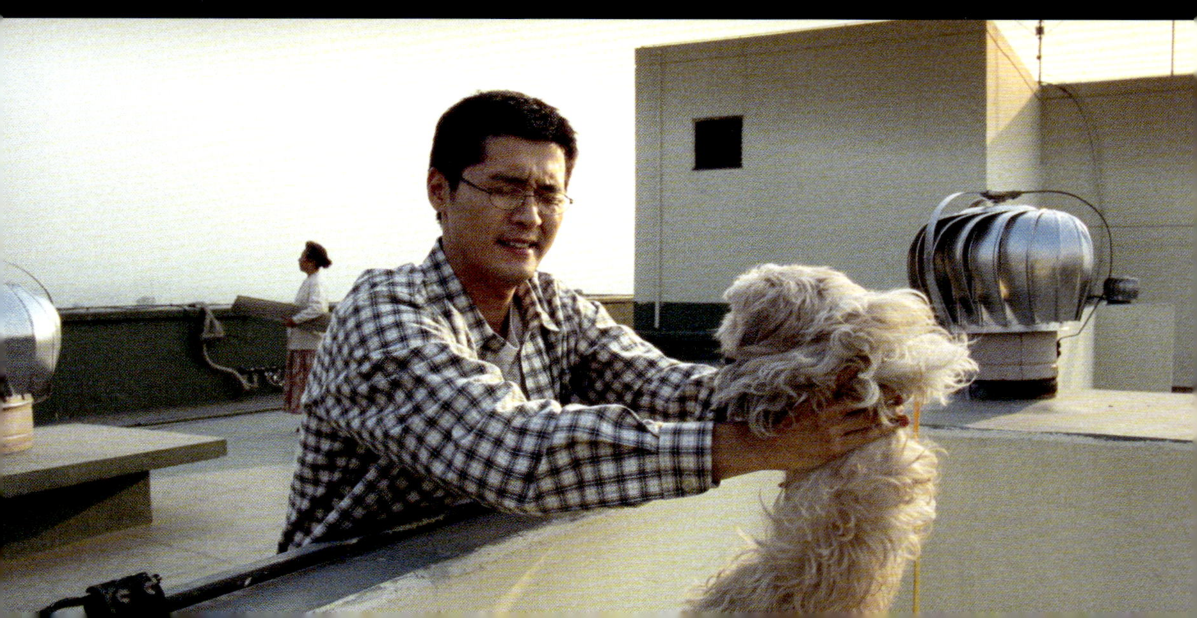

Barking Dogs Never Bite can be considered an autobiographical comedy that follows the developmental pattern of a thriller.

Bong considers his first feature, *Barking Dogs Never Bite* (2000), to be his most personal film. It draws, in part, on a childhood memory of a dead dog he found on the rooftop of a luxurious apartment complex. "It was so shocking," he says, "and I started creating stories of who might have done this…. I recalled some of those memories to come up with the story."

Opposite: Scenes from *Barking Dogs Never Bite*

Right: Draft script with the English working title *A Higher Animal*. Bong found this image of a boy holding a dog in French theorist Roland Barthes's *Camera Lucida: Reflections on Photography* (1980).

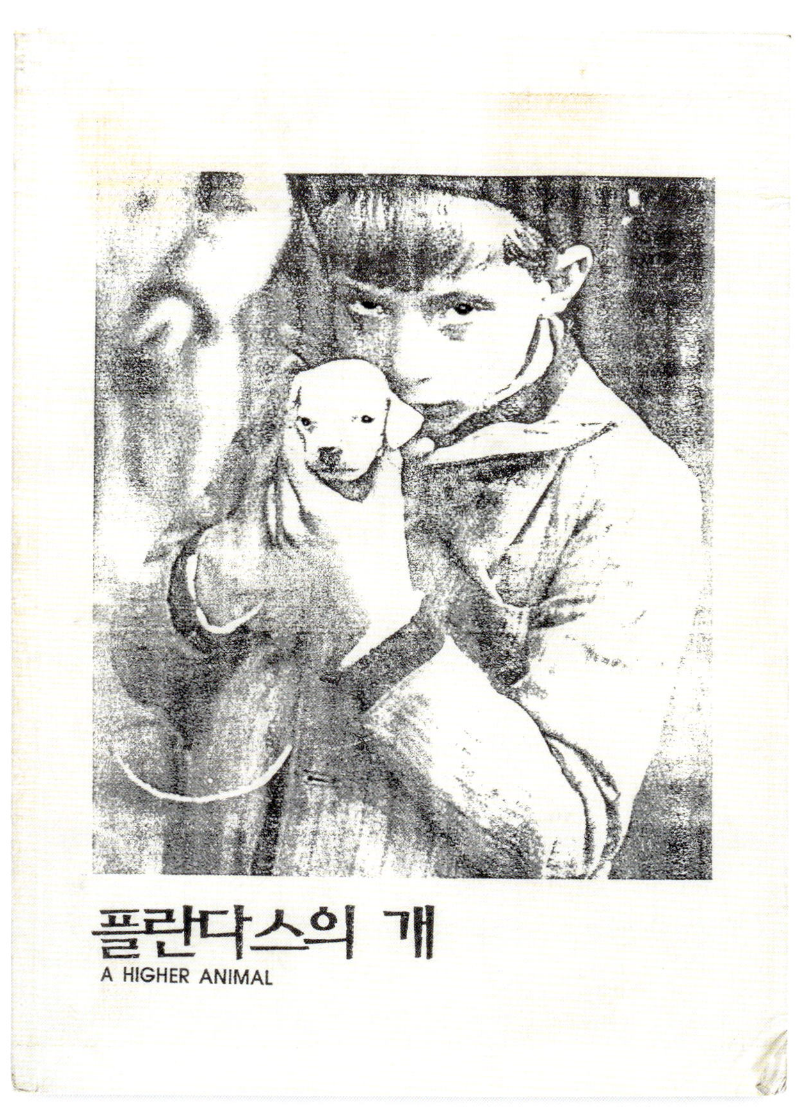

It centers around the killing of a dog in an apartment complex, a premise that raised eyebrows and puzzled many.

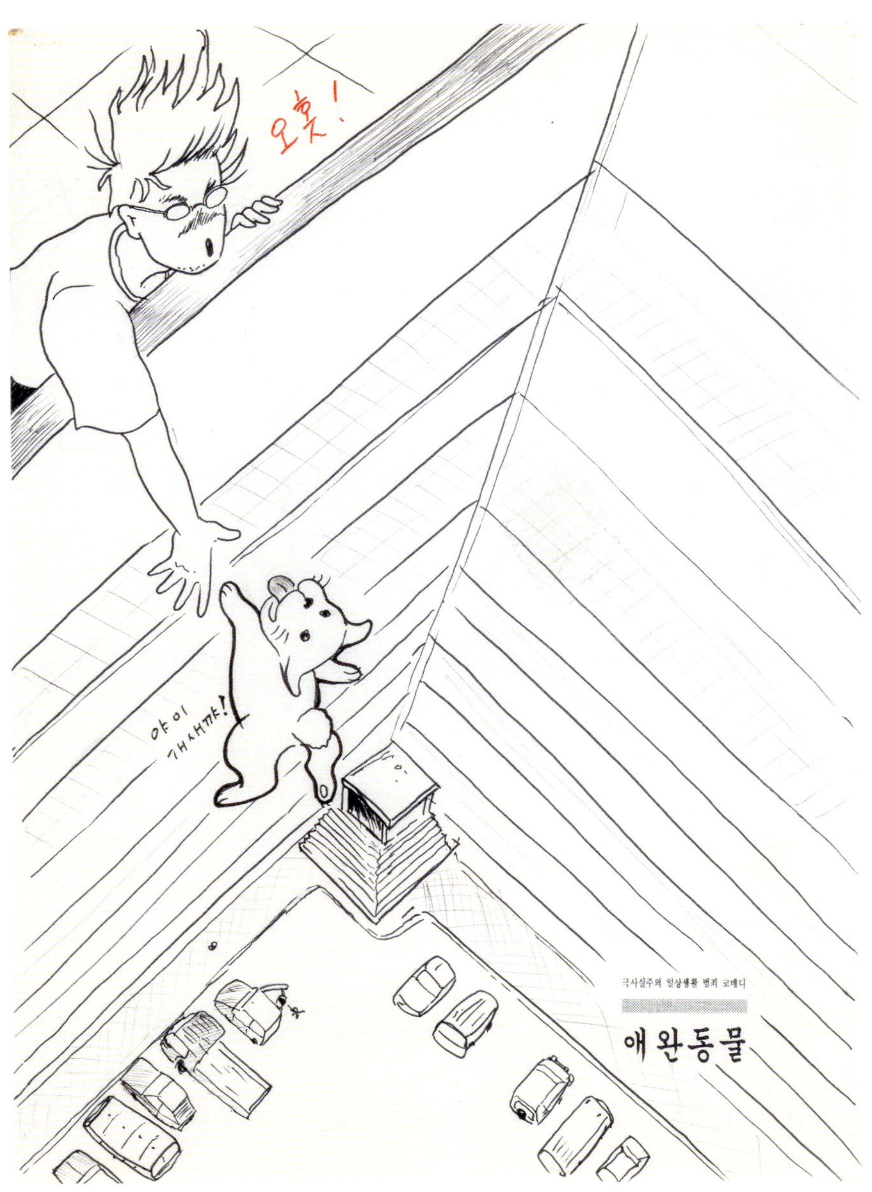

An unemployed professor and an apartment worker are brought together by a series of dognappings in their building. The film's mix of dark comedy, crime, and social commentary exemplifies the genre blending that will become a hallmark of Bong's style.

Left: Drawing by Bong. The Korean text at lower right describes the film as a "hyper-realistic everyday life crime comedy."

Opposite: Scenes from *Barking Dogs Never Bite*

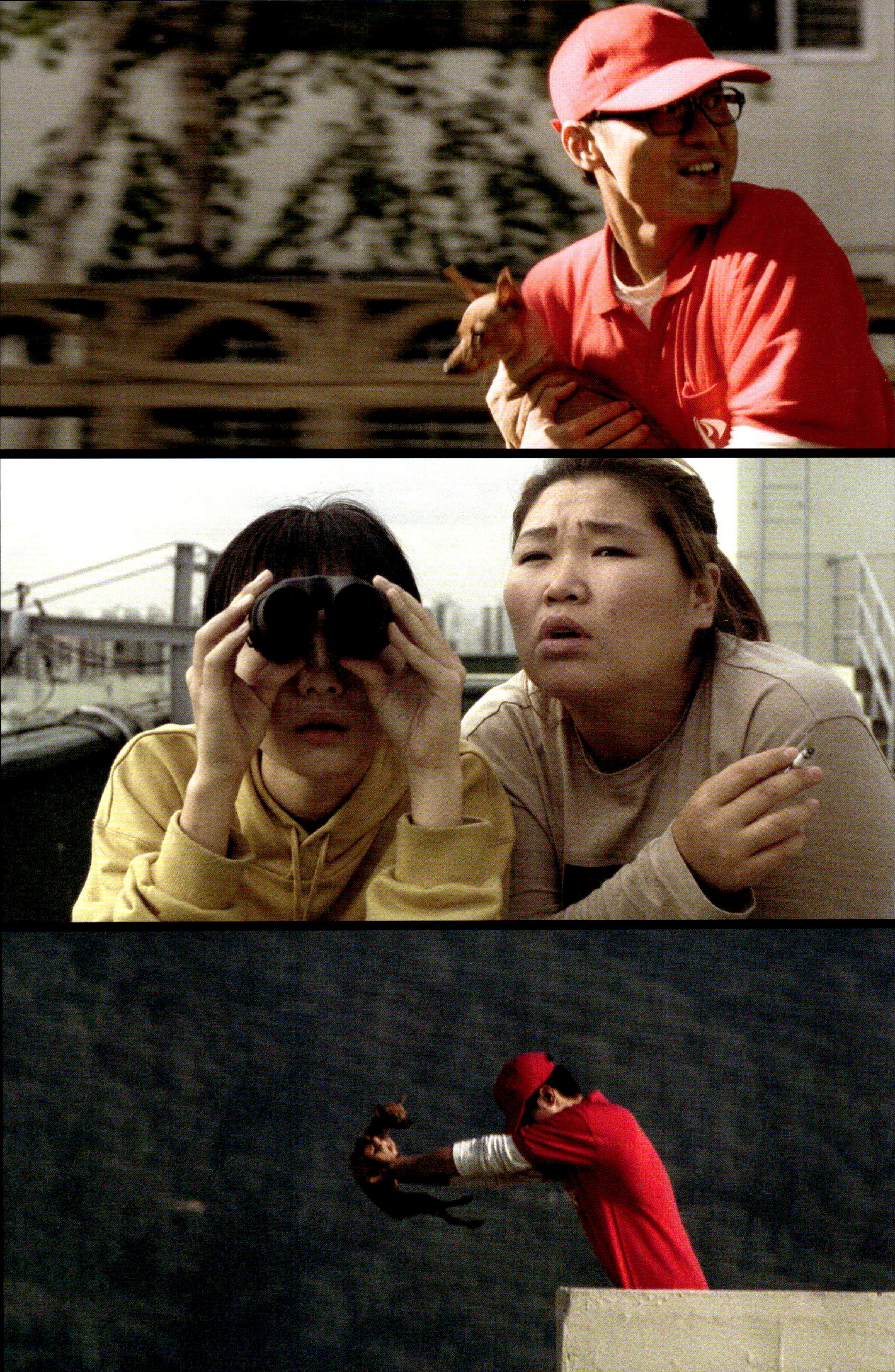

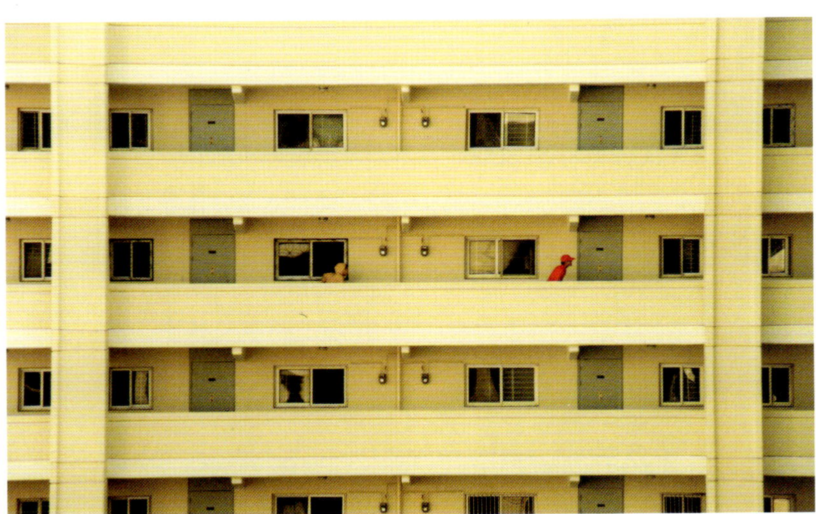

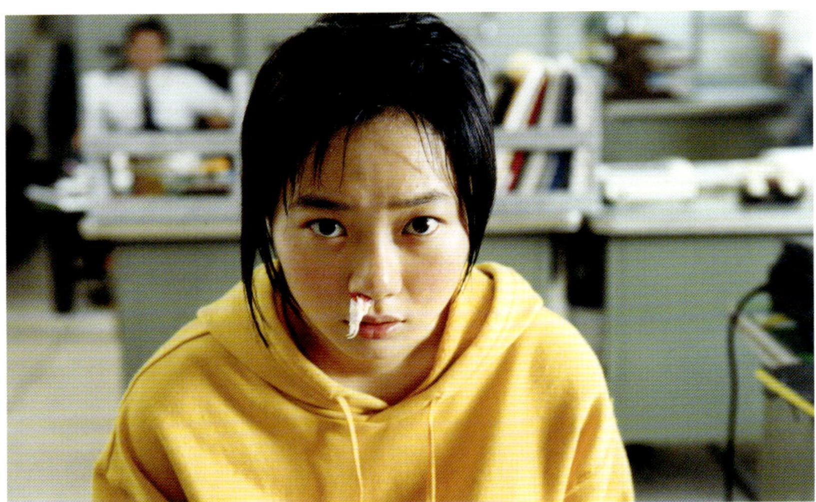

Misrecognition is important in my films. With *Barking Dogs Never Bite* in particular, that film was a series of misrecognitions and misunderstandings. I've always liked that kind of thing.

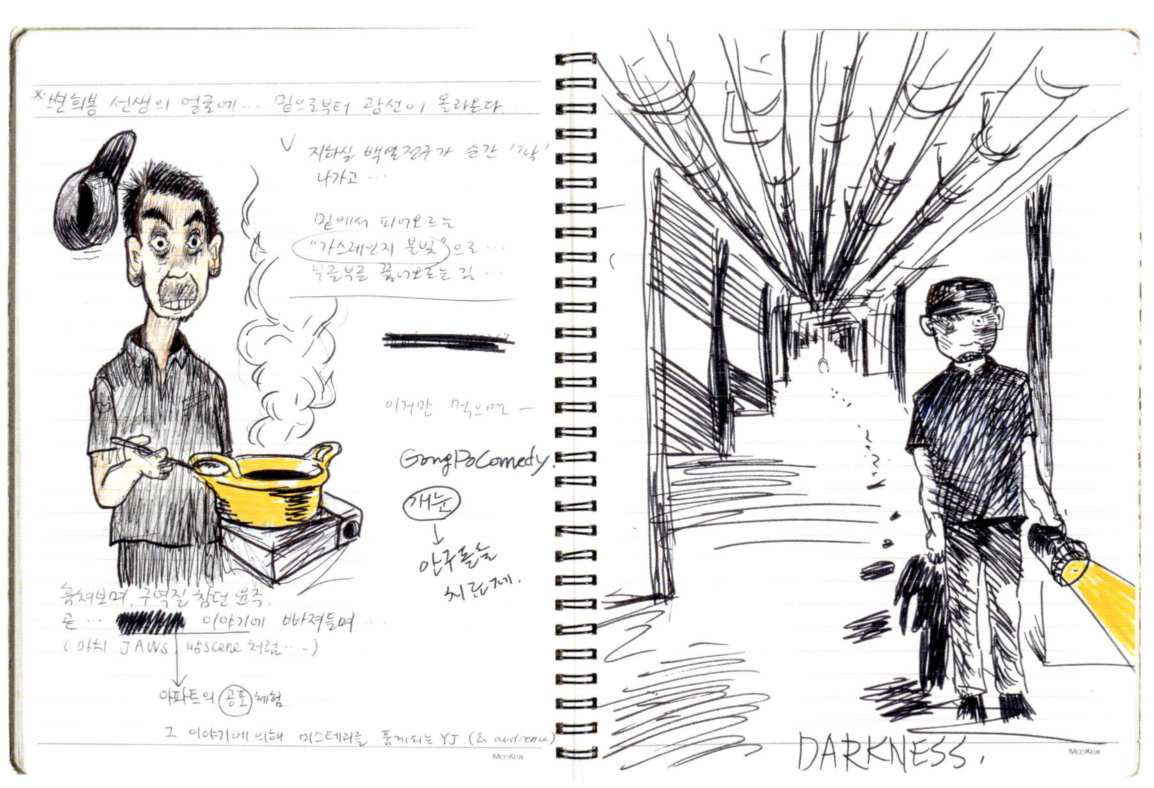

※ 변희봉 선생의 얼굴에… 밑으로부터 광선이 올라온다.
∨ 지하실 백열전구가 순간 '팍' 나가고…
밑에서 피어오르는 "가스레인지 불빛"으로… 부글부글 끓어오르는 김…
이거만 먹으며 —
GongPoComedy.
개눈
↓
안구로를 치단제.
울쳐보며, 구역질 참던 윤주.
은 … 이야기에 빠져들며 …
(마치 JAWS 밤scene 처럼… -)
↓
아파트의 공포 체험.
그 이야기에 의해 미스테리를 품게되는 YJ. (& audience)
MooKeuk
DARKNESS.
MooKeuk

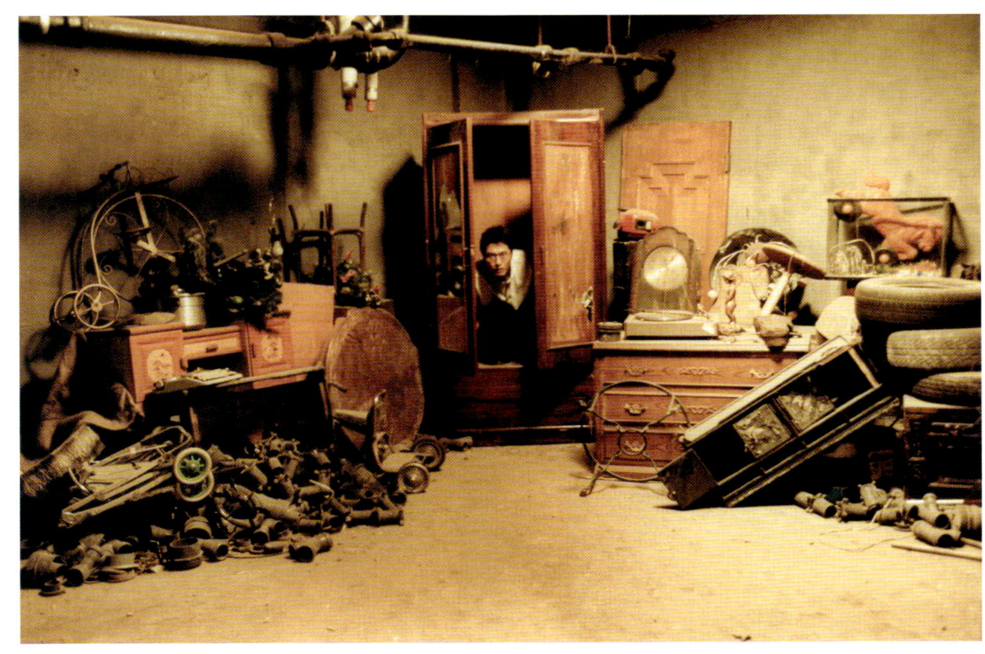

> I didn't realize it at the time, but looking back, I see that it captures two conflicting emotions: the desire to be a director and the fear of becoming a director.

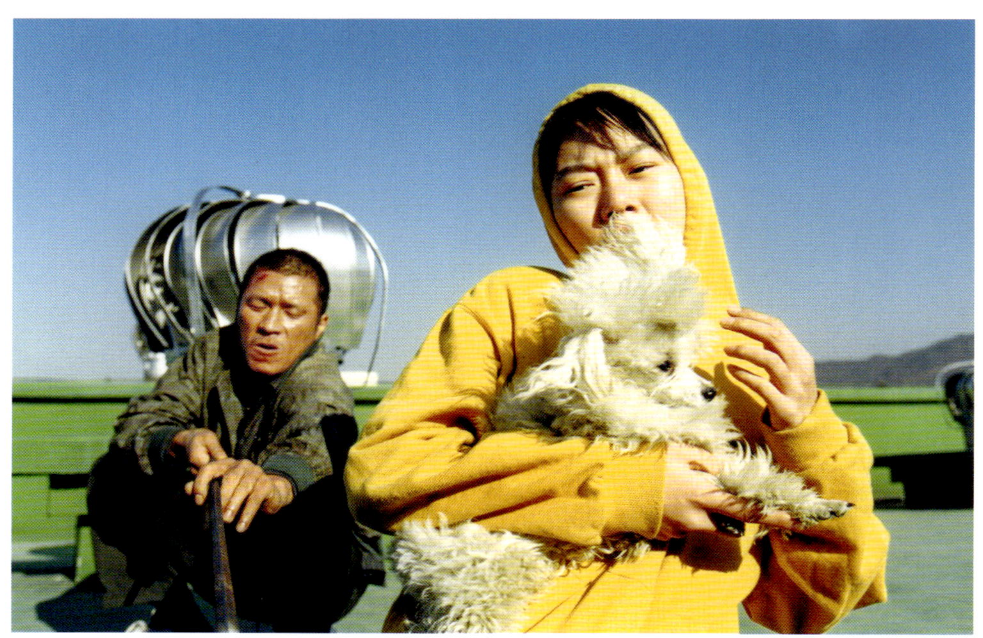

"The movie reflects my state of mind at that time," Bong says, recalling his move from independent short films to commercial features. "I was worried and caught in a strange transitional phase."

Left: Kim Roi-ha (left) and Bae Doona

Opposite: Scenes from *Barking Dogs Never Bite*

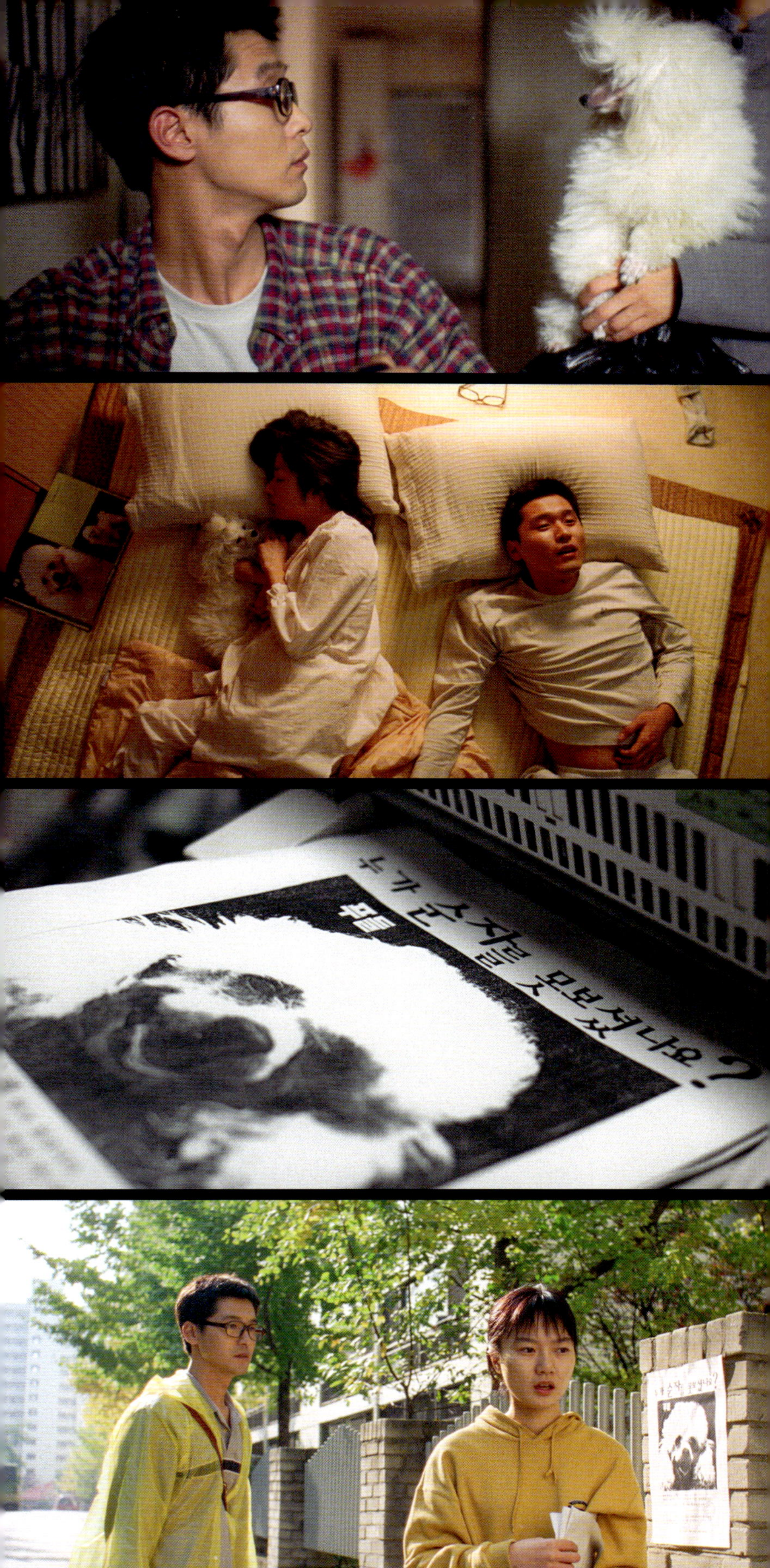
누가 강아지를 못보셨나요?
현상

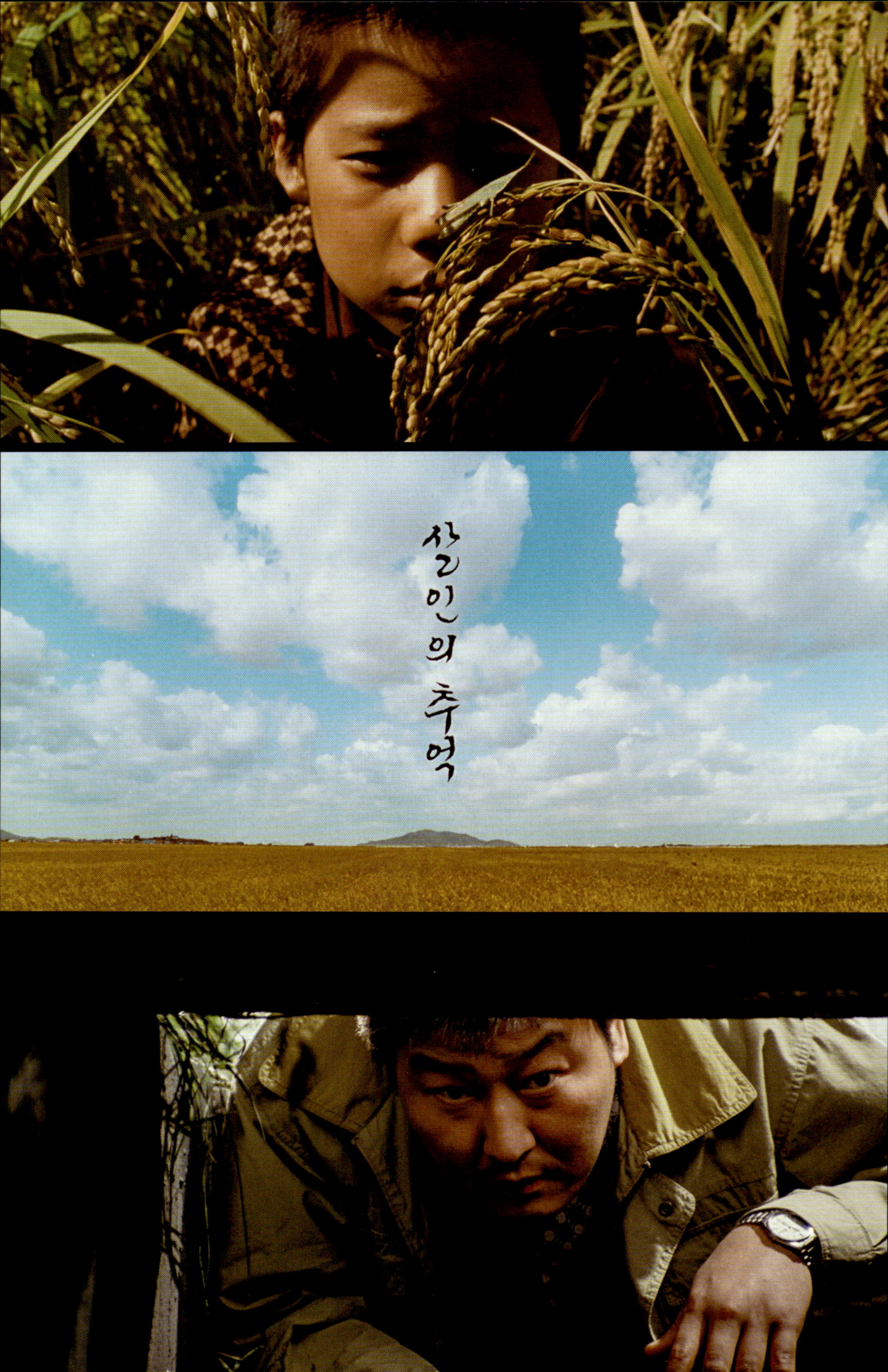
살인의 추억

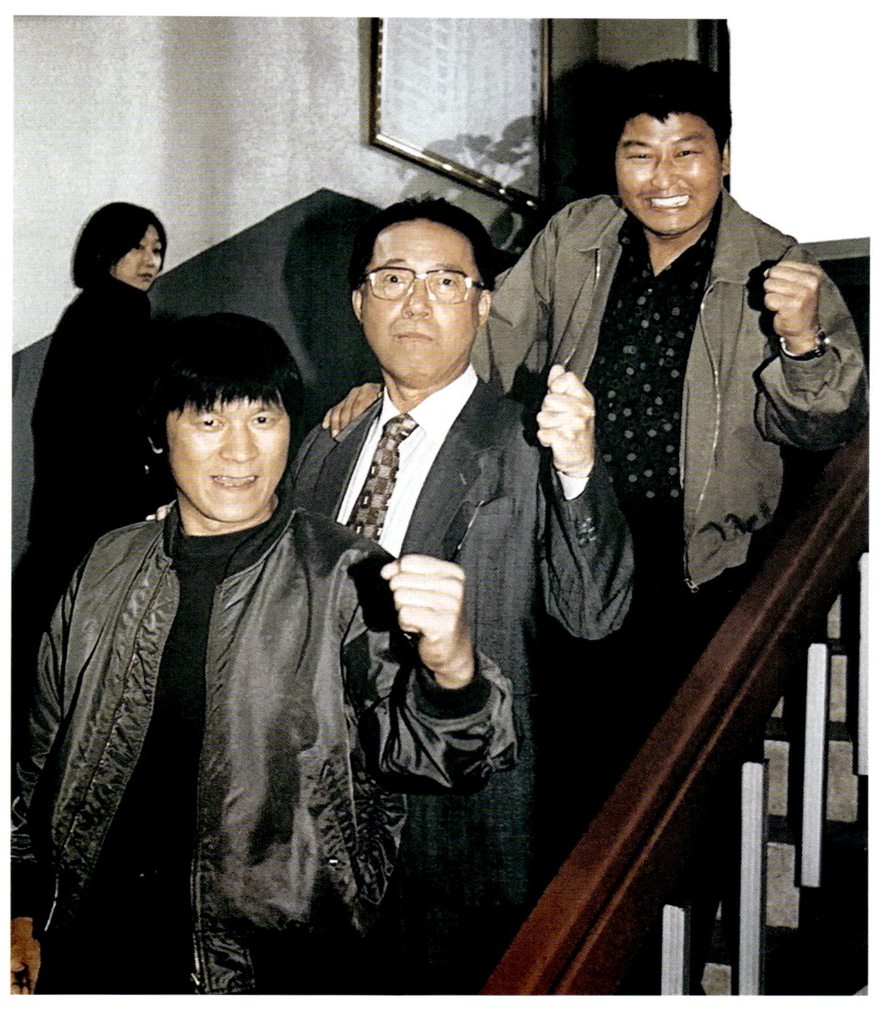

Memories of Murder is about the chaos of the '80s. This film was a reflection on why they failed to catch the actual killer and a reflection of how Korean society functioned in the '80s.

Bong based his crime thriller *Memories of Murder* (2003) on "the first real case of serial murder in Korea." The crimes took place in and around the rural city of Hwaesong between 1986 and 1991 and remained unsolved until 2019.

Above: From left, Park No-shik, Song Jae-ho, and Song Kang-ho on set. This scene was inspired by an archival photograph of the detectives celebrating the capture of a man they (wrongly) believed to be the killer.

Opposite: Scenes from *Memories of Murder*

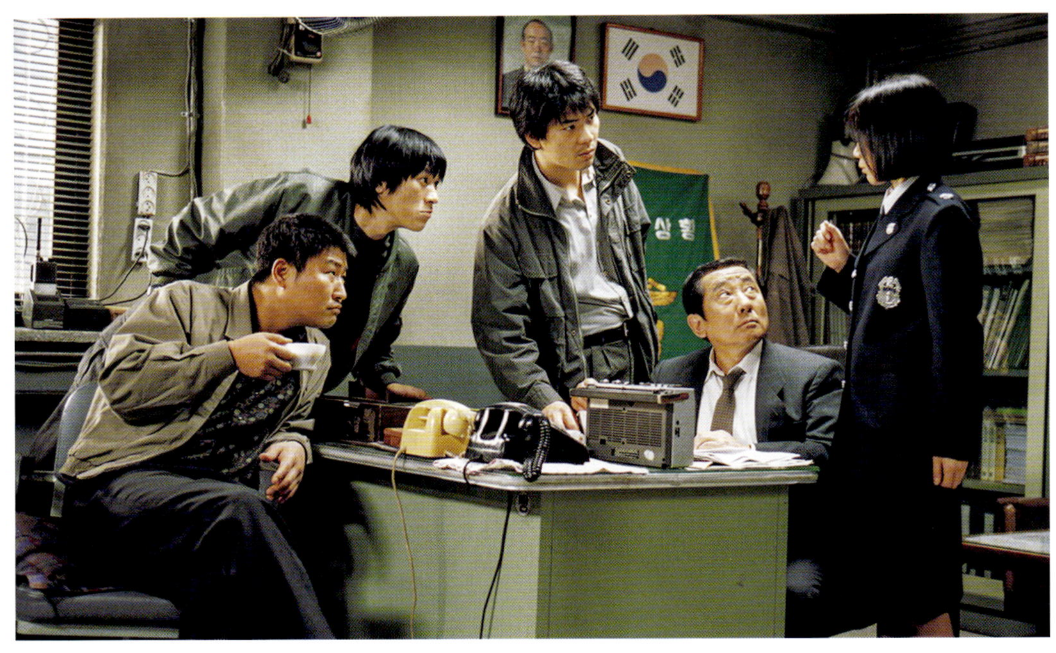

The detectives in Bong's police procedural are flawed and complex characters: incompetent, violent, corrupt, and arrogant but wholly obsessed with solving the crimes.

Above: From left, Song Kang-ho, Park No-shik, Kim Sang-kyung, Song Jae-ho, and Ko Seo-hie in *Memories of Murder*

There's an old tradition of crime movies in Korean cinema which are rather different from plot-oriented Hollywood thrillers, and I wanted to make something of that sort. The old-style Korean movies are essentially humane and emotional—that's what I like about them.

It's about a guy who really wants so badly to catch the criminal, but he lacks the skills to be successful. And it's a very sort of complicated human character that I felt only Song Kang-ho could play.

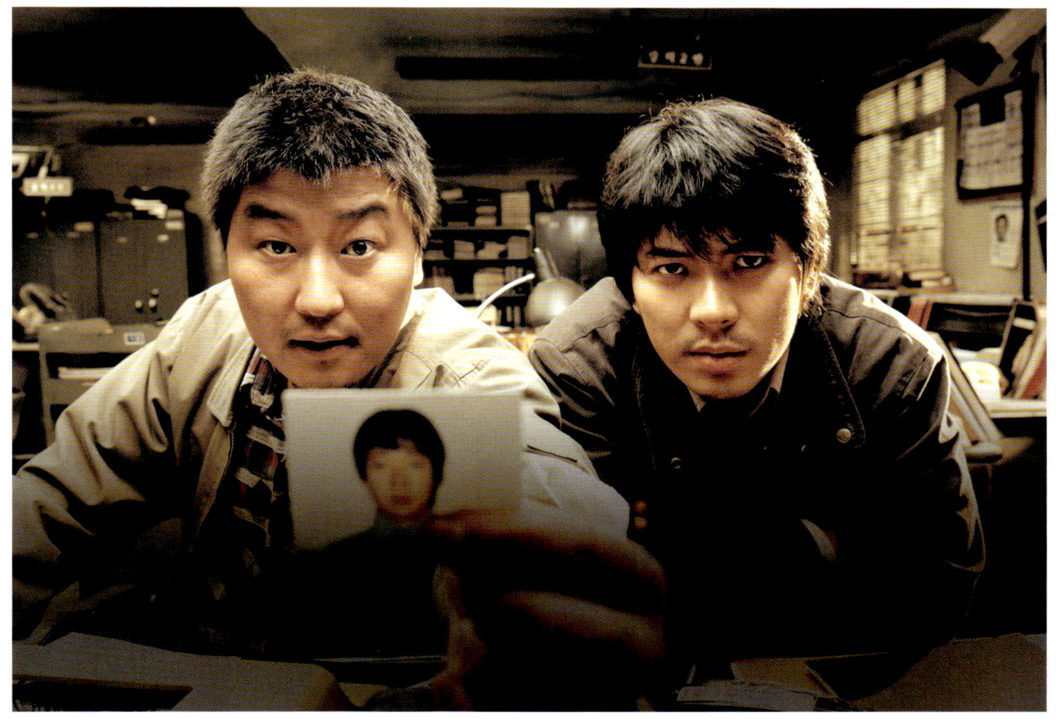

—

When I first started writing the script, people would ask me the genre, and I would wonder what to say. After a while I just invented the phrase "rural thriller." There could be the suave, intelligent detective wearing a trench coat, or a muscular detective with a handgun, but this movie doesn't follow those conventions. The ambiance is more that of a rotten tractor.

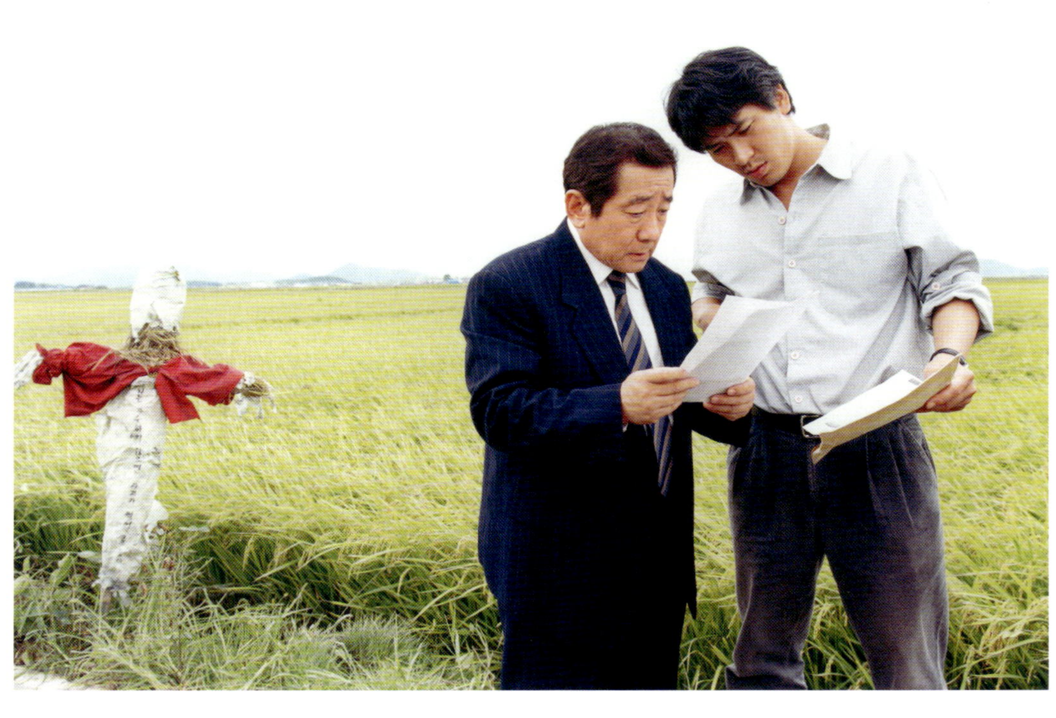

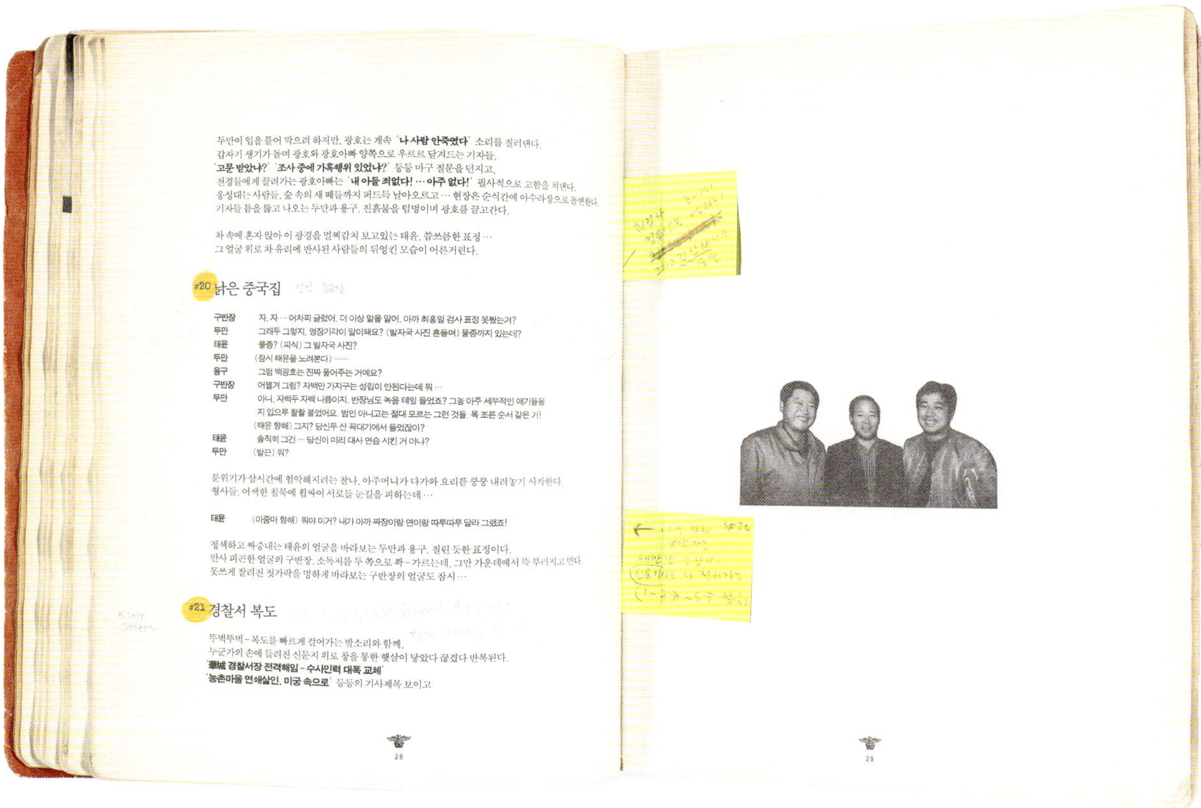

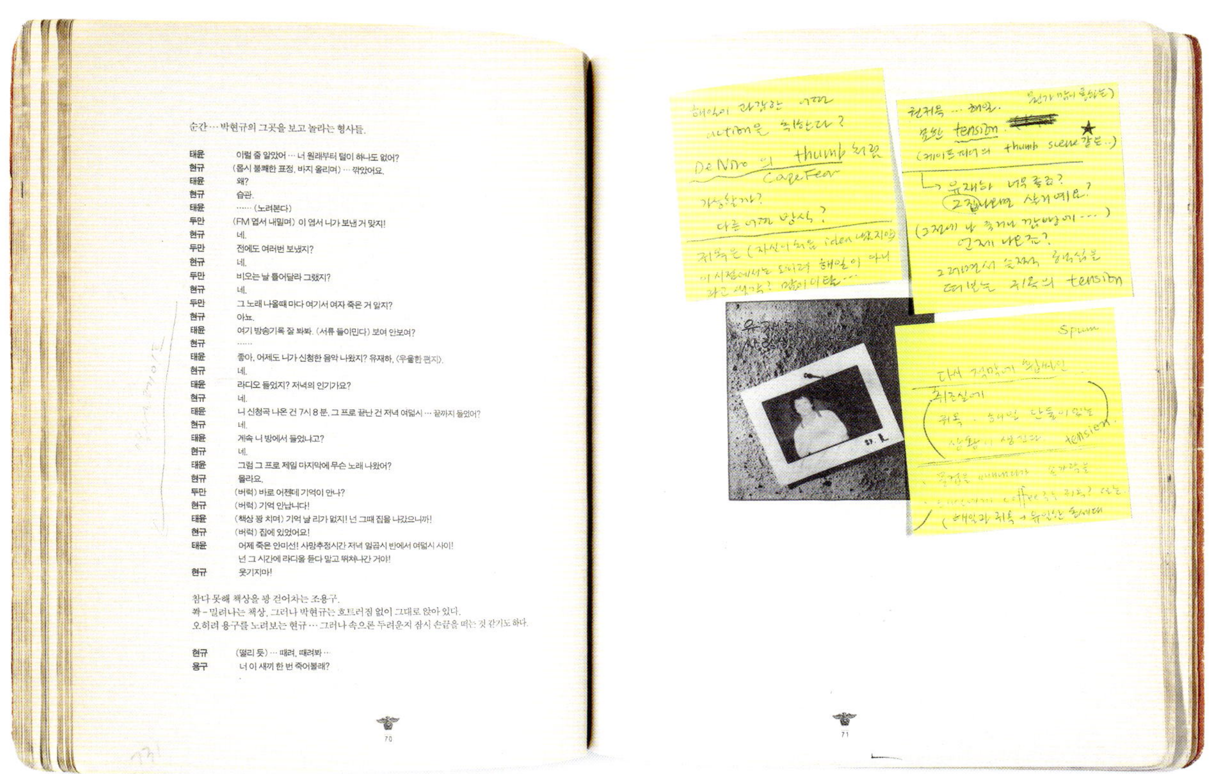

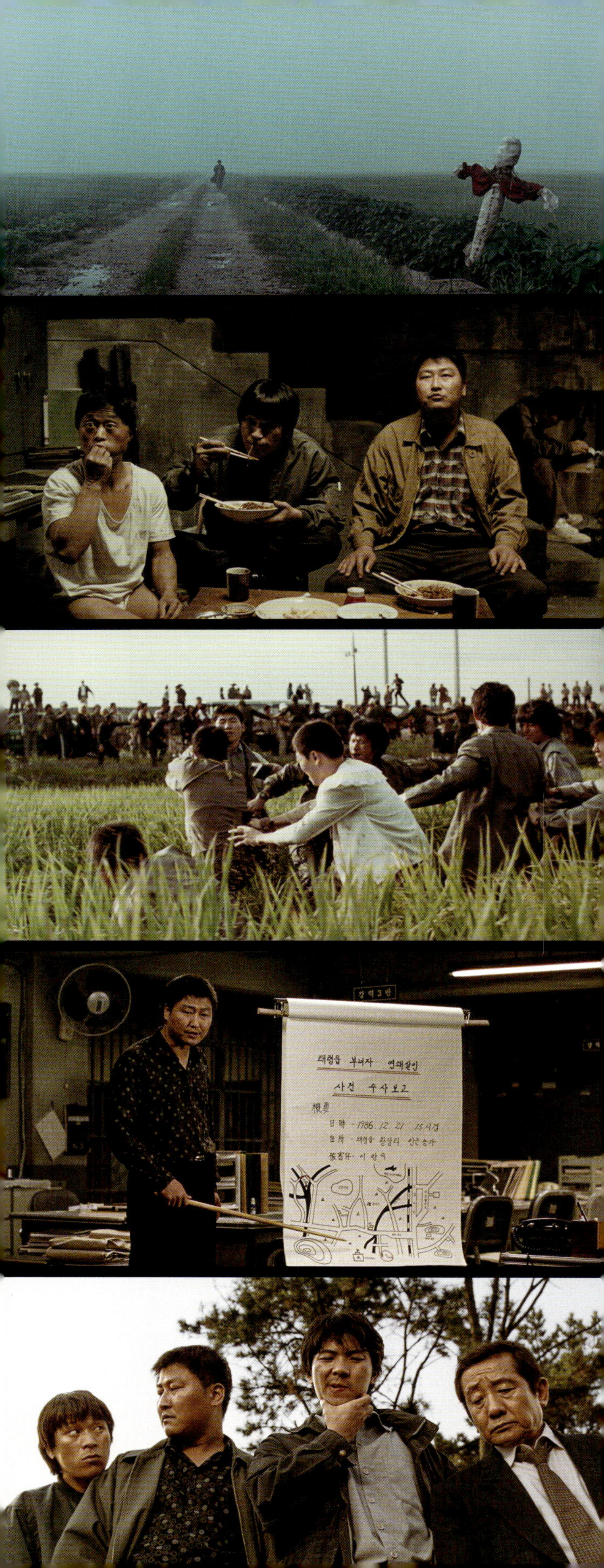
강력3반
태령읍 부녀자 연쇄살인
사건 수사보고
概要
日時 - 1986. 12. 21 15시경
住所 - 태령읍 창상리 인근 농가
被害者 - 이향숙

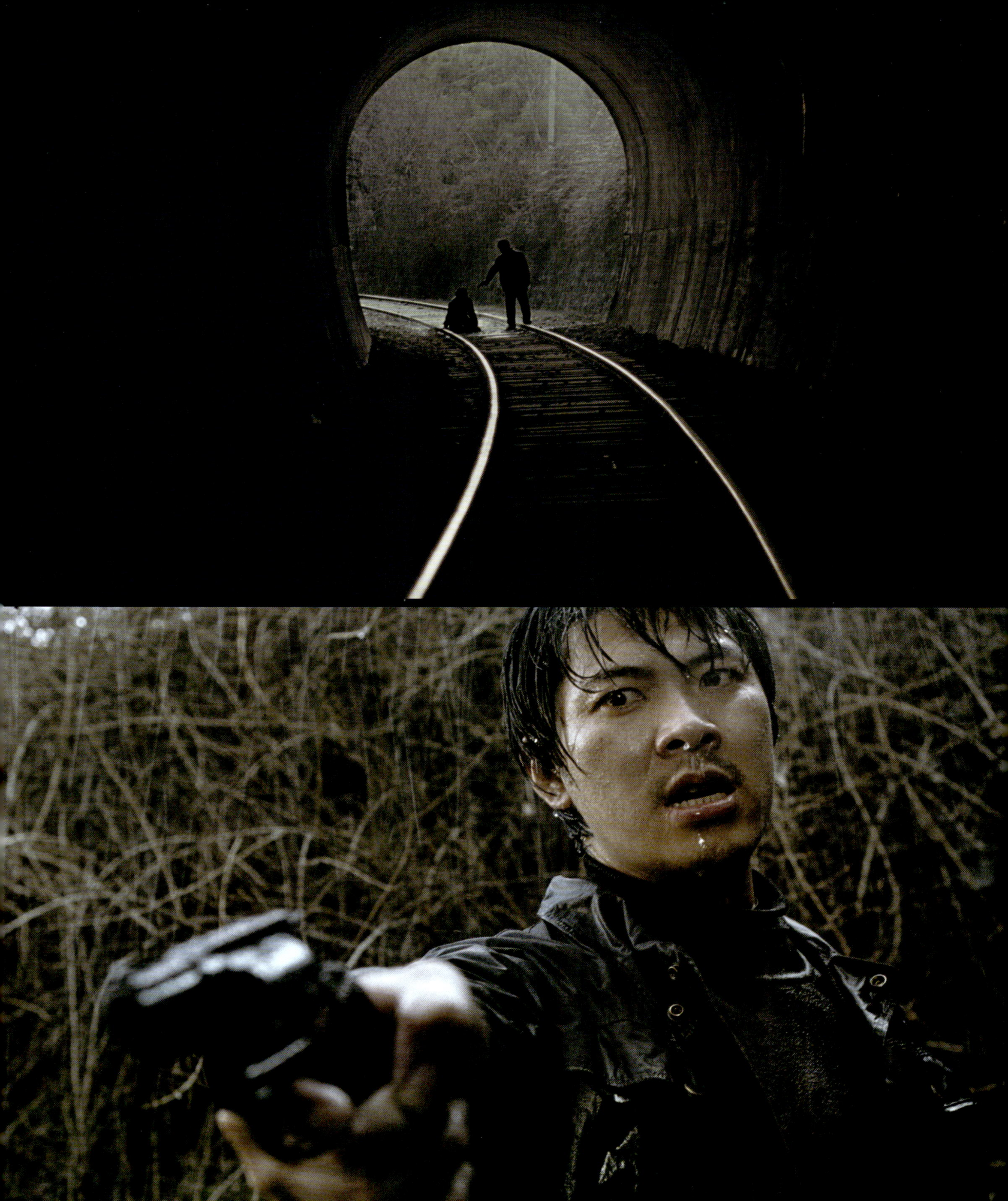

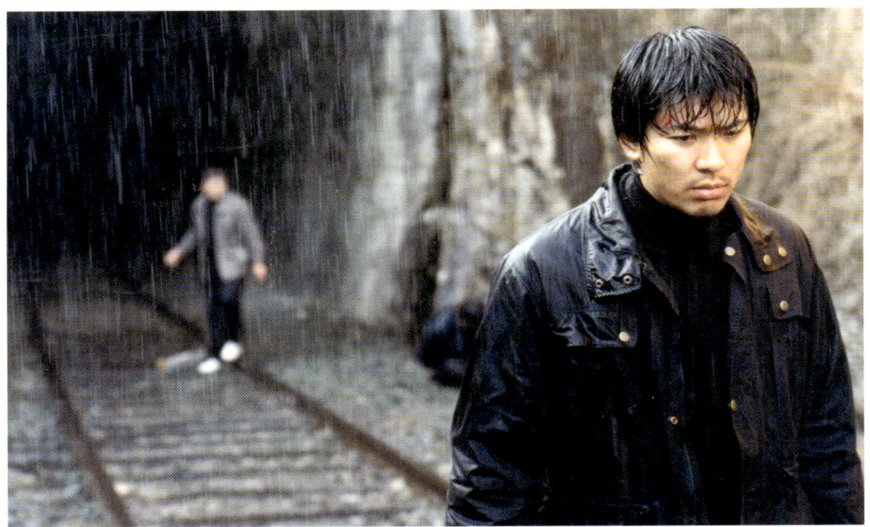

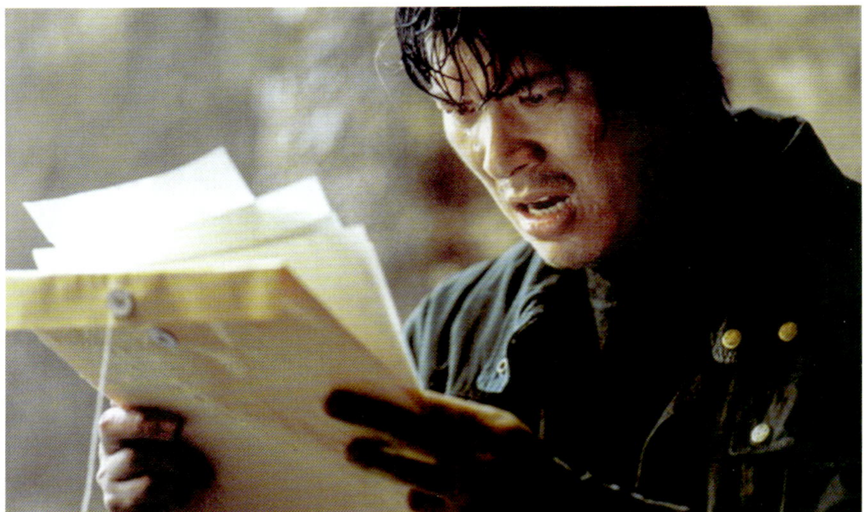

I attempted to focus on the characters' visceral feeling of ineffectiveness. The police detectives are doomed to fail in their investigations.

Without going through
the filter of thinking about
camera movements, place-
ment, and frame size … it's
impossible for me to come
up with a story. My brain
is optimized for cinema.

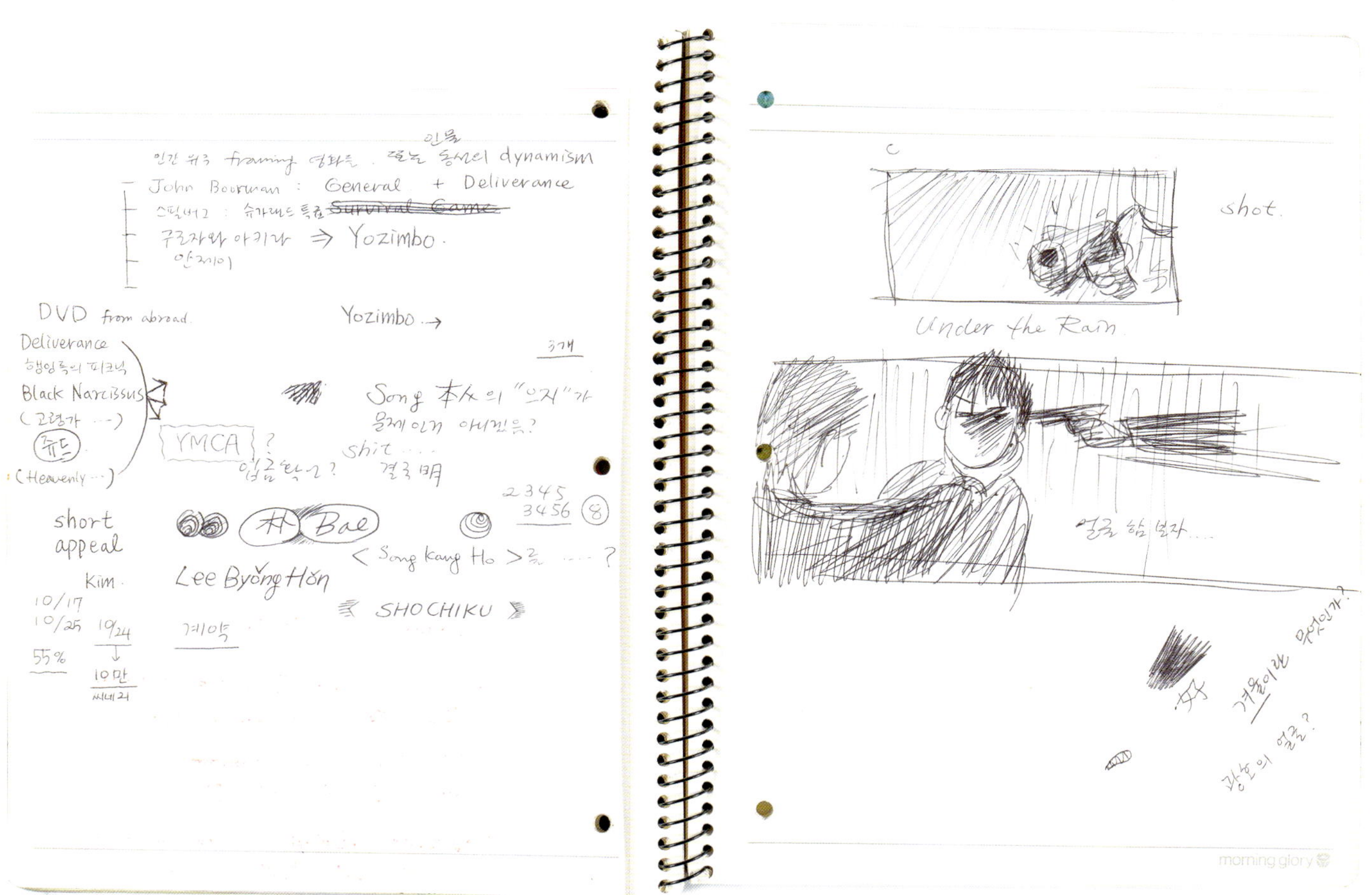

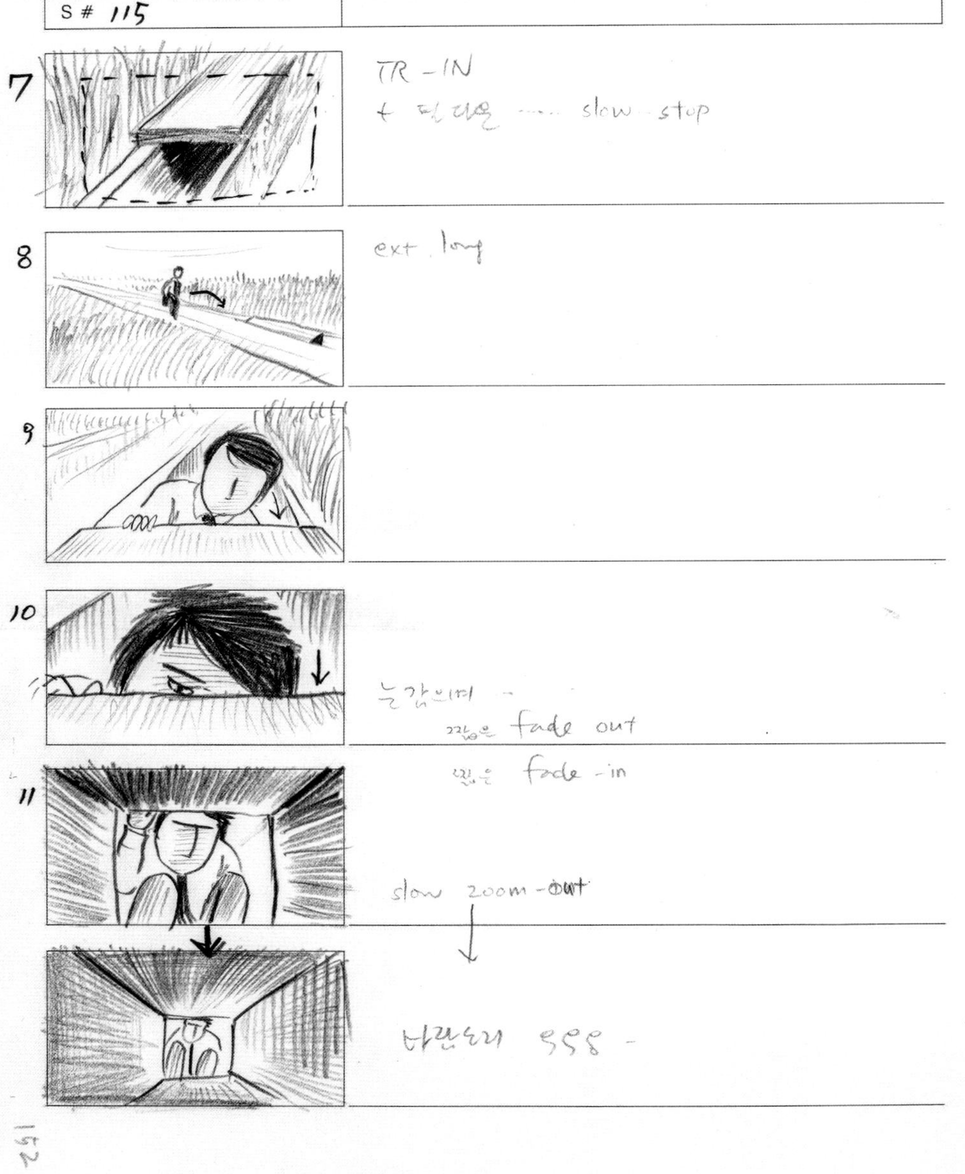

For each of his films, Bong draws detailed storyboards that illustrate key aspects of every shot: composition and framing, action and character movement, and camera angles and timing. This allows him to plan complicated set pieces, action, and visual humor long before filming begins.

Left: Bong's storyboard for *Memories of Murder*

Opposite: Scenes from *Memories of Murder*

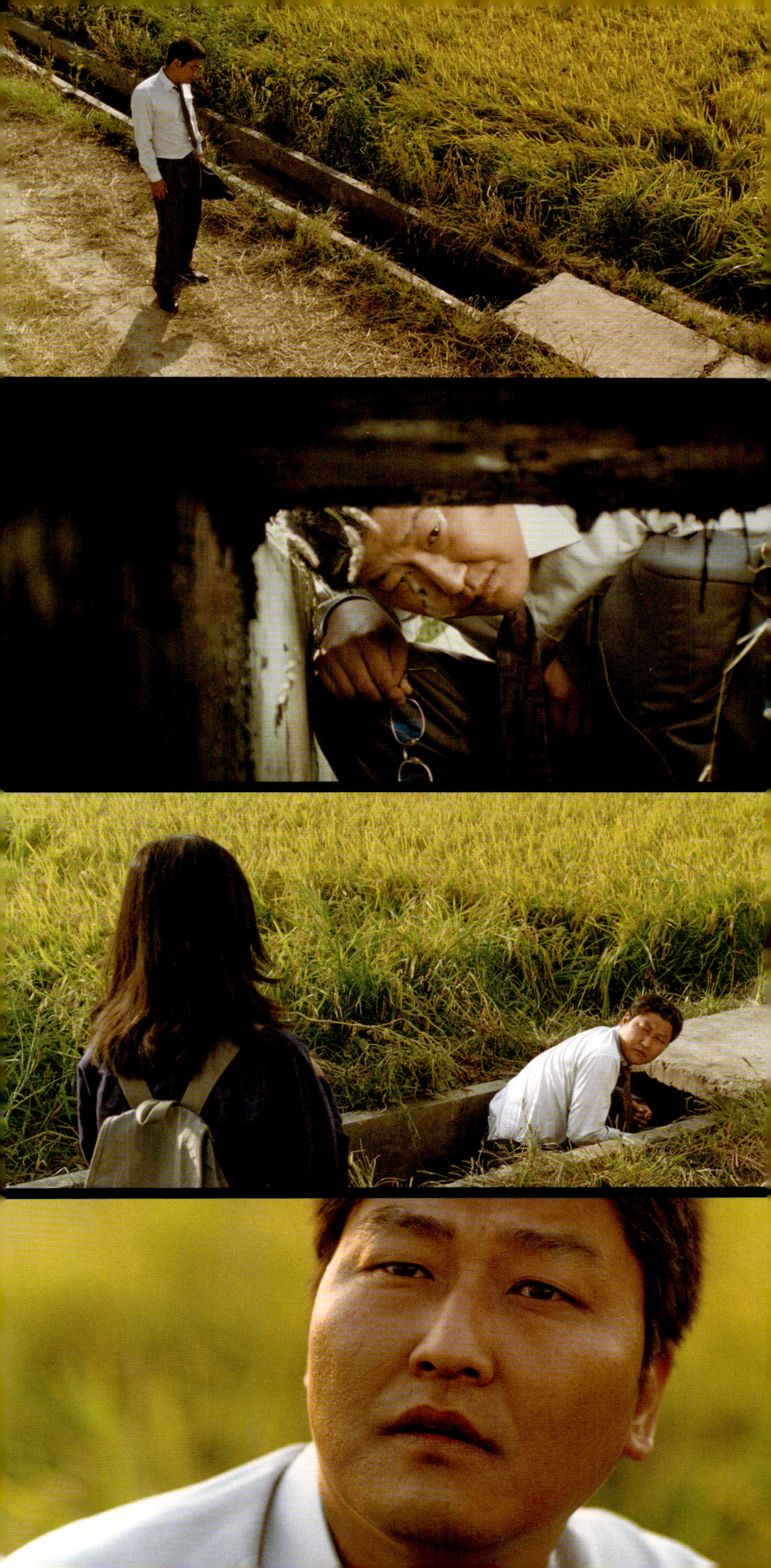

GUILLERMO DEL TORO

Director Bong and I were simpatico even before we met. When you encounter a filmmaker you share so much in common with—who values the tragedy and the comedy of heroes and villains equally, uses the same palette and compositional elements, loves monsters as symbols of universal truths or terrors—it's like you're starting a conversation in the middle. You already know each other from many movies ago.

What I find delightful is that he's profoundly enamored of cinema. Bong is not just an auteur but a film lover. This is something rare and precious. He doesn't exist high above the material or the medium; he swims in it. He's promiscuously well versed in cinema of all kinds—genre films, European arthouse, exploitation thrills, it makes no difference—and he's fascinating to talk shop with, director to director.

And then there is his tonal prowess. One of the most difficult resources for any director to acquire is tone. It's like the fingerprint of any filmmaker's soul. You cannot fake it, and you navigate it almost 99% through instinct. Think of the sentimentality, comedy, and precision of Charlie Chaplin and the scathing, raw, equally precise comedy of Buster Keaton; the heightened melodrama of Douglas Sirk, and the searing melodrama of Rainer Werner Fassbinder. To achieve what Bong does in blending comedy and melodrama in genres like crime or horror requires an incredible faith in tone. The tone cannot waver at all, or the entire structure will collapse. Everything has to coexist in a way that is completely true and unique to the director. That's why tone is so challenging and impossible to forge.

Cinema is a bit like world cuisine: You want a flavor you don't normally get at home. You're looking for an experience, not comfort food. Bong's cinematic language has flavor, an undeniable umami. I remember many years ago somebody asked me,

"What is Mexican about your films?" I said, "Me." I think the same is true for Director Bong. His movies have idiosyncrasies that feel handmade and hand-seasoned. Films like his don't come out of an assembly line. As it is with most international filmmakers, the films retain the essence of their maker's country and origins. It's impossible to erase that DNA. Genre is a universal language, but there's a localism and personality in how filmmakers subvert it.

Above all, Bong has an outlandish sense of humor. Even in one of his darkest works, *Memories of Murder*, there's a vein of humor and irreverence throughout. Those two things are not interchangeable; I think you can have humor that reaffirms who we are, the old humor, and an irreverent humor that is actually iconoclastic. I sense that Bong likes to exert the latter, allowing us to recognize things that are tragically uncouth or sadly funny about human nature and society.

When *Memories of Murder* came out, I thought it looked like a movie by someone who had been shooting films for 30 years. Then I read how young the director was and almost fainted in admiration. There's one brilliant daylight shot where they go to identify a crime scene, and it starts with a tractor crossing the land and ends in an almost perfectly circular way. The shot is two to three minutes long, with multiple elements moving up and down a hill and crossing the camera. It's a staging reminiscent of Steven Spielberg, John Schlesinger, or Roman Polanski—all masters of this kind of take—where the choreography makes the scene of a piece with the rhythm of the rest of the movie. *Memories of Murder* is like the work of an old master with the rabid, savage wit of a young filmmaker. It is, in my opinion, an extraordinary film. There's no way you can be a practitioner of our craft and come out of a movie like that without feeling profoundly inspired.

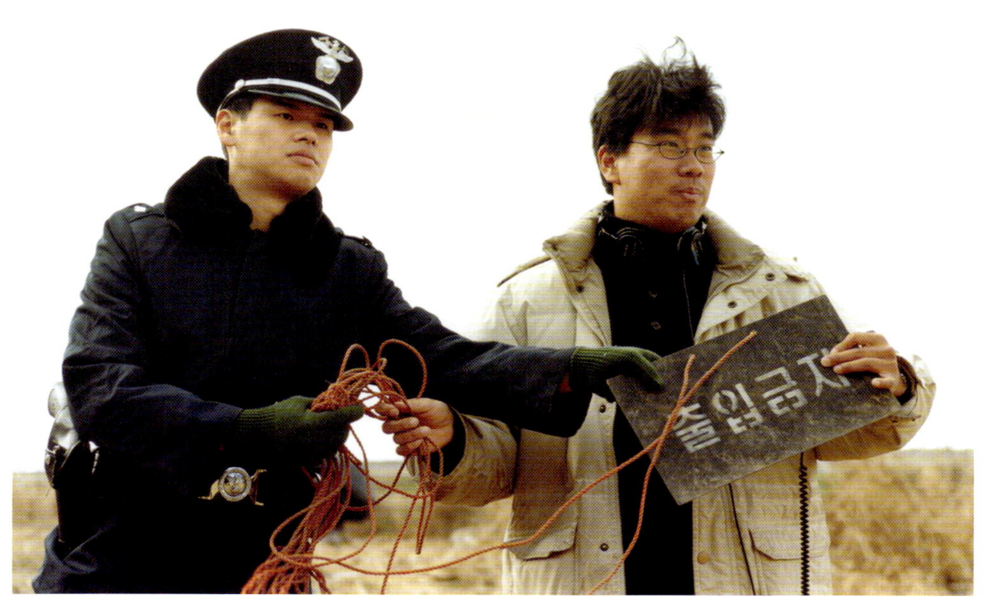

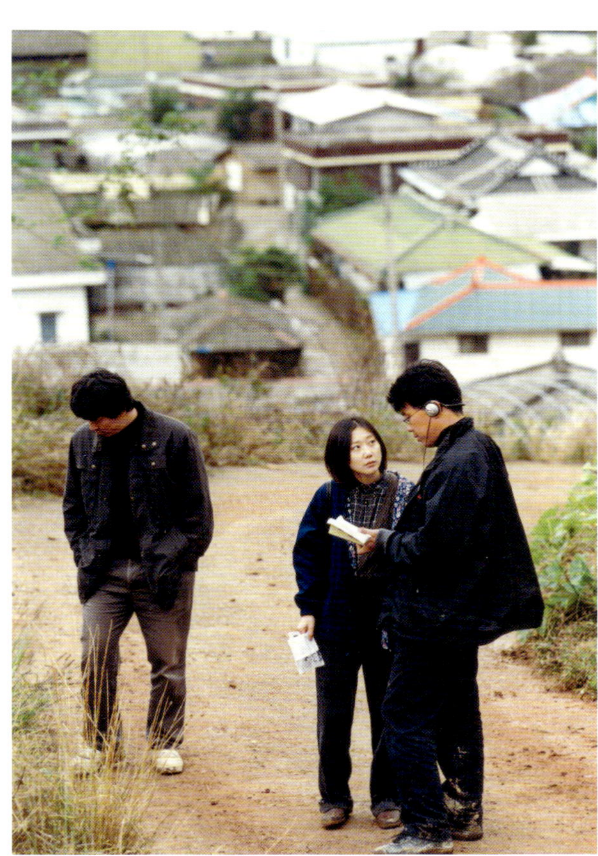

Bong and crew on location
during production of
Memories of Murder

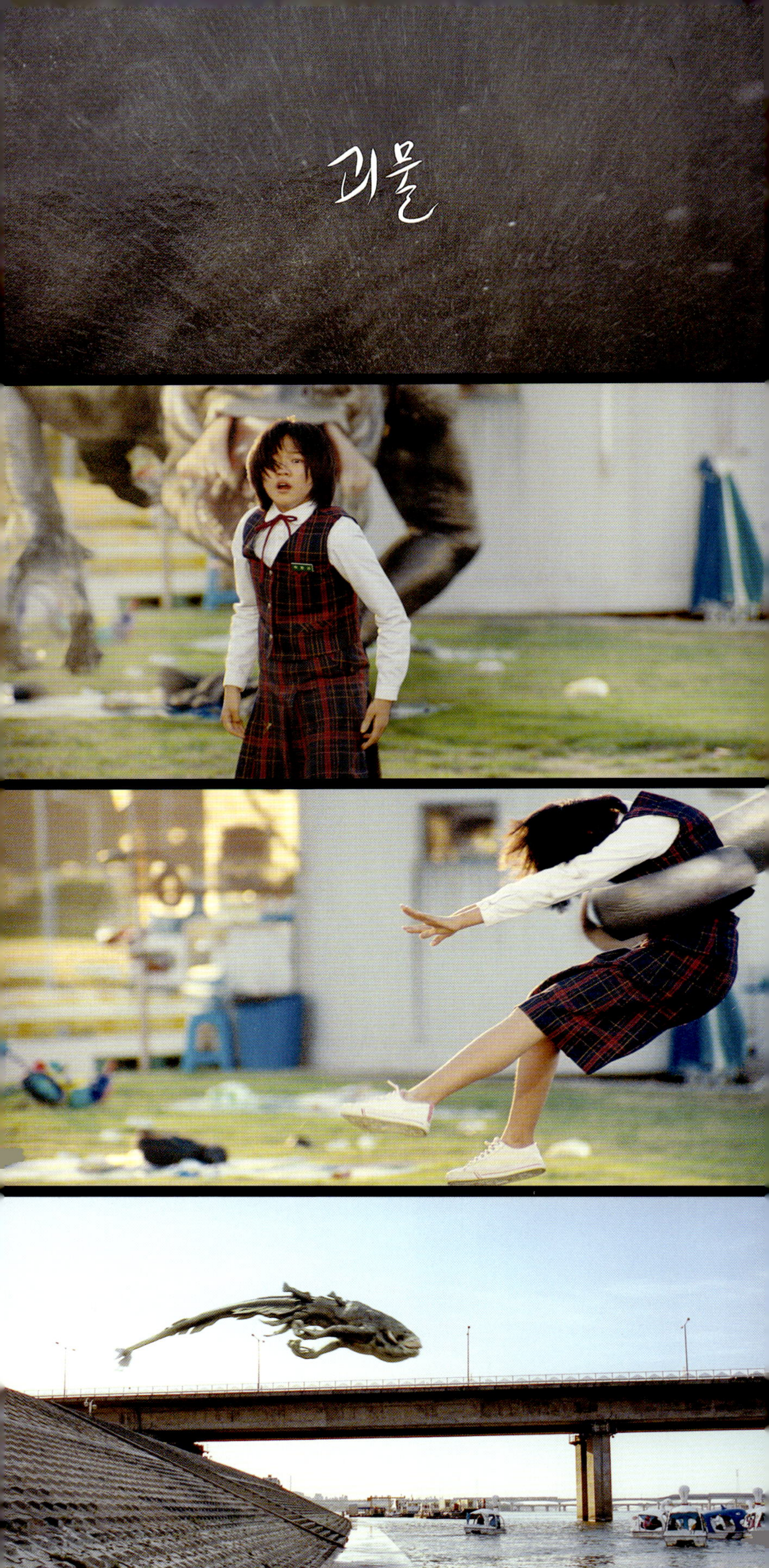

괴물

I don't think you can say *The Host* is a monster movie. It's more of a kidnapping movie. The kidnapper just happens to be a creature. It's all about the family coming together and what they overcome.

Bong's international breakthrough film, *The Host* (2006), focuses on one family's fight to save their daughter from a giant amphibian. A fan of the Loch Ness Monster since childhood, he says he "wondered what it would be like to move the mystery of a Western monster to the Han River."

Opposite: Scenes from *The Host*

Right: Song Kang-ho (center) and Ko Asung in *The Host*

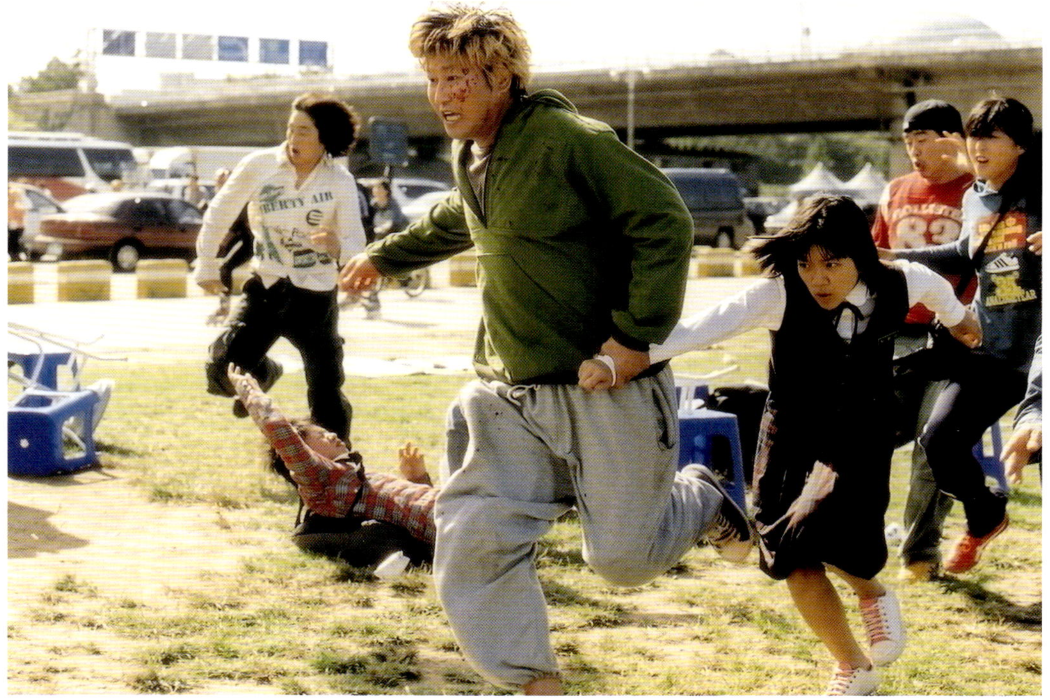

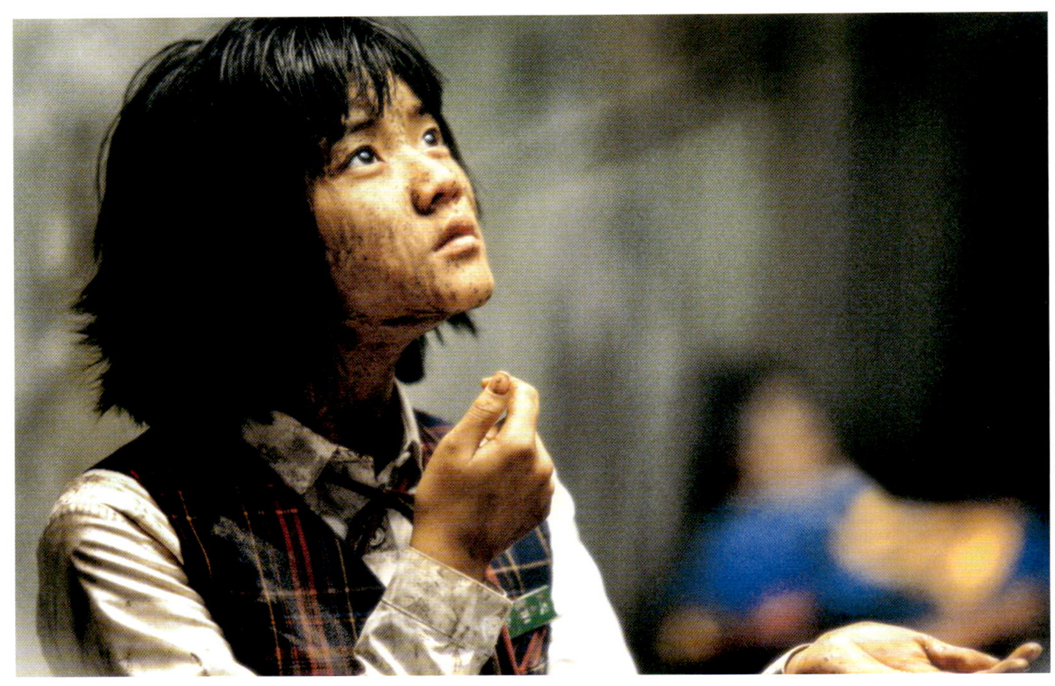

The Host subverts the monster film genre by showing its creature in clear daylight right at the beginning. "I had decided beforehand that there was one monster and it wasn't big," Bong explains.

Above: Ko Asung in *The Host*

Opposite: Concept art by Ha Kwang-min

I like putting these characters in impossible situations that they can't deal with. That's what makes powerful drama. When you have a superhero going on a mission, the outcome is too predictable.

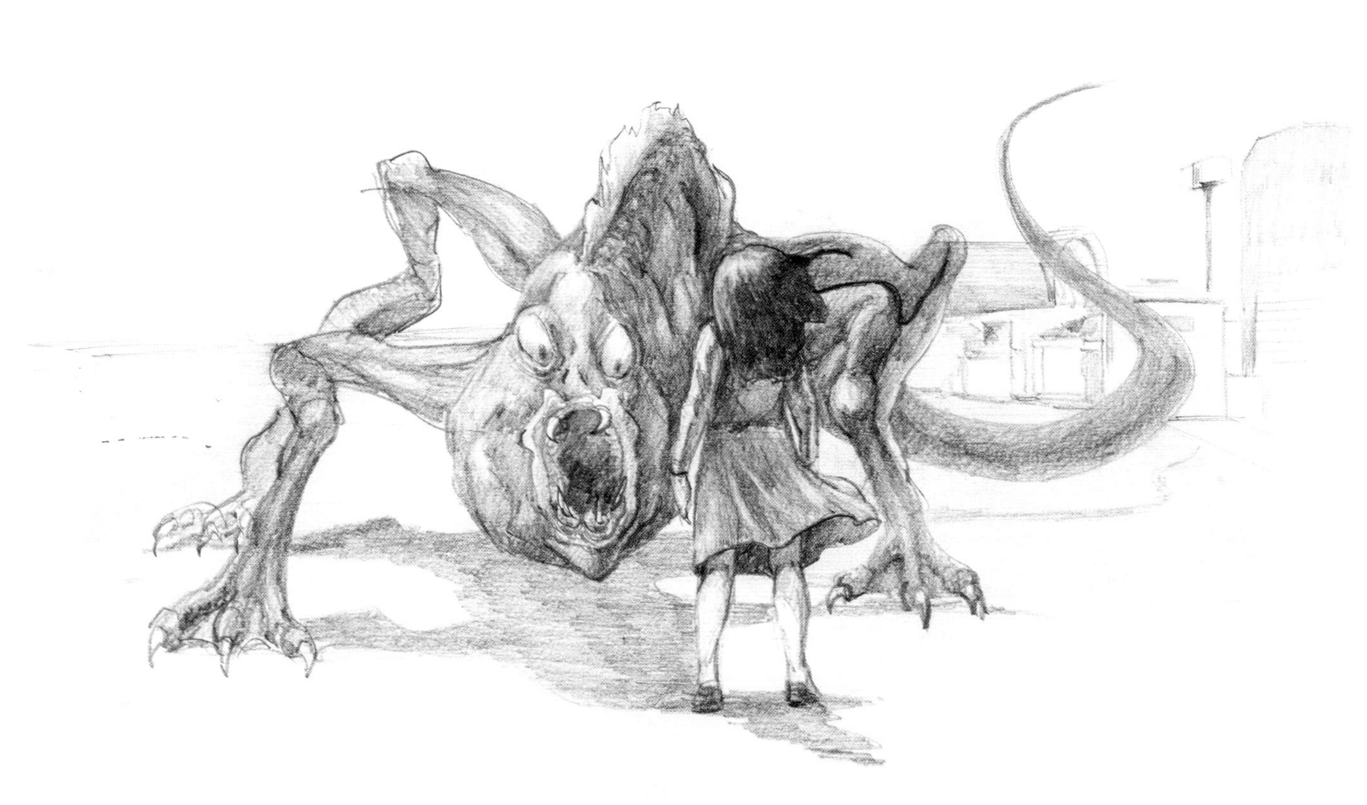

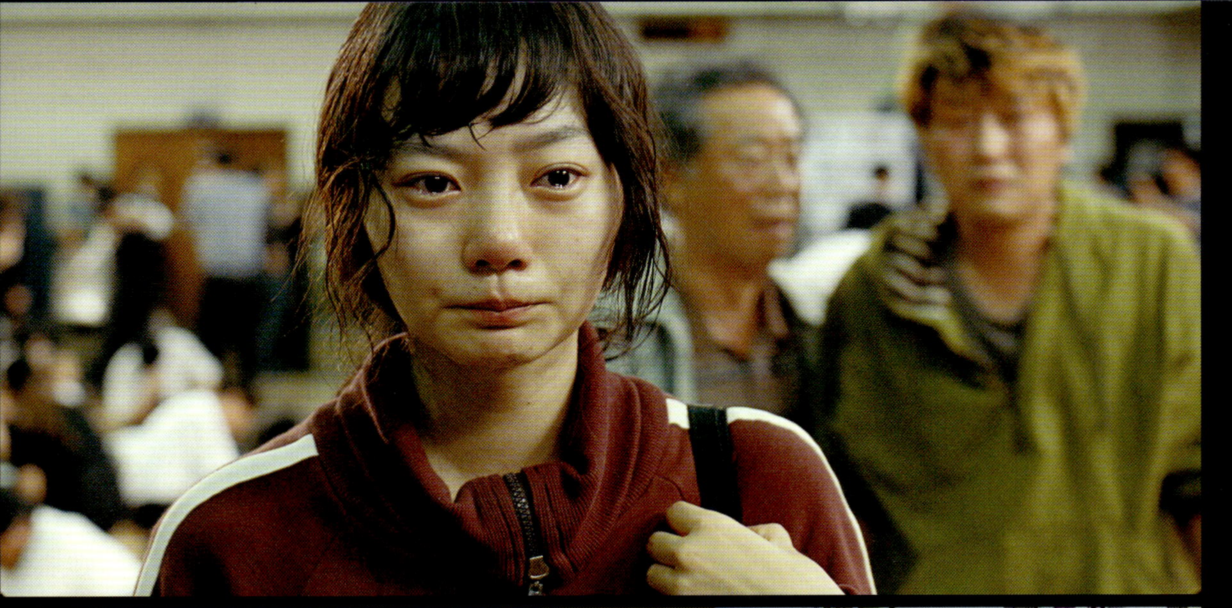

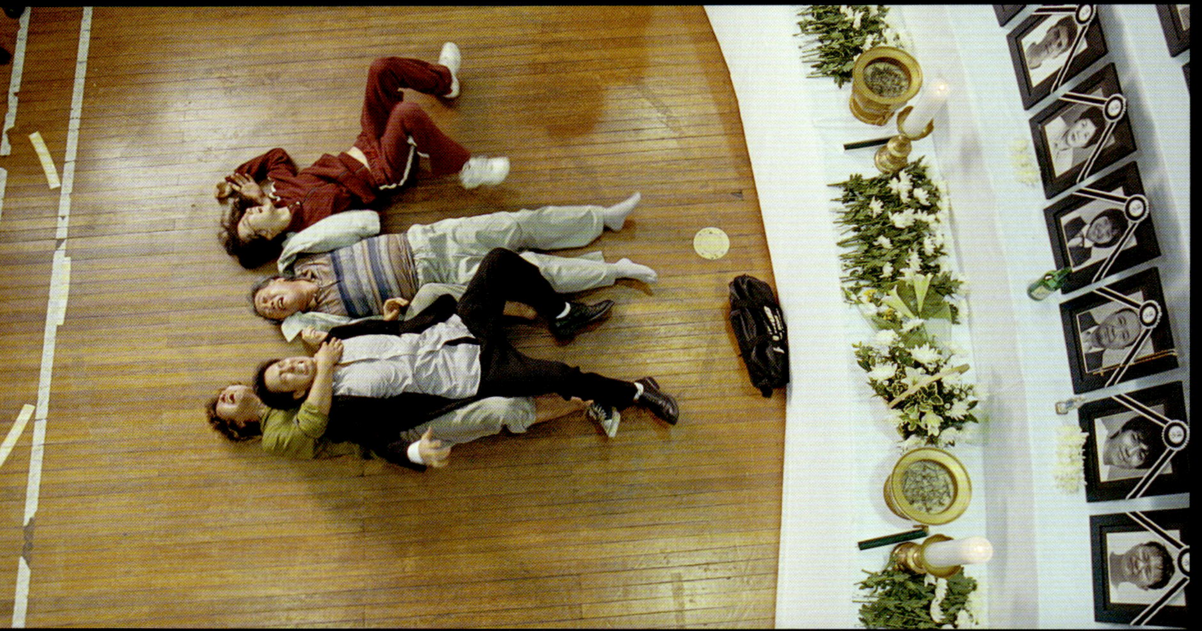

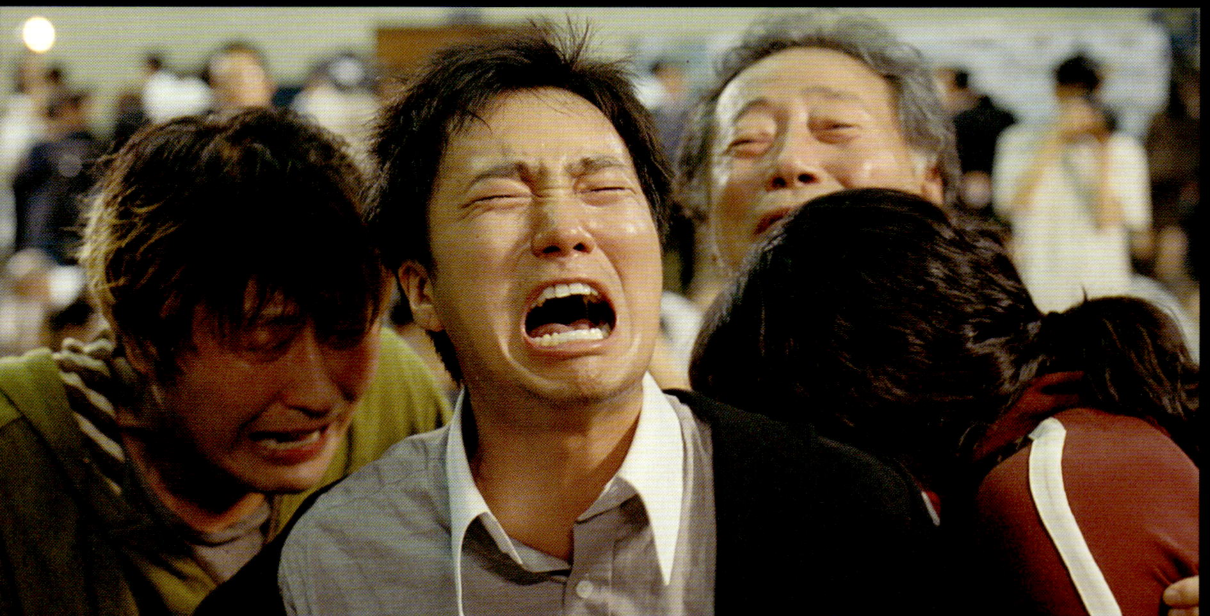

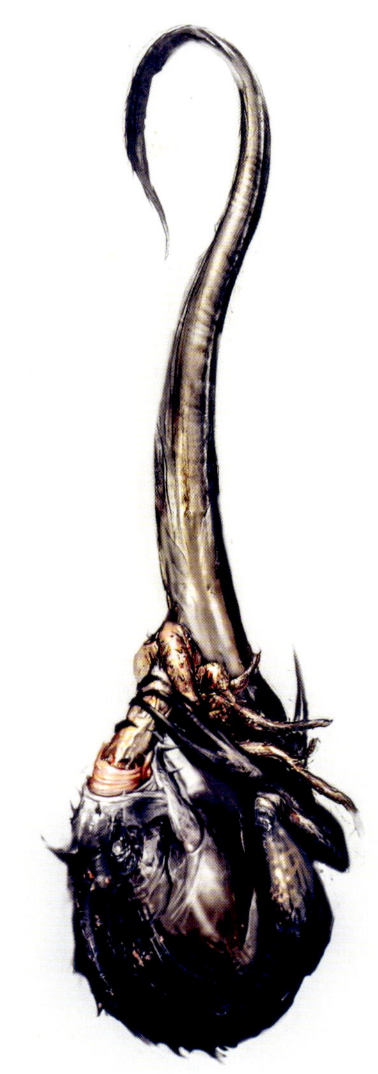

Bong described a vision of the creature "hanging upside down with its tail wrapped around a bridge over the Han River, like a bat or a cocoon." He worked with a team of concept artists to develop the creature's design.

Opposite: Scenes from *The Host*

Right: Concept art by Oh Woo Jin

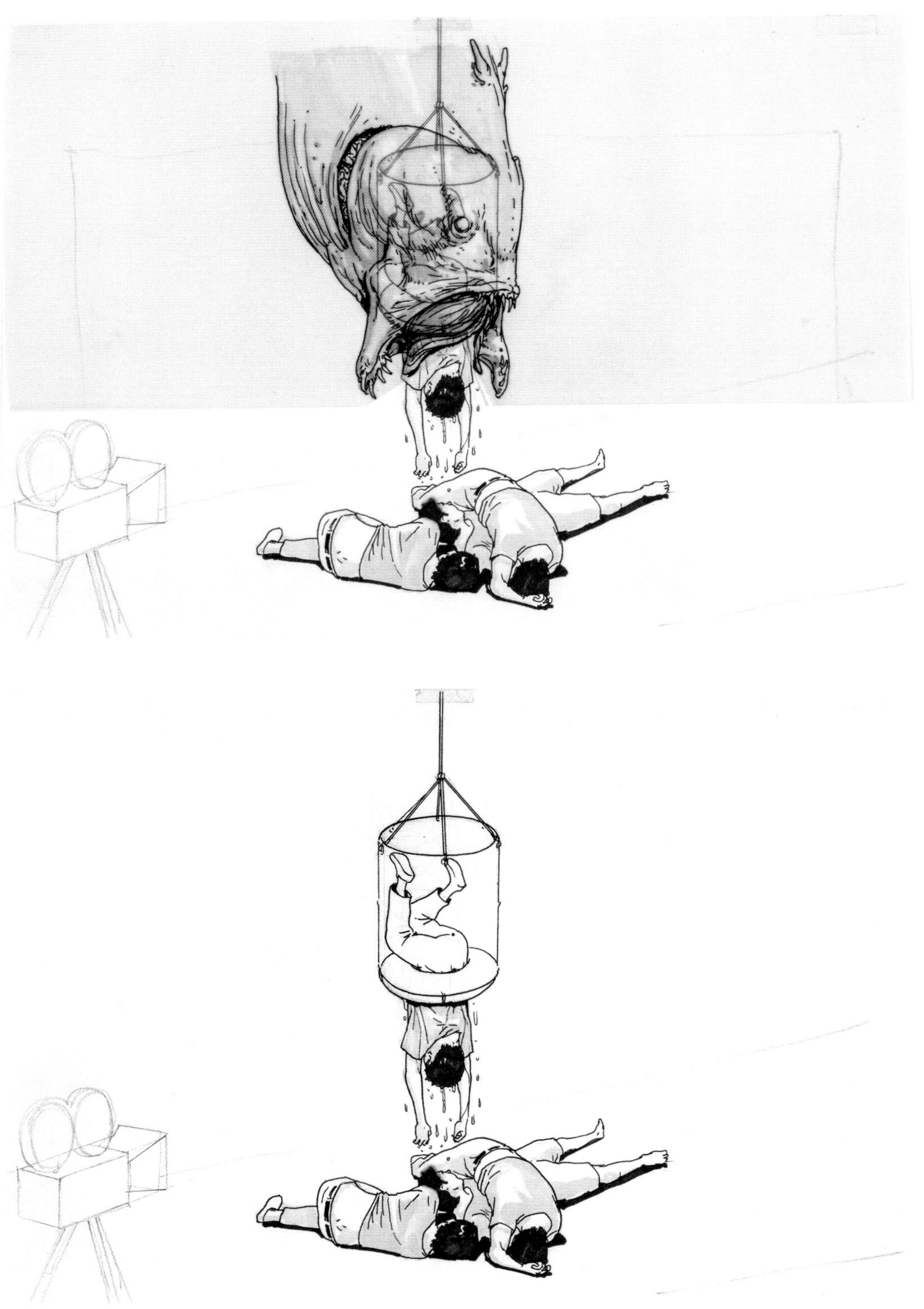

Bong used both practical effects and computer graphics for a scene in which the creature spits out a human body into its lair. "The design is based on a fish, so it has less personality than King Kong," he says. "But I tried to achieve some humanness through its behavior patterns."

This page: Concept art by Jang Hee Chul

Opposite: Concept art by Lee Jisong

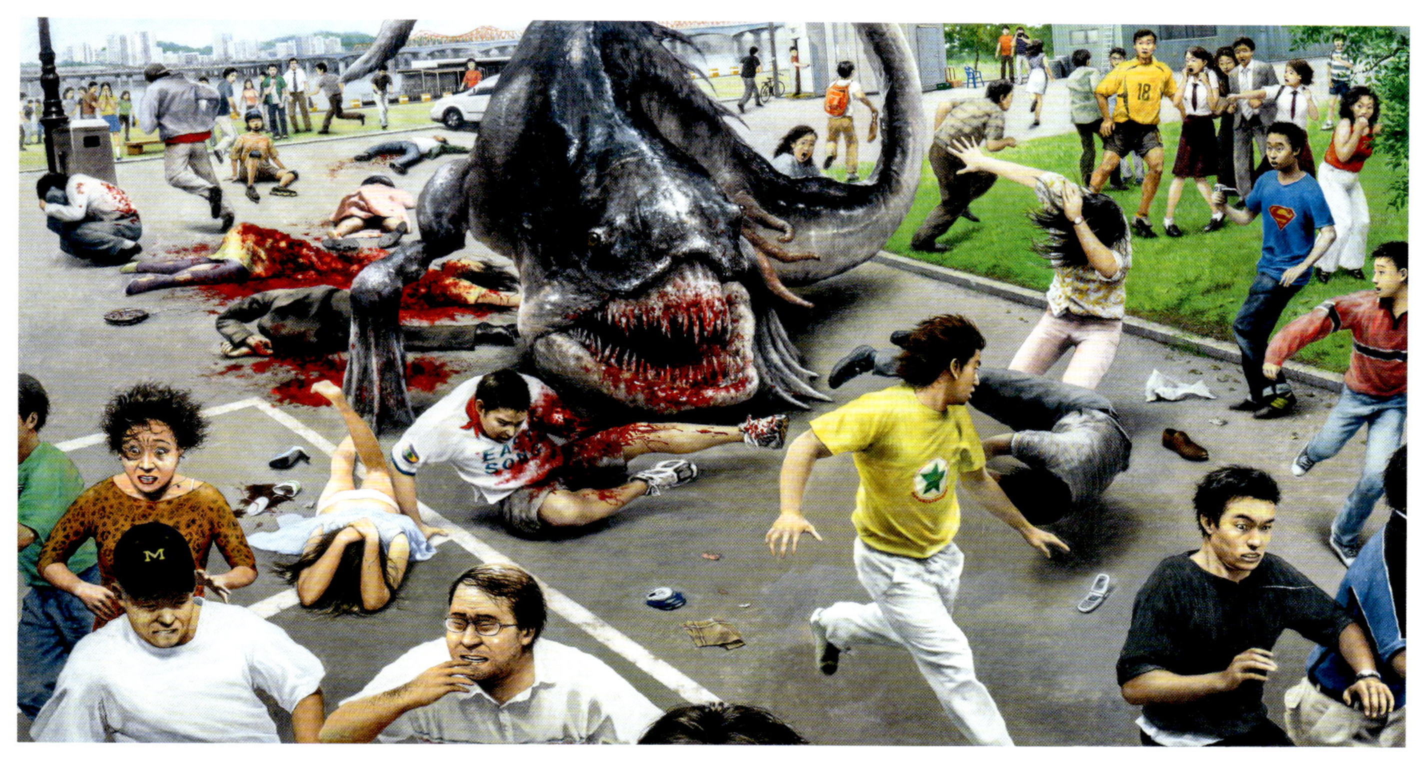

I wanted the creature to be clumsy and violent and even hysterical—a character without charisma. Not like Hannibal Lecter, who's full of charisma in *The Silence of the Lambs*, but like Steve Buscemi in *Fargo*.

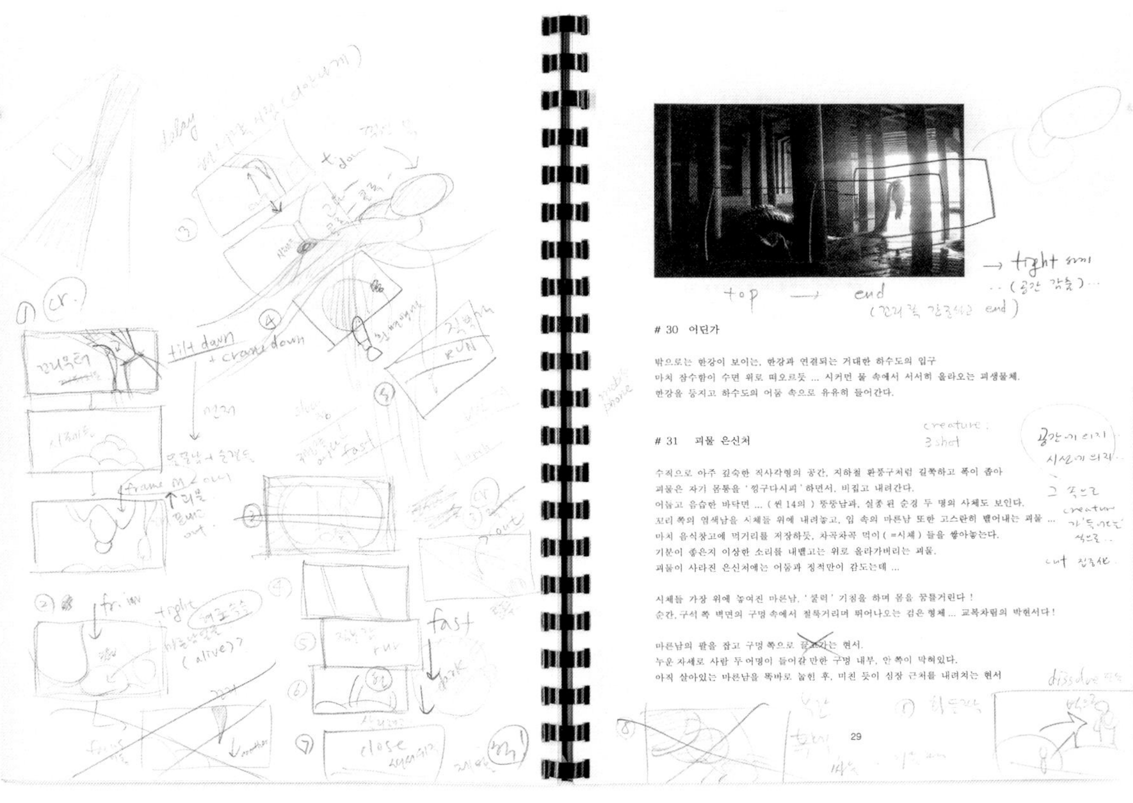

30 어딘가

밖으로는 한강이 보이는, 한강과 연결되는 거대한 하수도의 입구
마치 잠수함이 수면 위로 떠오르듯 ... 시커먼 물 속에서 서서히 올라오는 괴생물체.
한강을 등지고 하수도의 어둠 속으로 유유히 들어간다.

31 괴물 은신처

수직으로 아주 깊숙한 직사각형의 공간, 지하철 환풍구처럼 길쭉하고 폭이 좁아
괴물은 자기 몸통을 '끼구다시피' 하면서, 비집고 내려간다.
어둡고 음습한 바닥면 ... (씬 14의) 뚱뚱남과, 실종 된 순경 두 명의 사체도 보인다.
꼬리 쪽의 염색남을 시체들 위에 내려놓고, 입 속의 마른남 또한 고스란히 뱉어내는 괴물 ...
마치 음식창고에 먹거리를 저장하듯, 차곡차곡 먹이 (=시체) 들을 쌓아놓는다.
기분이 좋은지 이상한 소리를 내뱉고는 위로 올라가버리는 괴물.
괴물이 사라진 은신처애는 어둠과 정적만이 감도는데 ...

시체들 가장 위에 놓여진 마른남, '불러' 기침을 하며 몸을 꿈틀거린다 !
순간, 구석 쪽 벽면의 구멍 속에서 절뚝거리며 뛰어나오는 검은 형체 ... 교복차림의 박현서다 !

마른남의 팔을 잡고 구멍 쪽으로 끌고가는 현서.
누운 자세로 사람 두 어명이 들어갈 만한 구멍 내부, 안 쪽이 막혀있다.
아직 살아있는 마른남을 똑바로 눕힌 후, 미친 듯이 심장 근처를 내려치는 현서

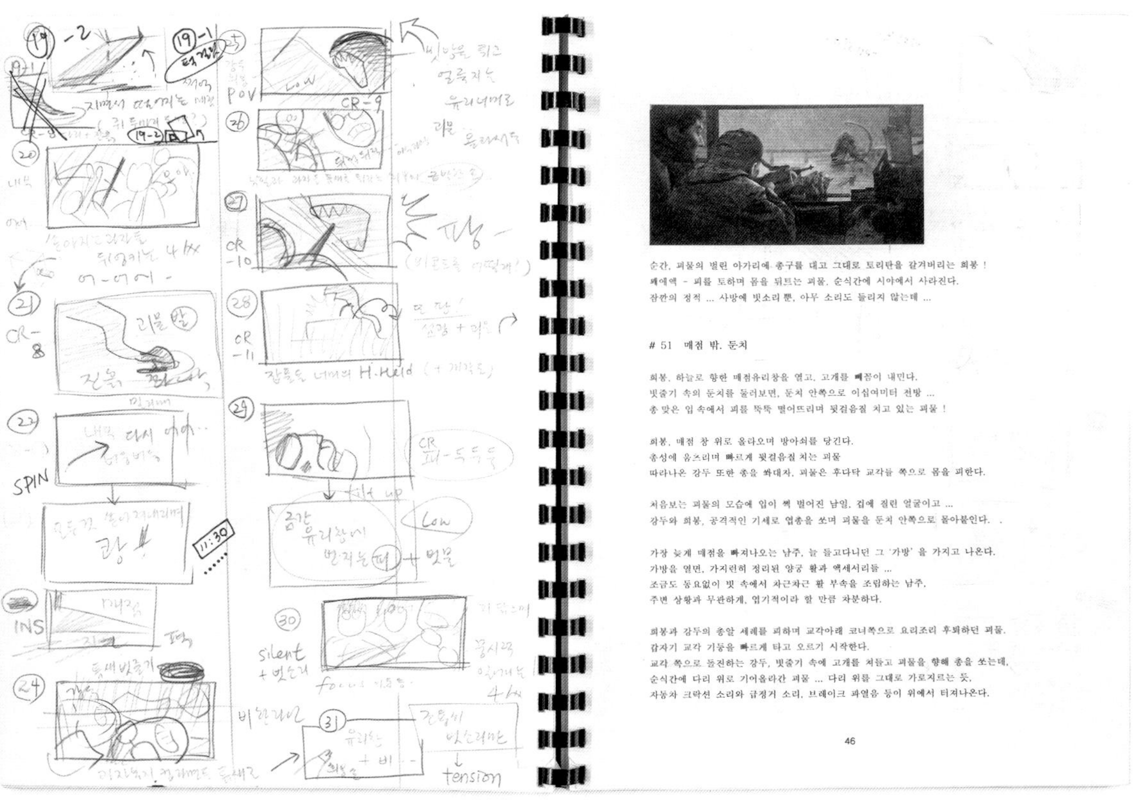

순간, 괴물의 벌린 아가리에 총구를 대고 그대로 토리탄을 갈겨버리는 희봉 !
페에액 - 피를 토하며 몸을 뒤트는 괴물. 순식간에 시야에서 사라진다.
잠깐의 정적 ... 사방에 빗소리뿐, 아무 소리도 들리지 않는데 ...

51 매점 밖. 둔치

희봉, 하늘로 향한 매점유리창을 열고, 고개를 빼꼼이 내민다.
빗줄기 속의 둔치를 둘러보면, 둔치 안쪽으로 이십여미터 전방 ...
총 맞은 입 속에서 피를 뚝뚝 떨어뜨리며 뒷걸음질 치고 있는 괴물 !

희봉, 매점 창 위로 올라오며 방아쇠를 당긴다.
총성에 움츠리며 빠르게 뒷걸음질 치는 괴물
따라나온 강두 또한 총을 쏴대자, 괴물은 후다닥 교각들 쪽으로 몸을 피한다.

처음보는 괴물의 모습에 입이 쩍 벌어진 남일. 겁에 질린 얼굴이고 ...
강두와 희봉, 공격적인 기세로 엽총을 쏘며 괴물을 둔치 안쪽으로 몰아붙인다. .

가장 늦게 매점을 빠져나오는 남주, 늘 들고다니던 그 '가방' 을 가지고 나온다.
가방을 열면, 가지런히 정리된 양궁 활과 액세서리들 ...
조금도 동요없이 빗 속에서 차근차근 활 부속을 조립하는 남주,
주변 상황과 무관하게, 엽기적이라 할 만큼 차분하다.

희봉과 강두의 총알 세례를 피하며 교각아래 코너쪽으로 요리조리 후퇴하던 괴물.
갑자기 교각 기둥을 빠르게 타고 오르기 시작한다.
교각 쪽으로 돌진하는 강두, 빗줄기 속에 고개를 처들고 괴물을 향해 총을 쏘는데,
순식간에 다리 위로 기어올라간 괴물 ... 다리 위를 그대로 가로지르는 듯,
자동차 크락션 소리와 급정거 소리, 브레이크 파열음 등이 위에서 터져나온다.

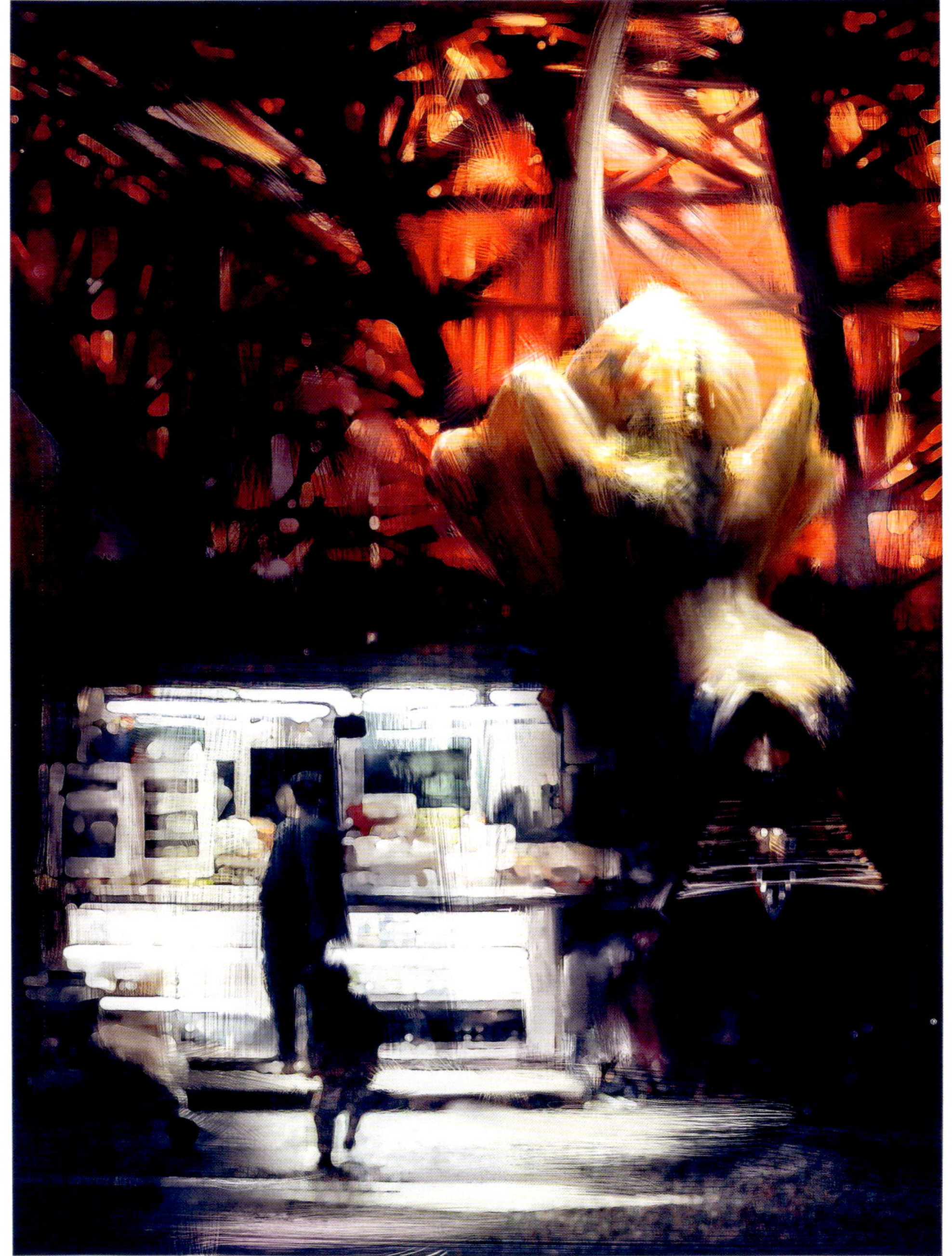

"It is a relay race of the weak to save one another," Bong says of the family's struggle. "While the nation, the government, and the society neglect them, they fight for themselves."

Opposite: Pages from Bong's annotated draft script

Right: Concept art by Oh Woo Jin

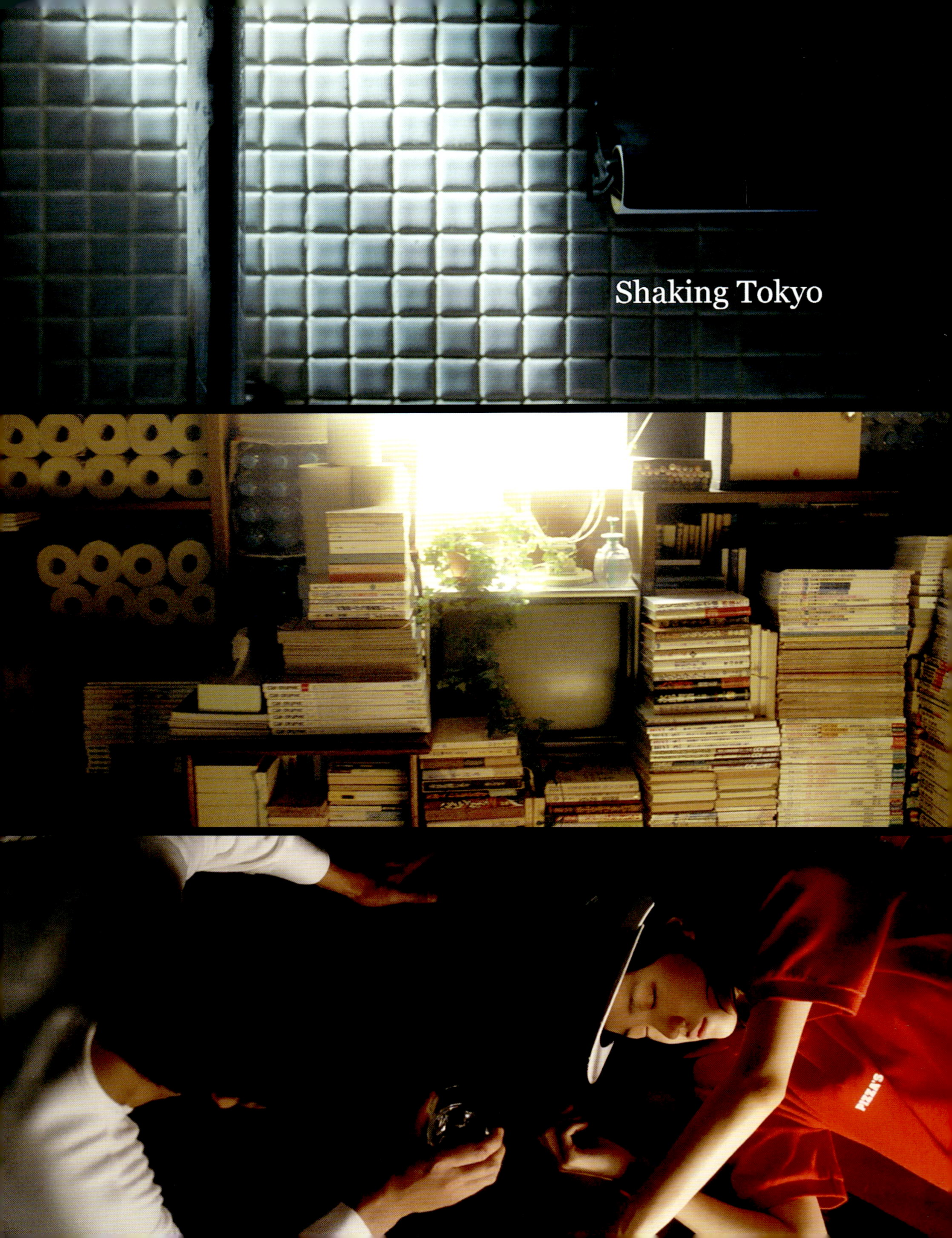
Shaking Tokyo

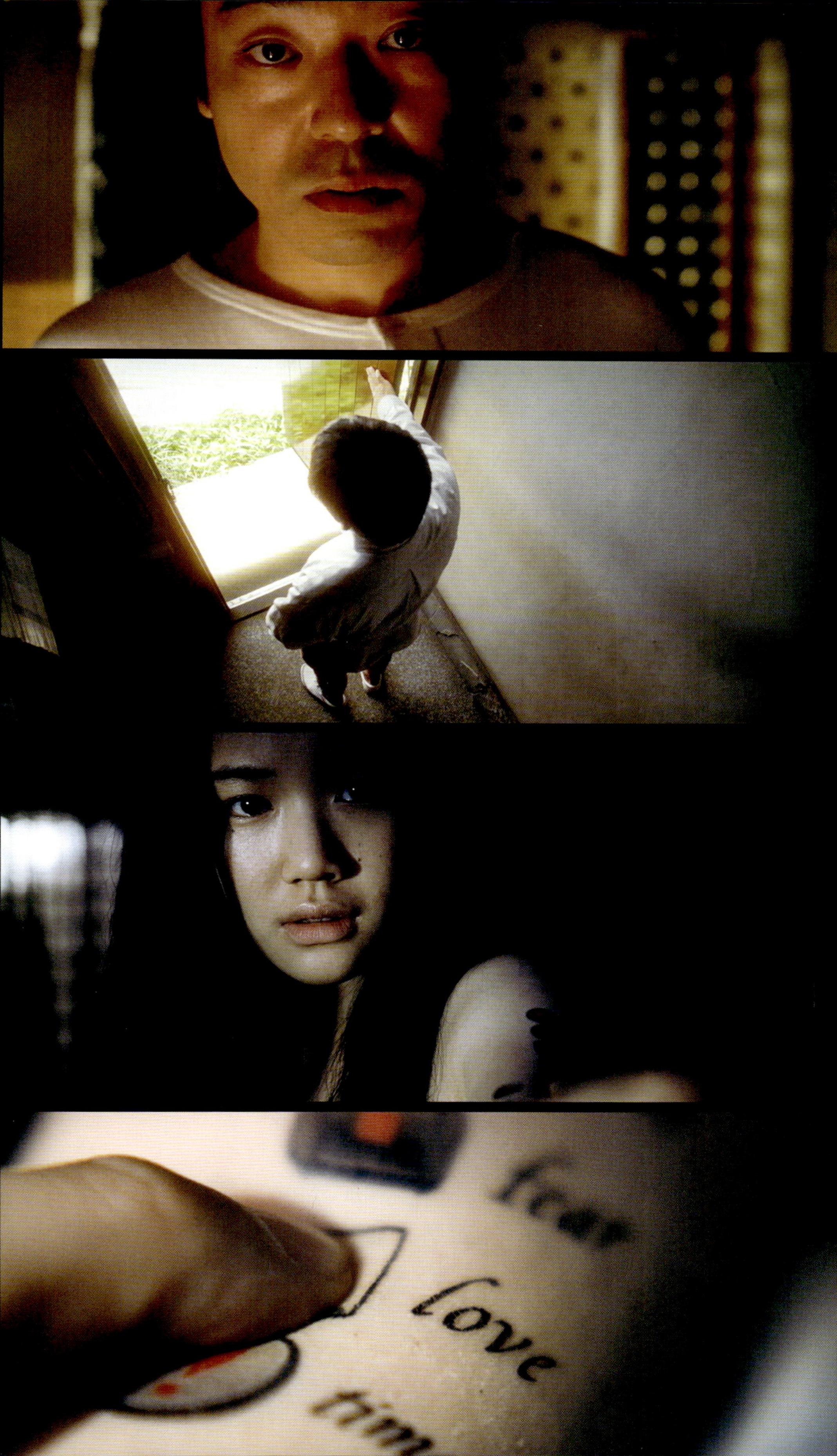
love

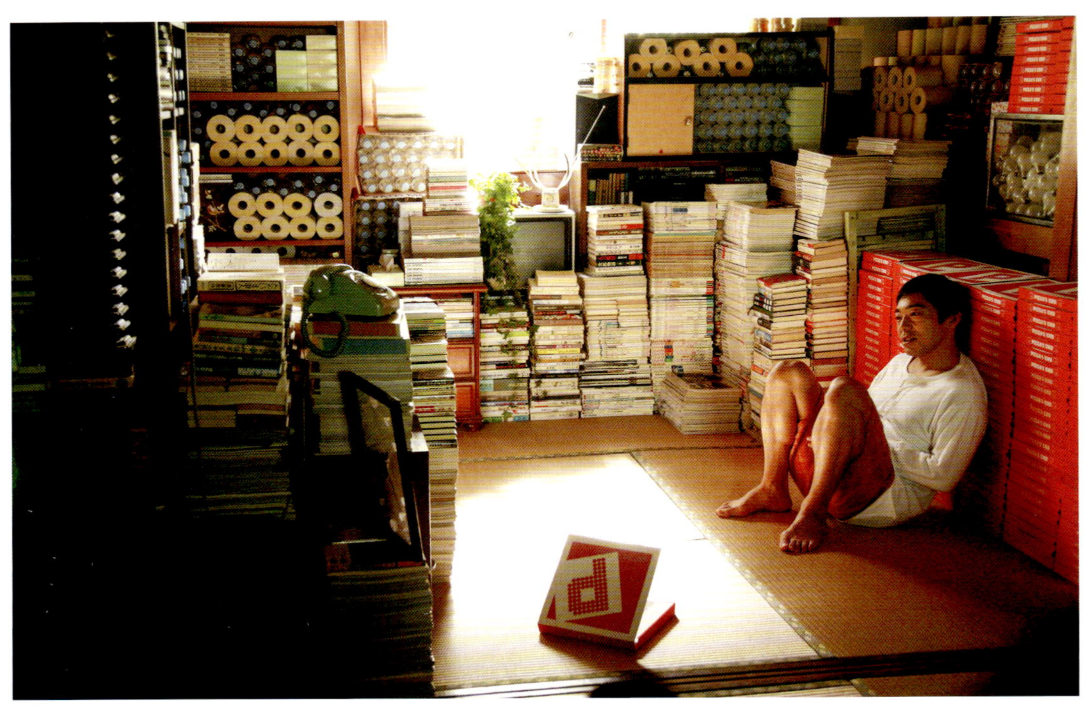

The fear of being isolated and unprotected has always been present in my work. I'm very comfortable portraying anxiety and fear in movies, but I can't do grand, heroic narratives.

Shaking Tokyo, Bong's contribution to the anthology film *Tokyo!* (2008), tells the story of a Japanese hikikomori, a social recluse who isolates at home until an earthquake creates an unexpected moment of connection. "I learned that even when you make a film in a foreign language, the emotions are the same."

Previous spread: Scenes from *Shaking Tokyo*

Above: Teruyuki Kagawa in *Shaking Tokyo*

Opposite: Pages from Bong's sketchbook for *Shaking Tokyo*

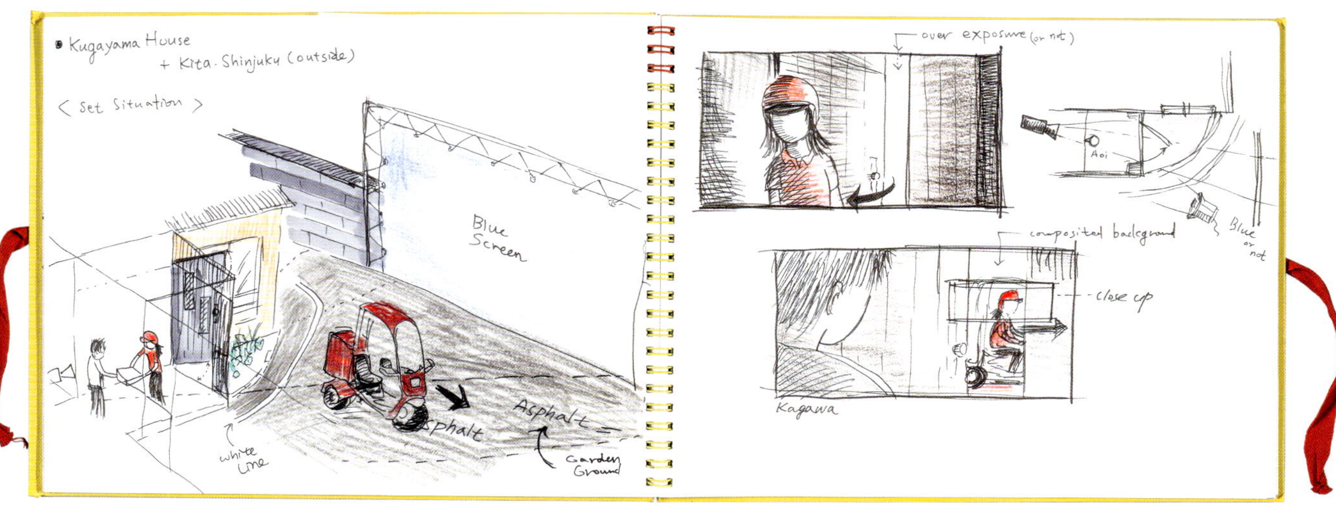

Kugayama House
+ Kita. Shinjuku (outside)
< Set Situation >
Blue Screen
Asphalt
Asphalt
white line
Garden Ground
over exposure (or not)
Aoi
composited background
close up
Blue or not
Kagawa

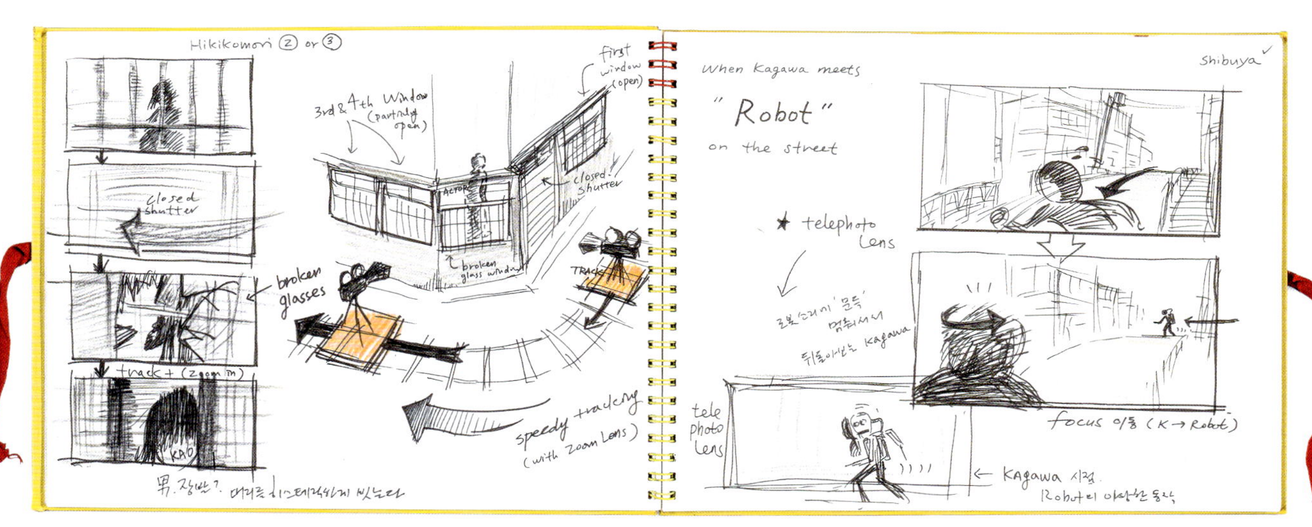

Hikikomori ② or ③
first window (open)
3rd & 4th Window (partially open)
Actor
closed shutter
closed shutter
broken glass window
broken glasses
TRACK
track + (zoom in)
KAO
speedy tracking (with zoom Lens)
When Kagawa meets
"Robot"
on the street
Shibuya
★ telephoto Lens
tele photo Lens
focus 이동 (K → Robot)
Kagawa 시점

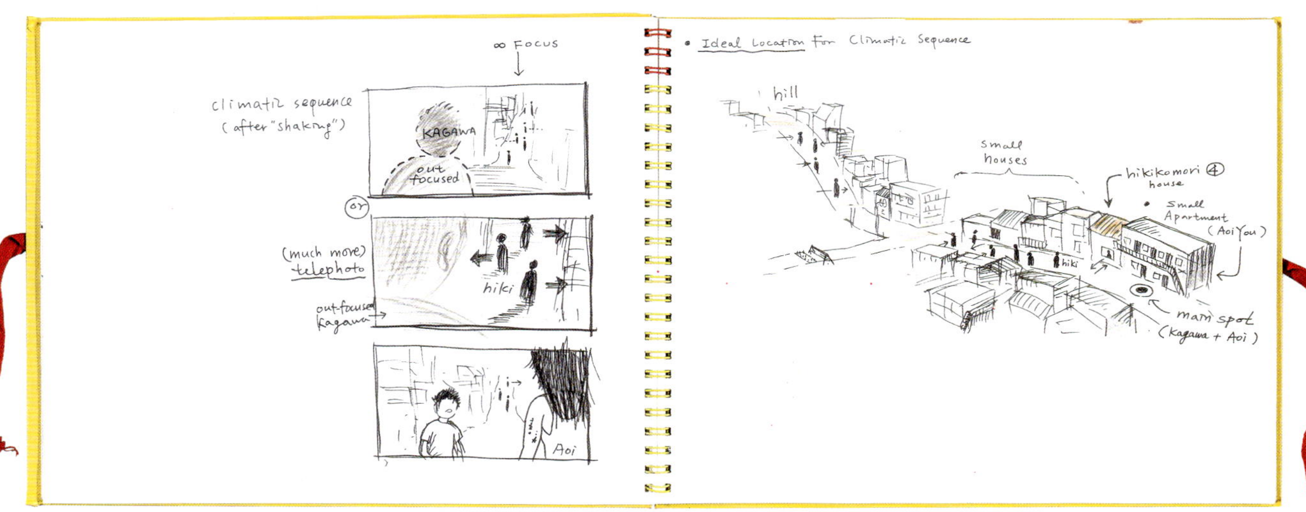

∞ FOCUS
climatic sequence
(after "shaking")
KAGAWA
out focused
(or)
(much more) telephoto
out focused Kagawa
hiki
Aoi
Ideal Location For Climatic Sequence
hill
small houses
hikikomori ④ house
Small Apartment (Aoi You)
hiki
main spot (Kagawa + Aoi)

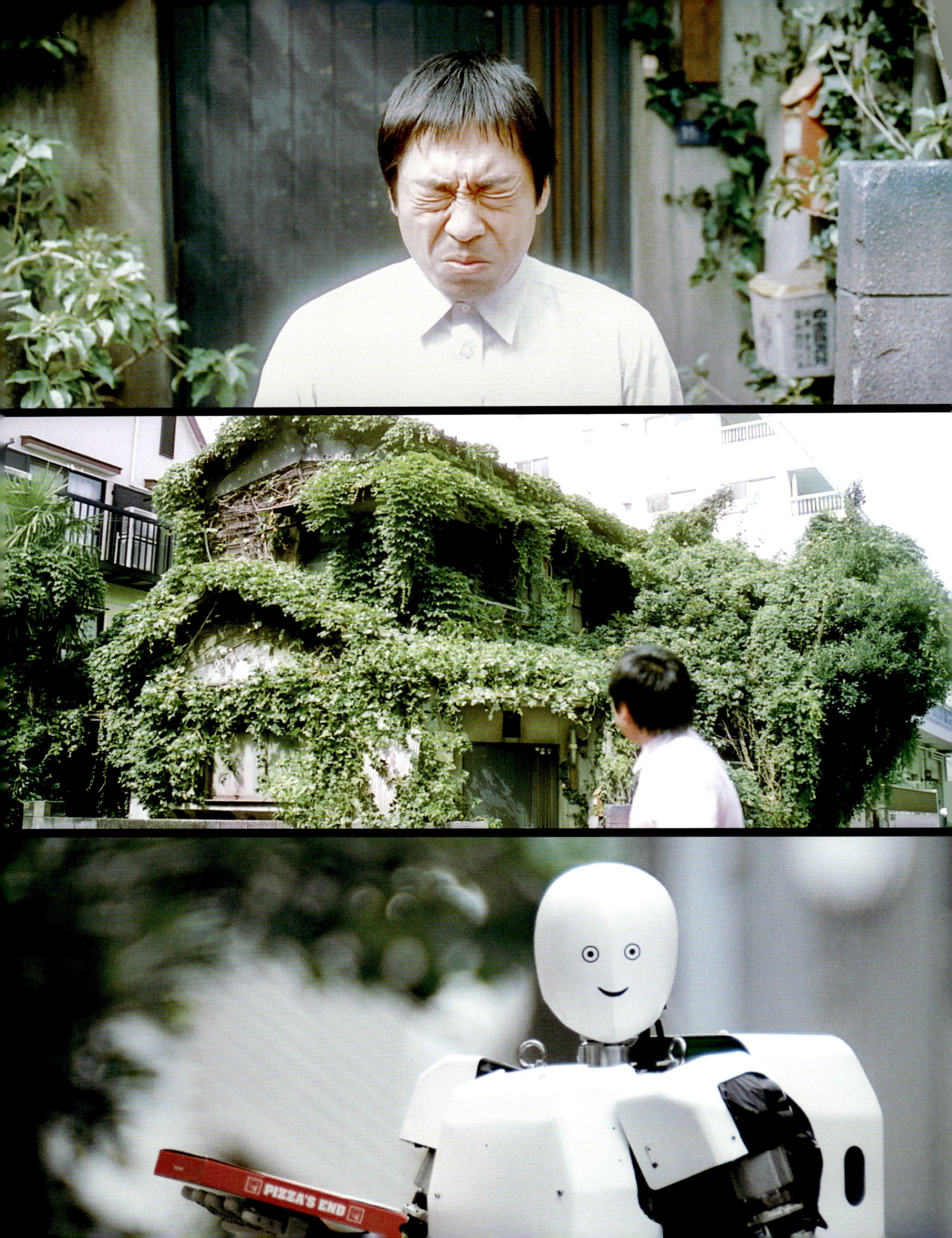
PIZZA'S END

LEE ISAAC CHUNG

Bong Joon Ho's *Shaking Tokyo* was one of those films that showed me filmmaking as a kind of magic. I watched in awe of how tightly woven it was—every detail so deliberately placed, not a single moment wasted. It reminded me of Anton Chekhov's belief that everything seen on stage must have purpose, even a seemingly insignificant object. For Director Bong, this translates visually, like the scholar's stone in *Parasite*, introduced quietly yet inevitably becoming central to the climax. Chekhov gave us everyday people whose simple acts set forward unexpected and profound outcomes. Director Bong takes this notion a little further, letting us watch ordinary lives on the edge of madness.

As a filmmaker, I'm humbled by his sleight of hand—his capacity to craft each frame meticulously, in a way that feels like genuine spontaneity. Take the emotional scene in *The Host*, where a family's grief over young Hyun-seo (Ko Asung) is staged with layers of activity in the foreground and background—a nightmare to get right on set—so that it can slip naturally and unexpectedly into slapstick comedy. Or watch the camera carefully rove the house in *Parasite* as the Kim family frantically improvises places to hide when the Park family comes home unexpectedly.

When *Parasite* came out, I expressed to Director Bong that he had made a perfect film. I have studied it for the way he composes and covers even the most mundane conversations, the way he expresses his themes, and the way he structures his screenplays. My favorite of his is *Memories of Murder*—a police procedural that transcends genre to explore Korean society's complexities through the lens of a true crime story. It is gruesome, unwavering, yet it never wallows in self-seriousness. The humor emerges naturally as ordinary people react to extraordinary pressures; the tone is unpredictable and fits the emotions of the story.

Many of Director Bong's characters remind me of the detectives from *Memories of Murder*, searching for meaning in a world that makes little sense. They are observers, often outsiders, awkward yet relatable. For instance, Ki-woo (Choi Woo-shik) in *Parasite* navigates the world of a wealthy family he's infiltrated, while he searches for his own sense of home within a world defined by absurdity and outrage. His final letter to his father is like a prayer and a coming of age that fits our times.

And speaking to our times might be clearest in Director Bong's science fiction films—*Snowpiercer*, *Okja*, and *Mickey 17*. Unlimited by place and time, these films push the tone of madness even further. Heroes are adrift and antagonized by powerful weirdos. I admit I once wondered if Director Bong had gone too far with these films—exaggerating his villains to behave like memes. With each new day, I am convinced I was wrong. Perhaps Director Bong's latest trick is showing us that the absurd is the ordinary.

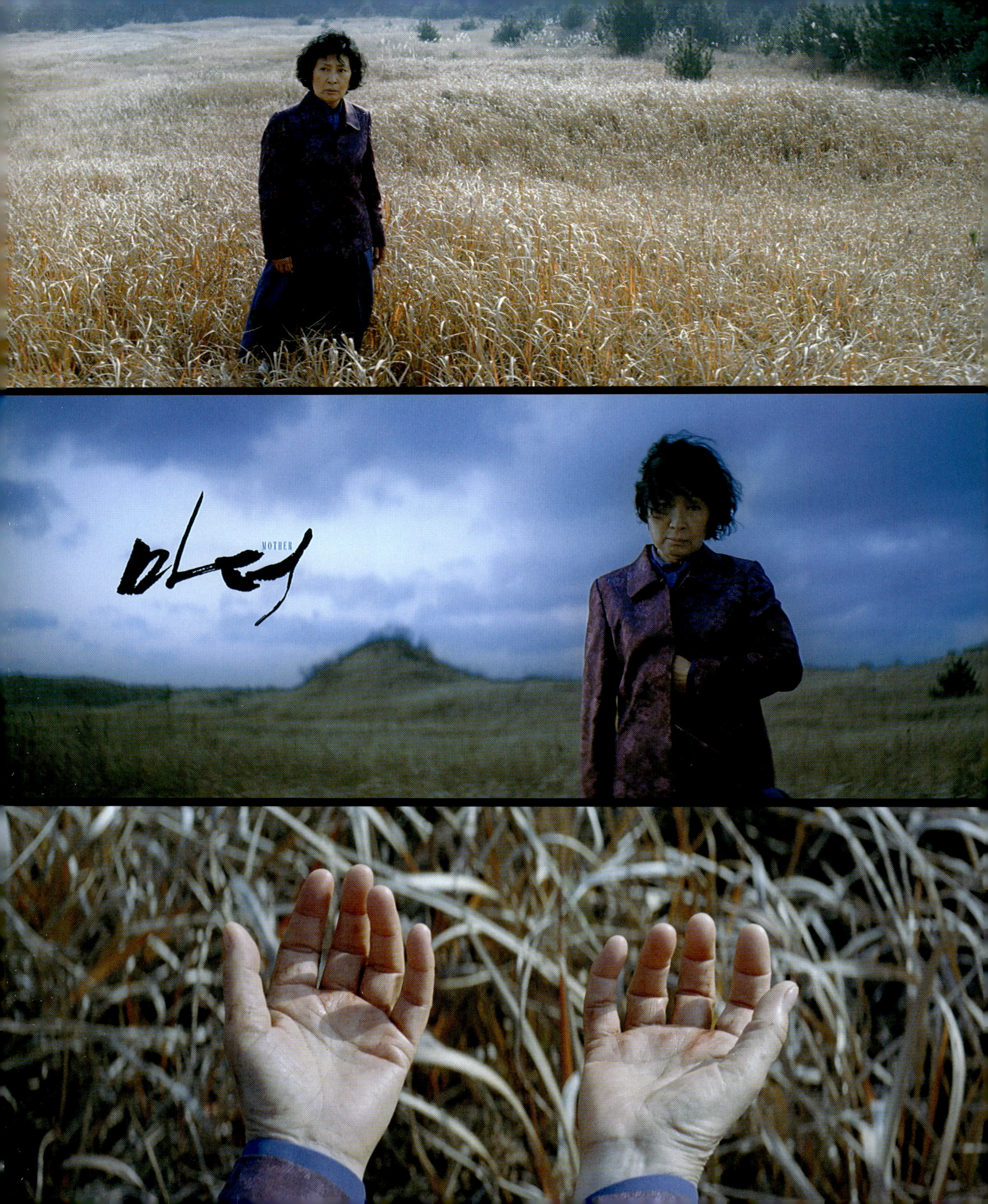

마더
MOTHER

The titular character in Bong's psychological thriller *Mother* (2009) is a woman driven to extremes to prove that her only son is innocent of murder. "When I was making *Mother*, I rewatched *Psycho*," Bong recalls. "I thought that maybe when Norman Bates's mother was alive, they might have had a similar relationship."

Opposite: Scenes from *Mother*

Right: Prop acupuncture kits used in *Mother*

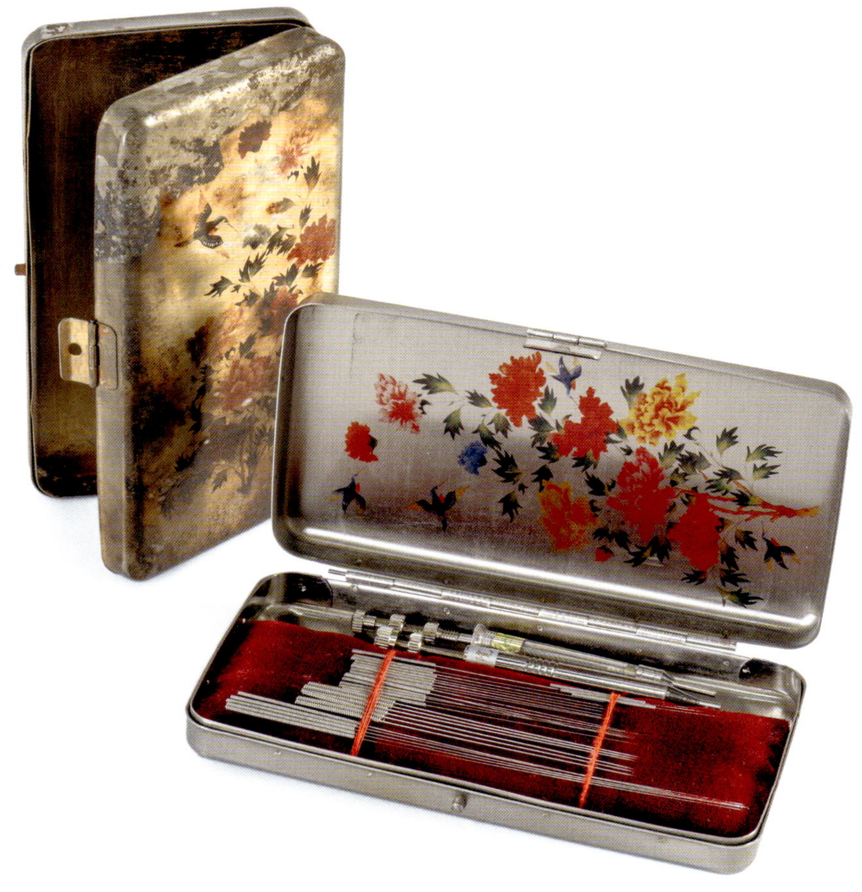

Of course it's a crime genre. But storyline-wise, it's about a mother and son. I wanted to express the explosive madness of a mother who's trying to save her wrongly accused son.

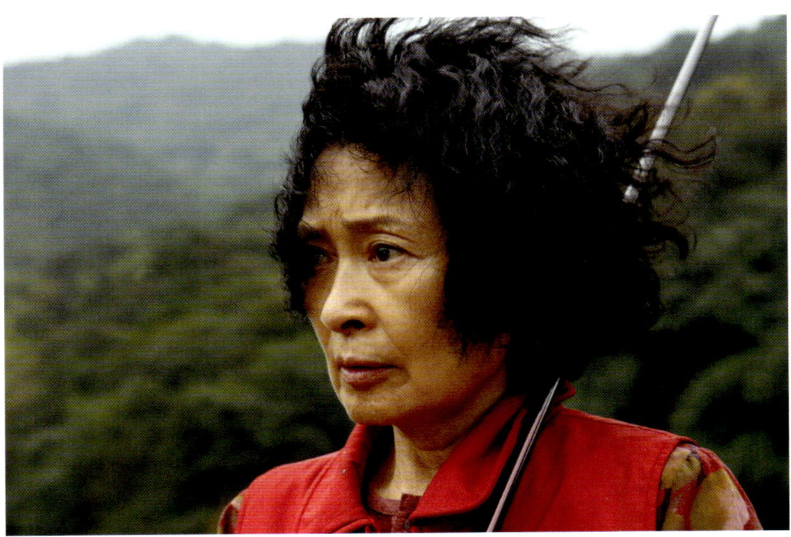

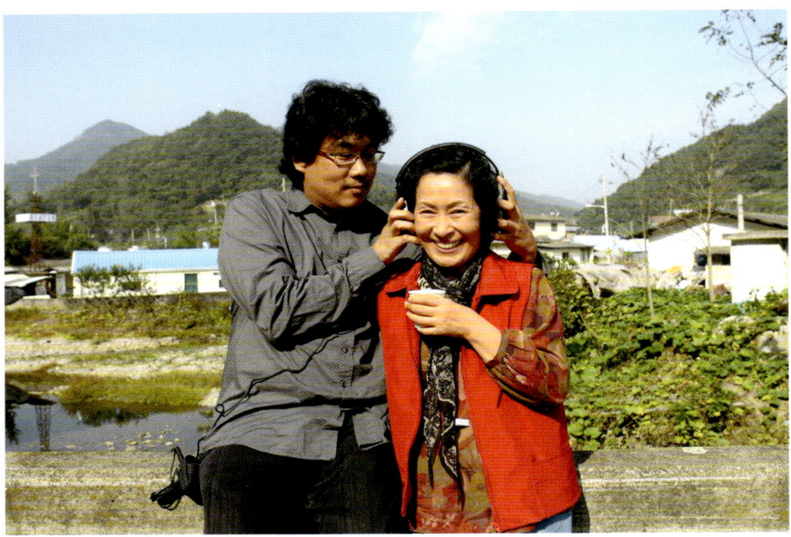

More than just being a great actor, Kim Hye-ja is quite an icon in Korea. She symbolizes the motherhood of the nation. I really wanted to explore that, delve deeper into this actor, and present her in a new light.

Bong cast beloved actor Kim Hye-ja, best known for playing kind and self-sacrificing mothers, against type. "It was actually because of her that I came up with the story," he says. "It wasn't as if I had other actors in mind, if she refused the role. It was because of her that I did this film."

This page, top: Kim Hye-ja as Mother

This page, bottom: Bong and Kim Hye-ja during production

Opposite: Scenes from *Mother*

I was interested in taking the
mother role to a much darker
place. I believe that, under
extreme circumstances,
mothers will do anything for
their children. It's very
touching, but it can also be
quite frightening.

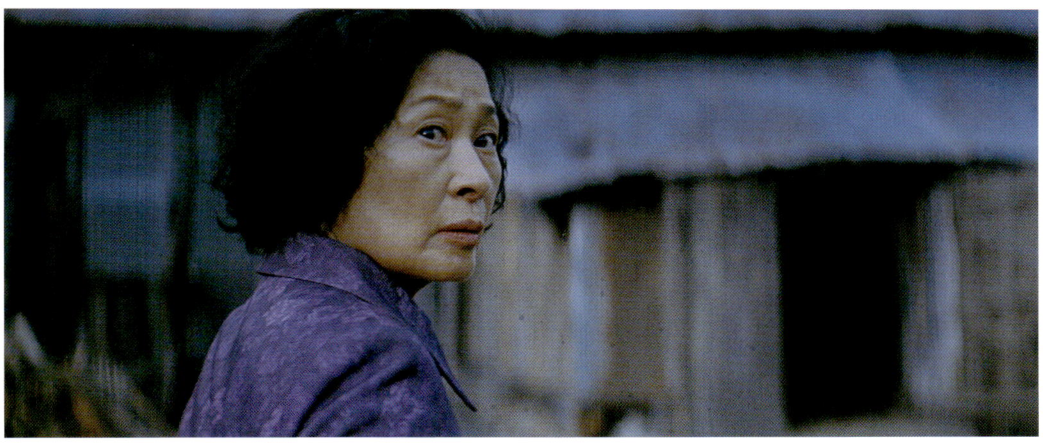

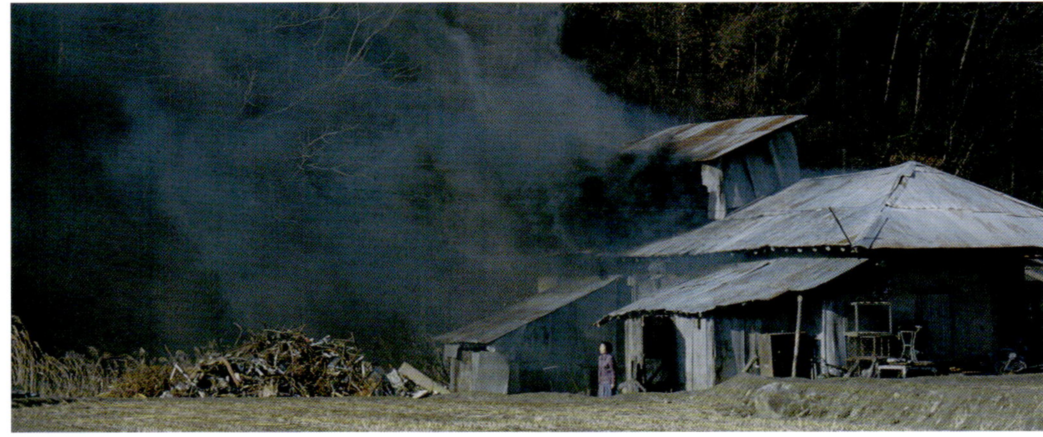

HONG KYUNG PYO

Making a film with Bong Joon Ho is so different from working with any other director. Long before shooting starts, we spend a huge amount of time planning out every single shot, the camera movements, and so on. Everything is decided beforehand. So you might think, after all that preparation, my job as director of photography would be fairly simple once we get to the set. But funnily enough, I'm even more busy on the set of his films than I am for other directors who don't prepare as much.

I guess it's because we execute the shots in such fine detail. The main elements of each shot have already been decided, but then we try so hard to make the execution of each shot perfect. There's no time to do that on other sets; you just do the best you can and move on. But my concentration and focus need to be at their peak whenever I'm working with Bong Joon Ho. Every day on set, it feels like two outs in the ninth inning.

You know he's such a nice guy, and he never loses his temper with anyone. That said, on the set, when he's looking at the monitor—really concentrating on it—there's a bloodthirsty edge to his gaze. It's a bit scary. You can tell when he doesn't like a shot. But then he'll turn and his expression will change completely, and in a calm, gentle manner he'll ask, "Do you mind trying that once again?" He never gets angry. I'm not sure where he gets that patience. But that in itself is a bit scary too. You can't help but try your hardest when you're working with him.

Over the years, his methods of filmmaking have remained very consistent. But there was a bit of a contrast between his approach to *Mother* versus *Parasite*. Much of *Mother* was shot on location, where the light and natural setting were constantly in flux, and he wanted that feeling reflected in the characters. We did a lot of location scouting, and then on the set we spent a lot of time waiting for the right conditions, whereas 90% of *Parasite* was shot on a set where everything was constructed, and it was always about the composition, the depth. Everything was incredibly precise—like, if the composition were off even a tiny bit, it would affect the emotions of the scene. With *Mother*, things were the slightest bit looser, but for *Parasite* the shooting concept was completely different.

Rhythm is always very important to Bong Joon Ho. He often sends me music when a film is in pre-production, just to give me a sense of the rhythm he wants to create in the film. Before shooting *Mother*, it was an aria from Bach's *St. Matthew Passion*, while for *Parasite* it was the intro music from Tchaikovsky's "June: Barcarolle," from *The Seasons*. It's not about the film's soundtrack, it's the rhythm of the film itself and the camera. He'll often say, "Film is all about rhythm."

I'm always amazed when I look at the storyboards he makes for his films. He draws them himself, and when you look at them, you can already see his ideas on how he will present the story. His visual analysis of the film is right there in the storyboard. Because he shoots with a single camera, you can see how the shots flow together and how the camera will move. He's the only director I know of where you can look at the storyboard and see his cinematic style. The rhythm of the film is already there in the images.

Opposite: Scenes from *Mother*. Won Bin plays Mother's adult son, Yoon Do-joon.

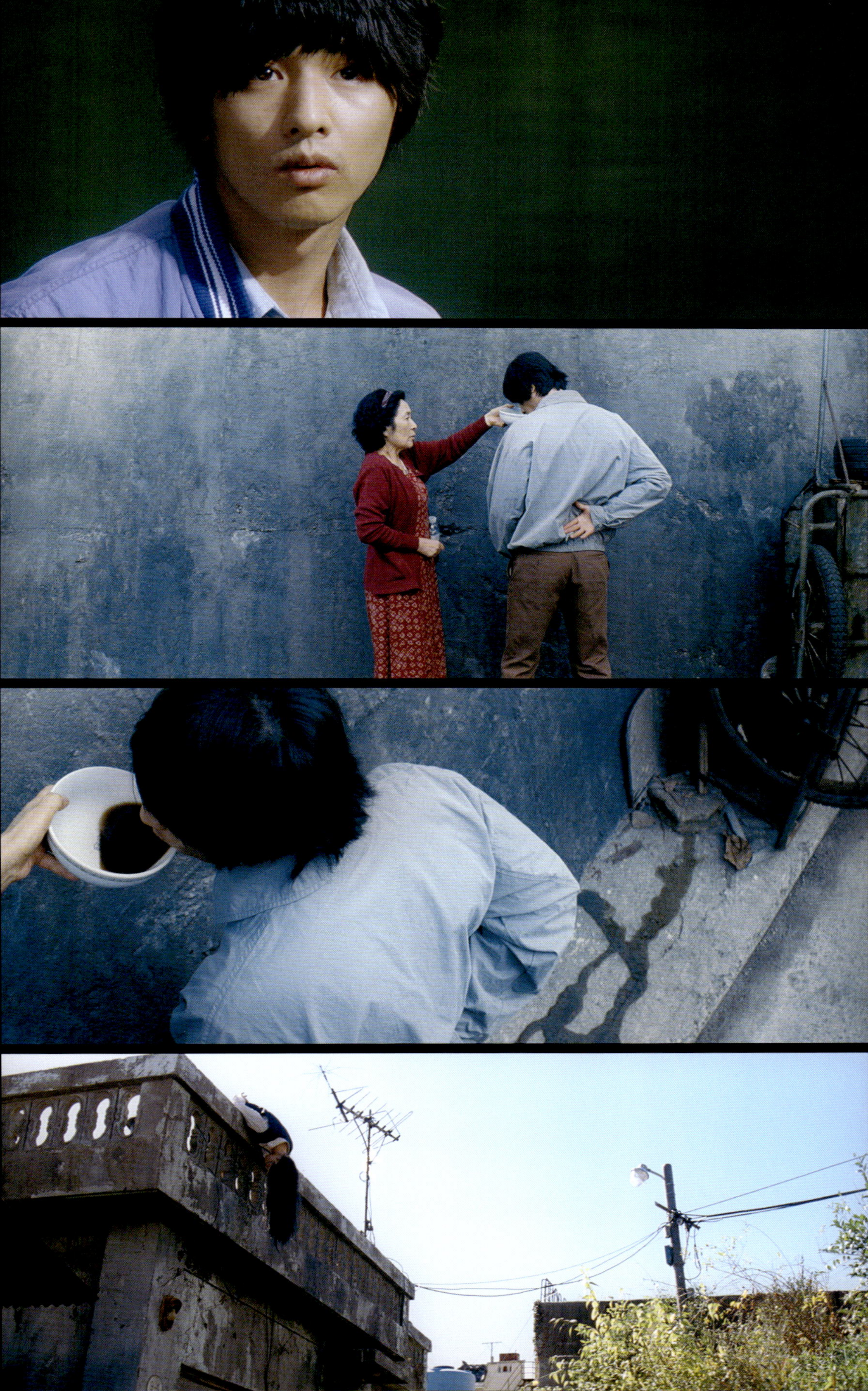

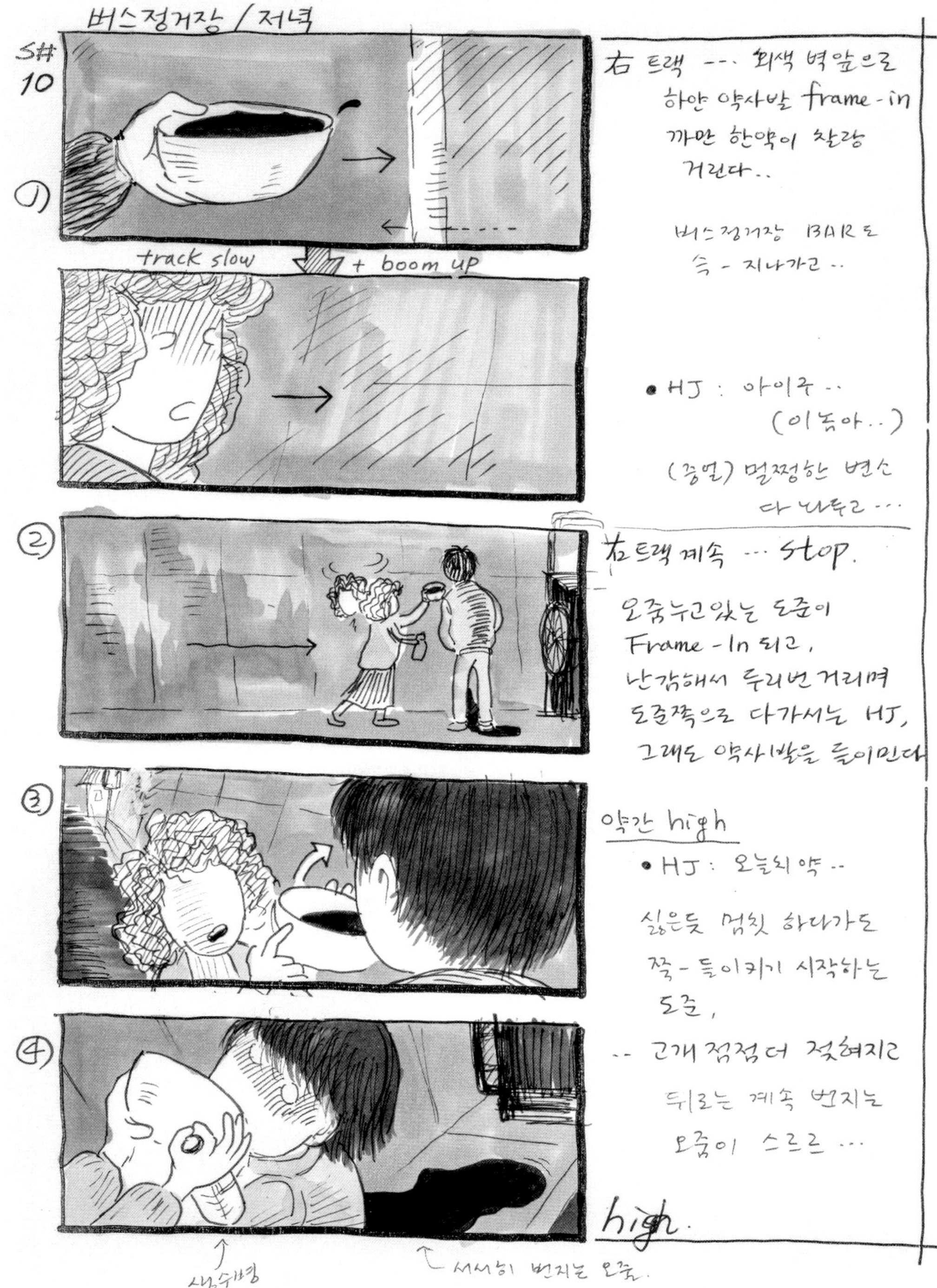

Mother features controlled visuals that alternate between wide landscape shots and close-ups of faces. "A director's job is really about shot construction and figuring out how to cut a scene and what to shoot," Bong explains. "It's not an arbitrary thing, where you get on set and try this and try that. You have to have a clear vision."

Left: Bong's storyboard for *Mother*

Opposite: Pages from Bong's sketchbook

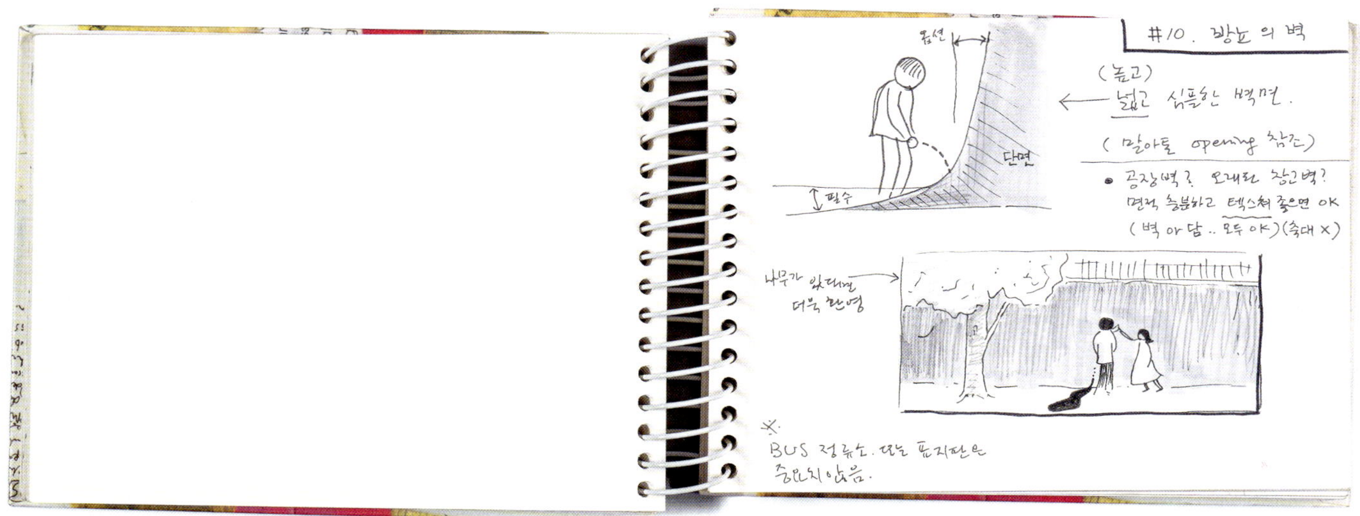

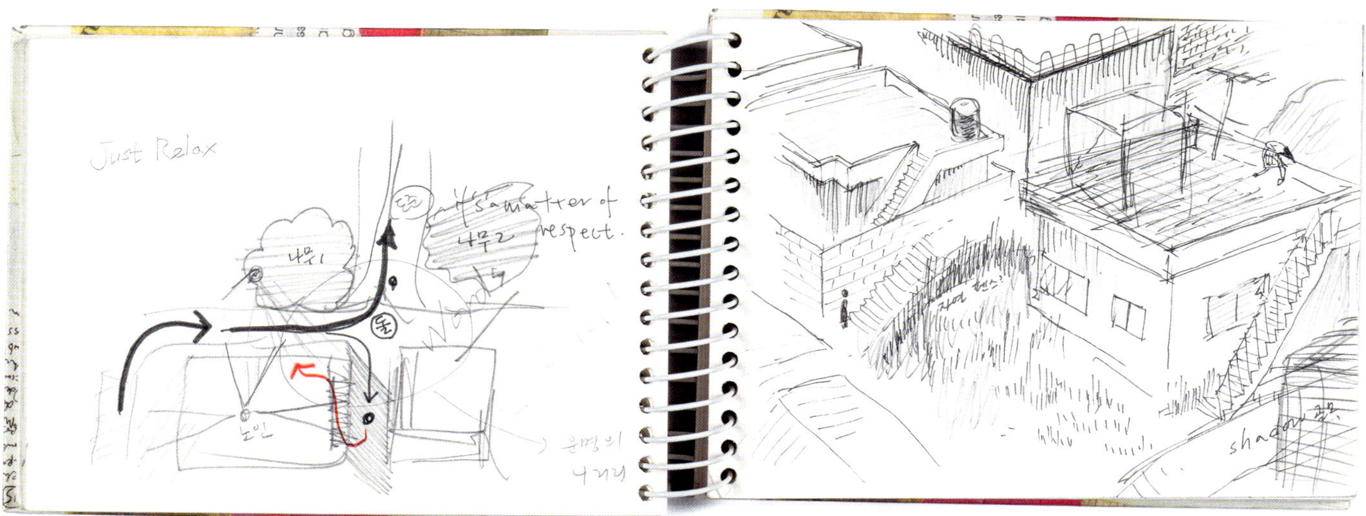

The relationship between mother and son is the focus, and every element in the story, from the murder in the village to some other minor incidents, is there to explore this relationship in its entirety.

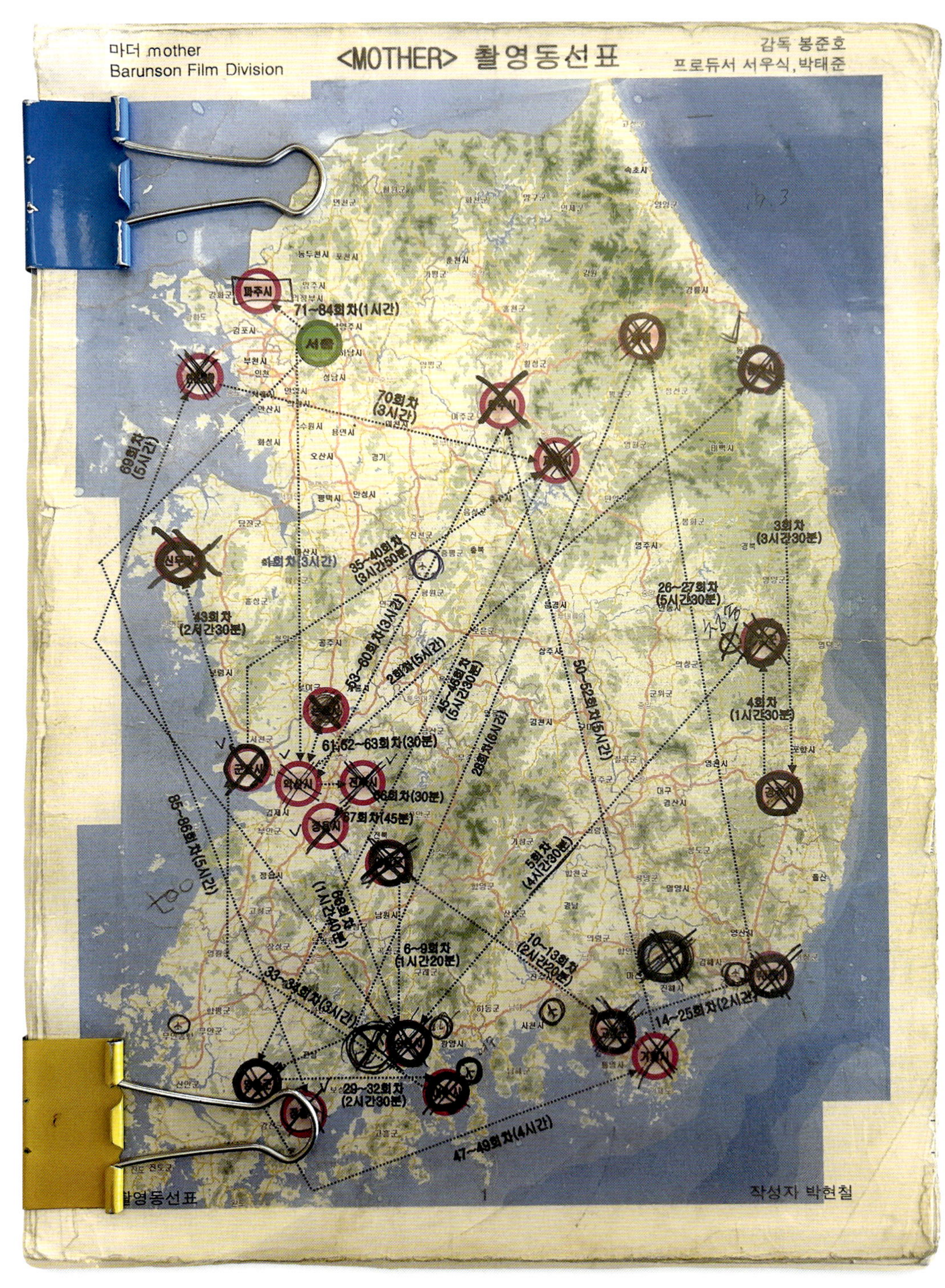

Bong's shooting script for *Mother*. The map on its cover indicates filming locations across South Korea.

SEO WOO-SIK

In the 1990s there were many young people who got their start in the Korean film industry, myself included. Around that time a rumor began to spread about a genius assistant director whose name was Bong Joon Ho. So I came to know about him then.

The first time I saw *Memories of Murder*, it was a real shock to see such a well-made film. I didn't realize it at first, but certain angles and shots remained lodged in my memory long after watching it. A few years later I visited the set of *The Host*, for the scene where the creature causes pandemonium among the crowds by the Han River. I had met Director Bong before then, but this was my first time seeing him in action, controlling a film set. In my eyes, he came across as exactly the kind of director that a producer would want to work with.

I began working with Barunson Group when they acquired the company I had been working with. They had recently signed directing deals with both Bong Joon Ho and Kim Jee-woon, something uncommon for the Korean film industry, and I ended up producing on the set of Kim's *The Good the Bad the Weird* and Bong's *Mother*.

As we started pre-production on *Mother*, I had a certain expectation about the depth of preparation we would do, but it went much further than I imagined. The film takes place in a fictional village sketched out by Director Bong, but our location-scouting spread out across the entire country. There is a Ferris wheel that appears in the film, and we visited all 70 Ferris wheels in South Korea. There is a Lotteria fast-food restaurant and a police substation, and we set out to document every Lotteria and police substation in the country. It became too much for the assistant directors and production assistants to handle, and so I ultimately brought in the cinematography team as well.

As shooting started, the logistical challenge of having so many locations across the country, and of shooting in sequence, was sometimes overwhelming. I ultimately divided up the production team by region, so for example one member of our team became the Busan producer, getting to know that area better than anyone and communicating directly with Director Bong rather than going through me. As the one responsible for balancing the great ambitions of the director and the practicalities of working within a budget on a given schedule, there were some instances of real stress for me.

But there were also moments of complete exhilaration. One of the scenes we prepared for most was the final sequence, where the main character, played by Kim Hye-ja, dances on the bus. Everything had to be perfectly aligned: the angle of the sunlight, the speed of the bus, the movement of the camera, the length of the shot, and so on. We prepared so much for that scene, but given the angle of the sun there was only enough time for two takes, and it had to be finished within that day. When we managed to pull it off, I remember Director Bong, director of photography Hong Kyung Pyo, and me celebrating like children: "We did it! It's going to come out so well!" It was then I felt the joy that comes from working so hard to execute something perfectly and then achieving it. In my career as a producer, *Mother* was the closest I've come to a pure expression of cinematic passion. I gave everything I had to that film.

Bong Joon Ho is remarkable in so many ways. One thing that strikes me about him is this: Most directors, when they reach a certain status, or when they reach the end of an exhausting shoot, might show signs of fatigue. But in the 15 years I've known him, I've never seen a hint of that from Bong Joon Ho. He controls himself in that way and is always striving to improve. I can feel that for as many decades as he makes films, he will always be challenging himself to do more, to do better.

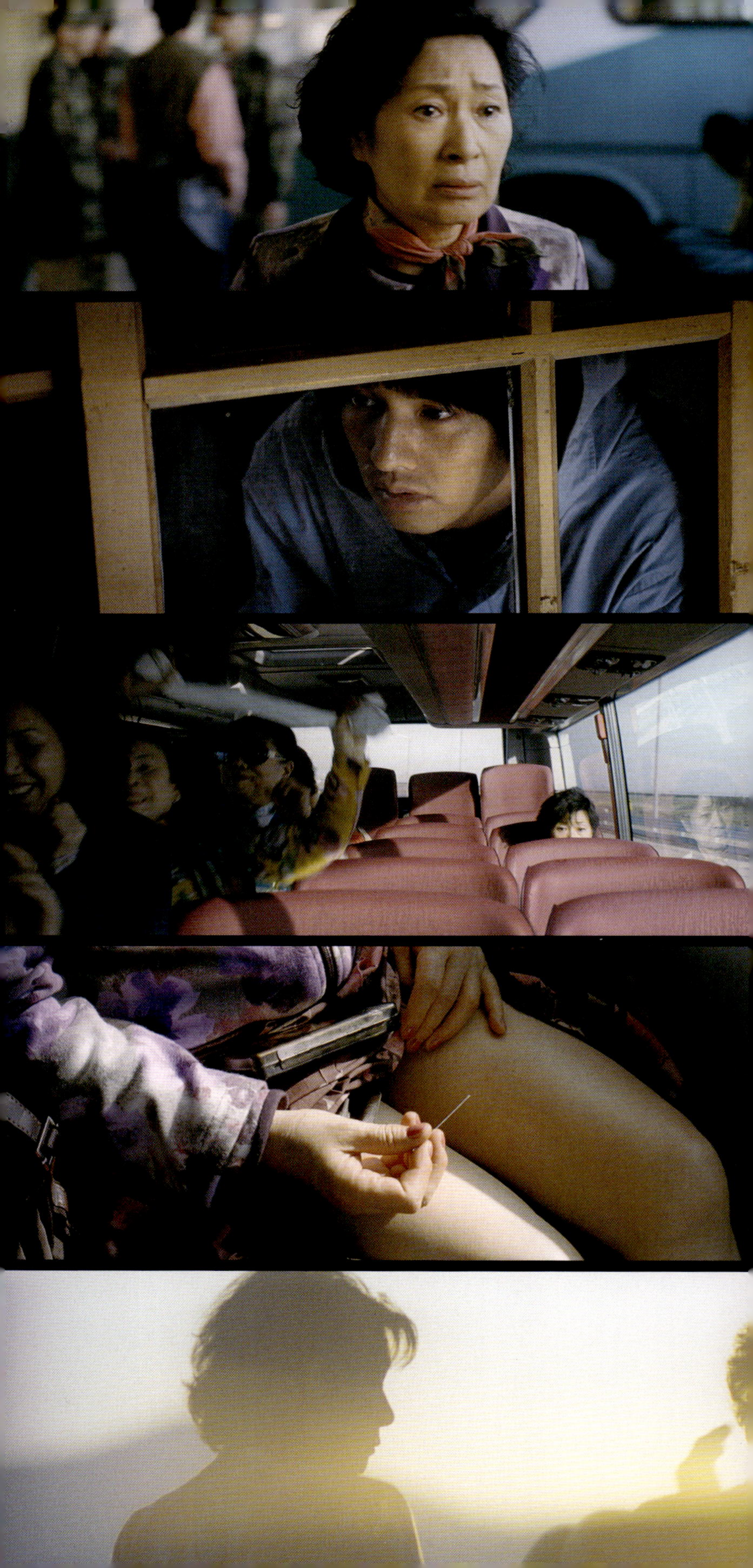

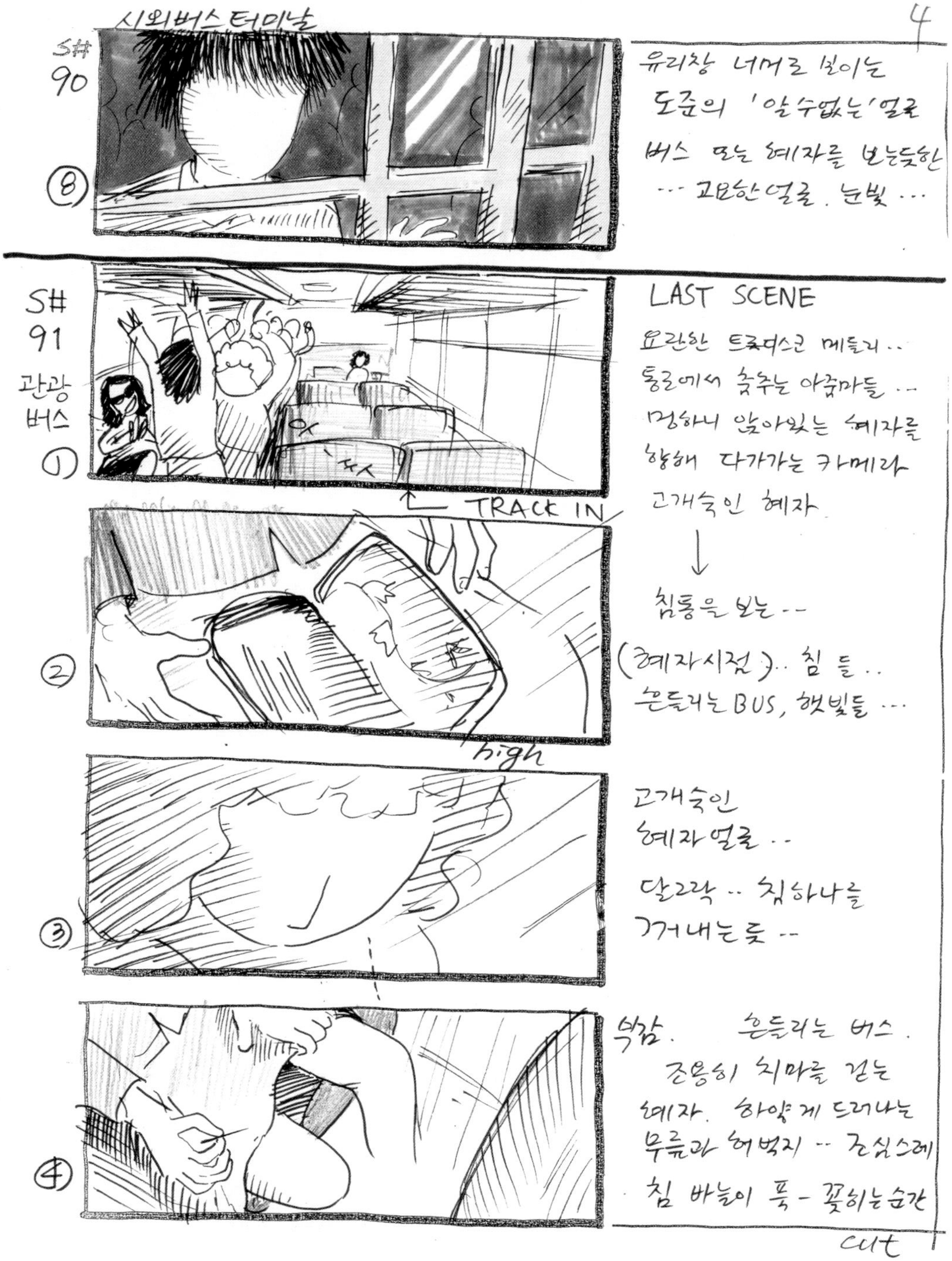

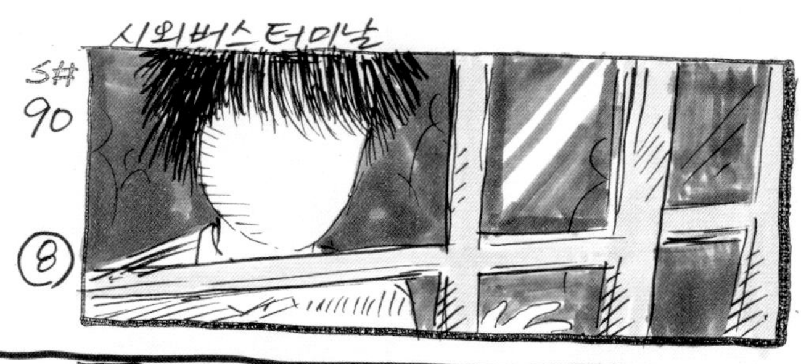

S# 90 ⑧

시외버스터미날

유리창 너머로 보이는
도준의 '알수없는'얼굴
버스 타는 혜자를 보는듯한
··· 고요한얼굴. 눈빛 ···

S# 91
관광버스 ①

LAST SCENE

요란한 트로트 메들리..
통로에서 춤추는 아줌마들 ..
멍하니 앉아있는 혜자를
향해 다가가는 카메라
고개숙인 혜자
↓
침통을 보는 --

← TRACK IN

② (혜자시점).. 침 들..
흔들리는 BUS, 햇빛들 ···

high

③ 고개숙인
혜자얼굴 ..

달그락 .. 침하나를
꺼내는듯 --

④ 박감.   흔들리는 버스.
조용히 치마를 걷는
혜자. 하얗게 드러나는
무릎과 허벅지 -- 조심스레
침 바늘이 푹 - 꽂히는순간

cut

"Visual ideas are usually my starting points," Bong notes. For *Mother*, he began with the idea of middle-aged women dancing on an express bus, something he refers to as a common sight in Korea. "I knew instinctively that this was how the movie had to end."

Left: Bong's storyboard for *Mother*

Opposite: Scenes from *Mother*

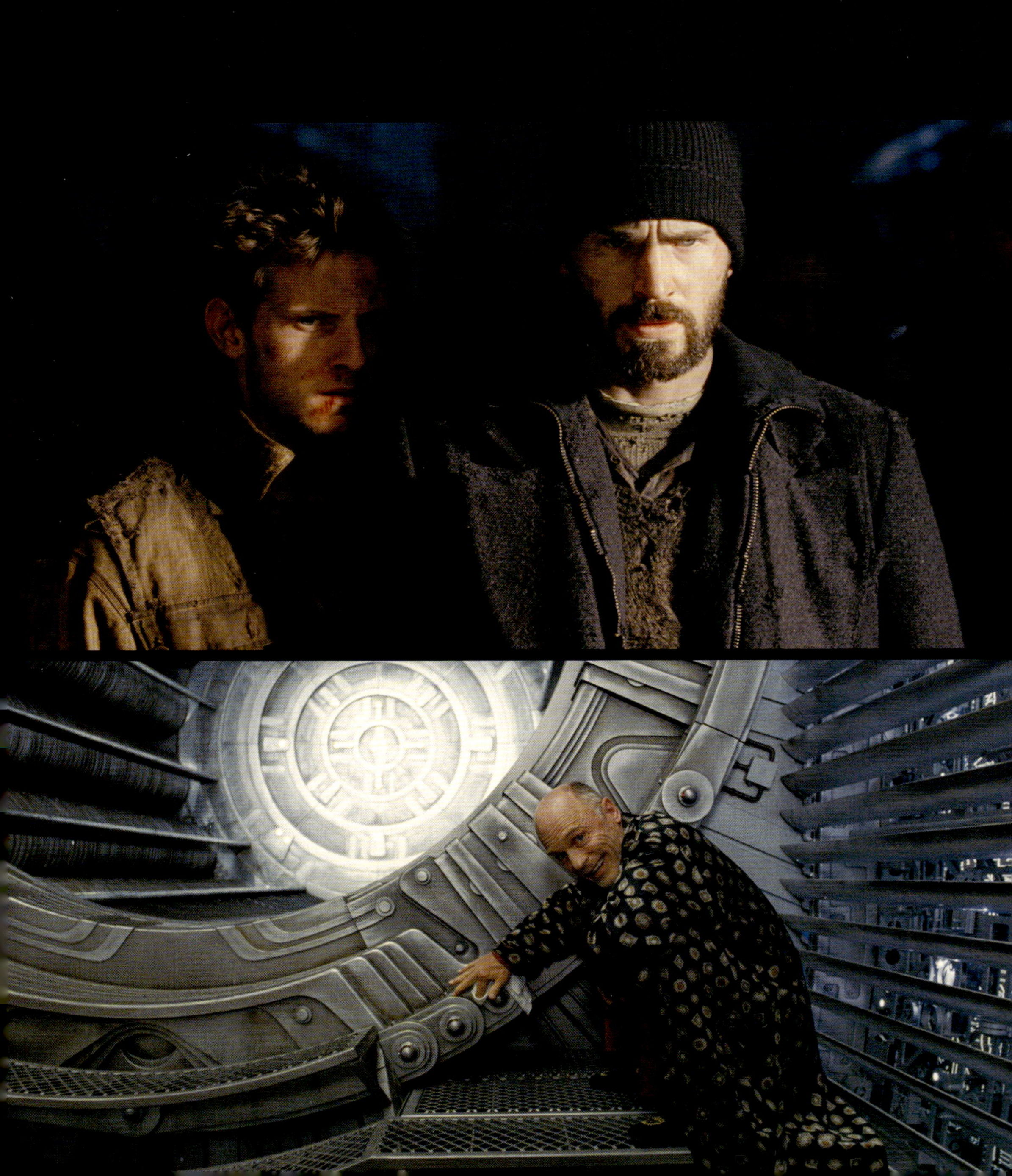

SNOWPIERCER

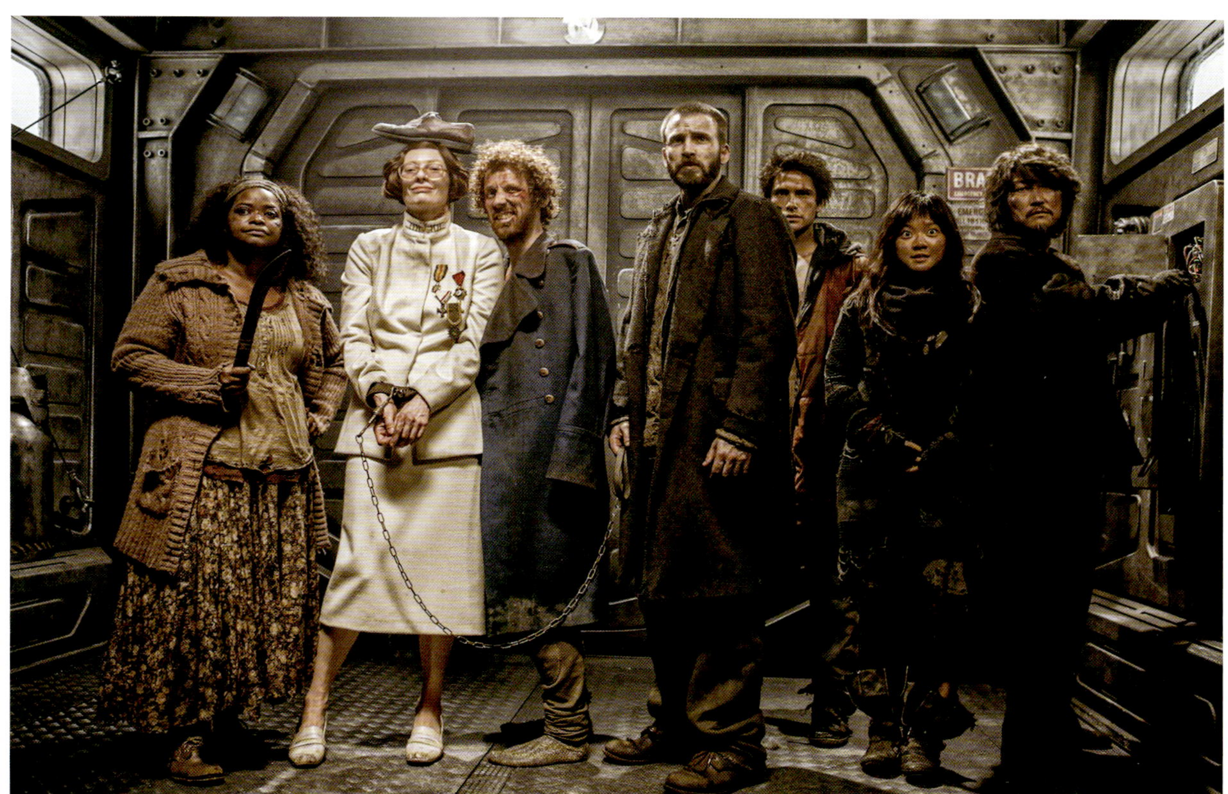

In *Snowpiercer* (2013), Bong's first English-language feature, the only survivors of a new ice age shelter together on a self-sustaining train circling the globe. Wealthy passengers occupy the front cars, while the poor live in the back.

Opposite: Scenes from *Snowpiercer*

Above: *Snowpiercer*'s international cast includes, from left, Octavia Spencer, Tilda Swinton, Ewen Bremner, Chris Evans, Luke Pasqualino, Ko Asung, and Song Kang-ho

From the very beginning of the scriptwriting process I had an idea of what I wanted to convey, and it's really a movie about systems—those who try to maintain the existing system on the train and those who want to destroy that system.

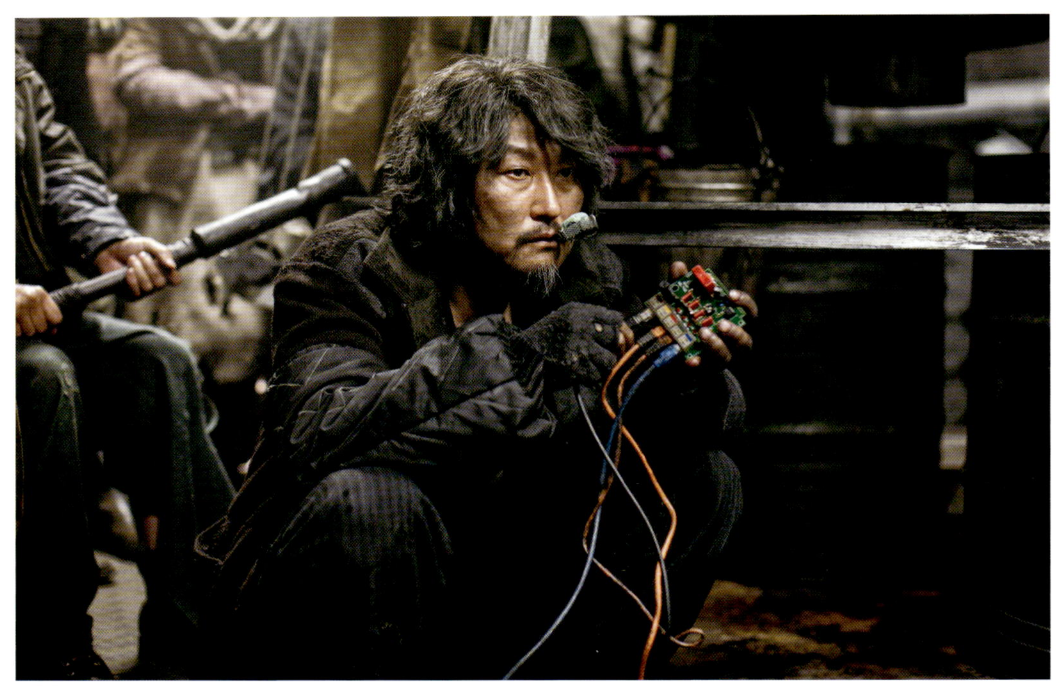

"Even during the writing of the script, I had to think about the space and locations of the train," Bong remarks. "This was a case where you couldn't separate the space from what happens in the narrative."

Above: Song Kang-ho plays Namgoong Minsoo, a security expert who can open gates between the train sections.

Opposite, top: Pages from Bong's sketchbook for *Snowpiercer*

Opposite, bottom: Storyboards for *Snowpiercer*, illustrated by Zoddd

It's a straight line—the long and narrow corridors of the train. So it's really about people trying to get to the front and move forward, and those who are trying to block that forward progress. It's really just a head-to-head encounter.

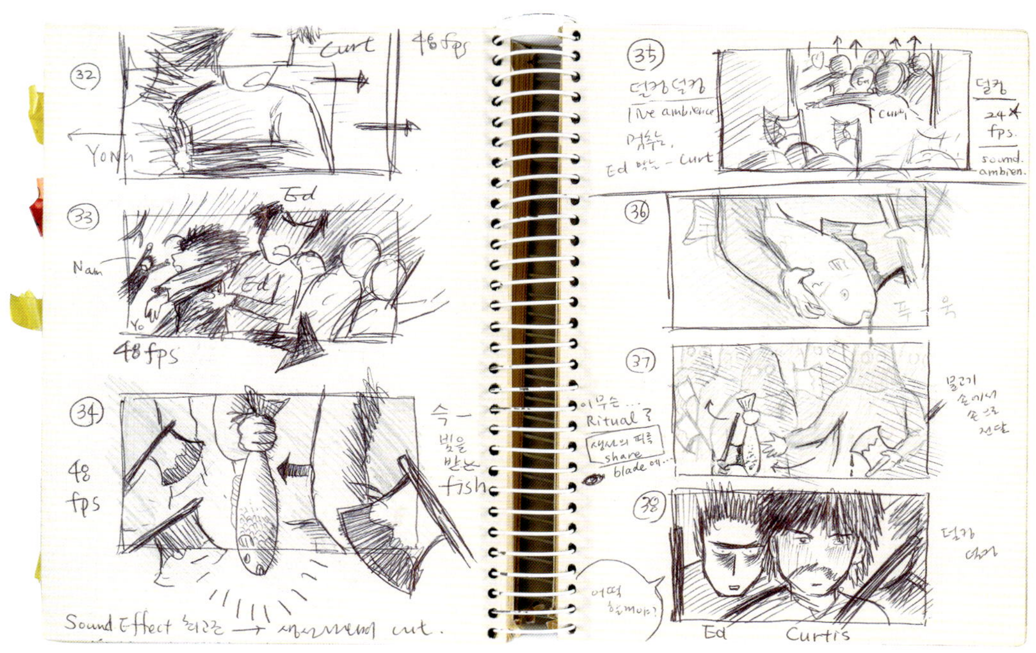

Curt
48 fps
Yona
Ed
Nam
Ed
Yo
48 fps
34
48 fps
Sound Effect
Ritual ?
share
blade
Ed
Curtis

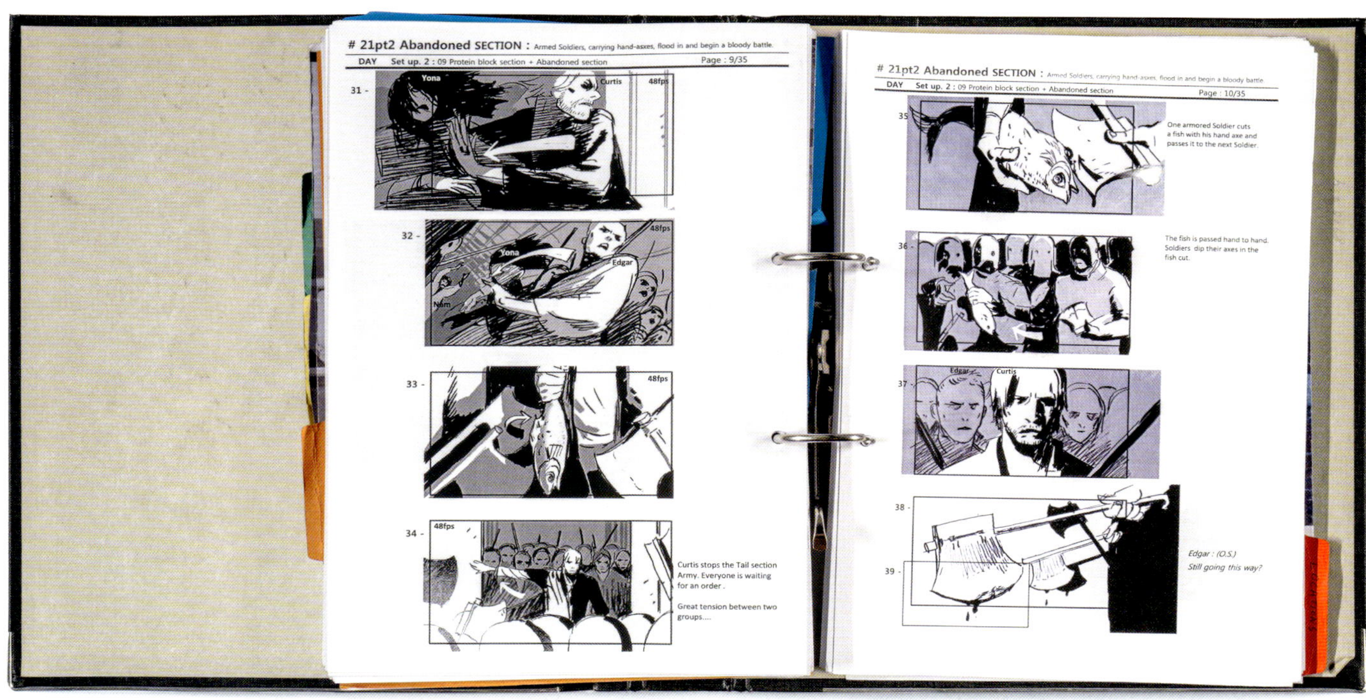

21pt2 Abandoned SECTION : Armed Soldiers, carrying hand-axes, flood in and begin a bloody battle.
DAY   Set up. 2 : 09 Protein block section + Abandoned section   Page : 9/35
31 -
Yona
Curtis
48fps
32 -
48fps
Yona
Edgar
Nam
33 -
48fps
34 -
48fps
Curtis stops the Tail section Army. Everyone is waiting for an order .
Great tension between two groups.....
21pt2 Abandoned SECTION : Armed Soldiers, carrying hand-axes, flood in and begin a bloody battle.
DAY   Set up. 2 : 09 Protein block section + Abandoned section   Page : 10/35
35 -
One armored Soldier cuts a fish with his hand axe and passes it to the next Soldier.
36 -
The fish is passed hand to hand. Soldiers dip their axes in the fish cut.
37 -
Edgar
Curtis
38 -
39 -
Edgar : (O.S.)
Still going this way?

I wanted the experience of making a true sci-fi film. What I like about the genre is that you can take a message and be really direct about it.

Below: Bong with (from left) Chris Evans, Song Kang-ho, and crew during production of *Snowpiercer*

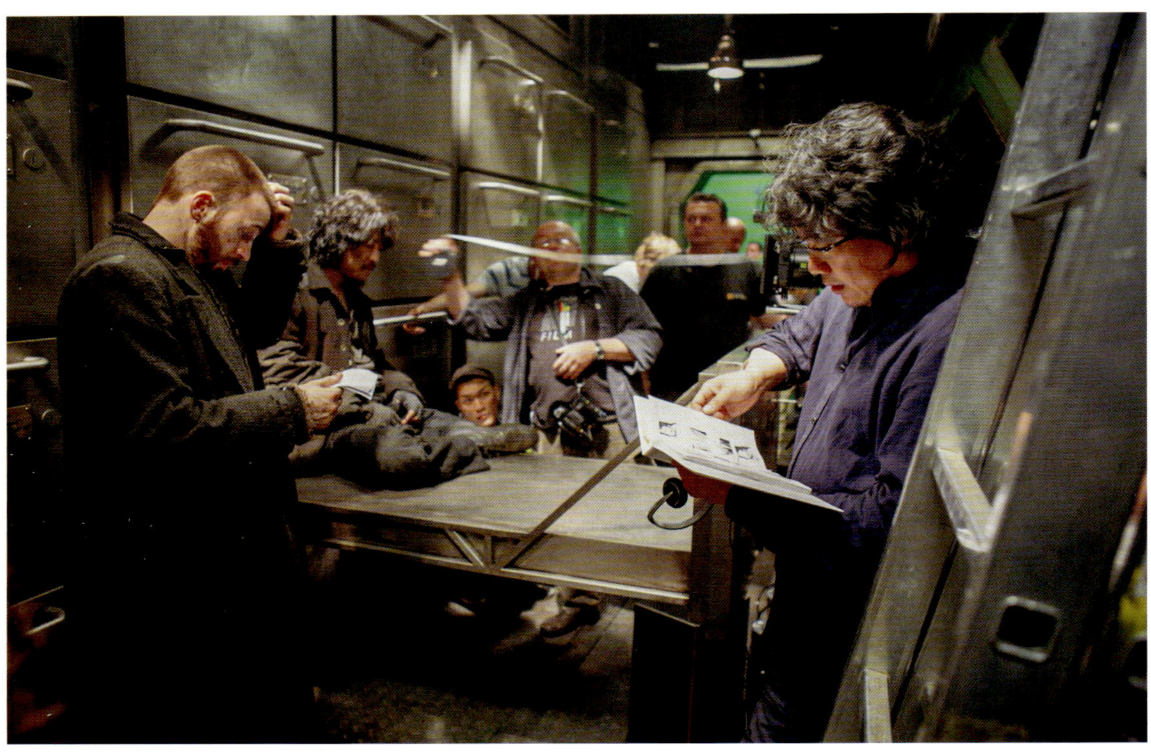

DOOHO CHOI

When I was enrolled at the Korean Academy of Film Arts (KAFA) in Seoul, my classmates lived in a house that we all used as our set. If we needed a bedroom or backyard or whatever the scene called for, we would shoot it there. One night we were in the basement filming a scene with Kim Roi-ha, a theater actor who would later play Detective Cho in *Memories of Murder*. Director Bong, who had graduated from KAFA four years earlier, showed up with a box of Bacchus, an energy drink you'll find on every Korean movie set. At that point, he had only made short films, but they had won prizes abroad at festivals.

Years later, around 2011, I was working as a producer in Los Angeles and got a call from Director Bong out of the blue. He said, "I don't know if you remember me, but I'm working on this movie called *Snowpiercer*. I need somebody in Los Angeles. Do you have any interest in working on it?" I said yes and got on a plane to Korea to meet with him.

Even though Bong had already made some great films, there weren't too many people in Hollywood who knew his work at the time. I arranged a meeting with a casting director, Johanna Ray, who had done a lot of films with David Lynch, and we started meeting actors. Tilda Swinton (as Minister Mason) and John Hurt (as Gilliam) were the first to sign on—John because he had seen *Mother*, and Tilda because she had seen *The Host*. After that, more people started paying attention.

Snowpiercer was Director Bong's first English-language film. Getting it financed was difficult. There was even a moment when we thought it was going to shut down. But once we were in production, things moved along smoothly. The transition to working with English-speaking actors and department heads, under union rules, was effortless for Director Bong. After a lengthy post-production process, it was released in Korean theaters and seen by nearly 10 million people. The US release was famously fraught, but, in the end the director's cut of the film was the one US audiences got to see.

From a production—and budget—standpoint, *Mickey 17* is the biggest of Director Bong's films so far, but his approach was the same as it was on *Okja* and *Snowpiercer*. He plans meticulously, but he is also ready to change something during a take if there's a new idea. He's fluid because he's prepared, and that also makes him efficient. What I've learned is that if he asks for something, it's because it's absolutely essential. When he identifies a problem, I put all my energy into solving it.

I've never asked him where he gets his ideas. In *Mickey 17*, there's a guy dressed in a pigeon costume that we called Pigeon Man. He shows up, and then he's gone. I don't know what it means. Sometimes I think he does things because it amuses him, but other times I feel like he can see the future. The stories he's told and wants to tell—about extreme weather events, genetically modified food, politics—are uncannily topical. I feel that he is an artist who makes movies that people want to see and puts them out at exactly the right moment.

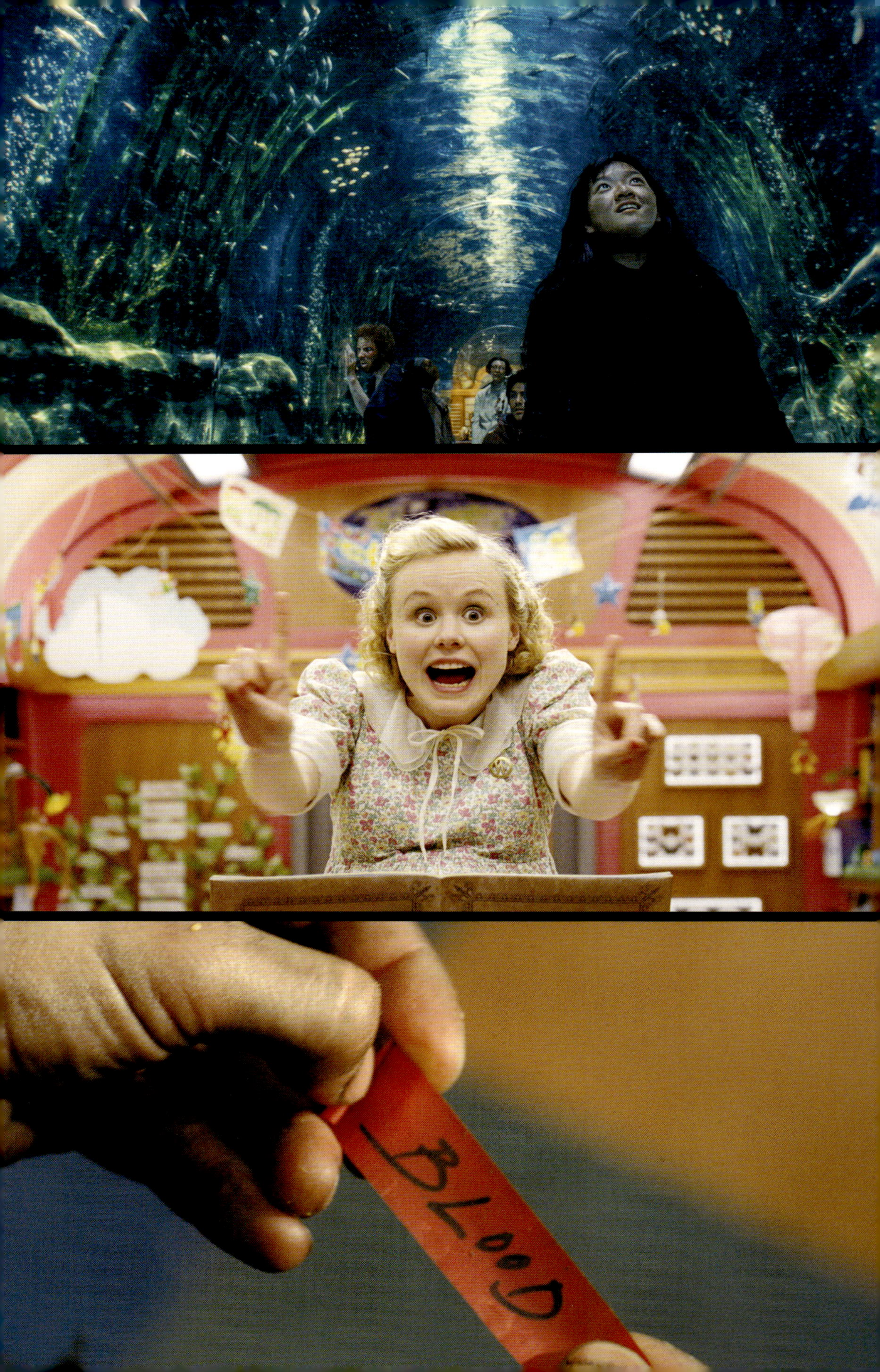
BLOOD

For *Snowpiercer*, Bong created a strong visual contrast between the front and back of the train. The opulent front section includes an aquarium car with a sushi bar and a candy-colored classroom led by Alison Pill as a deranged schoolteacher.

Opposite: Scenes from *Snowpiercer*

Right: Storyboard for *Snowpiercer*, illustrated by Zoddd

Below: Prop message capsule used in the film

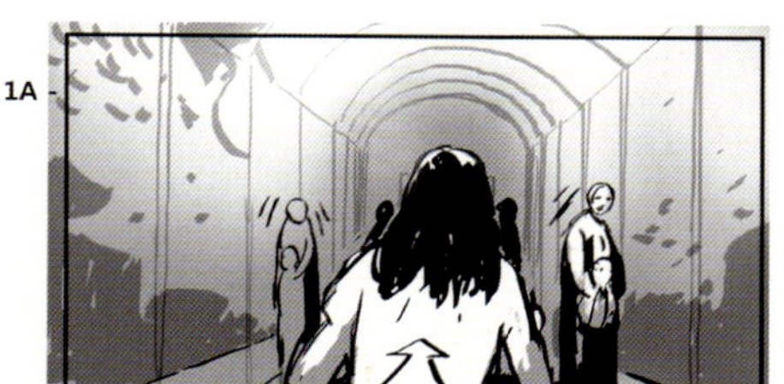

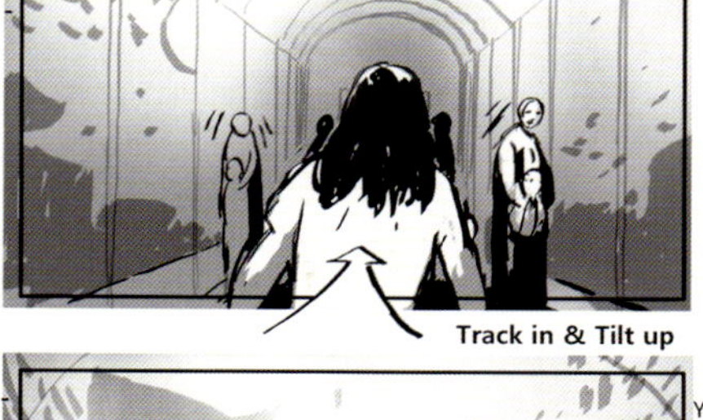

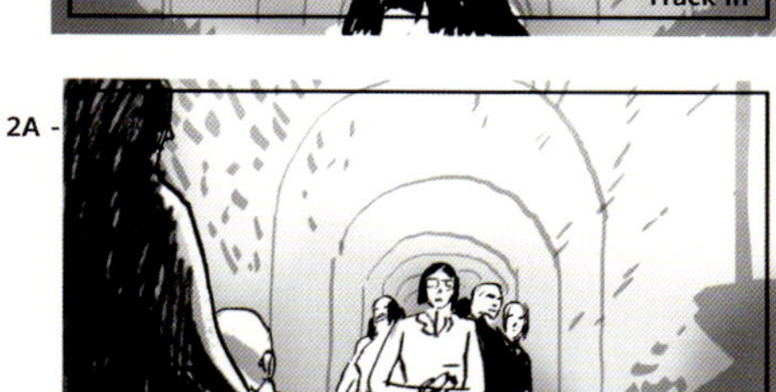

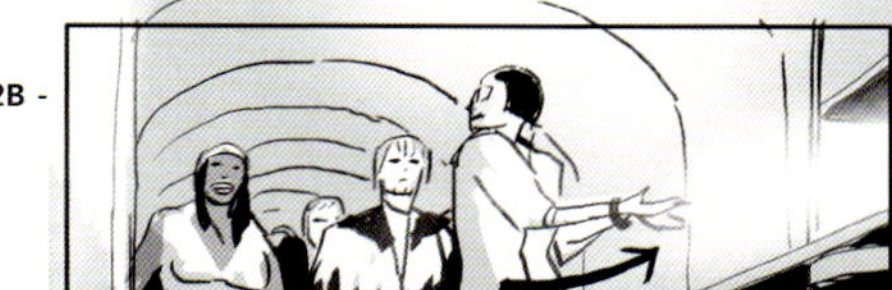

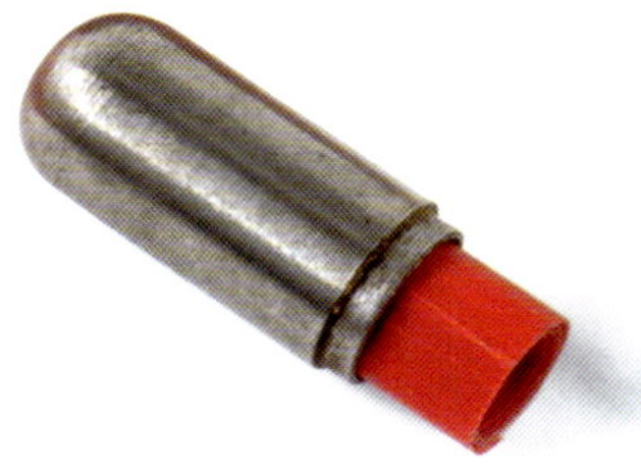
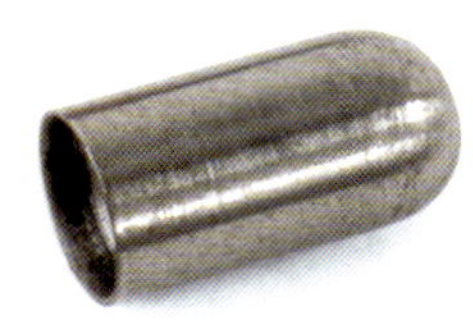

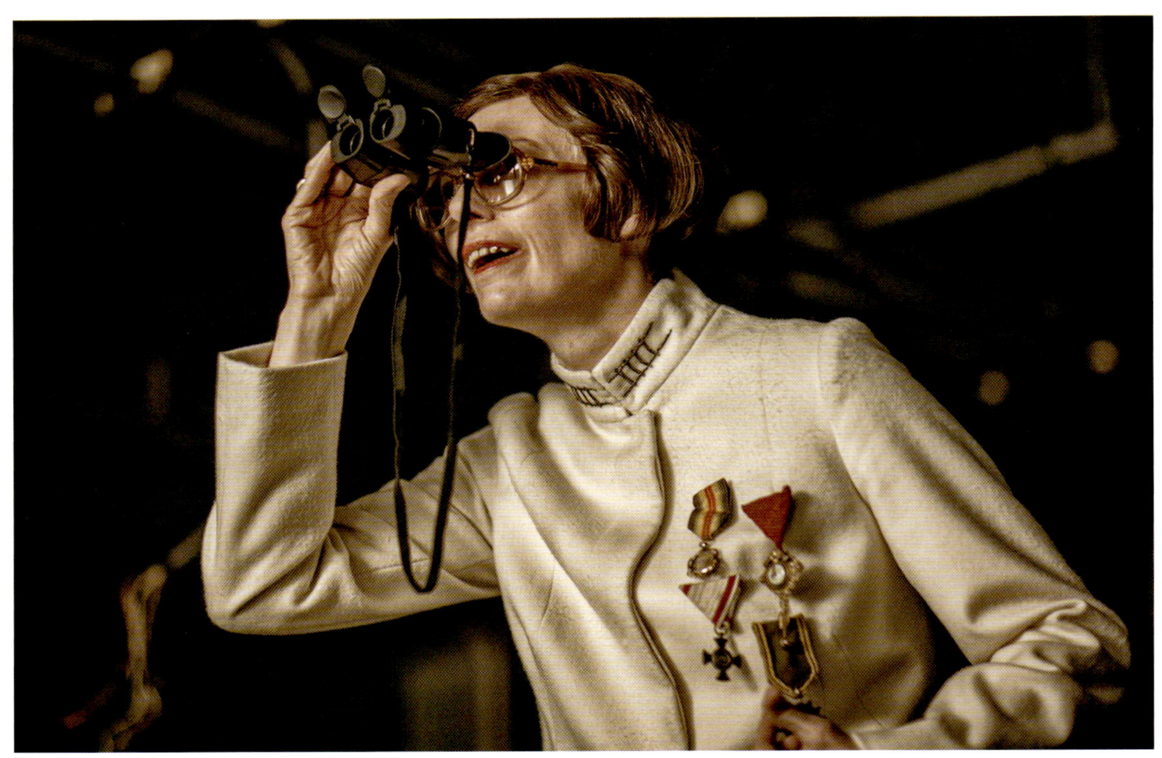

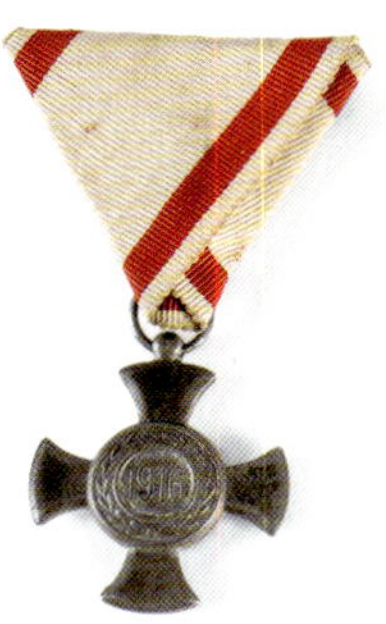

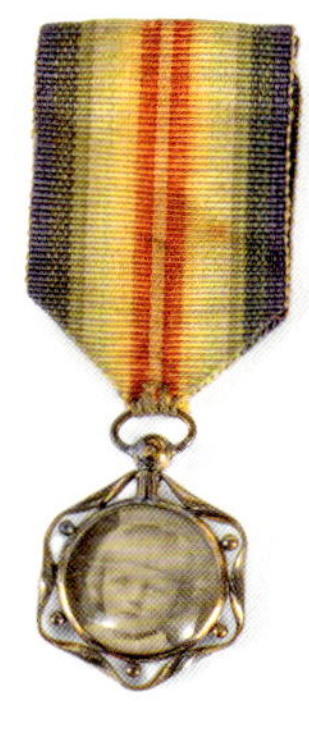

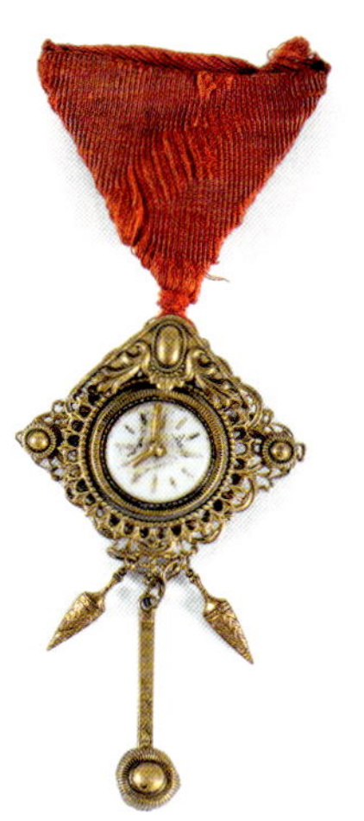

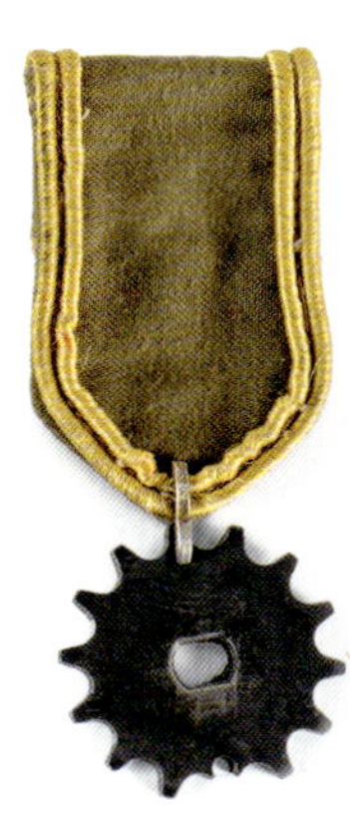

Bong originally wrote Minister Mason for a male lead but changed the role to cast Tilda Swinton. Her performance was inspired by sources ranging from her childhood nanny, whose accent she emulated, to authoritarian leaders Benito Mussolini and Kim Il-sung.

Left: Medals worn by Tilda Swinton as Minister Mason

Above: Swinton in *Snowpiercer*

CATHERINE GEORGE

In 2010, I designed the costumes for the Lynne Ramsay film *We Need to Talk About Kevin*, which starred Tilda Swinton. The film premiered at Cannes in 2011 when Director Bong was head of the jury for the Caméra d'Or section. As I understand it, Bong and Tilda met there to discuss *Snowpiercer*, and when he mentioned the look he wanted for the film, Tilda suggested that we should meet. That's how I got my first call from Bong Joon Ho.

The way Director Bong described *Snowpiercer* to me emphasized the human stories within the post-apocalyptic narrative. He always creates beautiful storyboards that help you jump right into his vision for a film. They help you understand the action and the characters, but Bong also stresses that we don't need to use the colors or costumes depicted in his drawings. He leaves plenty of creative space open for interpretation and collaboration. For *Snowpiercer*, the front section of the train had the lavish, glamourous feel of the Orient Express, while the back section was utterly destitute. As with many of Director Bong's movies, that class division element was key.

He has an encyclopedic knowledge of cinema, and we tapped into a global theme for the clothing on *Snowpiercer*. Bong wanted to show that people from all over the world had boarded the train, so we added styles from every continent. I researched the look of street vendors when designing the costume for Gilliam, the tail section leader played by John Hurt. I decided to put him in a very distressed, almost broken-down tweed jacket with a sarong-style piece underneath. This was blending two elements of the character's past life, in England and India, and John got a real kick out of it. For the children who were kidnapped from the tail section and forced to work in the engine room of the train, the amulets and trinkets sewn into their clothing are based on images I saw of child soldiers in Africa.

One of the looks for Minister Mason, the front section commanding officer played by Tilda, was based on a photograph of the Libyan dictator Colonel Muammar Gaddafi on an official visit to Italy. He arrived wearing some very homemade-looking regalia, which was said to have been made by him on the plane. So that was part of the concept for Minister Mason's regalia, that maybe she'd found the metal parts and ribbons around the train and assembled them herself. Director Bong especially enjoyed the political and absurd comedy of that.

Tilda played the twin heiresses Lucy and Nancy Mirando in Bong's next film, *Okja*. Our references for those characters were high-profile female CEOs. One of Lucy's key costumes is the Korean hanbok-style dress that she wears on stage to celebrate Mija's arrival in New York. Bong wasn't entirely convinced about the hanbok until I discovered a Chanel version that checked all the boxes for Lucy. We thought her character, a high-end luxury trendsetter, would embrace it as a superficial gesture indicating support for Mija and her cultural traditions.

Director Bong is always open to hearing about and discussing the details of costume development while he's prepping. For his most recent film, *Mickey 17*, we added strategic openings to Robert Pattinson's costume, with snaps, so the medical team would have access points. Director Bong came up with the idea that we should add a bum flap to Mickey's pants, and the next day that was in the storyboards as part of the scene. We've done three films together now, and I am always impressed by his decisiveness when I present images and ideas to him. Once you show him something that sparks, he doesn't forget it.

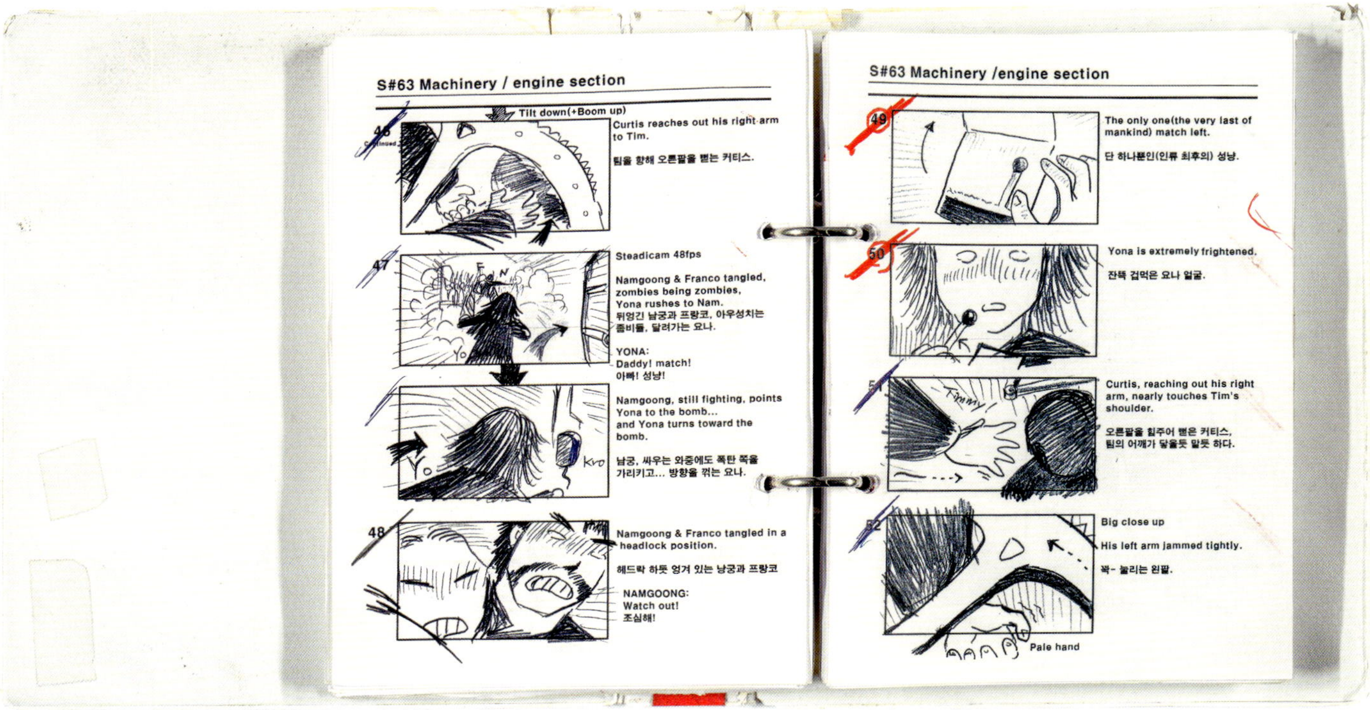

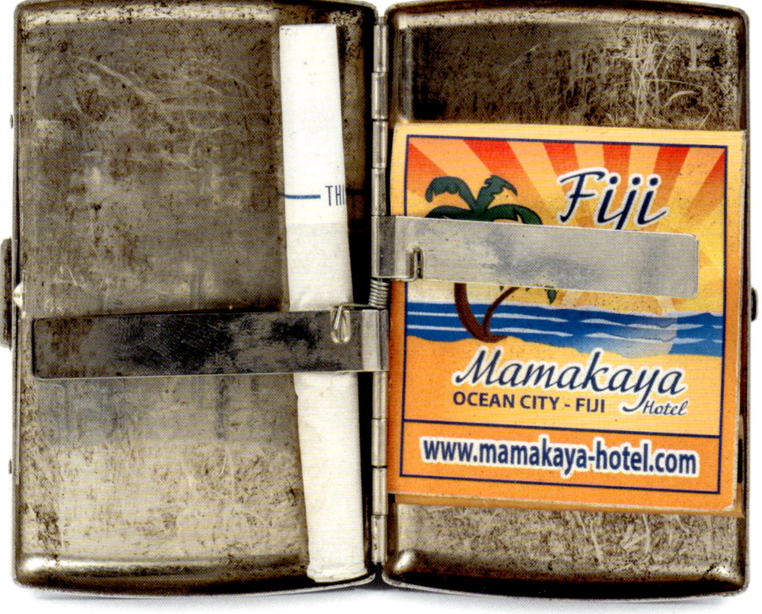

Above: Pages from Bong's storyboard binder

Right: Prop cigarette case, cigarette, and matchbook used in *Snowpiercer*

Opposite: Scenes from *Snowpiercer*

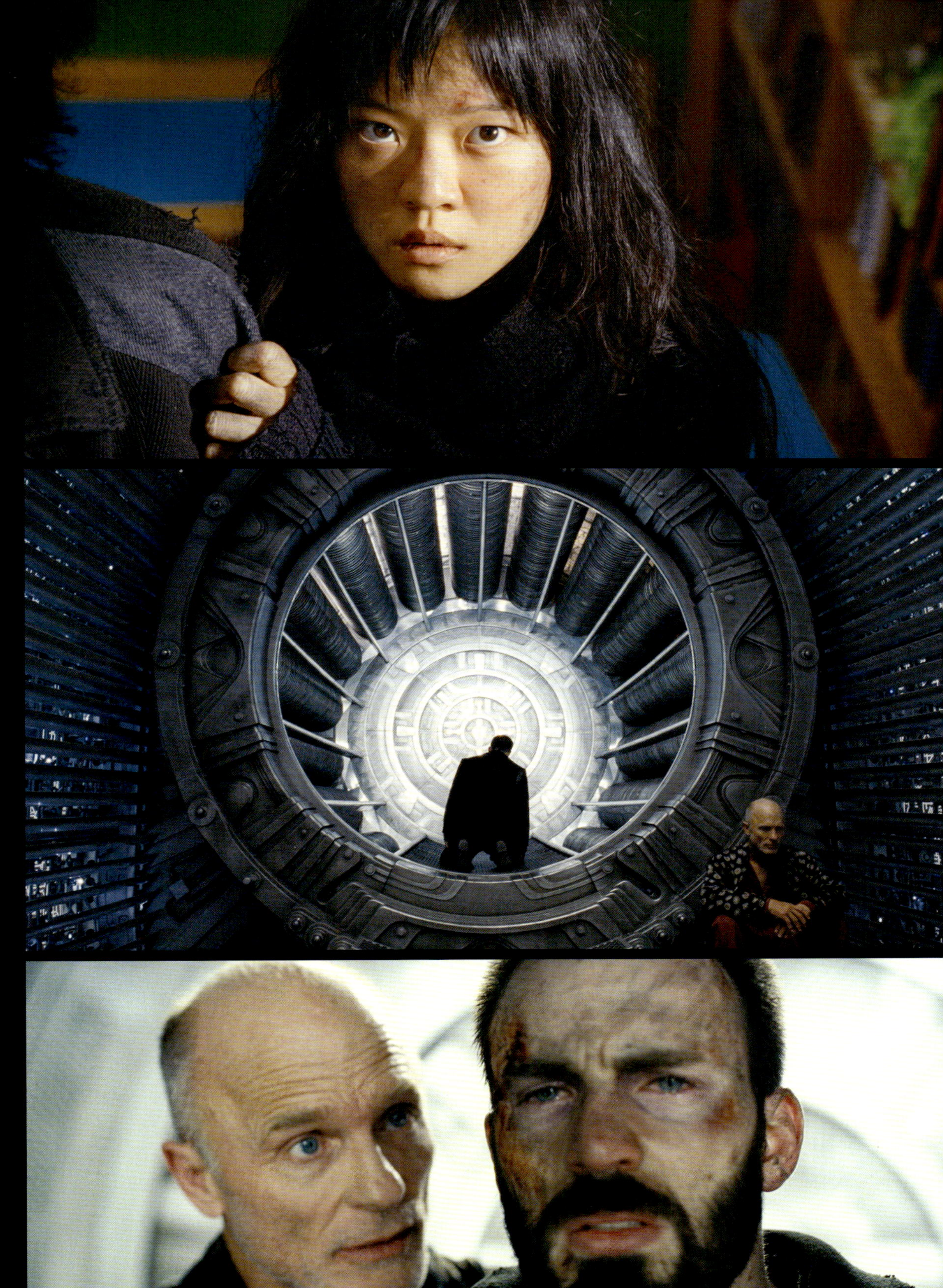

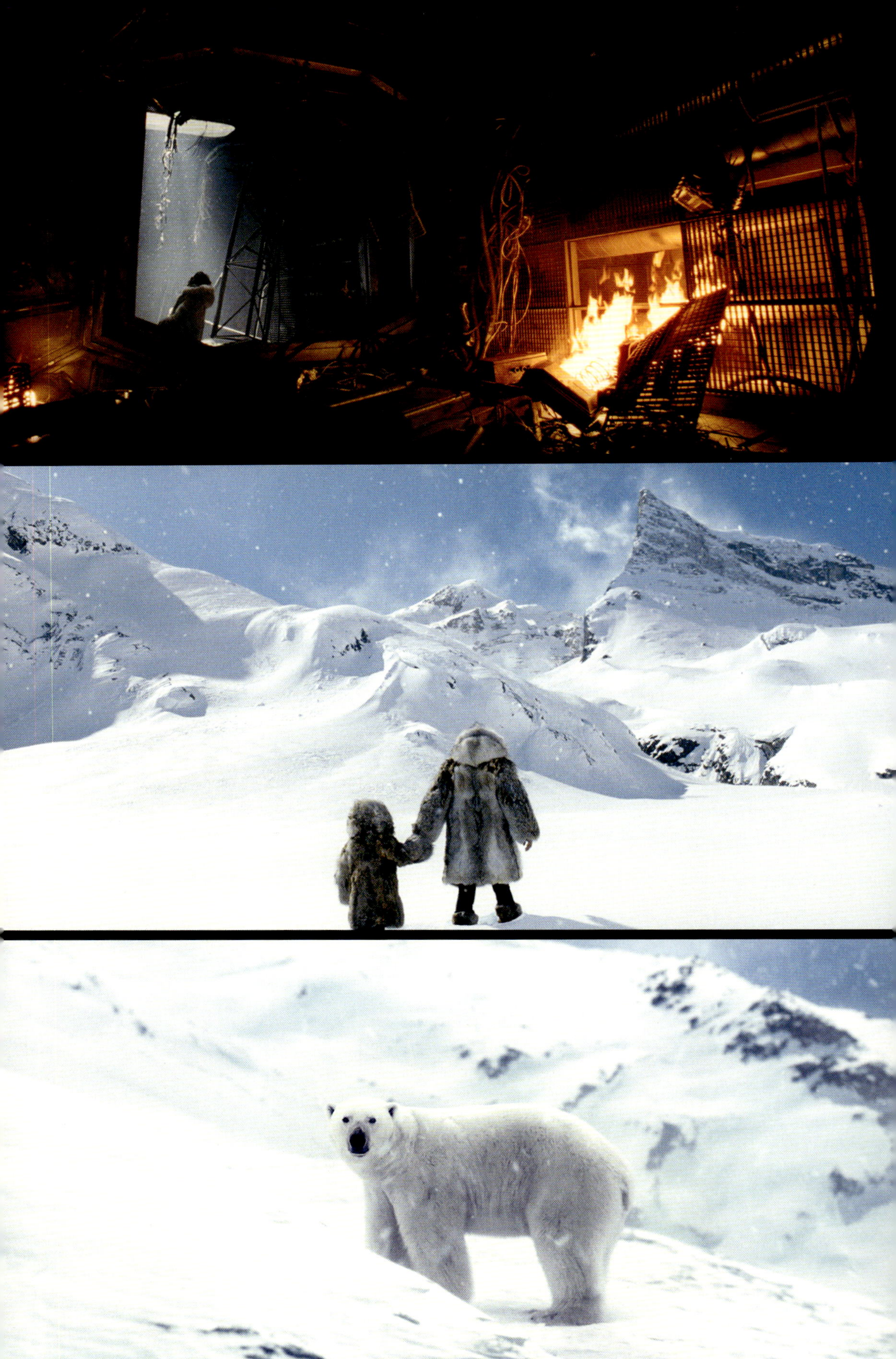

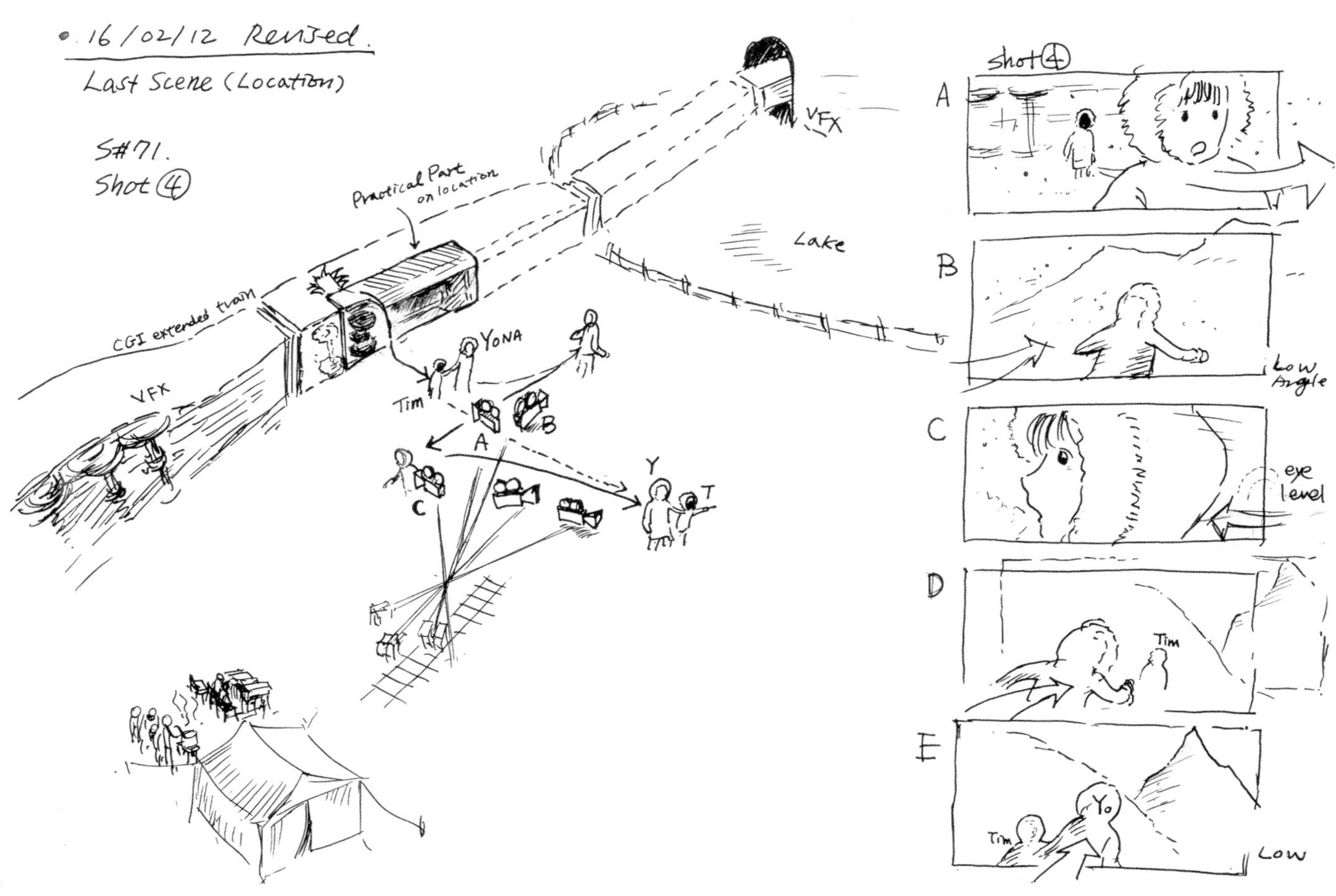

"Outside the train, life is actually returning," Bong says of the film's ending. "It's nature that's eternal, and not the train."

Above: Bong's storyboard and schematic for the final scene of *Snowpiercer*

Opposite: Scenes from the ending of *Snowpiercer*

It has violent energy and destruction on the train, but I've always insisted that it has a happy ending—there's hope at the very end.

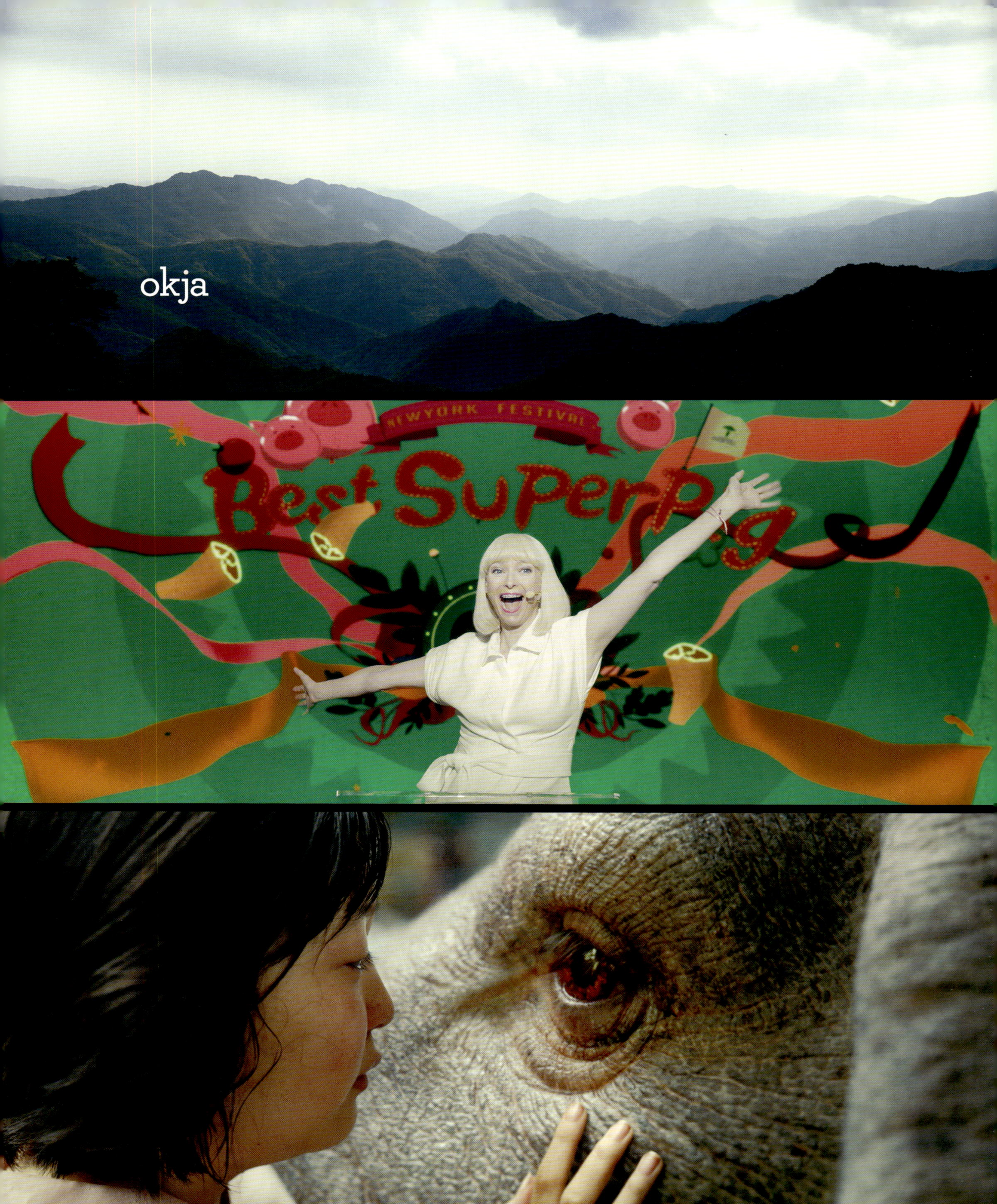
okja
NEW YORK FESTIVAL
Best SuperPig

Okja is primarily a love story between Mija and Okja—the girl and the animal. The things that come between them and end up tearing them apart could be seen as the political element to the film.

Part fantasy fable, part ecological thriller, *Okja* (2017) centers on a young girl's fight to save her beloved bioengineered "super pig" from the corporation that created her. The film's visuals juxtapose the bright colors of corporate advertising with the bleak realities of a globalized food industry.

Opposite: Scenes from *Okja*

Right: *Okja* concept art by Zoddd

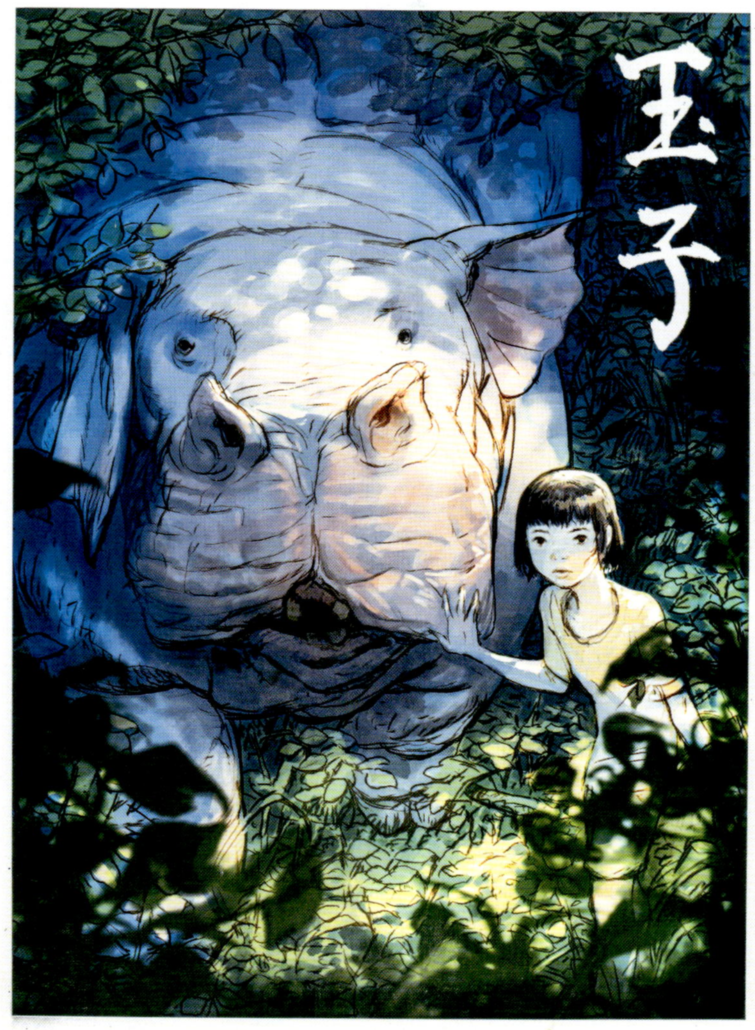

—

The starting point was two aspects of this creature: It has to be massive in size, and it has to look kind, introverted, and sad.

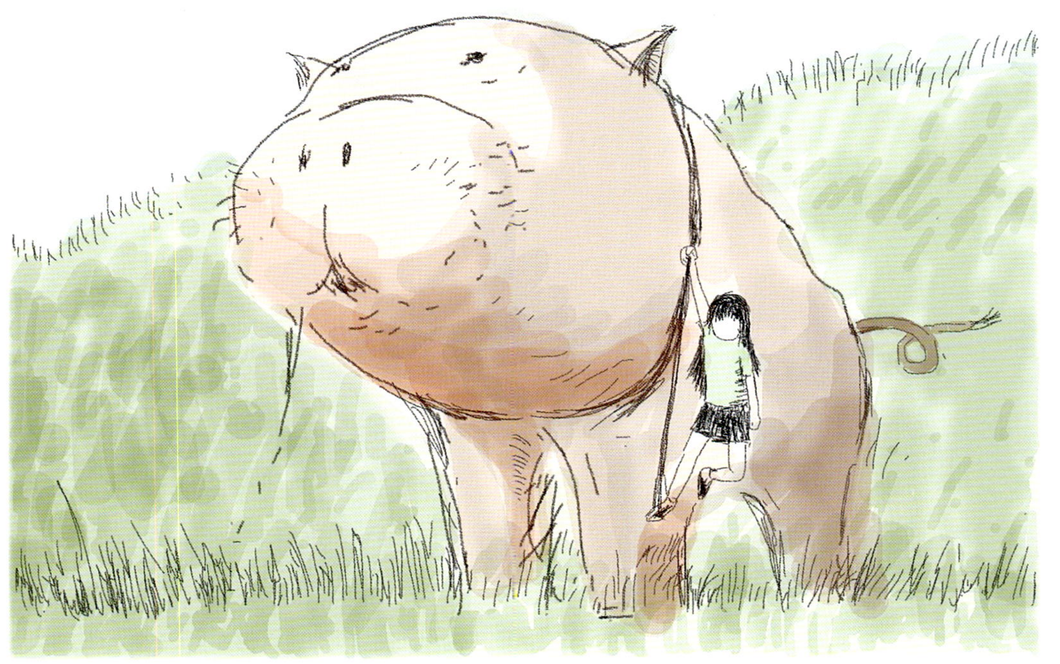

Okja is a CGI creature, but "the audience, after five seconds, has to believe that it's an actual animal that exists in this world," Bong says. "And also it had to be very lovely."

Left: Bong's early concept drawing

Opposite, top: Okja model by Jang Hee Chul

Opposite, bottom: Okja as rendered in the film

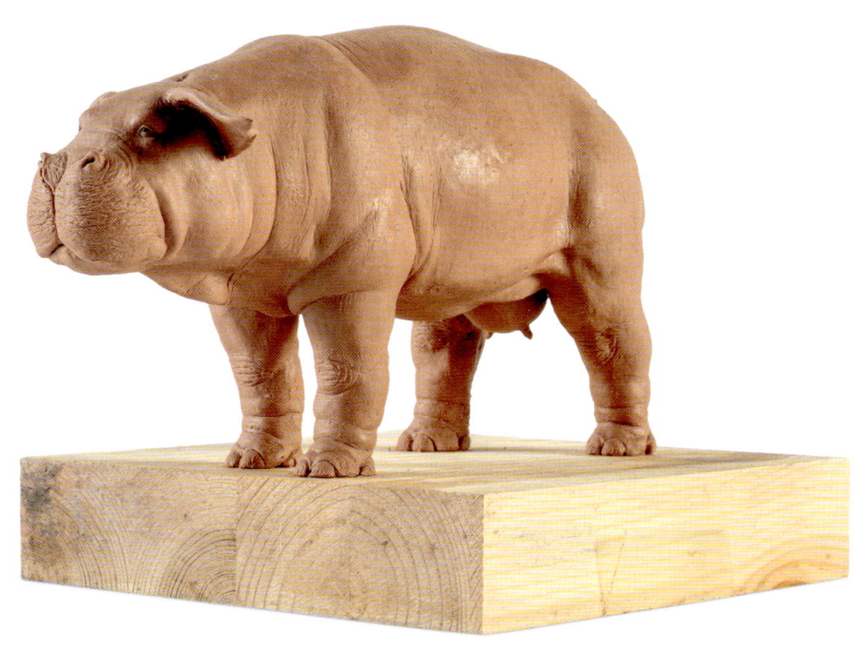

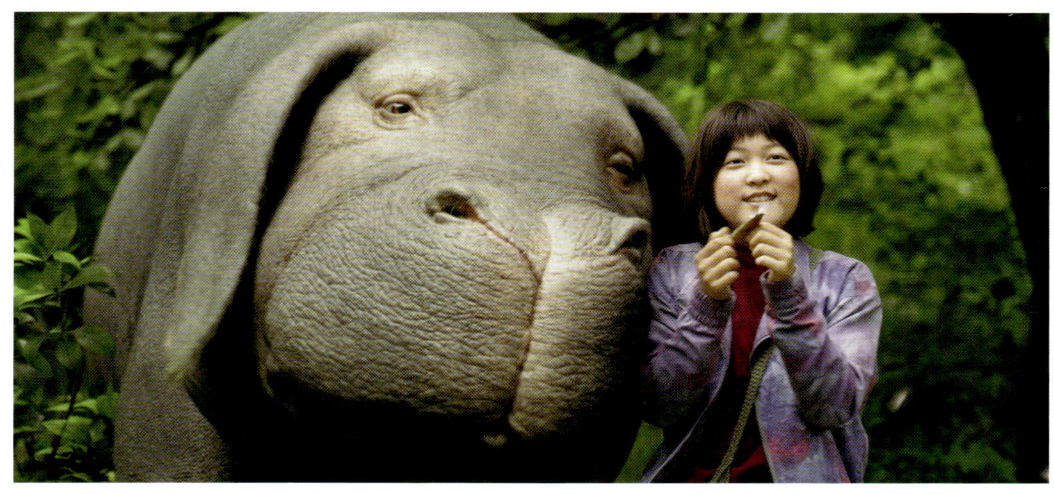

I wanted to make a realistic-looking animal, but an animal that nobody had ever seen in their life.

The visual effects team created a scale puppet of Okja to give the actors something physical to interact with while filming. Animator and on-set creature puppeteer Stephen Clee's interpretation of Okja's movements and mannerisms helped visualize the deep bond between the creature and Mija.

Opposite: Ahn Seo-hyun and Stephen Clee during production of *Okja*

Below: Concept art by Sandro Kopp

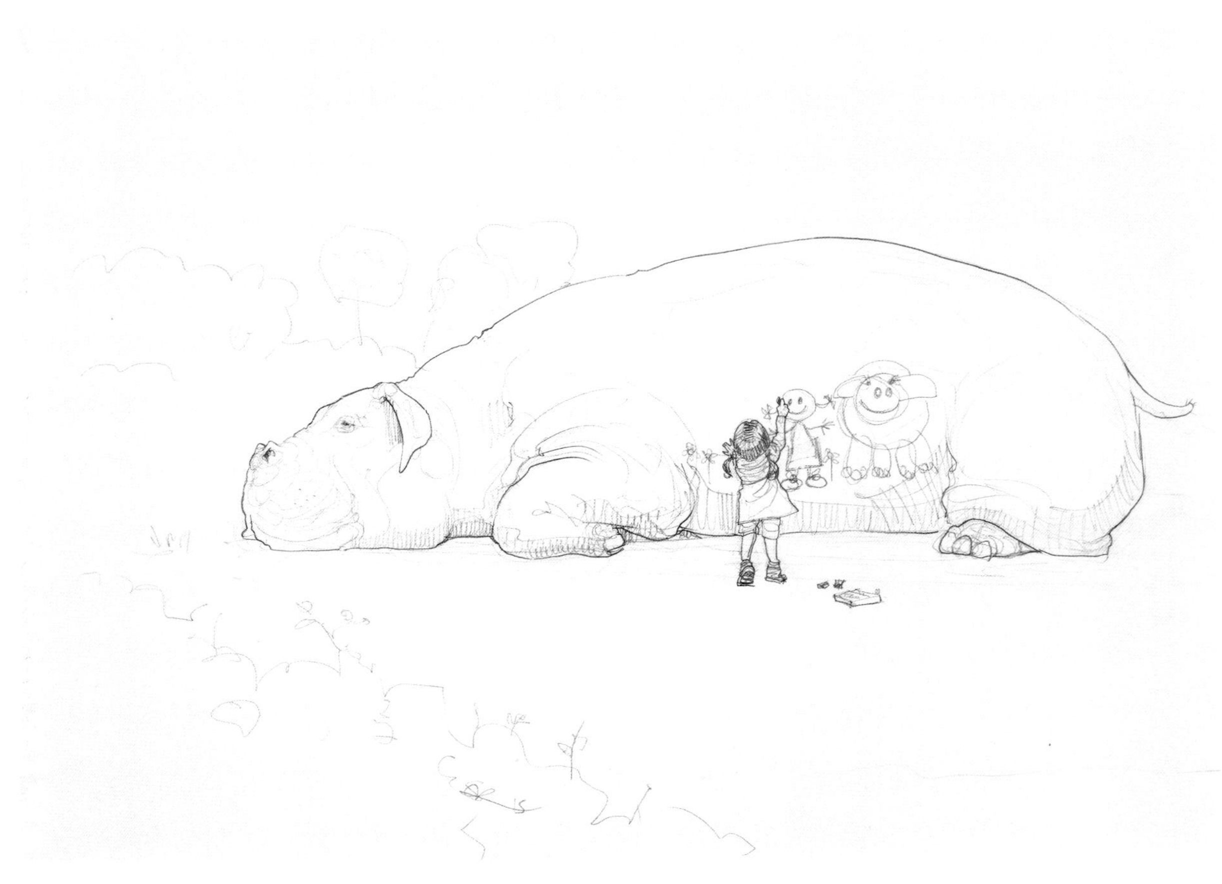

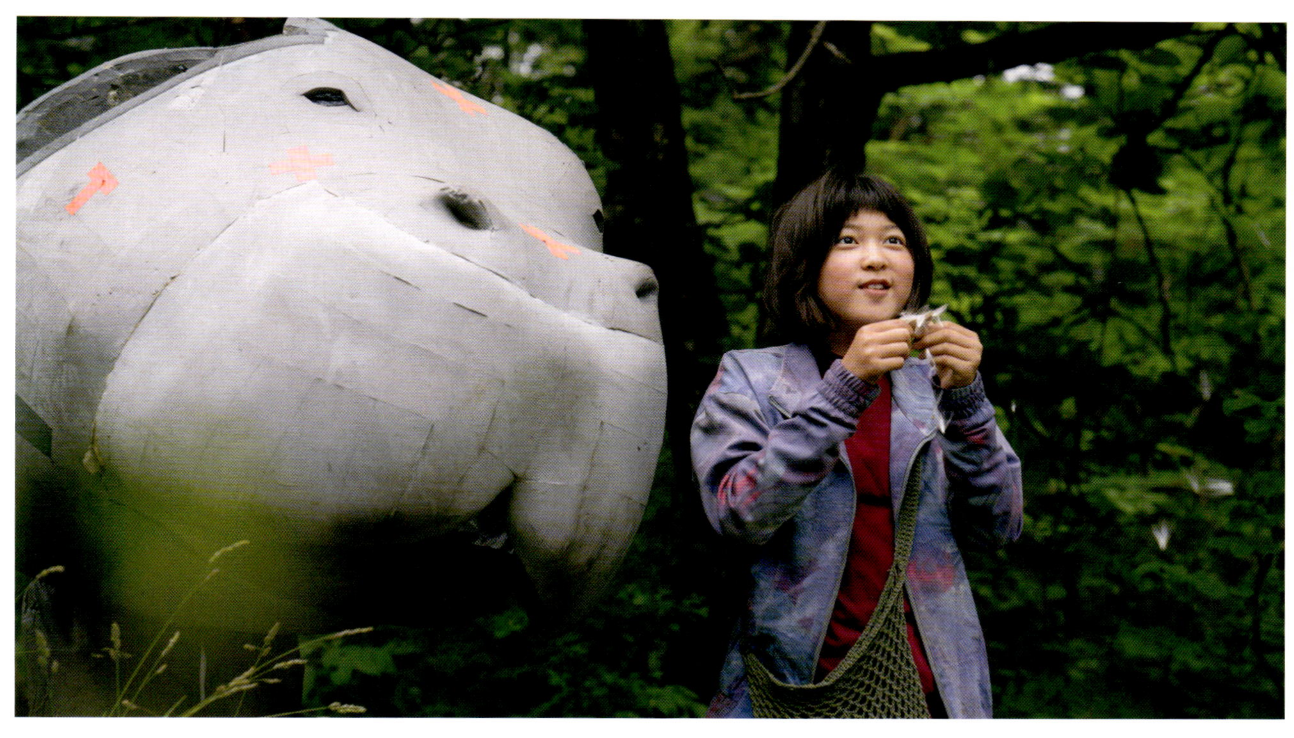

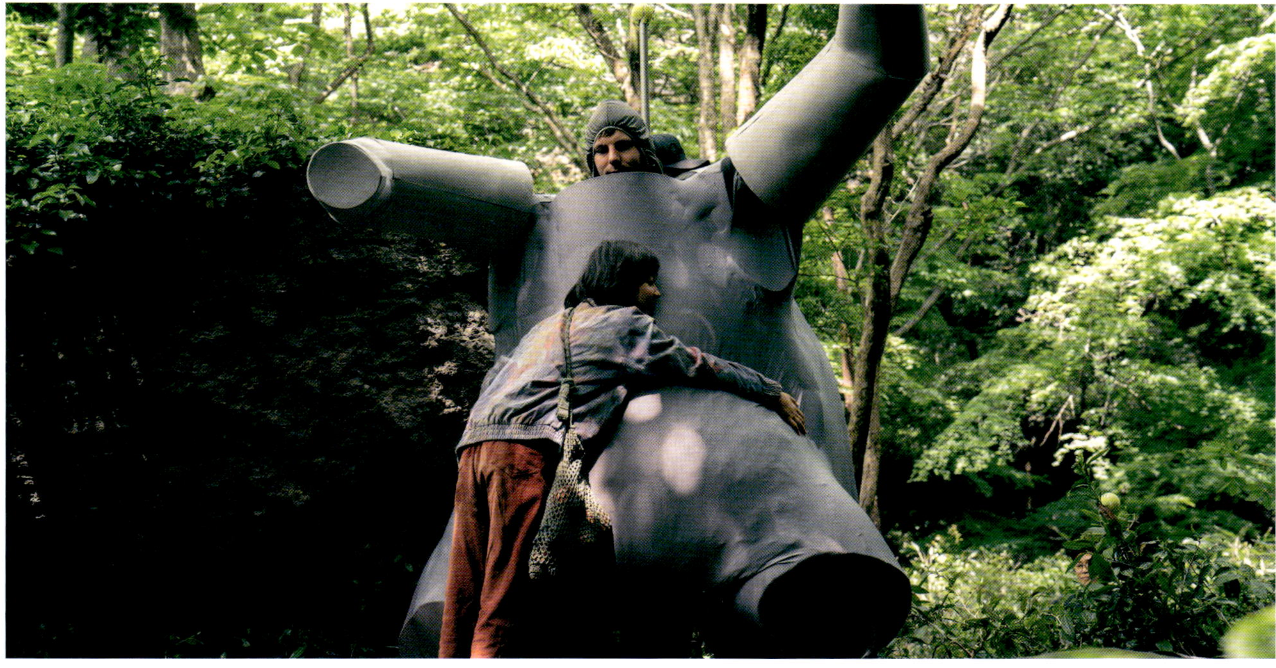

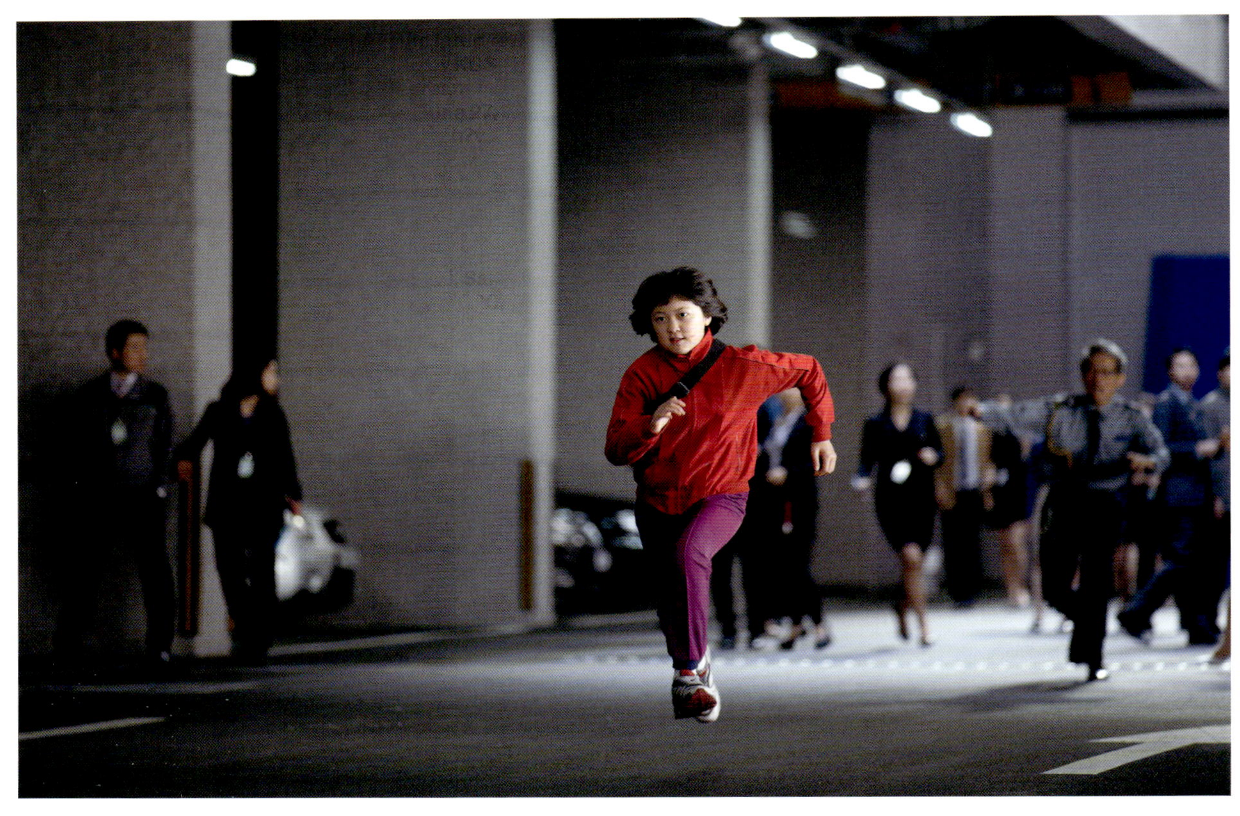

The energy that Mija possessed,
it had to be unstoppable. No big
corporations could get in her way,
her heart never stops beating,
there's this unstoppable energy
she had to have constantly.

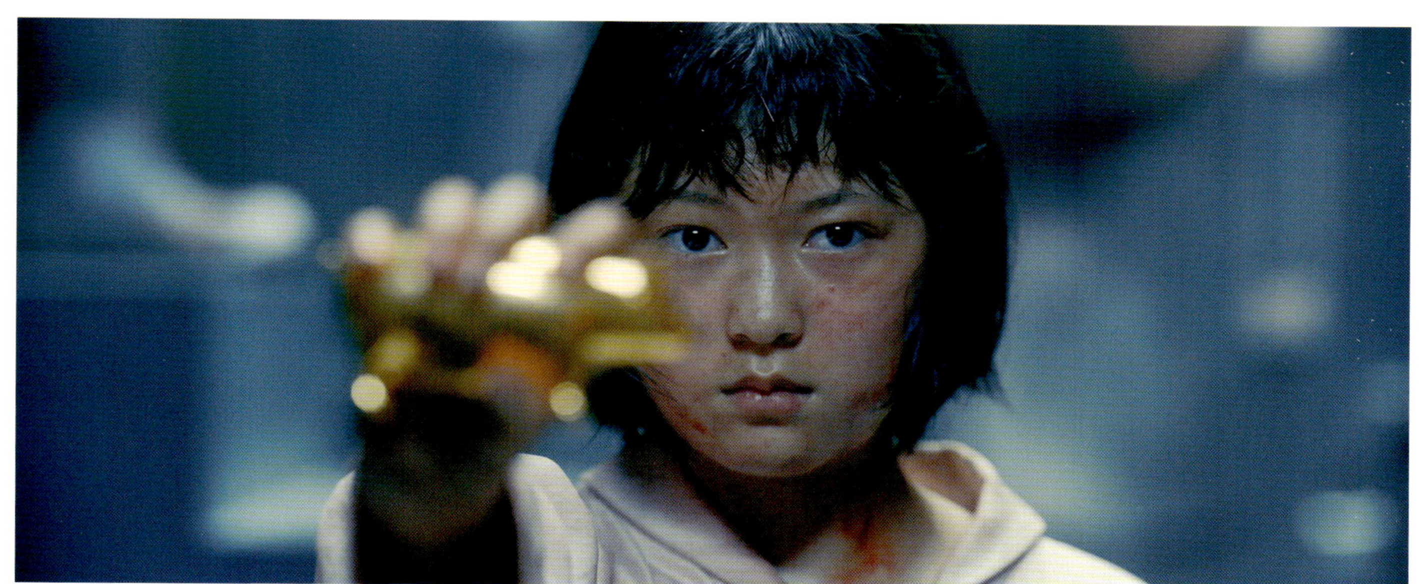

Mija's grandfather gives her a golden pig when *Okja* is taken away by the Mirando Corporation. She later uses the golden figurine to negotiate for Okja's freedom.

Opposite and above: Ahn Seo-hyun as Mija

Right: Prop golden pig used in *Okja*

Following page: Scenes from *Okja*

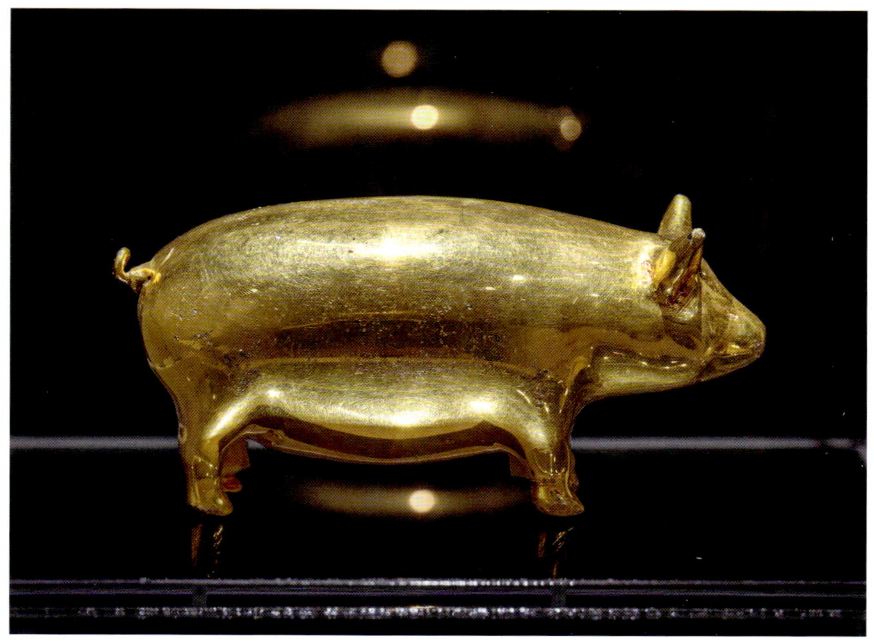

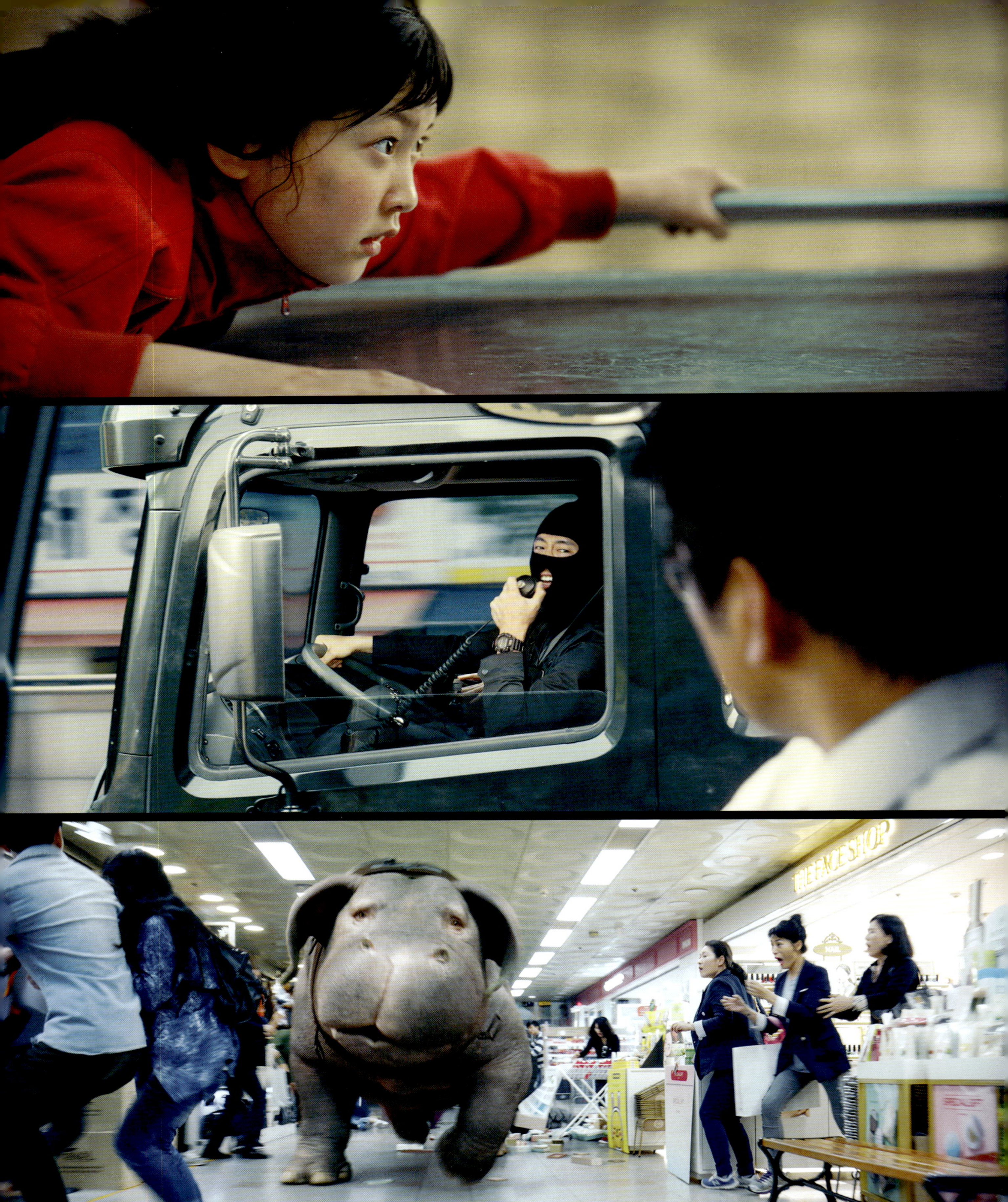

JUNG JAEIL

In my teens and twenties I was a total cinephile, practically living inside the cinematheque. Among the filmmakers I idolized in my youth was one in particular whom I was able to meet and work with later in my life, and that's Bong Joon Ho. The first time I met Director Bong was at the premiere of the film *Sea Fog* (2014). I had been the music director on that film, and he was executive producer. Then a long time passed, and one day out of the blue I got a phone call from him. He said he'd come visit me, then he came and handed me the script for *Okja*.

Up to that point I had been involved in a lot of different activities: I had released an album, composed for dance performances, and done some installations. I was surprised to find out that he knew about all of them. Most of the people I work with aren't familiar with all the things I've done. Apart from that, I was just a little stunned that this master director wanted to entrust the score of his $50 million film to someone like me, who didn't have that much experience. But we went over his ideas for the score in depth. The instructions he gave me then were very concise and clear, but he didn't say anything about the musical style he preferred—that was up to me.

Working with Director Bong, there needs to be a lot of emotional layering to the music. There are times when sadness, humor, fear, and joy all accumulate in the course of a single scene, and the music must reflect that. He wants it to feel unique and a bit odd. "It needs to be strange," he often says. For the chase sequence in *Okja*, I struggled to come up with an appropriate style. Then I suddenly thought of Balkan music, with its brass, like something Goran Bregović and Emir Kusturica might use. When I suggested that, Bong got really excited.

We met many times when *Okja* was in production and post-production to discuss the music. He even accompanied me to Budapest for the recording of the score. For *Parasite* and *Mickey 17* as well, he often visited the studio to see the music being recorded, watching by video call if he couldn't come in person. He told me once that it made him happy to see the music that would go into his film being recorded.

Okja is cleanly divided into four different stages: Gangwon Province, Seoul, New York, the slaughterhouse. So it wasn't really necessary to put unifying elements into the score. He wanted these abrupt shifts in tone as the film progressed. But *Parasite* was very different. He gave me the script as soon as he finished writing it, and shared a lot of the music that had come to his mind during the writing process: Handel, Vivaldi, Bach. There are two excerpts from Handel operas that appear in the film; those were decided on almost from the start. The very first line of the script reads, "Despairing music, full of hope." I pondered over that for a long time, thinking, "What could that possibly mean?"

When you spend time with Director Bong, you can really feel his love for music. He plays guitar and a bit of piano. Of course, many directors are influenced by music, but even so, I think it's rare to find a director who loves music as much as he does. When listening, he likes to shift between very different genres, from classical to 1970s funk, to contemporary music. And as a person, he's someone who really values artistic partnerships, which isn't so common in the Korean film industry. He's a warm person. Cynical, sensitive, and complicated, but warm. You can feel that warmth in his new feature, *Mickey 17*. His director of photography, Hong Kyung Pyo, has said that Bong Joon Ho has the ability to bring out the full potential of whoever he's working with, and that's been true in my case too. Working on his films can be exhausting, but it's tremendously rewarding.

STEVEN YEUN

I first met Bong Joon Ho at a café in Seoul in 2014. I was four years into a television show that was my big break, and he was already a legend. I was honored to sit with him. I have no memory of what we even spoke about. I do remember we spent a lot of time in random silence. It was awkward then, but now I know that we just tend to do that with each other. I also remember that he was incredibly gracious to me. A few months later, I got an email from him out of the blue asking me to be a part of his next film, *Okja*.

Since then, I've had the pleasure of working with him twice and spending time with him outside of work several times. When he's in Los Angeles we grab dinner, and when I'm in Korea we will grab a coffee and talk. The conversations never have a specific purpose. Usually it's checking in, and other times it's to talk deeply about the things we are concerned about in the world. On one visit to Seoul, we sat on a stoop of a house in a very wealthy neighborhood and smoked cigarettes. He said, "You know? I think this is the house of a pretty fucked-up guy." I knew who he was talking about. We laughed at how weird the moment was because there was a security camera pointed right at us. Then we ashed our cigarettes on their stairs and left.

Another time, I was in London, and I had spent an entire evening tossing and turning in bed. I was worried about work and what I was doing next—a typical actor moment. It was three in the morning, and I was in the middle of one of those anxiety-ridden doom spirals when all of a sudden I get a call: "Hello, Steven. It's Bong." Truly an incredible call to receive if you are ever lucky enough to get one. He told me another director wanted to meet with me and was interested in me for a role. He said, "You should really meet with him." Of course, I didn't need much convincing as the other director was Lee Chang-dong. That phone call would eventually lead to me being a part of

the film *Burning* (2018), which was a life-changing experience for me.

Director Bong has appeared many times in my life, usually at just the right times. I owe him a lot. What I can say in my experience with him is that he wears his heart on his sleeve—hidden under a sleek trench, with a nice tote hanging off his arm and an iPad inside, which collects all his sketches and thoughts and everything else. Maybe he's mysterious to some, but often he shows you glimpses of his kindness and leadership. He's a master storyteller, a benevolent observer, a hilarious comic, and an empathic soul. He fights for the things he believes in and selflessly lets things land at the right places. He is a true artist.

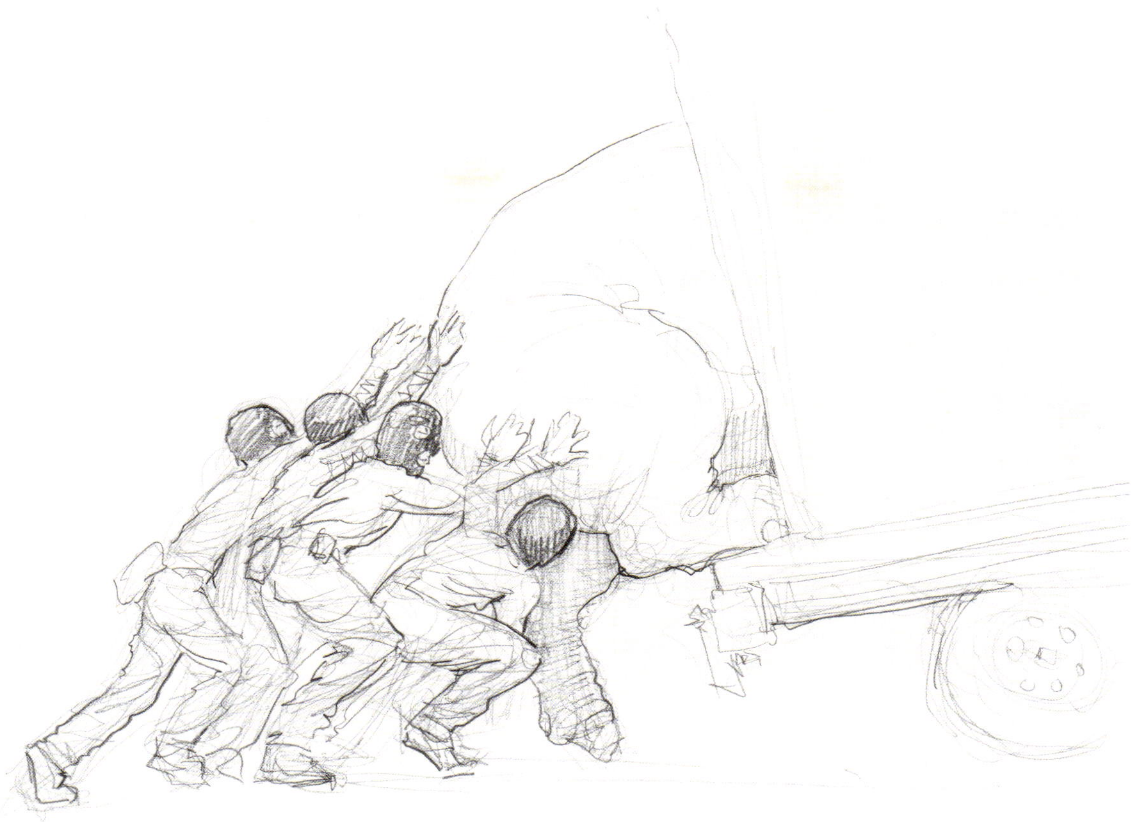

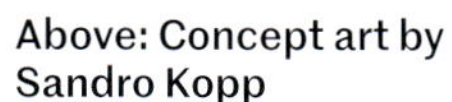

Above: Concept art by
Sandro Kopp

Right: Steven Yeun and
Ahn Seo-hyun in *Okja*.
Yeun plays a member of
the Animal Liberation
Front, an animal-rights
activist group.

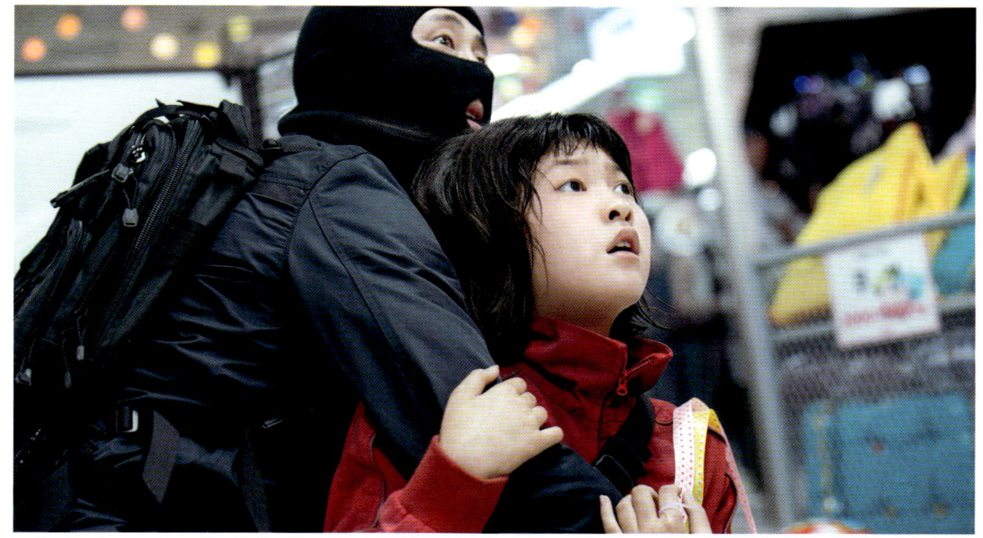

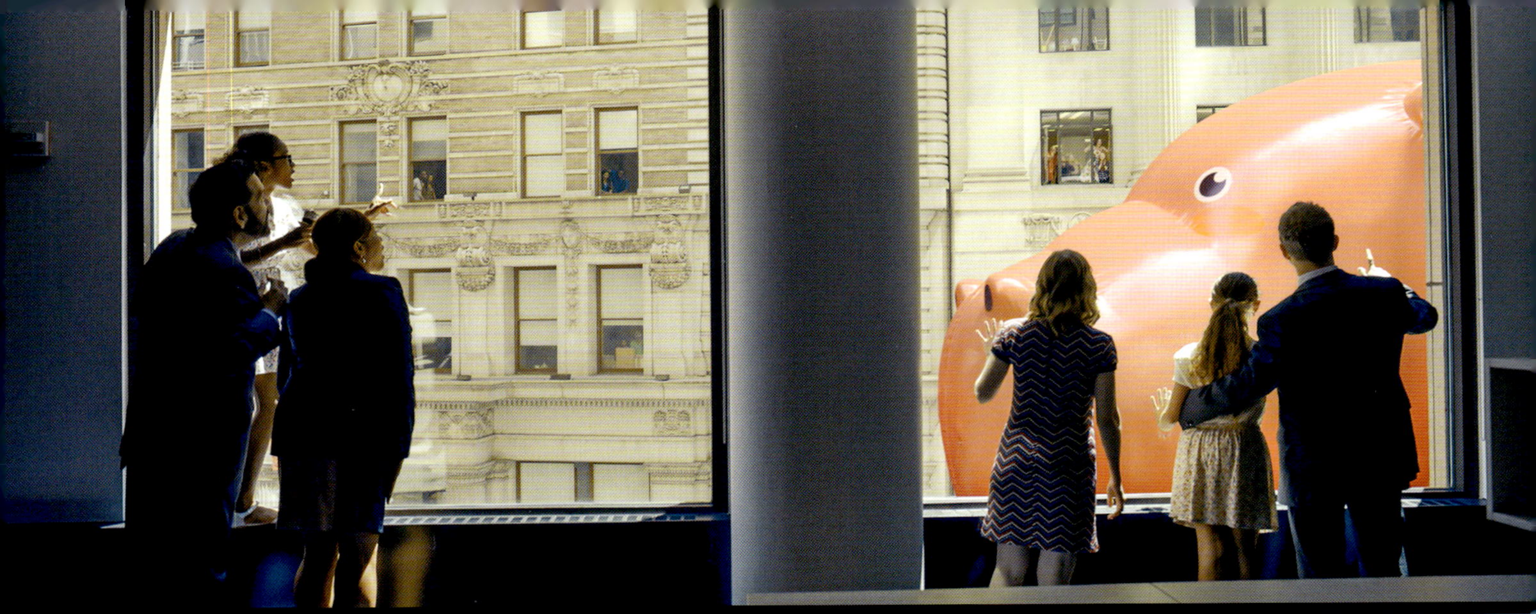

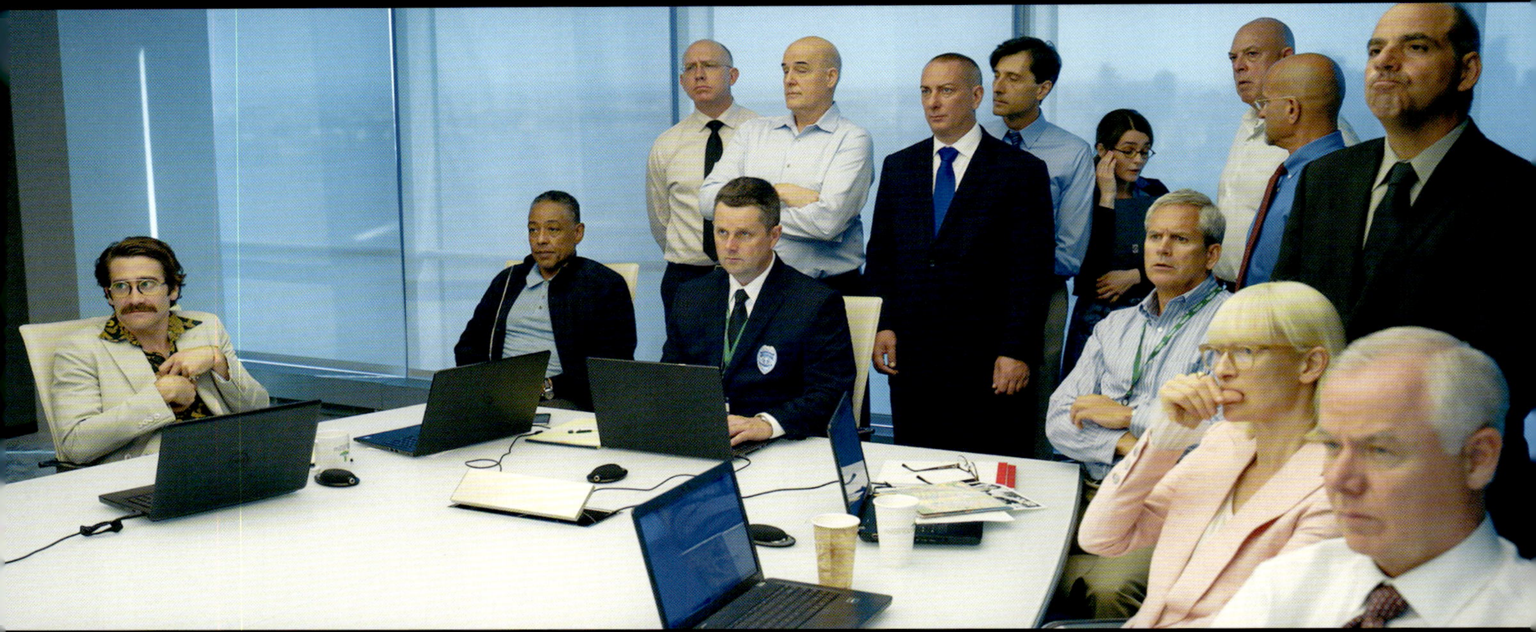

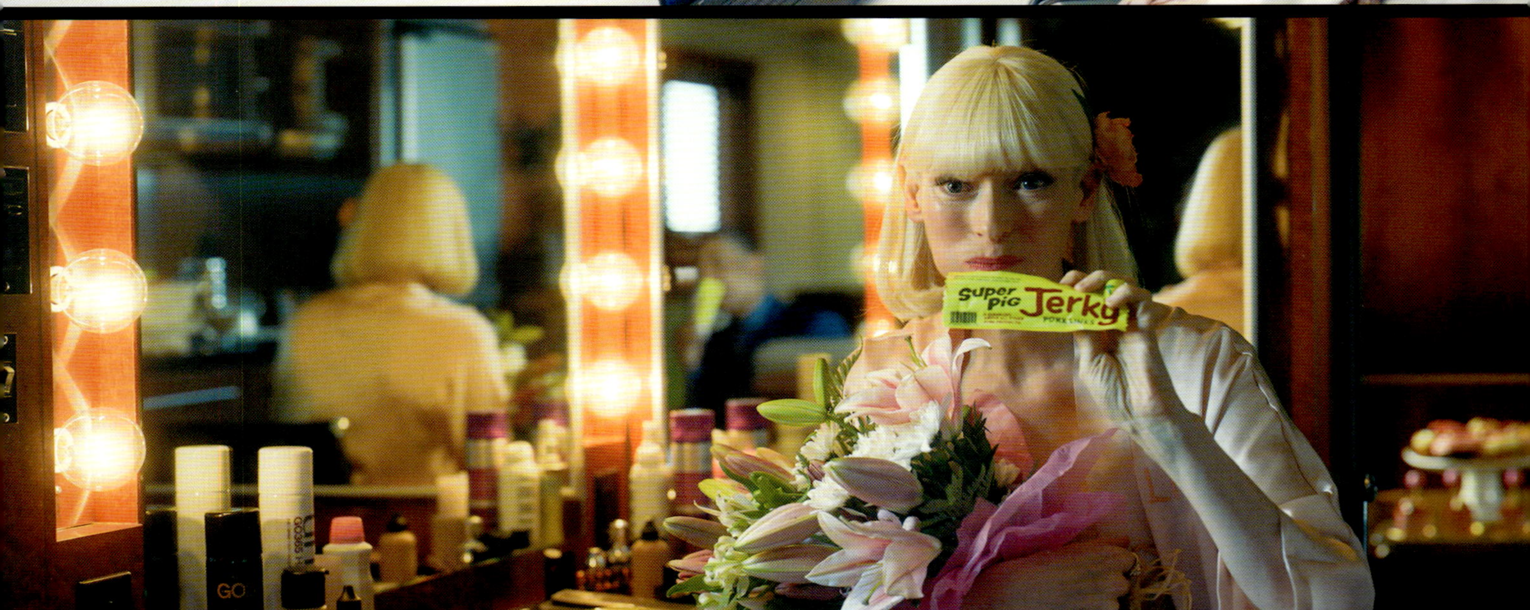
super pig Jerky
PORK SNACK

For the composition of one scene in *Okja*, Bong drew inspiration from an iconic photograph of President Barack Obama and his team watching the strike on Osama Bin Laden. His handwritten notes (below) indicate the placement of the film's cast.

Opposite: Scenes from *Okja*

I wanted to express the terror of how the power of multinational corporations sometimes exceeds that of nations.

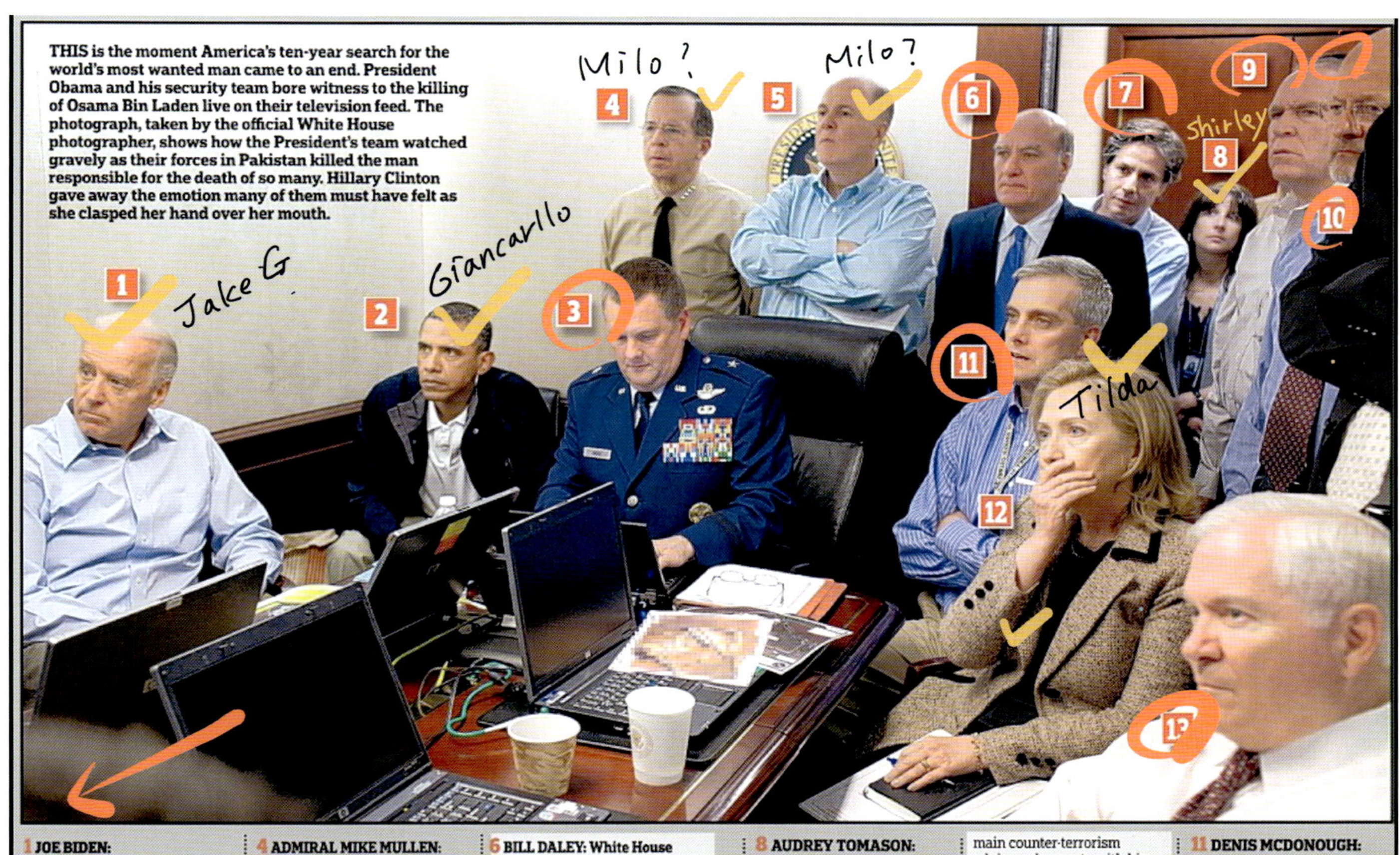

THIS is the moment America's ten-year search for the world's most wanted man came to an end. President Obama and his security team bore witness to the killing of Osama Bin Laden live on their television feed. The photograph, taken by the official White House photographer, shows how the President's team watched gravely as their forces in Pakistan killed the man responsible for the death of so many. Hillary Clinton gave away the emotion many of them must have felt as she clasped her hand over her mouth.

1 JOE BIDEN: U.S. Vice President

2 PRESIDENT OBAMA

3 BRIGADIER GENERAL MARSHALL 'BRAD' WEBB: Assistant Commanding General, Joint Special Operations Command. A former U.S. Air Force helicopter pilot, he is responsible for preparing special operations forces for missions around the world.

4 ADMIRAL MIKE MULLEN: Chairman of Joint Chiefs of Staff. The highest ranking military officer in the U.S. armed forces and the principal military adviser to the President.

5 TOM DONILON: National Security Adviser. A post appointed directly by the President, he is not connected to any government department and is so meant to be able to offer independent advice on national security.

6 BILL DALEY: White House Chief of Staff. The post is dubbed the 'second most powerful person in Washington' and his role includes overseeing White House staff and the President's schedule.

7 ANTONY BLINKEN: National Security Adviser to Joe Biden. Blinken helped Biden to craft policy on the Iraq and Afghan wars, Pakistan and Iran's nuclear programme. He also served on the National Security Council during Bill Clinton 's presidency.

8 AUDREY TOMASON: Director for Counter-Terrorism. A Harvard graduate who joined the Americorps voluntary work programme, she is one of several directors at the Office of the Co-ordinator for Counter-Terrorism.

9 JOHN BRENNAN: Deputy National Security Adviser for Homeland Security and Counter-Terrorism. President Obama's main counter-terrorism adviser who meets with him every day. His responsibilities include overseeing plans to defend the U.S. and responding to natural disasters.

10 JAMES CLAPPER: Director of National Intelligence. The retired air force general is the President's main adviser on intelligence matters (such as CIA operations) related to national security.

11 DENIS MCDONOUGH: Deputy National Security Adviser. He was a former foreign policy adviser to the President and was a key player in Mr Obama's decision to send an extra 30,000 troops to Afghanistan for the 'temporary surge'.

12 HILLARY CLINTON: Secretary of State

13 ROBERT GATES: Secretary of Defence

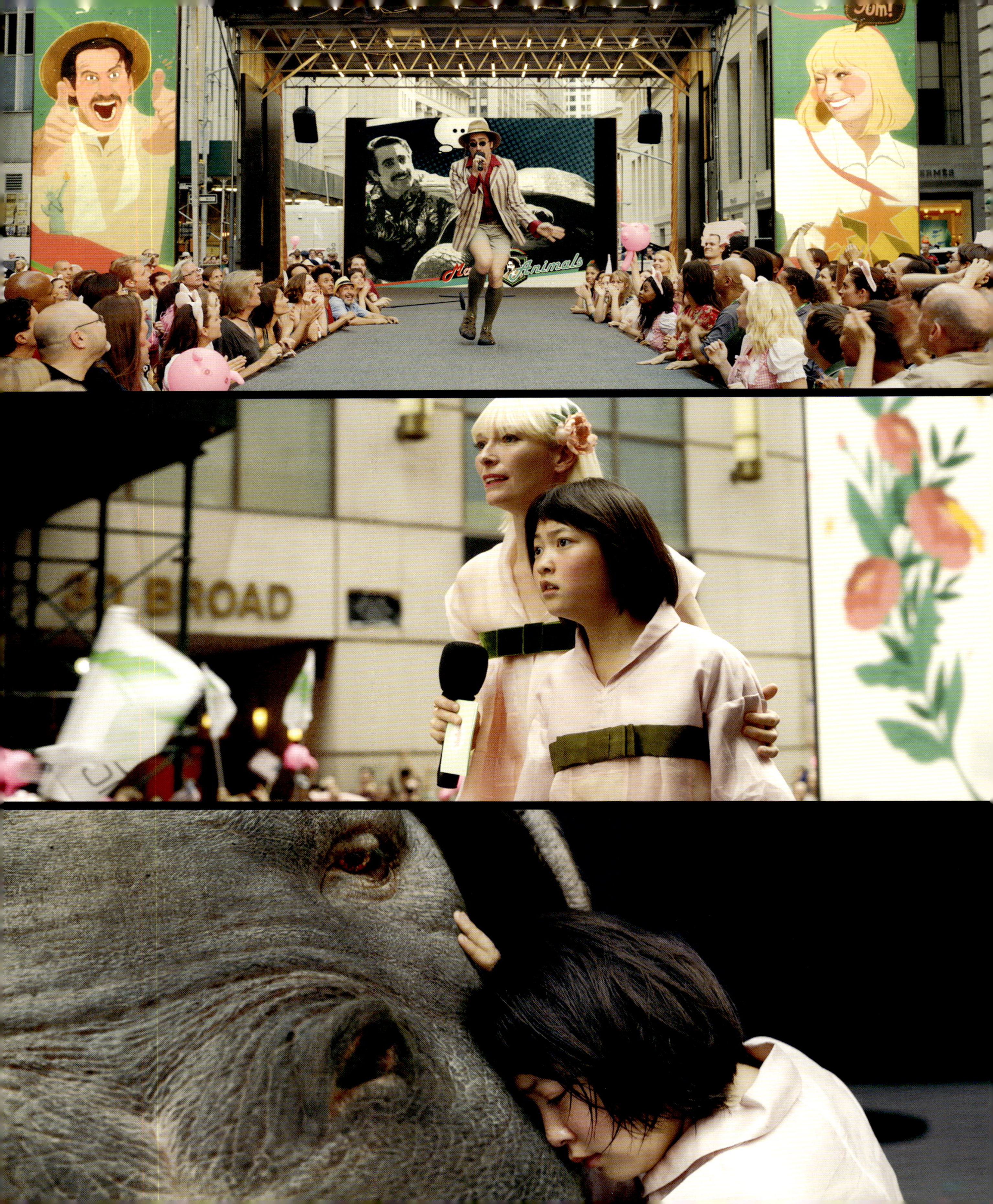

BROAD

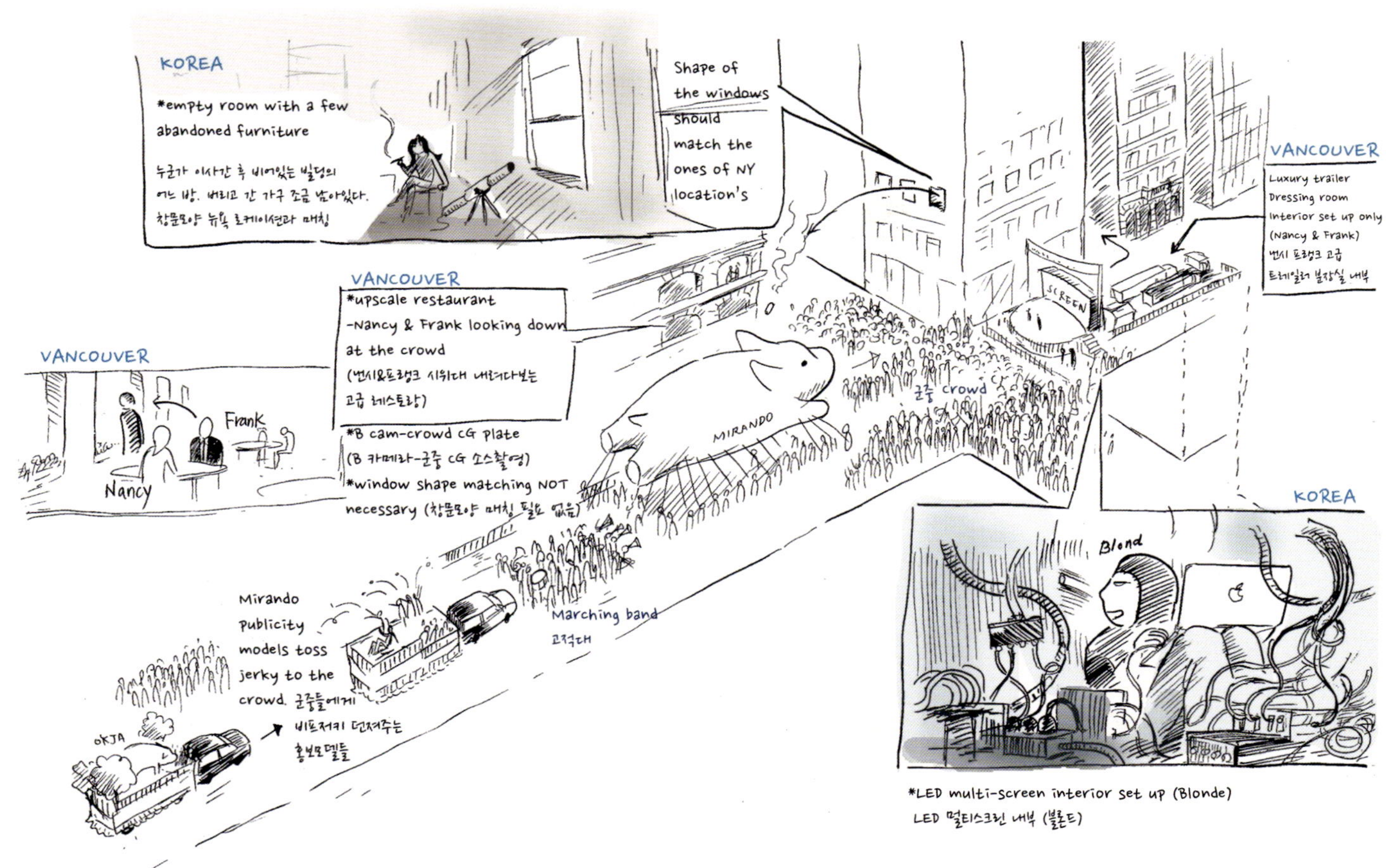

If you look at the characters, they are all from different places, different worlds, and they all come together because of Mirando, this global multinational biotech company and what it's doing and their interests around the world. It's like a web that connects everybody together.

Above: Planning drawing for the parade scene in *Okja*, which was filmed in Lower Manhattan, with additional footage shot in Vancouver and Seoul

Opposite: Scenes from *Okja*

Tilda was involved from the very beginning. She was instrumental in the creation of her characters…. Even though she's credited as a co-producer she's much more than that. It's a creative partnership that runs much deeper.

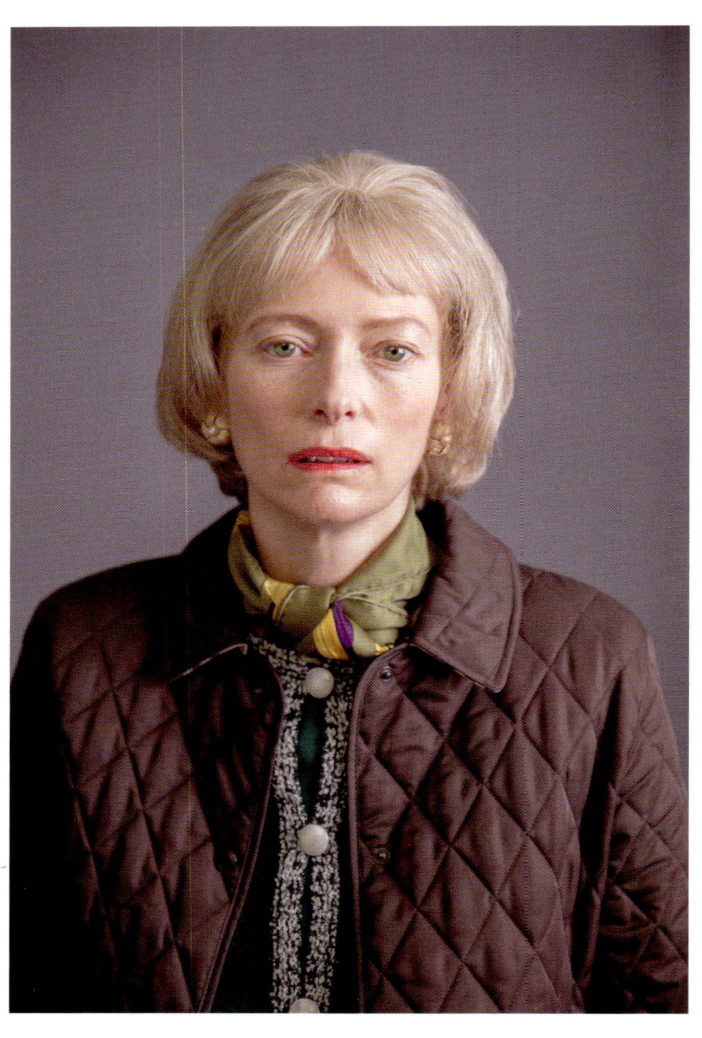

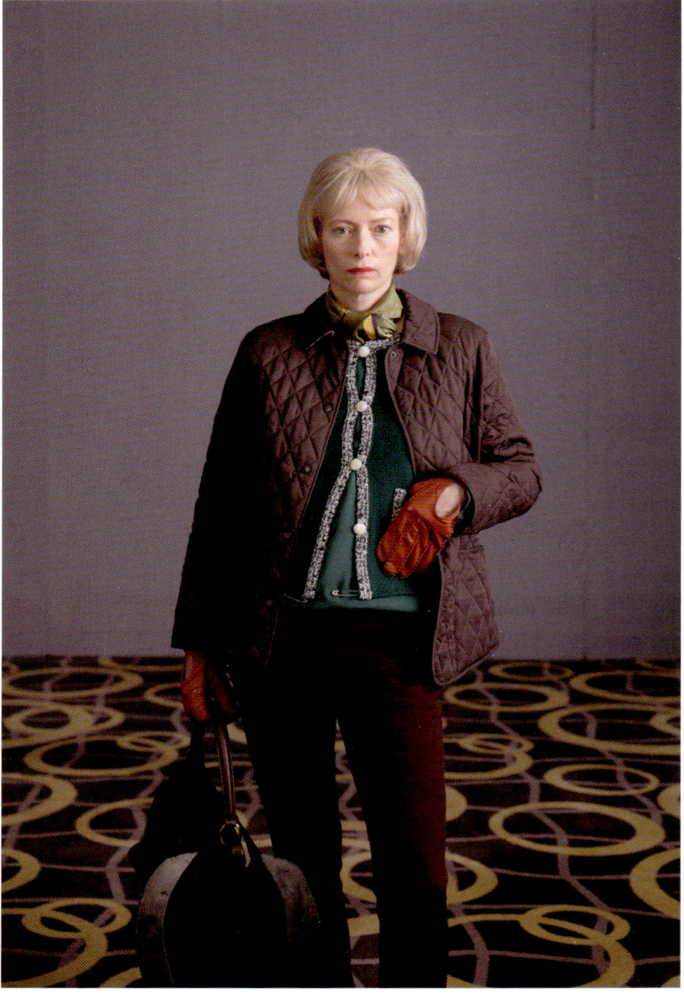

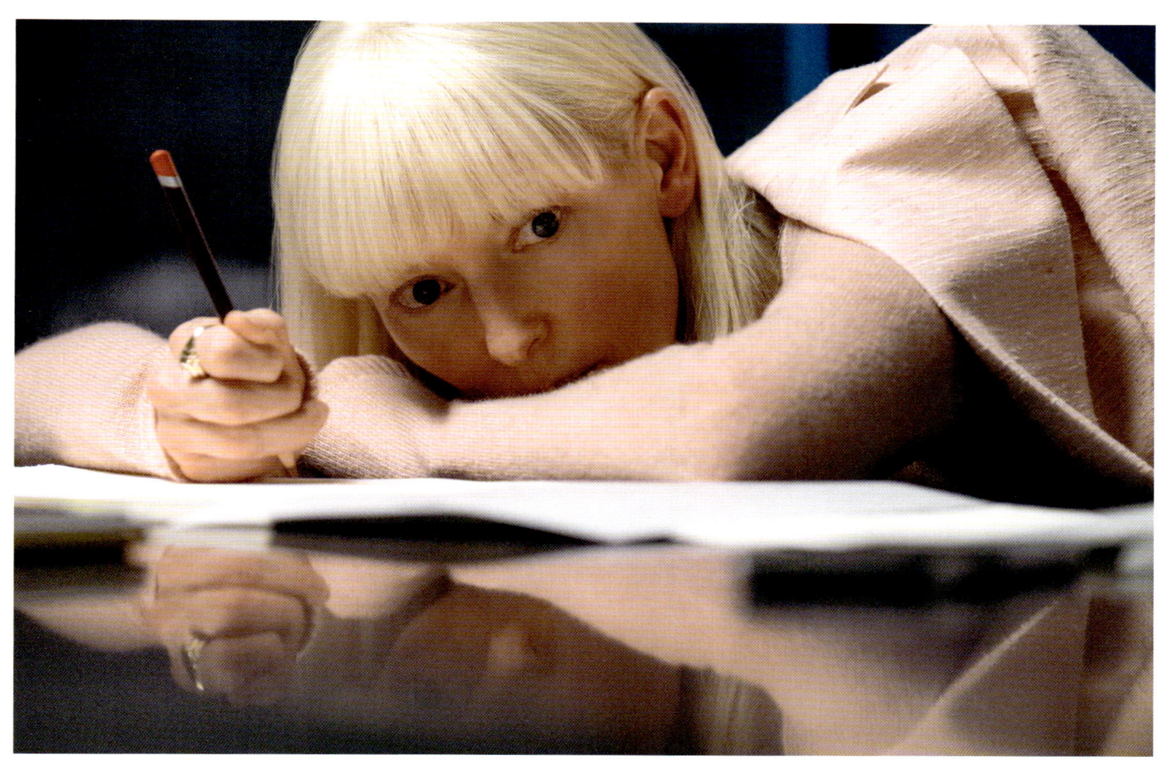

Tilda Swinton plays a dual role as twin sisters Lucy and Nancy Mirando, the current and former CEOs of their family's namesake corporation.

Opposite: Wardrobe test photographs for Tilda Swinton as Nancy Mirando

Above: Swinton as Lucy Mirando in *Okja*

We had many discussions about story and the character. But also we would converse about current events…. Inevitably those discussions found their way into the story as a separate layer to the overall arc.

DEDE GARDNER AND JEREMY KLEINER

When we first met Bong Joon Ho, it must have been 2006 or 2007, because we had just seen his latest film, *The Host*, and loved it. Song Kang-ho stars as the sort of hapless father in an allegory about the US military presence in Korea that is also a family story, a genre movie, and a creature movie all in one. It's brilliant. Anyway, we met Director Bong at the Chateau Marmont and had a great chat. Our production company, Plan B, had the rights to a graphic novel that he was a fan of, *Black Hole* by Charles Burns, so that was something we bonded over.

We wanted to work with him, so we sent him a couple of scripts and stayed in touch over the years, looking for the right opportunity. When he finished *Snowpiercer*, we watched it and were just rolling on the floor laughing at the incredible character Tilda Swinton created in Minister Mason. We heard about the next project Bong was planning, *Okja*, and lobbied his agents to get the script. Reading it, we got to the slaughterhouse in the third act and said, "We have to do this. We have to get involved in this film." The innocence of the young girl character, Mija, juxtaposed with the inequities of the adult world was just this beautiful contrast. He needed the money to make the movie and create the Okja creature in VFX the way he envisioned, but he also wanted final cut and needed an R rating. While some of the traditional studios were more reticent, Netflix was bullish. Ted Sarandos, who knew and loved his work, said, "I love Bong Joon Ho, tell me where to be," and then he greenlit the film in the room. It was just incredible.

Our job as producers is really to create the framework in which Bong can deliver things the way he intends and maintain the artistic freedom he needs. On set, it's dazzling to be around someone so confident. Bong knows exactly what he wants. He thinks about everything in advance but, in his way, absorbs our thoughts and ideas too.

His storyboards map out exactly what is being shot each day, and everyone can see the plan. It's all transparent, so there's resounding confidence on set.

What's amazing is that his work is tonally coherent, even though it contains multitudes—comedy, slapstick, different genres, creatures, all kinds of extremes. Sometimes it feels like Luis Buñuel, sometimes like Stanley Kubrick, sometimes like Charlie Chaplin. When we began working together, we asked him, "Where do your films come from? What's the fount of inspiration?" He told us about growing up under essentially a military dictatorship, where there was a lot of harshness and very silly authority figures. He has firsthand experience of both the buffoonery of authoritarianism and the deadly serious nature of it. All of his movies are antiauthoritarian. You can especially see it in *Parasite* and *Mickey 17*.

Director Bong is one of the great humanists of our time. He's just like, it's all true: We are despicable and we are glorious and we are everything in between. This is how it is on this spinning orb. Some of us were born luckier than others, so let's just put it out there inside of narratives that are thrilling and sexy and scary and sad. The human spirit and the beauty and humanity of people in obscene systems, in horrible and crazy situations—Bong gets all of this better than anyone. He doesn't think in terms of borders and languages and restrictions. He starts with a beating heart and the human experience.

Opposite: Scenes from *Okja*

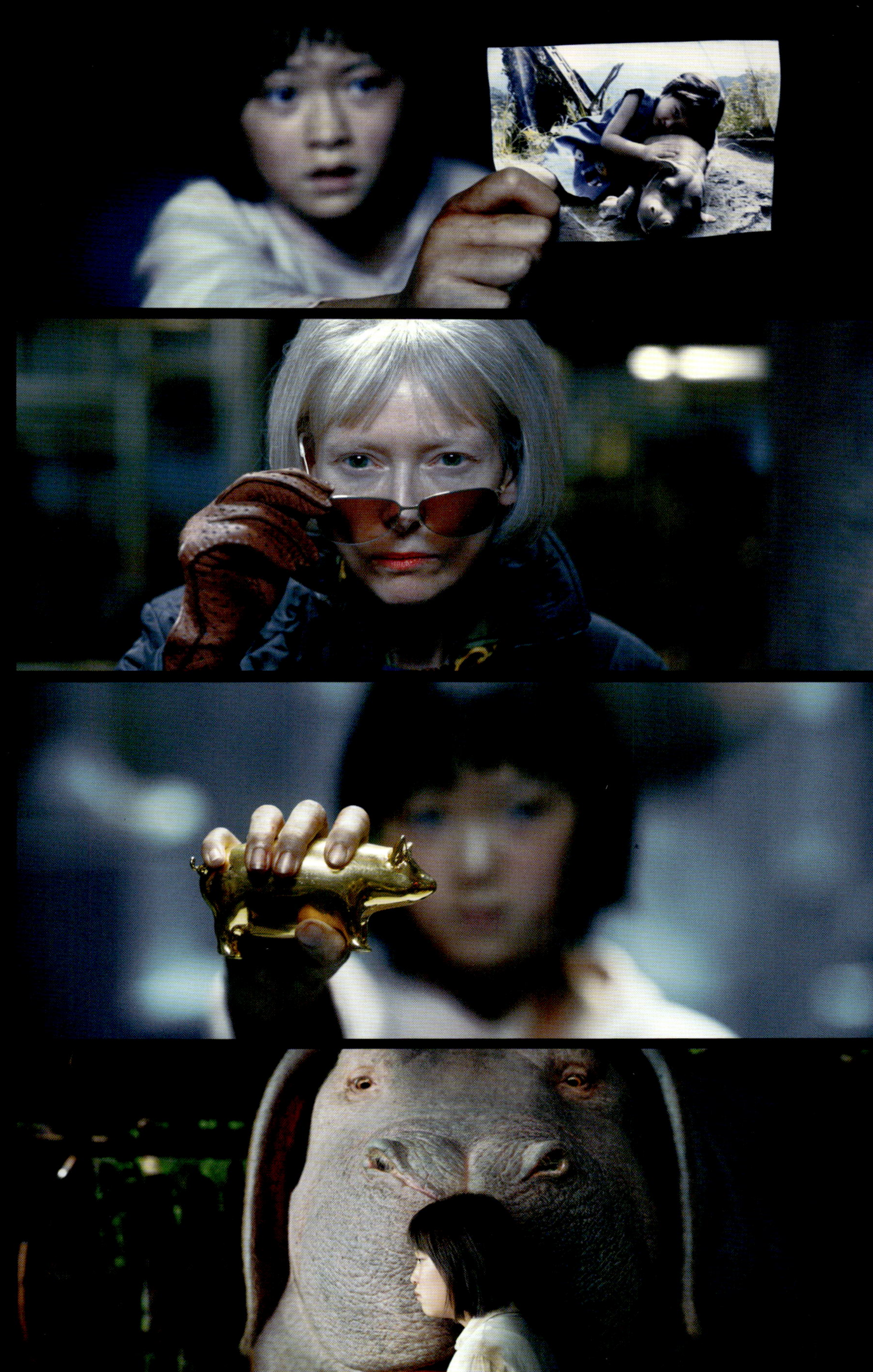

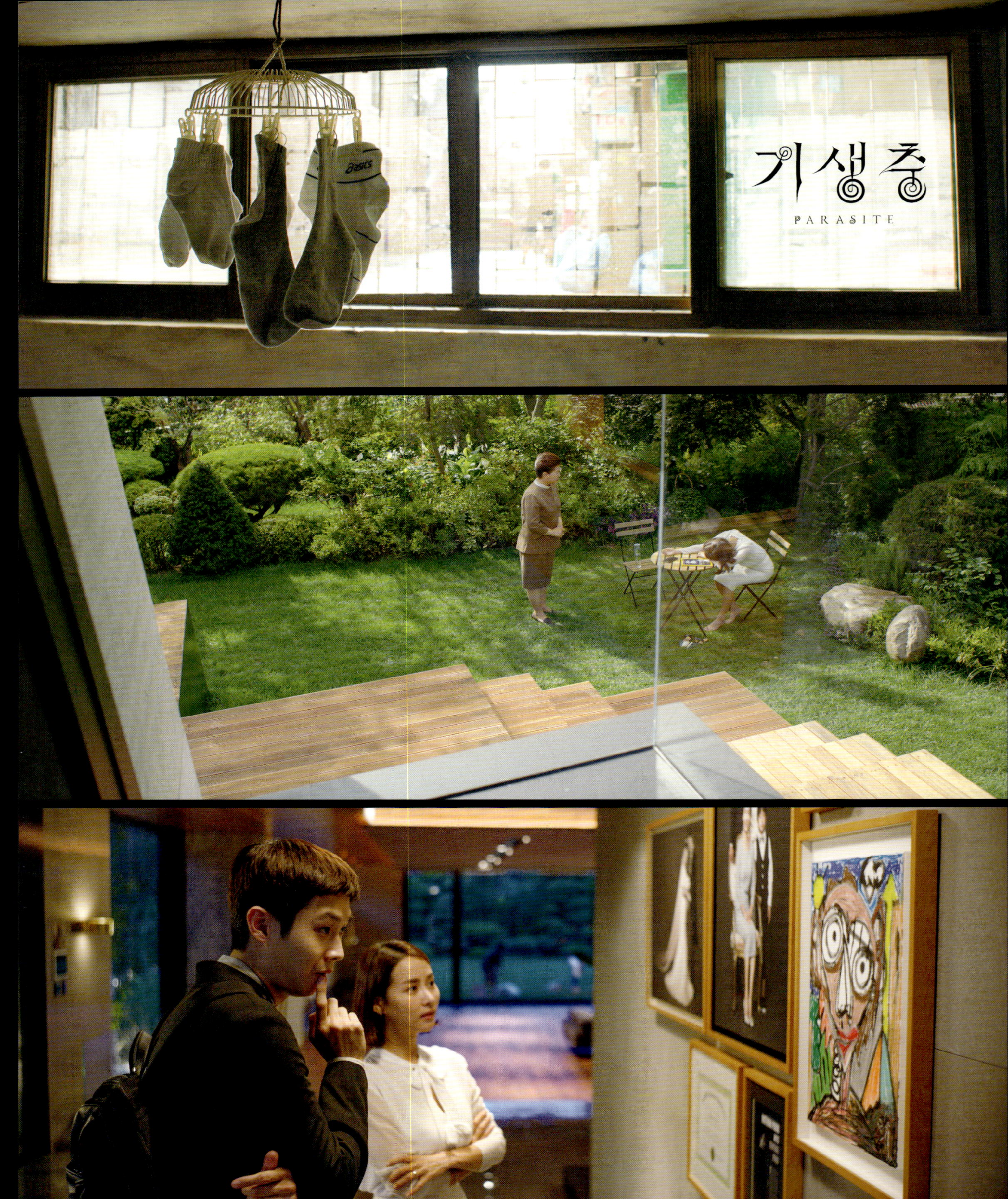

기생충
PARASITE
asics

In our society, the rich and poor are always spatially divided. What is particularly interesting about *Parasite* is that it shows them crossing these boundaries, coming close enough to smell each other.

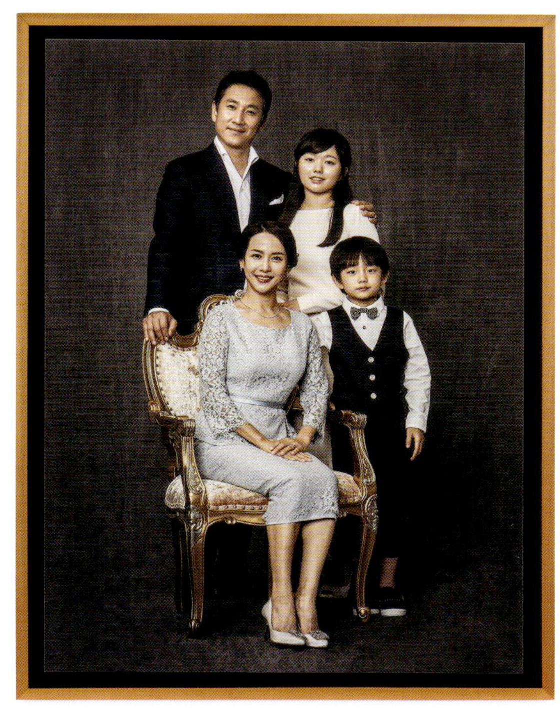

Parasite (2019) follows the working-class Kim family in Seoul as they scheme their way into the lives and home of the wealthy Park family.

Opposite: Scenes from *Parasite*

Above: Park family portrait created for *Parasite*

Right: From left, Choi Woo-shik, Song Kang-ho, Chang Hyae-jin, and Park So-dam as the Kim family

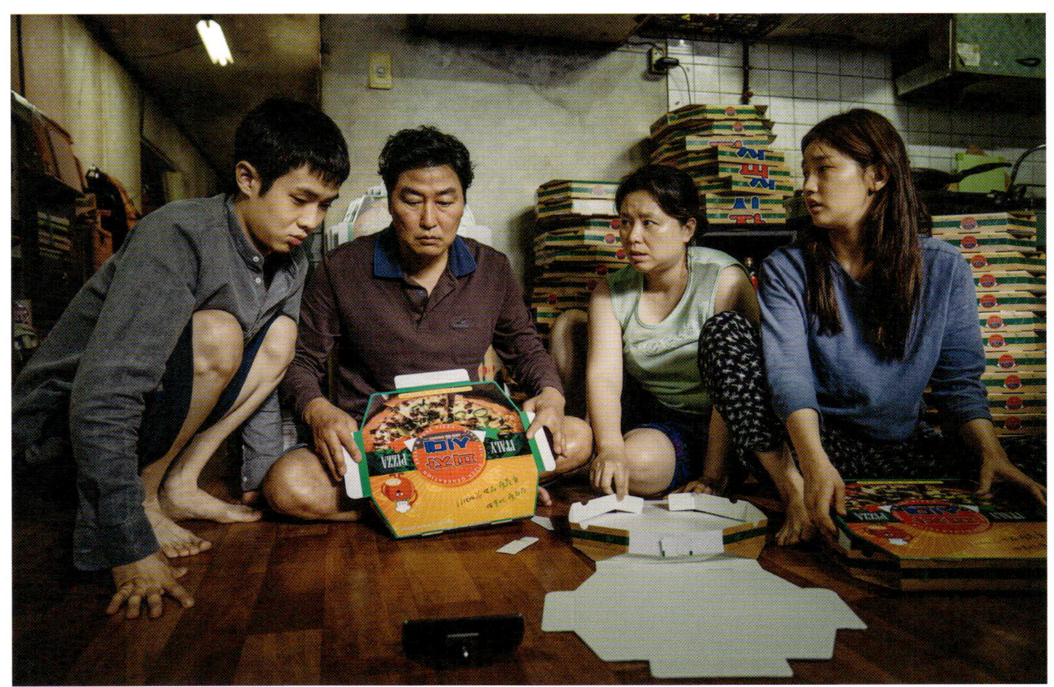

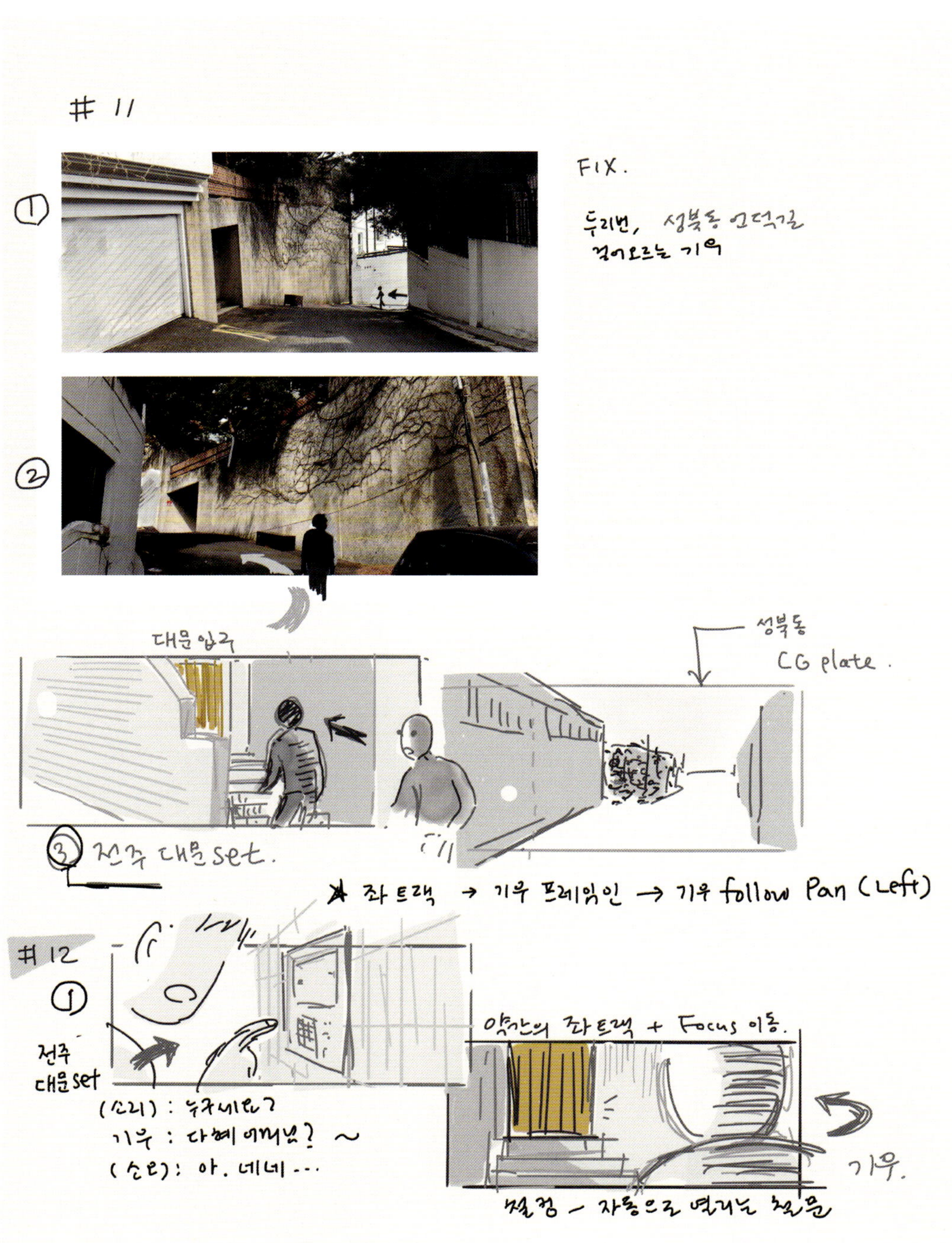

Bong says he "tried to express a sentiment specific to the Korean culture" with *Parasite*, but "all the responses from different audiences were pretty much the same.... Essentially, we all live in the same country, called Capitalism."

Opposite: Choi Woo-shik as Kim Ki-woo

Left: Bong's storyboard for *Parasite*

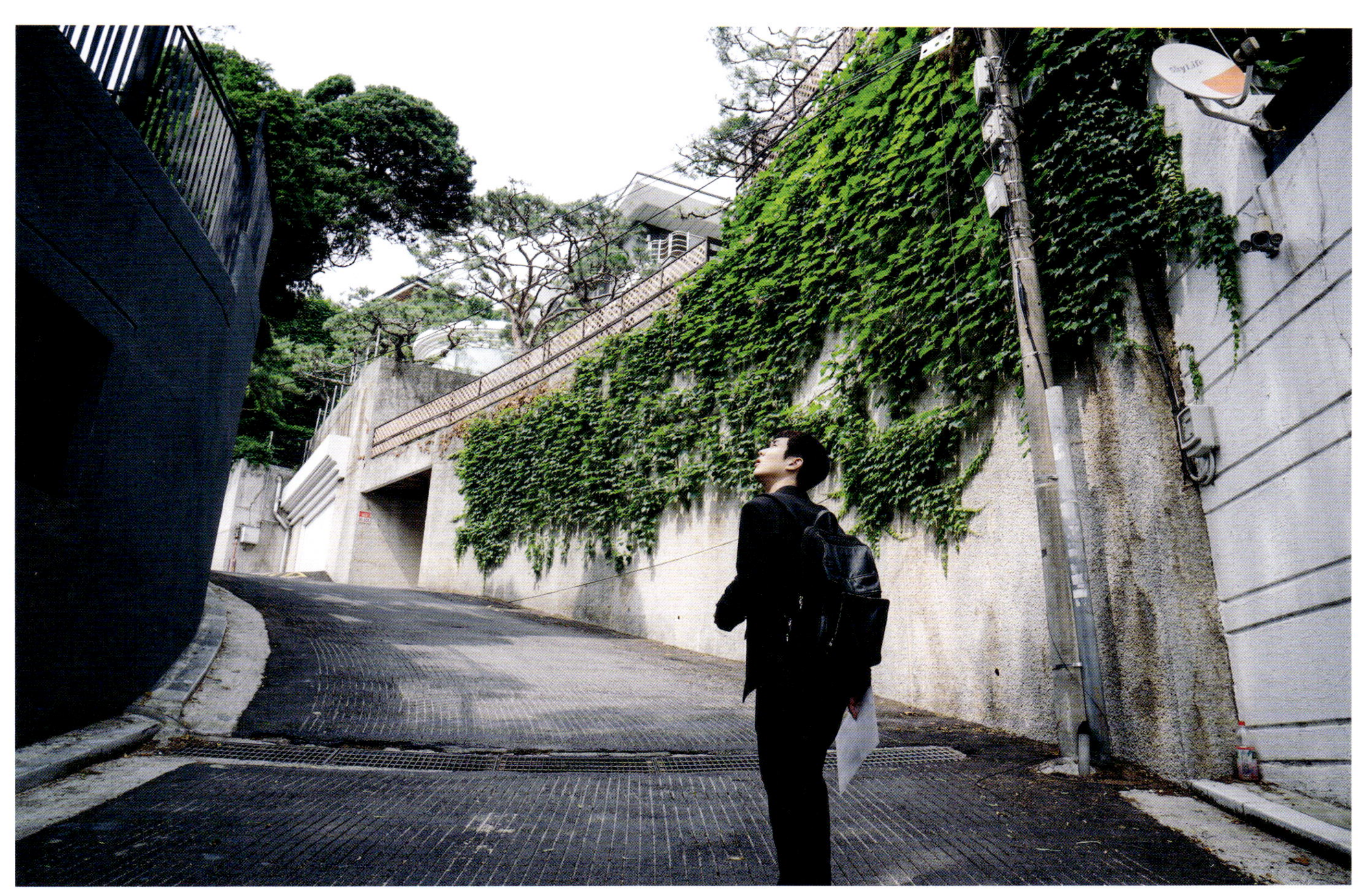

In the film, everything is aligned vertically. Water only flows from top to bottom, from rich neighborhoods to poor ones, and it never flows the other way.

MIKY LEE

When I saw Bong Joon Ho's first film, *Barking Dogs Never Bite*, in 2000, I was immediately drawn to his bold artistic style and satirical storytelling. I thought, "This director has something to say, and he knows how to say it differently." The blend of black comedy and insight into human nature really stood out to me. I felt that he was a filmmaker pushing the boundaries of storytelling, and I was sure that moviegoers, especially those of younger generations, would love his films.

I still remember the moment we first met in the early 2000s. Bong was a walking encyclopedia of world film—Korean, Japanese, Hollywood, French, Russian, Italian, and more. He spoke about cinema with such immense passion and depth. Listening to him talk inspired me to watch more films and also seek out films from a wider group of filmmakers. He once told me he loves writing in bustling cafés, where he can watch people and feel and absorb the energy around him as he works. It seems like the more he's focused, the more he opens up all of his five senses—and maybe even a sixth—to his surroundings. Another time he told me he rides the subway in disguise and observes others while staying unnoticed, even though he's six feet tall and has crazy hair. To this day, I still don't know his trick to being a chameleon. From time to time, when I see a tall person with curly hair on the street, I think to myself, "Could that be Director Bong?"

In 2009, when we were at the Cannes Film Festival together for the midnight screening of *Mother*, Bong told me about a French graphic novel he planned to adapt. It was *Snowpiercer*. We met the writers, and I knew that this could be the beginning of a meaningful global collaboration. With Bong's unique storytelling touch, *Snowpiercer* became a critically acclaimed film that people all throughout the world watched and continue to watch to this day.

When I visited the *Snowpiercer* set in Prague, the actors and film crew—those responsible for the costumes, makeup, production design, cinematography, and more—were from all over the world. They told me how happy they were to have finally worked with Director Bong and how much they loved being a part of his creative world. We celebrated and wrapped up the final day of shooting in Prague with karaoke. It was joyful, and everybody sang, just like we do in Korea.

Years later, when *Parasite* was released in the United States, people were saying they watched it because their children had recommended it to them. Usually it's the other way around, but this time it seemed like young people were actively urging their parents to watch the movie, telling them, "You have to see this!" It showed that great storytelling transcends borders, languages, cultures, and generations. On the night of *Parasite*'s big win at the Oscars, I was sitting with the actors, next to Song Kang-ho. When they announced that Bong had won for Directing, Song said, "I have a weird feeling we're going to win Best Picture." I said, "Me too, and when that happens, I'll be sitting here, cheering and clapping!" And then we won! It was like a wave hit us and carried us up to the stage.

The team took my arm and we walked up together. We waited for Bong to speak, but then he turned to me and said, "I've said enough. You should say something." So, I just started with the truth: how much I adore him, how deeply he has impacted Korean audiences, and how that impact was now rippling across the world. Throughout all these years, Bong has continued to be that same person that I met so long ago—finding inspiration in the familiar, and then inspiring others through the unique stories he creates.

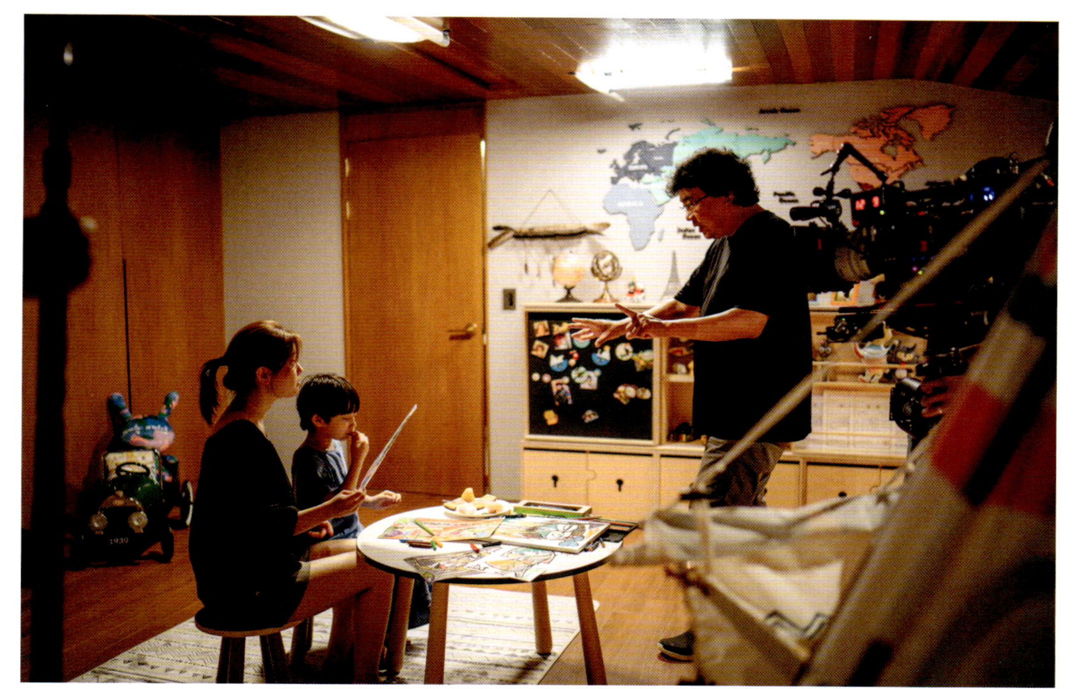

Bong with Park So-dam (left) and Jung Hyun-jun during production of *Parasite*

When I watch classic films from 50 years ago, they still feel very contemporary and current, and I love that feeling. I want people to remember this film as an honest record—an honest portrayal of the times that we currently live in.

Most of the narrative happens in two spaces, and all the houses you see in the film—the rich house, poor house, neighborhood surrounding the poor house—were built from scratch.

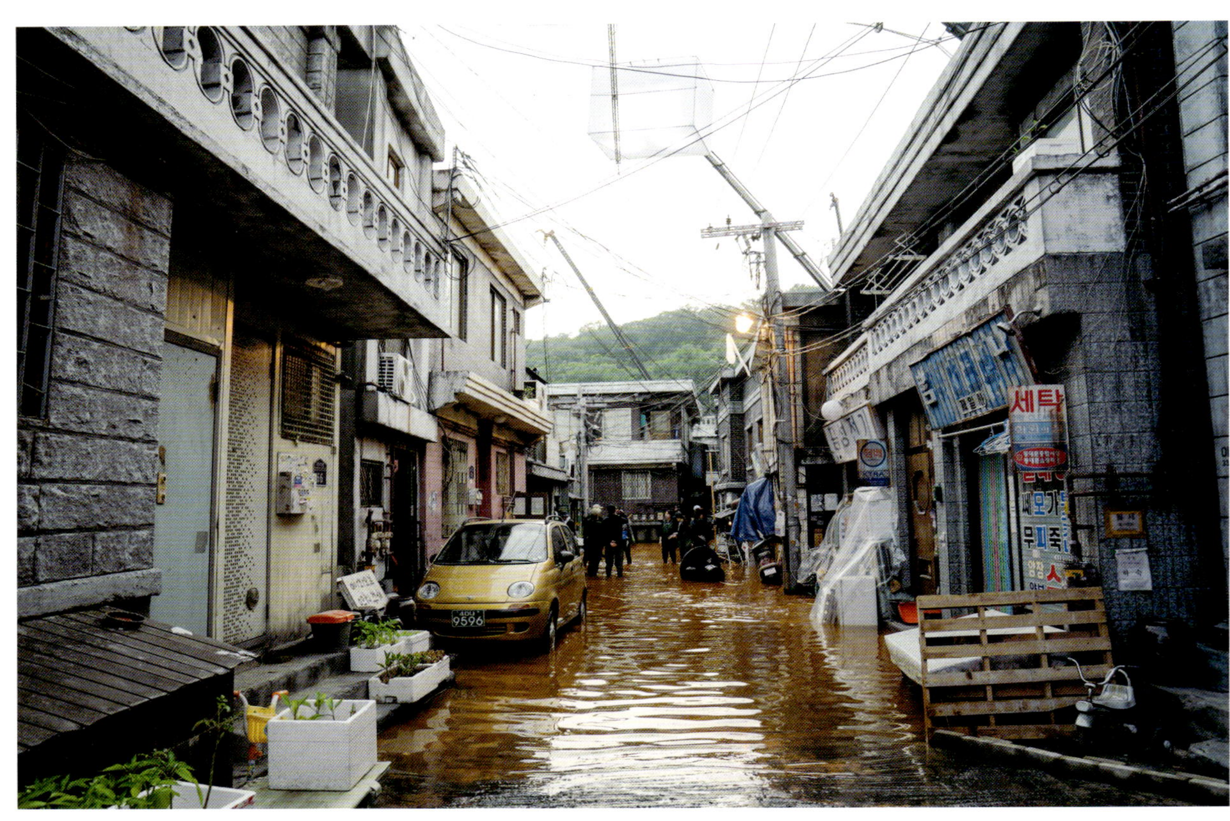

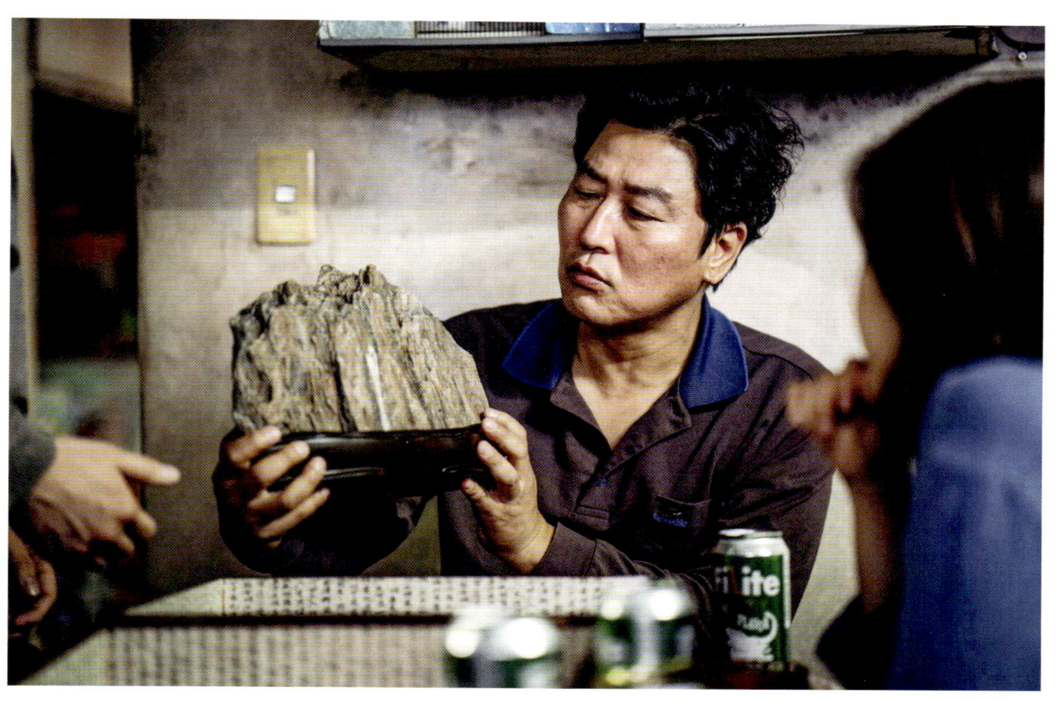

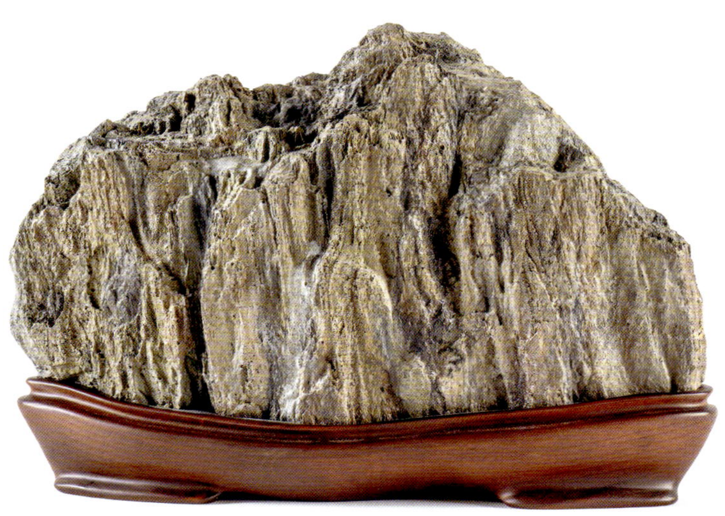

"Korean audiences are very perceptive about interpreting and analyzing all the symbols in films," Bong says, "so I was having fun with that. Is it still a symbol if a character outright tells you that it is?"

Opposite: Set constructed for the flooding sequence in *Parasite*

Above: Song Kang-ho as Kim Ki-taek

Left: Prop suseok from *Parasite*

LEE HAJUN

When making films, Bong Joon Ho is incredibly meticulous. His storyboards are so detailed that even with a quick glance one can get an in-depth understanding of each scene he plans to shoot. His screenplays are densely packed with precise description as well. In Korea he has earned the nickname "Bongtail"—a combination of "Bong" and "detail"—and the reason he puts such effort into this preparation is so that he can communicate with his actors and crew as clearly as possible.

As a production designer, I have had many conversations with Director Bong about how space connects to his stories. When he was describing one scene in *Parasite*, I remember him saying, "He presses himself flat to the floor and hides under the enormous living room table. Like a cockroach." The actors' movements and emotions were always connected to the spaces they inhabit. His words "The space must be designed with the actors in mind" have become the most important guiding principle for my work ever since.

After long discussions with Director Bong, we decided that in *Parasite*'s production design we would use color, texture, lighting, and architecture not simply as backdrop but as elements that visually reveal the class structure of the story. In the wealthy Mr. Park's home, a neutral color palette of gray, beige, and wood tones—and the textures of wood, stone, steel, and glass—creates a sophisticated and leisurely atmosphere. In contrast, the Kim family's semi-basement home has faded wallpaper, mold stains, and dull colors under bluish fluorescent lights, reflecting the hardship of their lives. I used to live in a semi-basement home myself, and based on my memories and studying other homes, we would consider how much sunlight should come in, how the wallpaper would change color, and how the view outside through the window should look.

We also talked a lot about the symbolism of the stairways. "The stairs are not simply a way to pass from one space to another," he would tell me, "but a way of dividing the classes." In Mr. Park's home, the gently inclining stairs reflect the leisure of the upper class, while the rough stairs leading down to the Kims' semi-basement home reveal an ambiguous position between aboveground and underground. The steep stairs leading to the underground bunker in Mr. Park's home can be read as a total decline.

Director Bong writes his screenplays while sitting alone in cafés. Most writers will confess that the process of writing is a lonely struggle, and only by enduring and overcoming it can one earn the right to glory. On the set, where he collaborates with others to bring his vision to life, he knows how to balance the possible and the impossible. He's very skilled at coping with the unexpected changes that arise during film production. He always speaks to his crew with respect and without being the slightest bit remote or removed. In fact, he's constantly sending and receiving text messages, showing images to his crew, and always strives to help everyone share in his vision.

In 2020 at the Academy Awards, Director Bong said the following as he accepted his Oscar for Directing: "When I was young and studying cinema, there was a saying that I carved deep into my heart, which is 'The most personal is the most creative.'" He went on to say this was a quote from "our great Martin Scorsese," his fellow nominee whose films he studied in school, and he paid respect to the other three nominees. Those who know Bong Joon Ho well would have recognized the humanity and humility he expressed in this moment. In awards acceptance speeches as elsewhere, he communicates appreciation and praises the work of others. These are my observations of the details that characterize Bong Joon Ho.

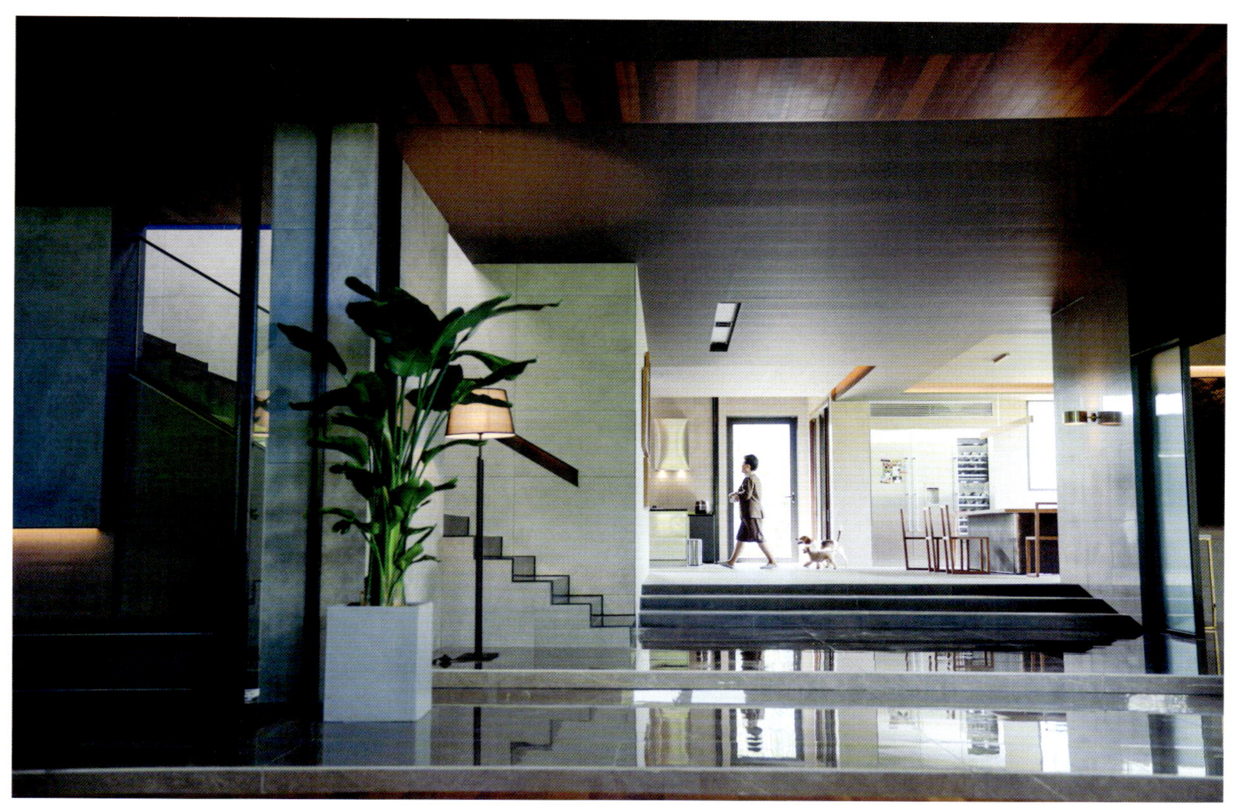

Parasite production stills taken in the Park family home. Bong states, "The story is about actual class realities, and I didn't want the feeling of people acting on a manufactured set."

When you have actors that good, moments can be shot like a documentary…. We didn't need a lot of rehearsals and went with the feeling on set.

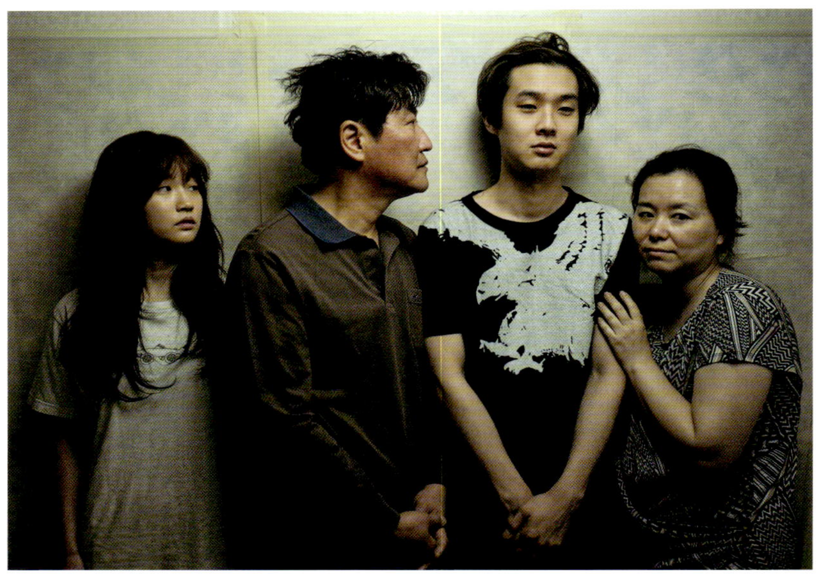

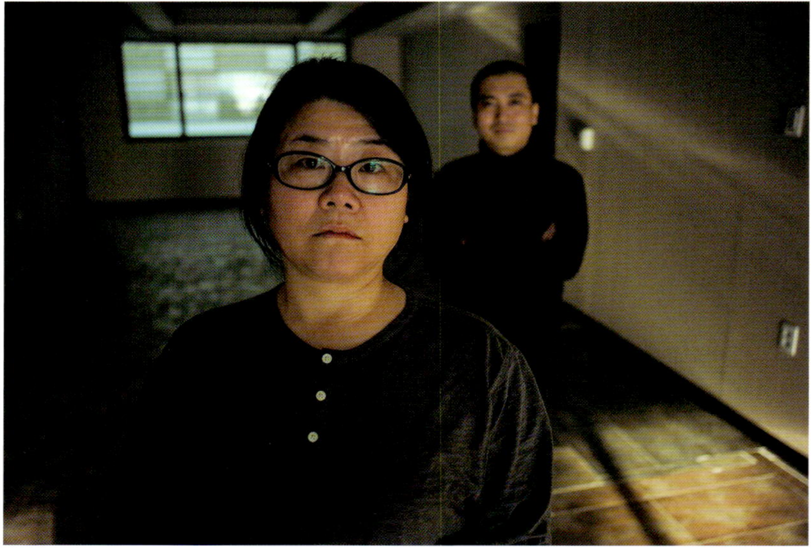

Top: From left, Park So-dam, Song Kang-ho, Choi Woo-shik, and Chang Hyae-jin, photographed by Bong

Bottom: Lee Jung-eun, who plays housekeeper Moon-gwang, and Park Myung-hoon, who plays her husband, photographed by Bong

CHOI WOO-SHIK

It was during auditions for *Okja* that I met Bong Joon Ho for the first time. I'm not sure how it is in other countries, but in Korea actors are expected to act a bit deferential to directors, to be on good behavior—it's just the industry's standard actor-director relationship. But right away, with Director Bong it felt different. He created a very free, relaxed atmosphere, and he seemed even more interested in me as a person than as an actor.

I was nervous when shooting *Okja*. I had comparatively less experience then, and the large scale of the project was something new to me. I play a small role, but I really didn't want to disappoint him. By the time we shot *Parasite*, I was more familiar with his working style, but the role of Ki-woo was so much bigger that I was even more nervous.

One thing that was challenging was to act in those scenes that had so many moving parts: the actors walking through the house, the back-and-forth of the dialogue, the moving camera, the lighting, and all the other technical elements. I had never done shots like this before. I had to focus so that I didn't mess up the take for everyone else, but there was also something very exciting about it. I grew to really enjoy it.

During the flooding scene in *Parasite*, there's a moment where I'm running with Song Kang-ho through the water toward my house. Suddenly Director Bong asks me, "You know water lizards? Can you run like a water lizard?" Before shooting, while reading the screenplay, I hadn't really come up with a good image for how my character would run, but ... a water lizard? Amazingly, though, it's somehow perfect. It looks strange, but that just makes it more memorable. Actually for *Parasite*, Director Bong often mentioned animals or insects when telling us how to act. When we were going down the stairs, he told us to descend like spiders.

I'm sure Bong Joon Ho must feel a lot of anxiety every time he makes a new film, but even so, he was always the most positive, happy person on set. You can see his love of filmmaking and that he enjoys new challenges. He's also always on the side of the actors and crew. He's famous for this—he knows the names of every single person on set, plus their backgrounds, what sort of things they like, and so on. He shows more genuine curiosity toward the people he works with than anyone else I know.

Sometimes he was almost like a psychological counselor for us. If he could tell that someone was feeling anxious, he'd take them to this place behind the monitor with an electric fan, and have them sit there and listen to classical music. I remember sometimes sitting there for 10 or 15 minutes, not speaking to anyone, just listening to music.

If by any chance my mother's prayers are answered, and I get to work with Bong Joon Ho again, I think next time I'll feel a bit more at ease. My attitude while shooting *Parasite* was, "Since he cast me for this role, I really have to make sure I do well, so that I don't disappoint him." But now I realize that when he cast me, he already knew everything. He knew my capabilities as an actor, what I look like on screen, and what I bring to a character. If he casts me, then I just need to focus and do my best. Even for actors who walk briefly across the back of a shot, he never casts them without knowing exactly what it is that they can give him. So next time I think I'd be less nervous, knowing I got that role for a reason.

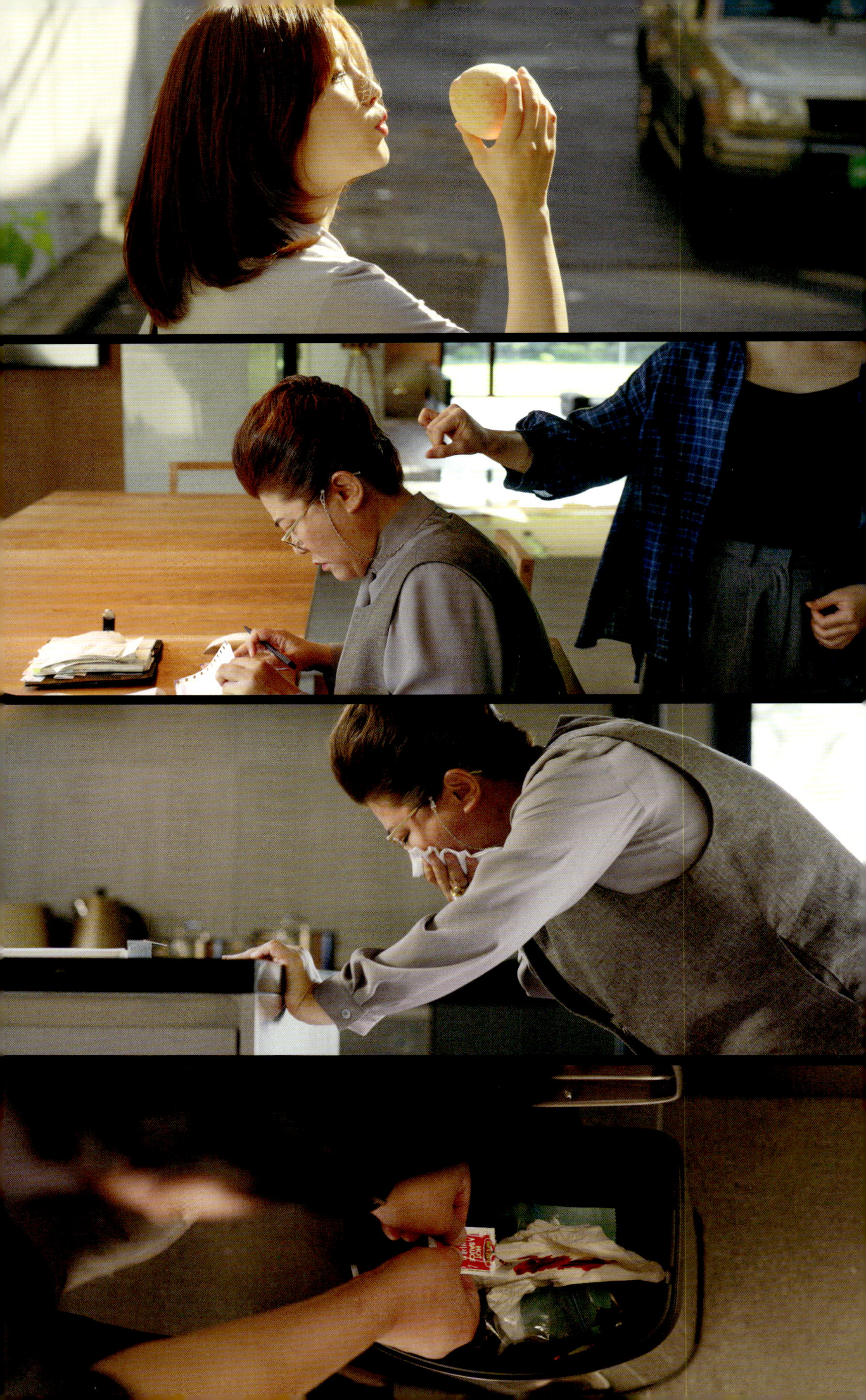

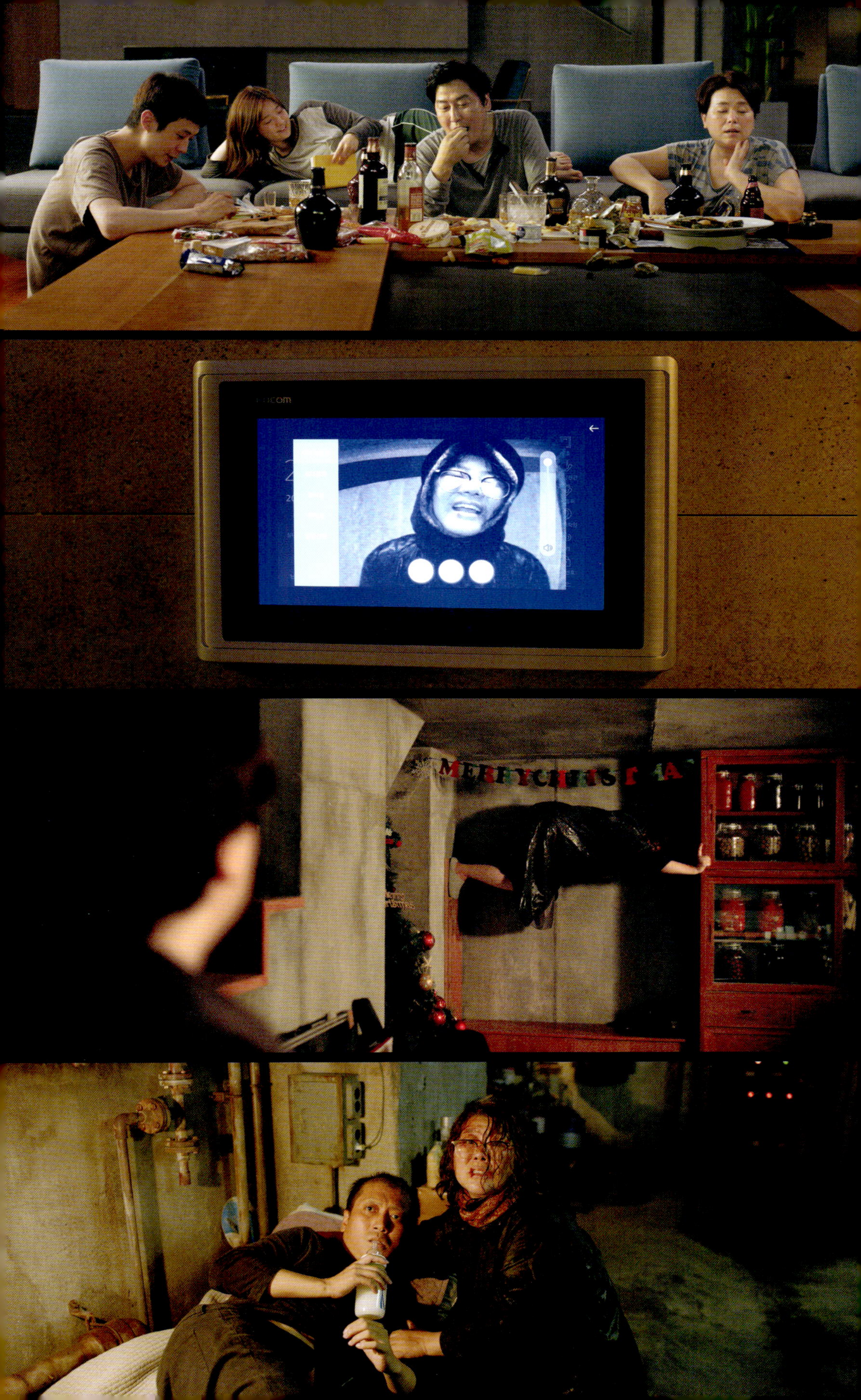
MERRY CHRISTMA

A lot of the families in my films are sort of in a big mess. They malfunction as a family. I feel the best when I write characters like that.

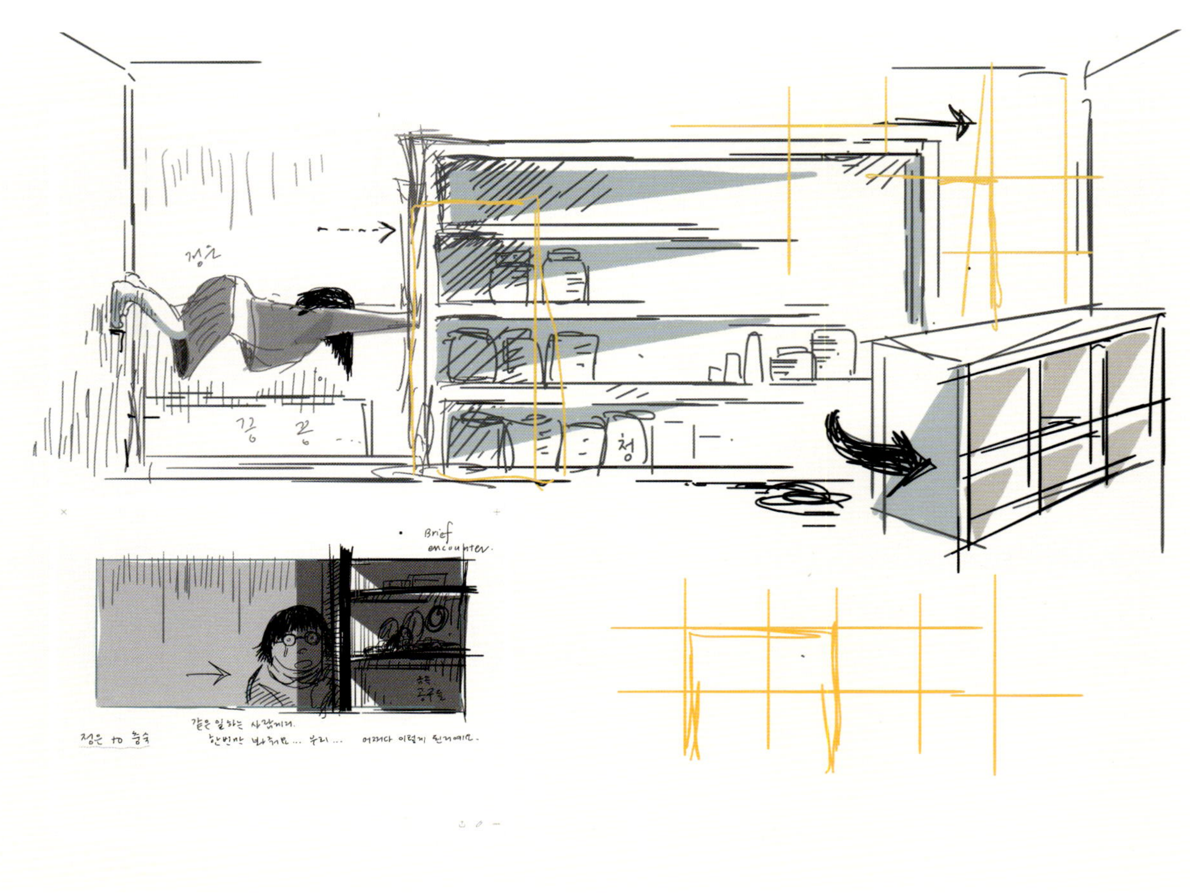

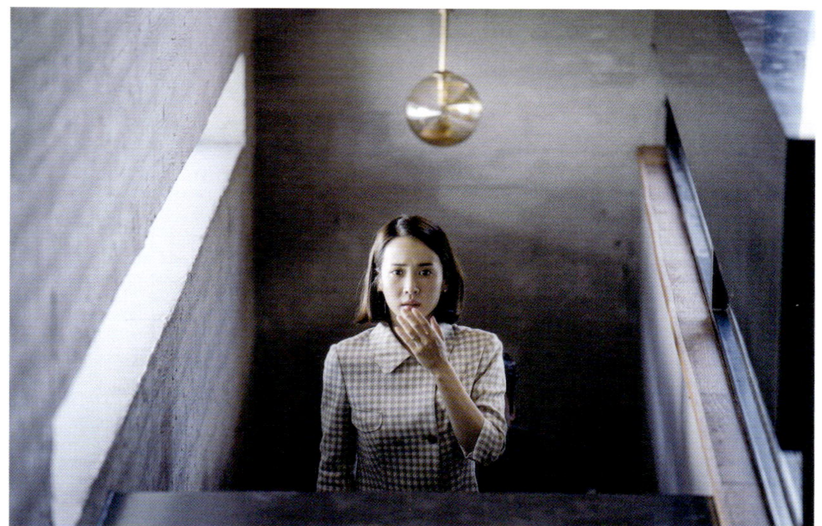

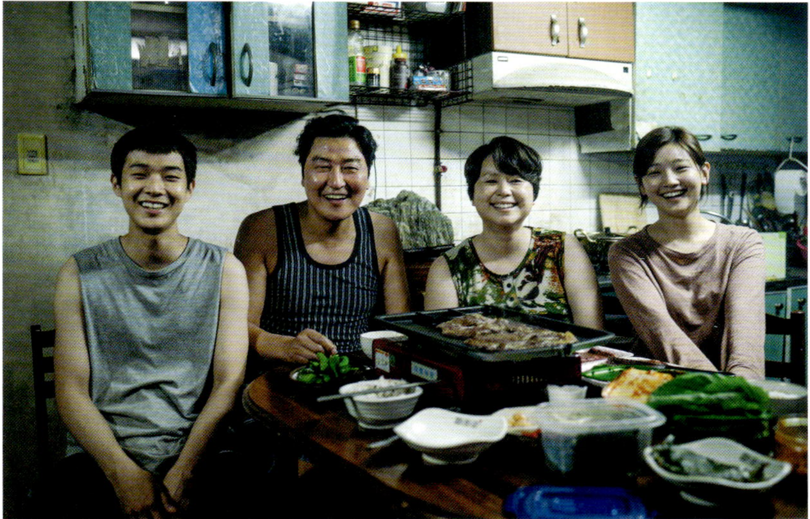

My films generally seem to have three components: fear, anxiety, and a sense of humor.... At least when we laugh, there's a feeling that we're overcoming some kind of horror.

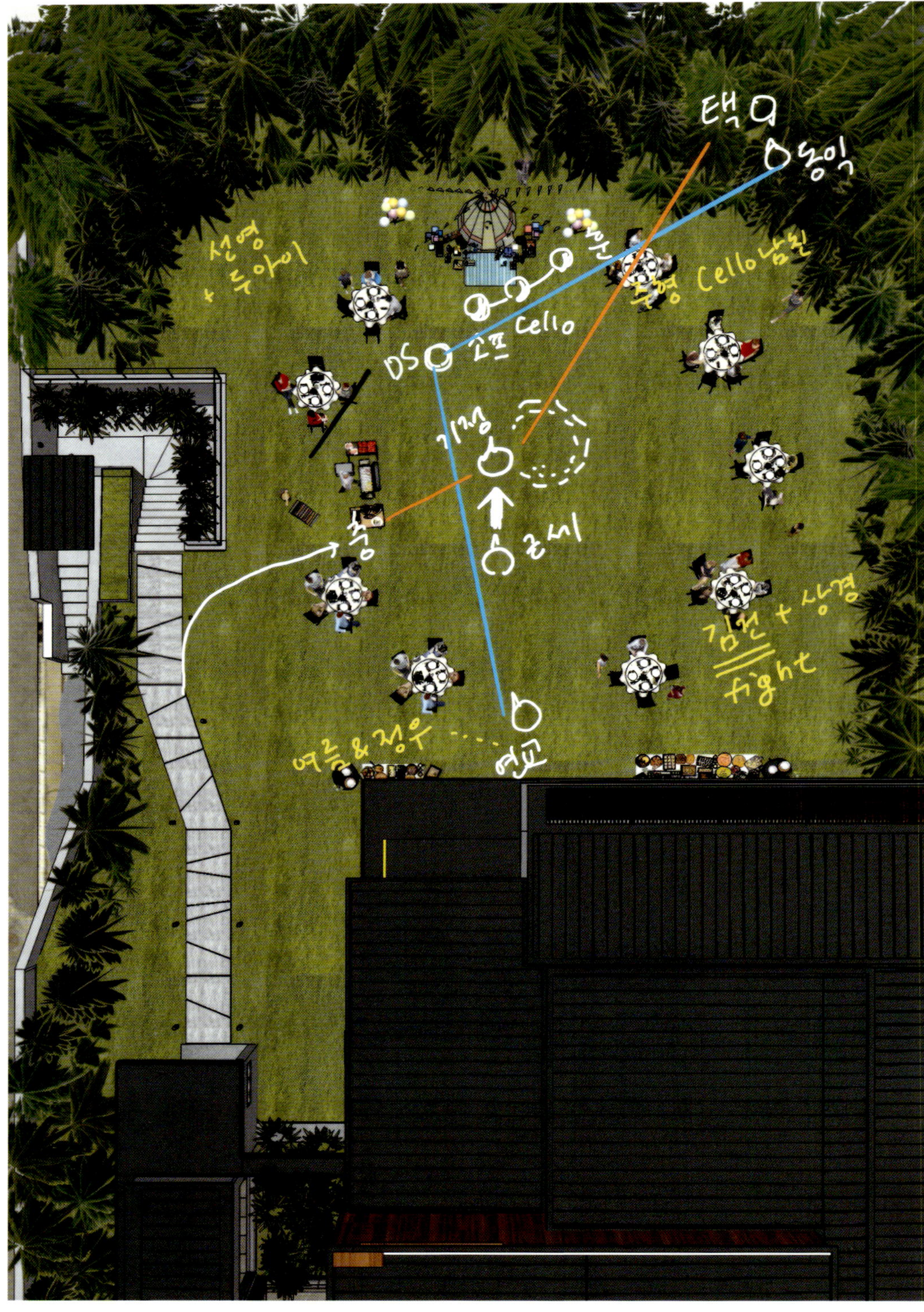

"In this film, it's very difficult to separate the good ones from the bad ones," Bong says. "Even the rich characters are not your conventional, typical, greedy villains that you see on screen. I was sympathetic to everyone."

Left: Bong's planning drawing for the backyard scene in *Parasite*

Opposite: Cast and extras during production

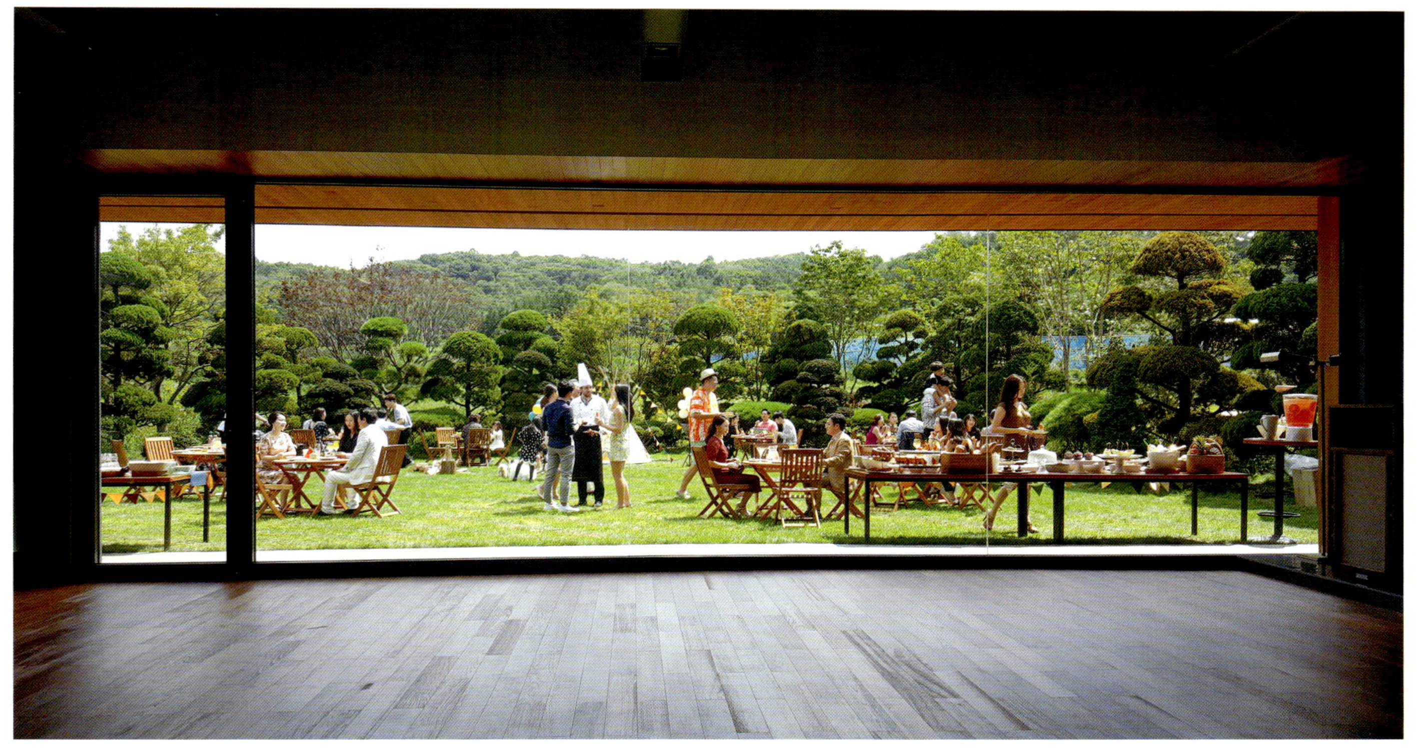

I had specific requirements in terms of what the characters would or would not be able to see from certain positions, where they could eavesdrop, how they would move from one position to the next, and the like.

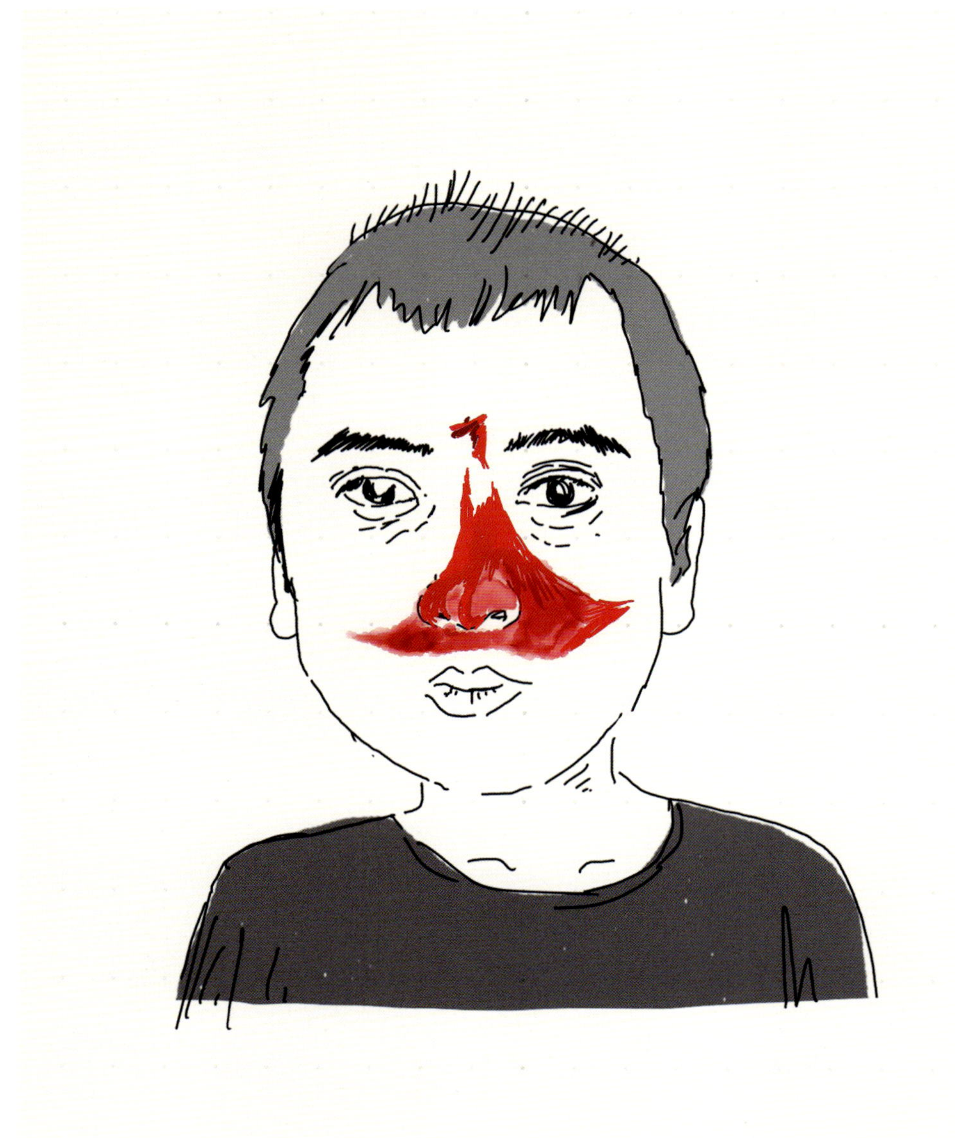

Left: Bong's concept art for Geun-sae, the housekeeper's husband in *Parasite*

Opposite: Scenes from *Parasite*

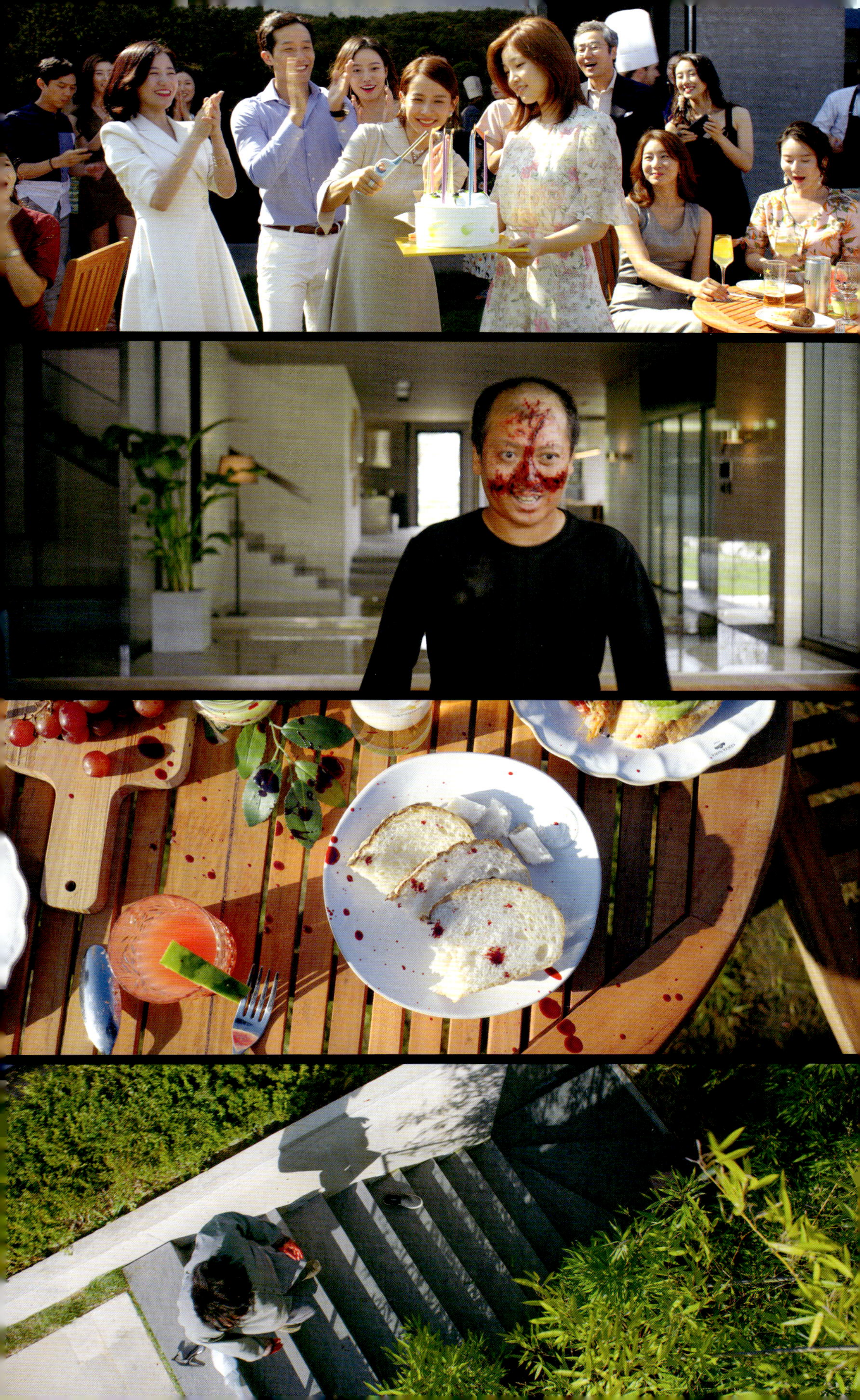

MICKEY 17

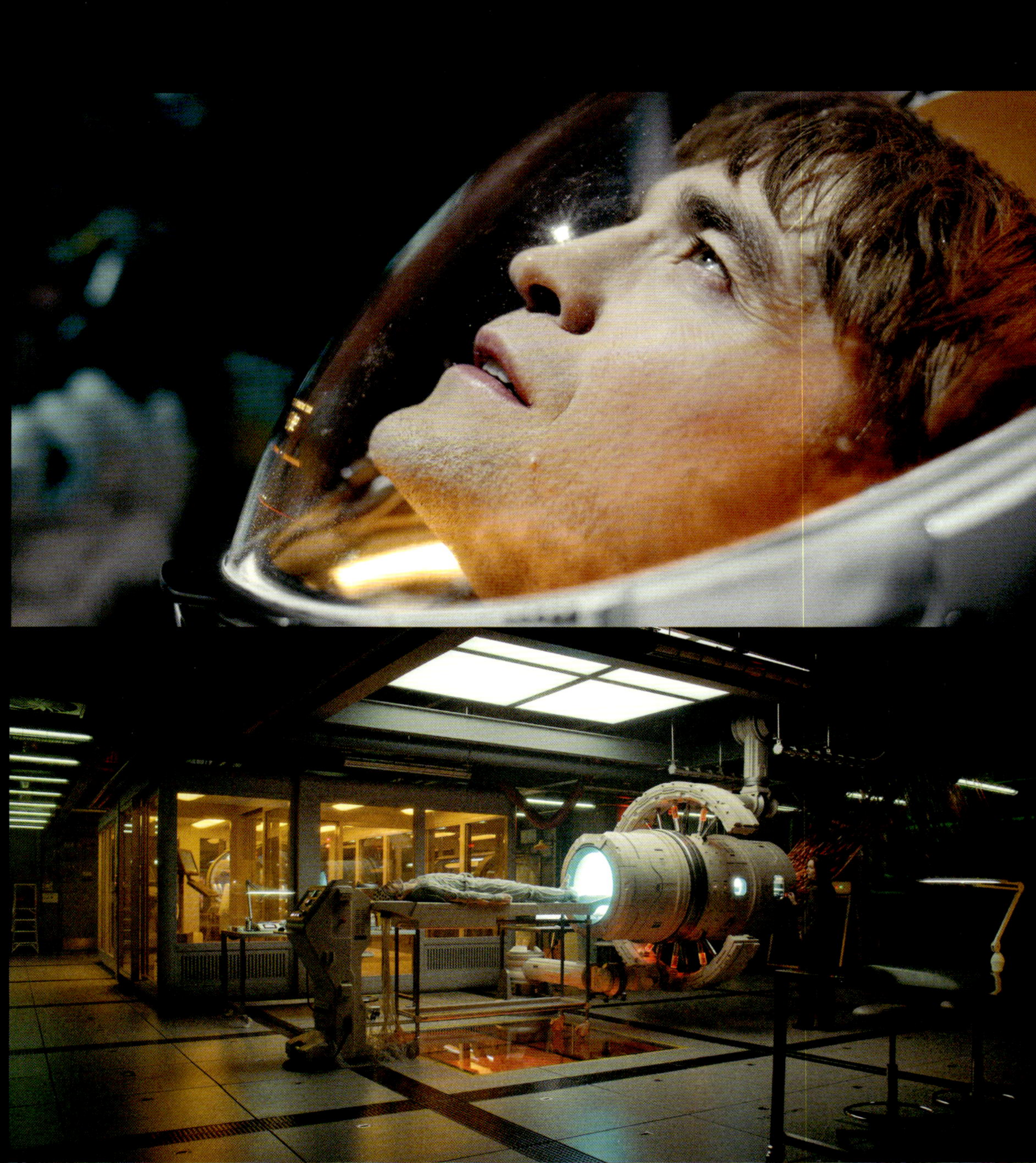

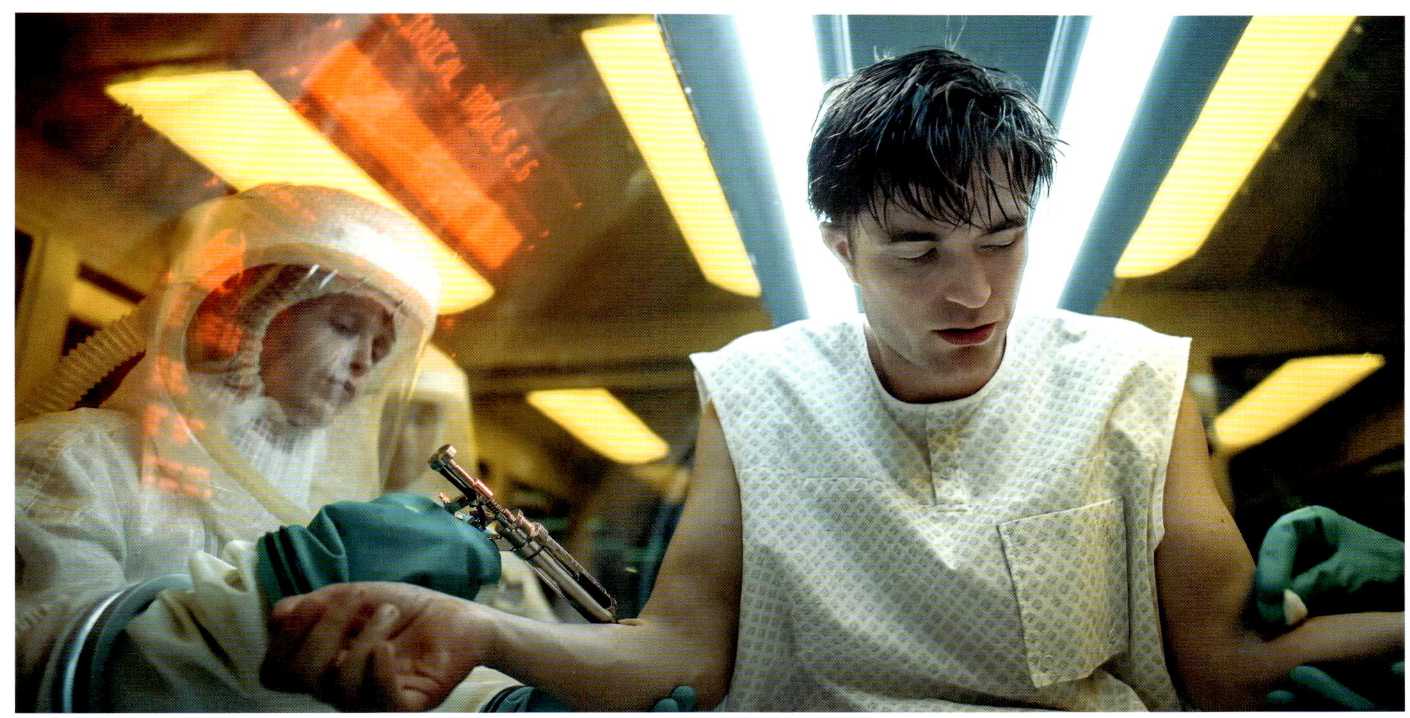

In Bong's sci-fi film *Mickey 17* (2025), Robert Pattinson plays an "expendable" worker who performs the most dangerous labor on a space mission to colonize the ice planet Niflheim. Each time Mickey dies, a new Mickey is printed out with his memories intact.

Opposite and above: Robert Pattinson as Mickey

It's a story of a simple man who ultimately ends up saving the world.

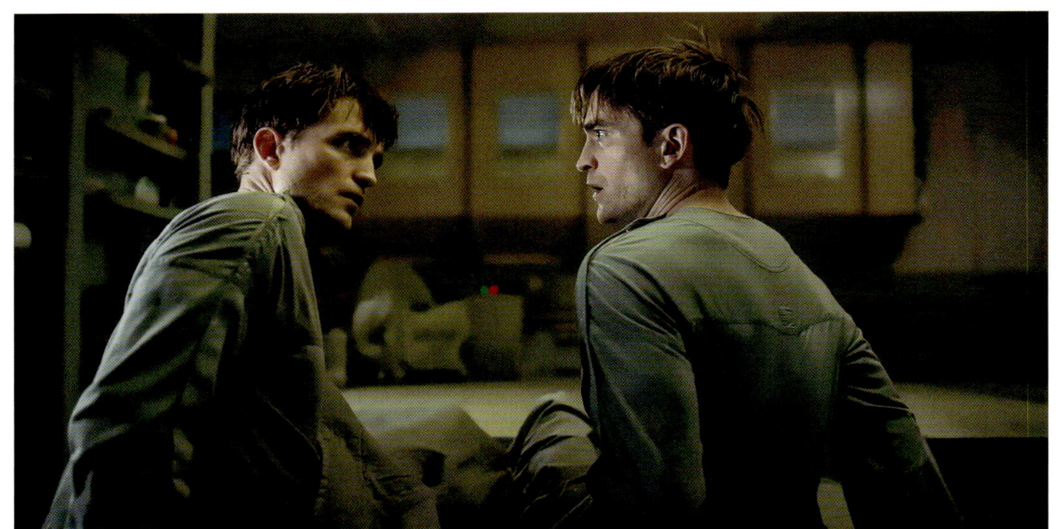

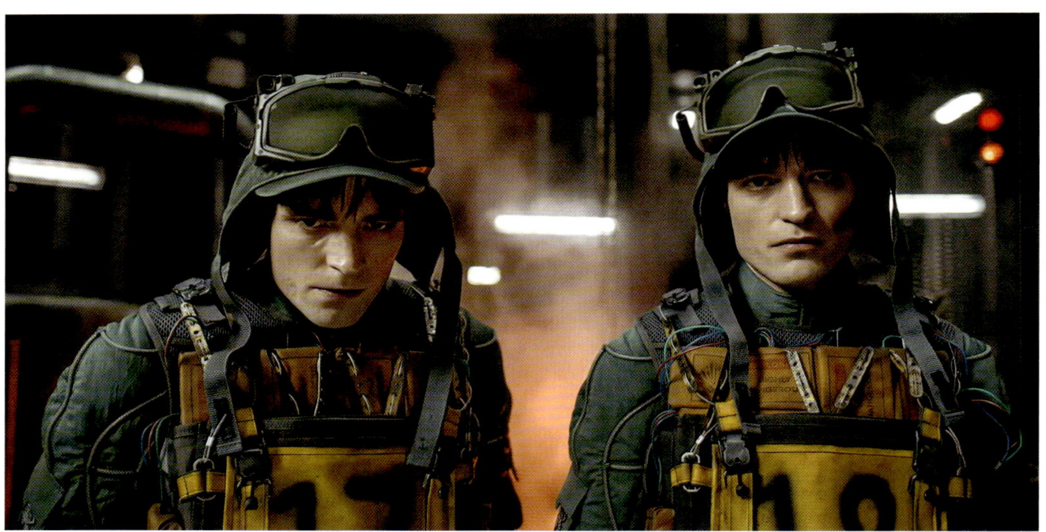

The role demanded duality,
shifting between the pitiful and
slightly stupid Mickey 17 to the
manic yet charismatic Mickey 18,
so I had Robert Pattinson in
mind from the start.

ROBERT PATTINSON

I wanted to work with Bong Joon Ho basically since I became an actor. I saw *Memories of Murder* as a teenager, and it deeply stuck with me. When we began discussing *Mickey 17*, I watched it again and realized, many years later, that something about the performances in that film had appealed to me on a primal level. I could see little things I'd picked up and incorporated into so many of my other roles. The body language and physical comedy in *Memories of Murder* is so singular and so uniquely Bong. It felt like an alien amalgam of so many things I loved, from Laurel and Hardy to Jim Carrey, to Tarantino and the French New Wave.

You can watch five seconds of any scene in any Bong Joon Ho movie and know immediately that it's his. There are very few directors you can say that about. In my experience, the people who make it to his level of iconic status get there because they care so deeply about their work. That's certainly true of Bong, but when we first met and started talking about working together on *Mickey 17*, I was struck by his humility. He was nervous about the script and anxious to know if I liked it. Meanwhile, I'm thinking, "You didn't even have to send me the script, I'm already in!"

There's an interesting balance with Bong, where everything is incredibly well-organized without feeling regimented. He initially seems a little Hitchcockian, where he already knows exactly what he wants for the edit, but then he's also so pleased to let you follow your most ridiculous instincts and is incredibly open to using even the most audacious ideas. He's deeply funny as a filmmaker and as a human. Bong is incredible at elevating the banal into the surreal and being provocative in such a well-meaning way.

There's also a disarming sweetness to him that he manages to expand to an entire movie set. It puts everybody at ease, with seemingly very little effort. It's a deceptively powerful ability. He imbues everyone with a sense of anticipation; you really feel like you're doing something important when you're working with him. I think everybody who works with him feels like that.

To get to work with someone so exceptionally talented who has dedicated his life to this art form—and isn't jaded by it at all but who remains so excited by it, who approaches each new project with the same enthusiasm and wonder as the last—it's a priceless gift. Everyone should experience working with Bong Joon Ho. He's the absolute best.

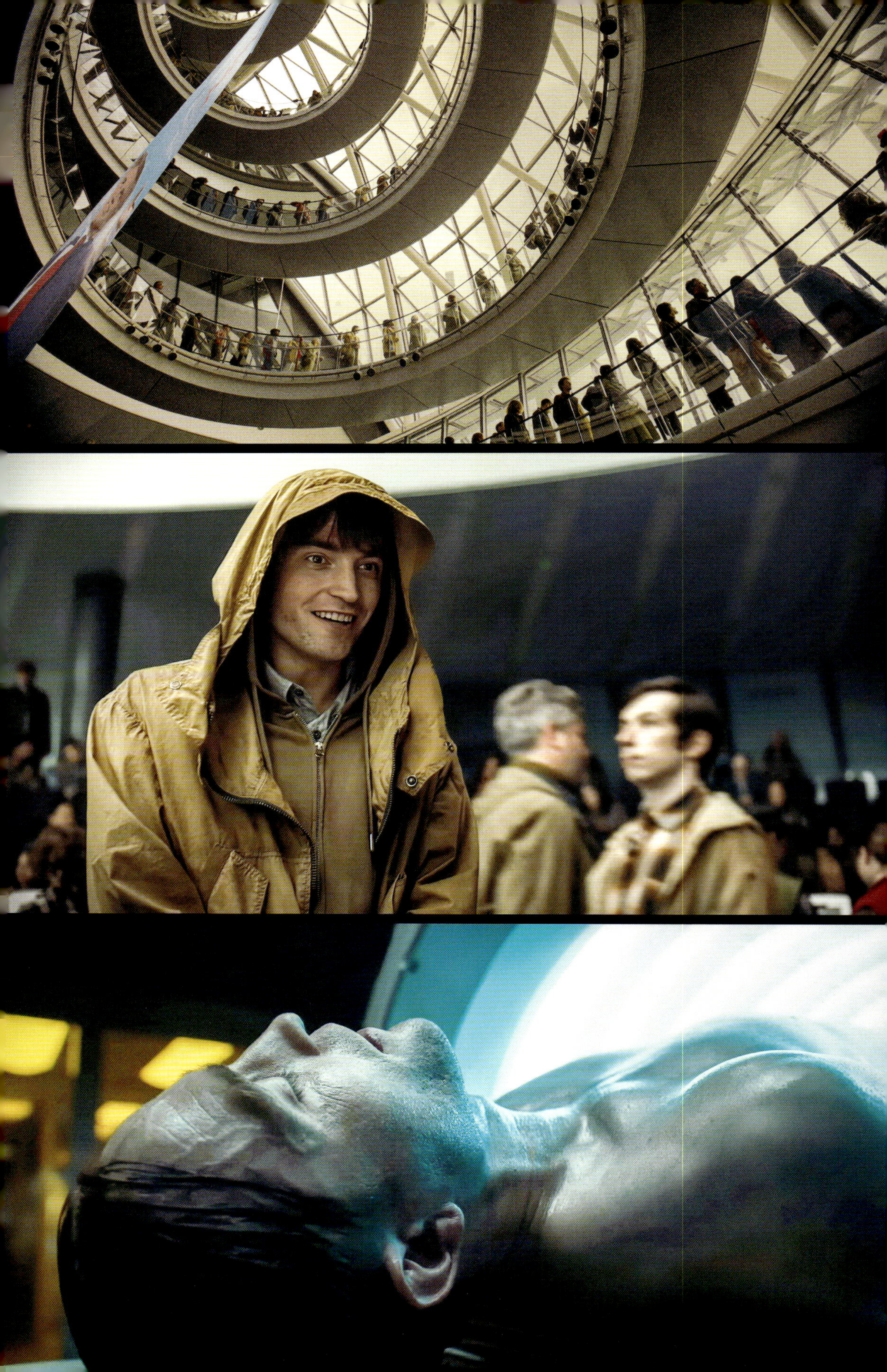

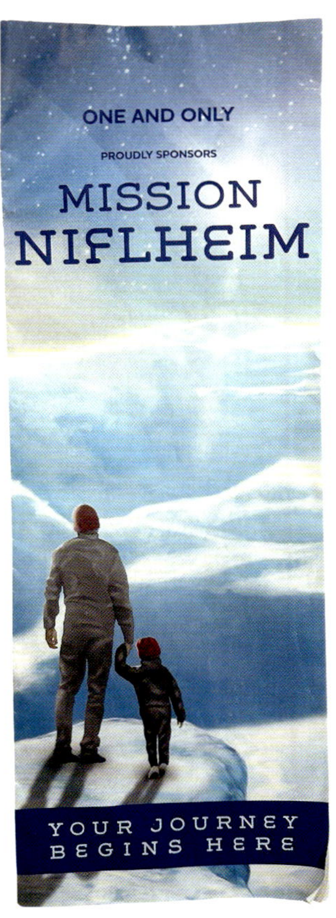

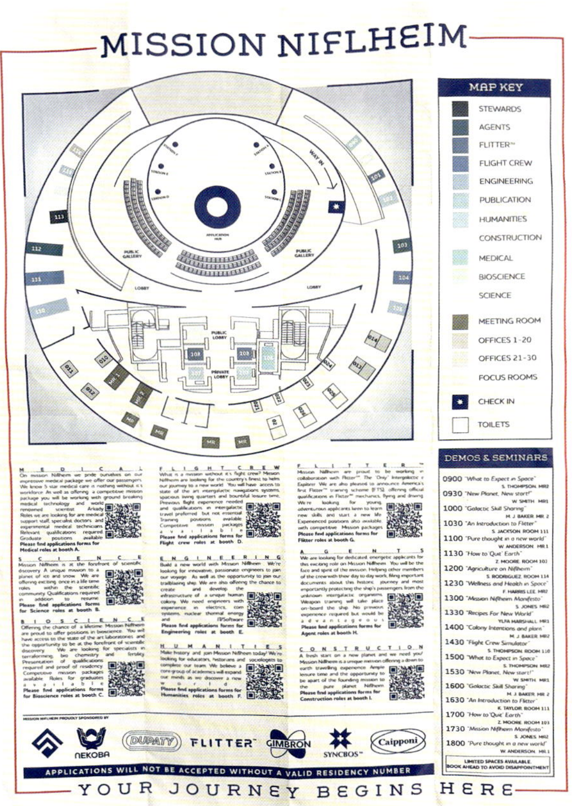

Like many of Bong's protagonists, Mickey is an ordinary person caught up in a dehumanizing system. "Many of my characters are confused. They're in the middle of a situation and don't know what's going on. It's sad and comic at the same time."

Opposite: Scenes from *Mickey 17*

Above: Prop brochure advertising Mission Niflheim

Right: Bong and Robert Pattinson (right) on set

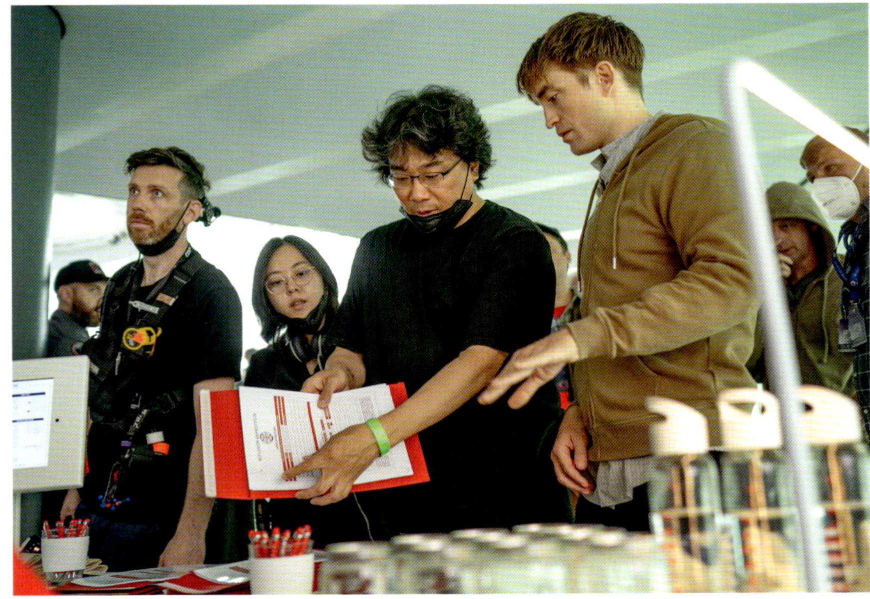

DARIUS KHONDJI

I took my kids to see *The Host* in a big cinema in Paris. It was the first film by Bong Joon Ho that I'd ever seen, and I thought it was terrific. It never crossed my mind that I might someday work with him. Years passed, and one day a friend doing post-production work on *Snowpiercer* emailed me and said Director Bong wanted to meet. We met up a few times, and the conversations were fantastic. He told me about these characters taking shape in his mind, a giant pig and a little girl, and gradually it became clear that he wanted me to be the cinematographer for his next project. This is how we started working together on *Okja*.

On set, Bong directs with an incredible fluidity, and he knows the lenses, techniques, and formats as well as we, the camera people, do. He's an inspiration for the people working around him, partly because you can tell it to him straight. If you give Bong an idea, he won't necessarily take it. But he'll take it right away if it makes for interesting storytelling, and if he thinks the camerawork can move the story forward in a powerful way.

His storyboards are like complex opera scores made up of shots. He works like a musician—carefully arranging notes, creating layers. The camera's movements are planned to fall in sync with the actors' rhythms, including how they talk. Bong directs the camerawork in terms of mood and characters and scenes. That's what's important to him. He'd never say, "Are we going to use the techno crane here?" We pick a very good camera operator, the key grip, who goes through all the preparation with us so that we can immediately translate Bong's direction into motion. On *Mickey 17*, the shot list was so full that I thought of the emperor in *Amadeus* (2014), telling Mozart, "It has too many notes!" But you shoot trusting that it will all come together.

Making *Mickey 17* felt like a real puzzle. We didn't approach it as a science fiction film. Bong loves science fiction—and I do too—but he wanted to make this film, which is about a spaceship traveling to colonize a distant planet, more as a comedy with contemporary political nuance. He wanted it to feel like something that could happen on Earth, so the spaceship became, in my mind, like a big, old, dirty garage that just happens to be traveling through space. The story he wanted to tell was more important than the genre.

Director Bong is one of the hardest workers I have ever met. He's constantly thinking about the film he's working on. When I work with him, I come home at night and literally collapse. Few people in filmmaking have the genuine strength and power to make things happen the way he does. At the same time, he's also very playful. He has this magical ability to make you feel that the fantastical characters in his films are alive in the world. He's kept the spirit of a young kid, developing his mind through play like we do in the first years of life.

Bong would say he's been influenced by Alfred Hitchcock, Jean-Pierre Melville, Park Chan-wook, and Robert Bresson. That's all true, of course, because he's a cinephile. But he's a very special director in his own right, the kind you rarely meet. I never use the word "genius," but for filmmaking I think Bong is pretty close—a total original.

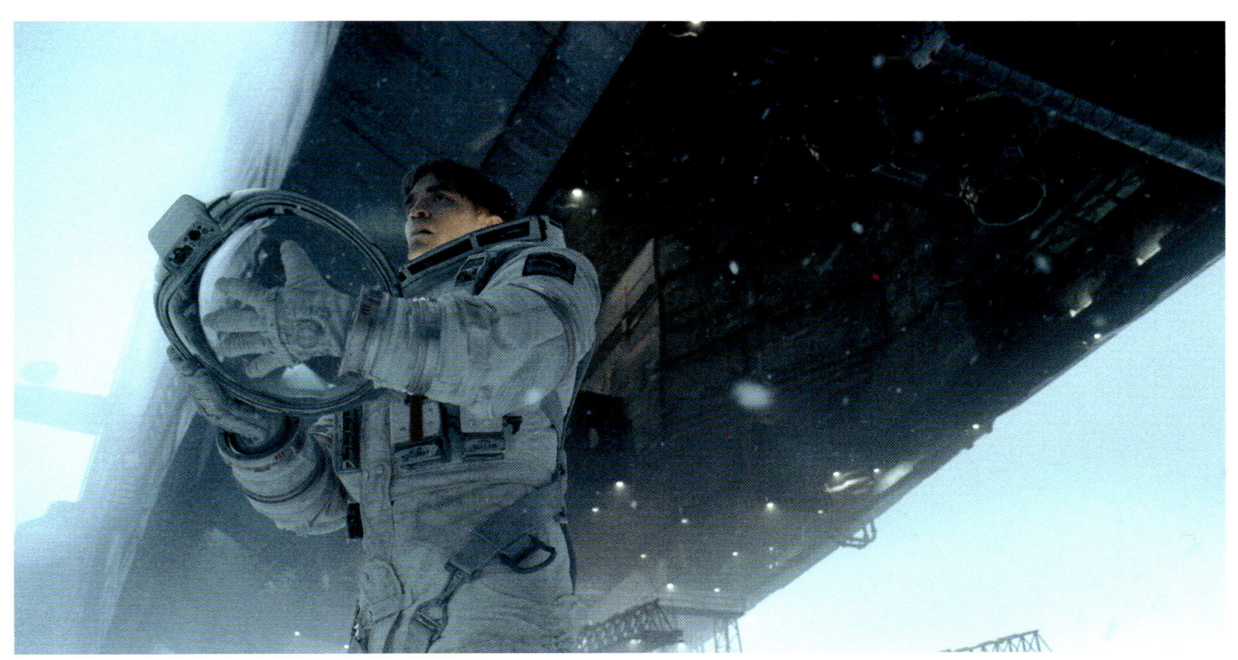

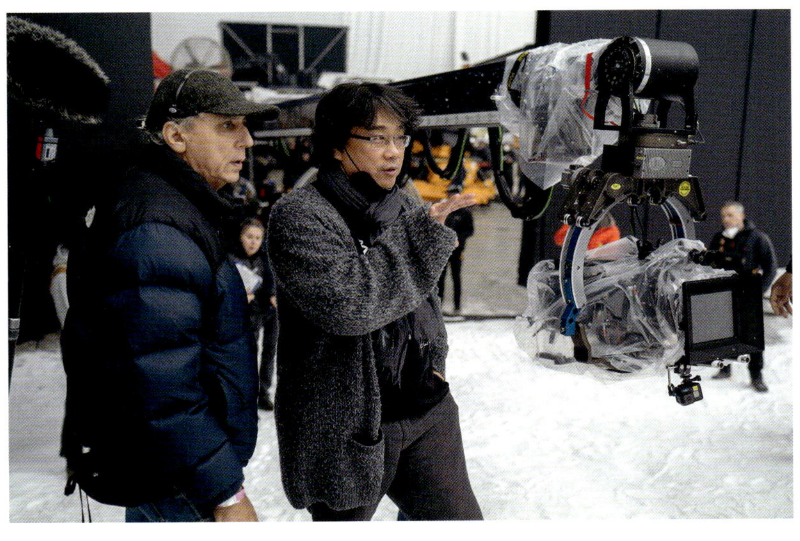

"Every time I make a film, I feel like I become a new person," Bong remarks. "So, I feel like I know what Mickey goes through. I've made eight films. I was Bong 1, and now I'm Bong 8."

Above: Robert Pattinson in *Mickey 17*

Left: Bong and cinematographer Darius Khondji (left) during production

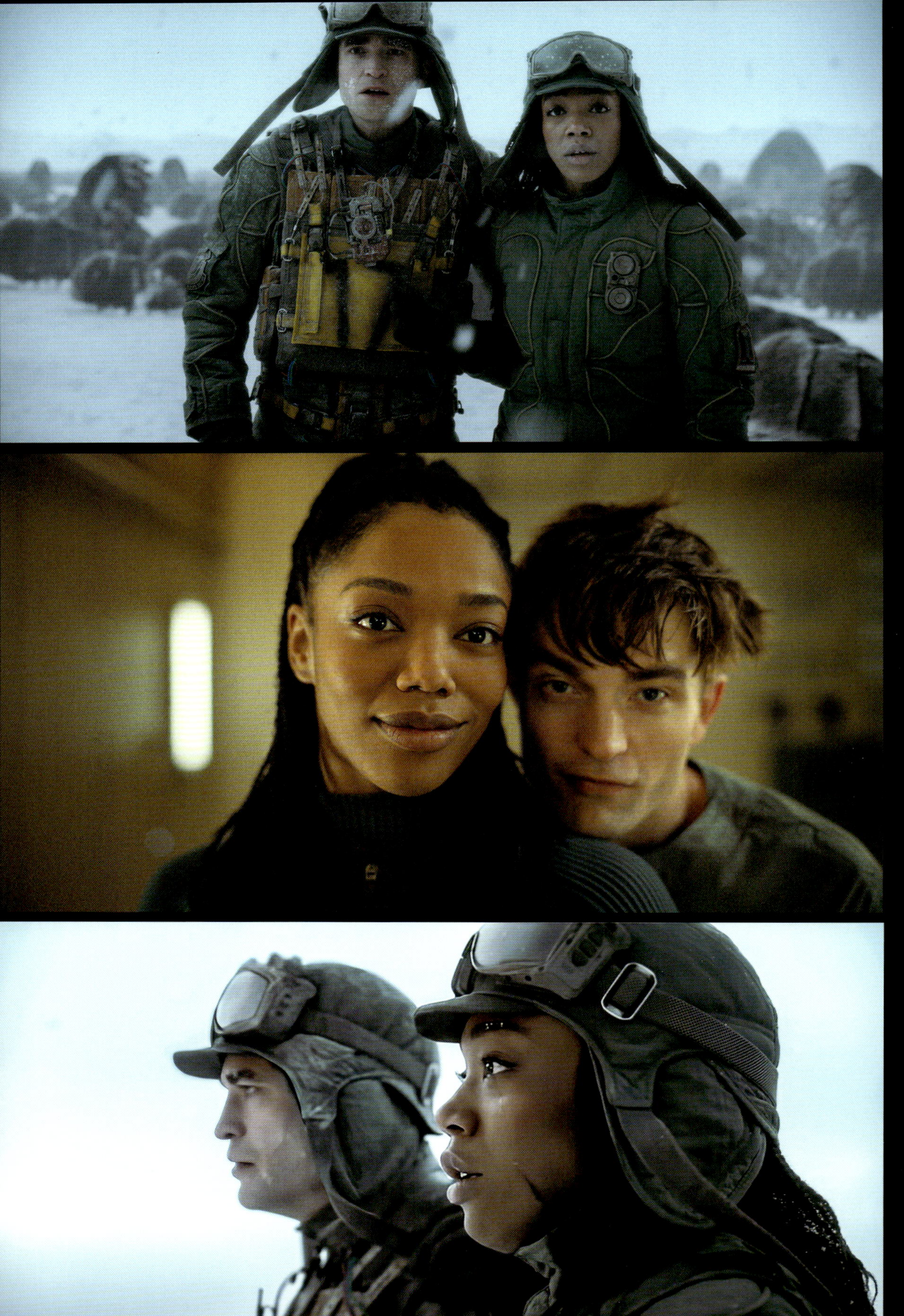

I really loved how their love was portrayed, and I didn't want to lose that aspect in my adaptation. So, for the first time in my work, I think, love was introduced as a theme.

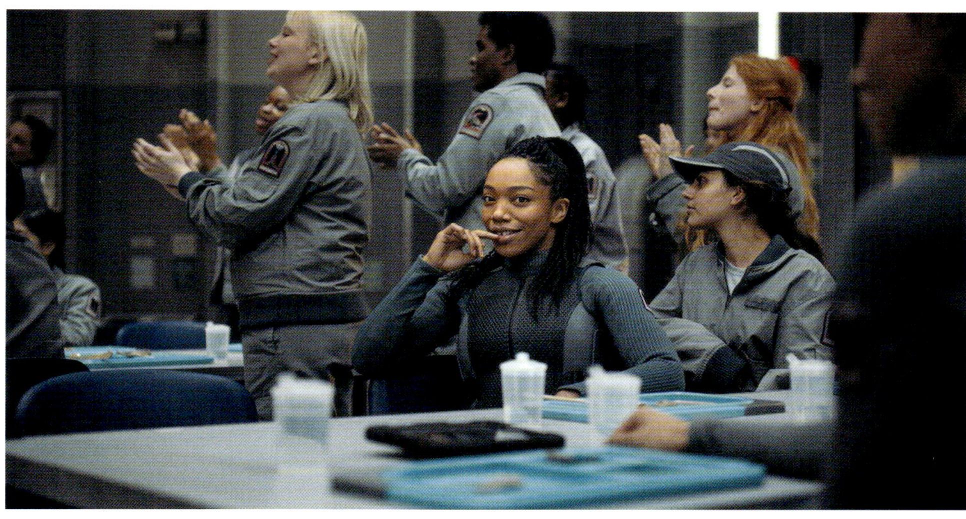

Bong adapted his story from the sci-fi novel *Mickey7* (2022) by Edward Ashton. "When I adapt a work, I tend to make a lot of changes," he says. "But the one thing I wanted to keep from the original was the love story between Mickey and Nasha."

Opposite and this page: Naomi Ackie and Robert Pattinson in *Mickey 17*

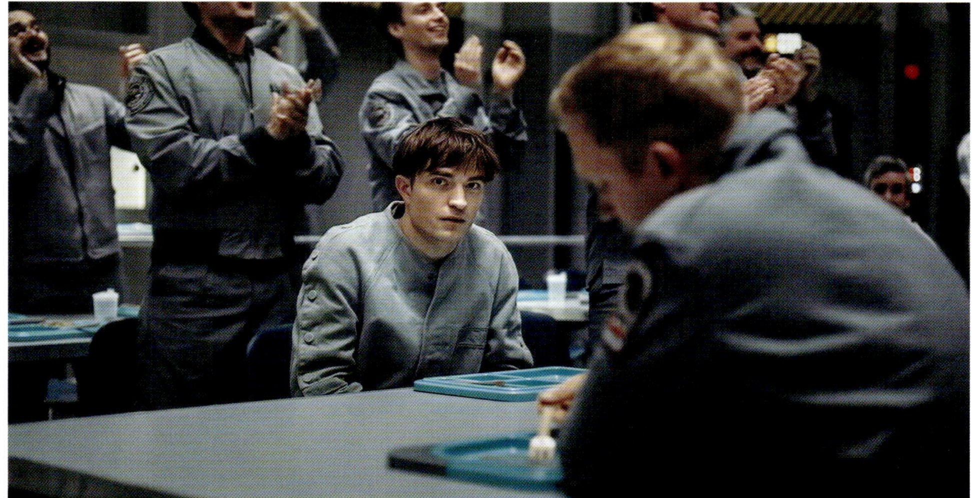

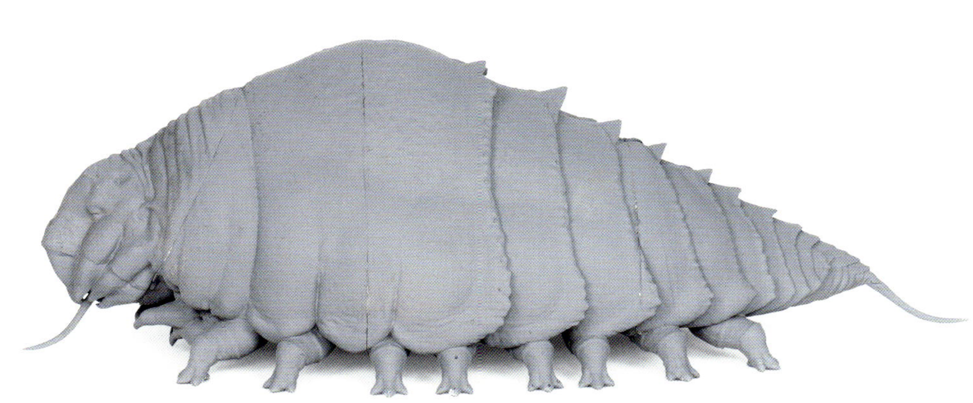

In *Mickey 17*, the creepers are creatures native to Niflheim. "In the very early stage of creature design, we shared many images of armadillos and croissants," Bong says.

Left: Model of Mama Creeper by Jang Hee Chul

Below: Concept art for Baby Creeper

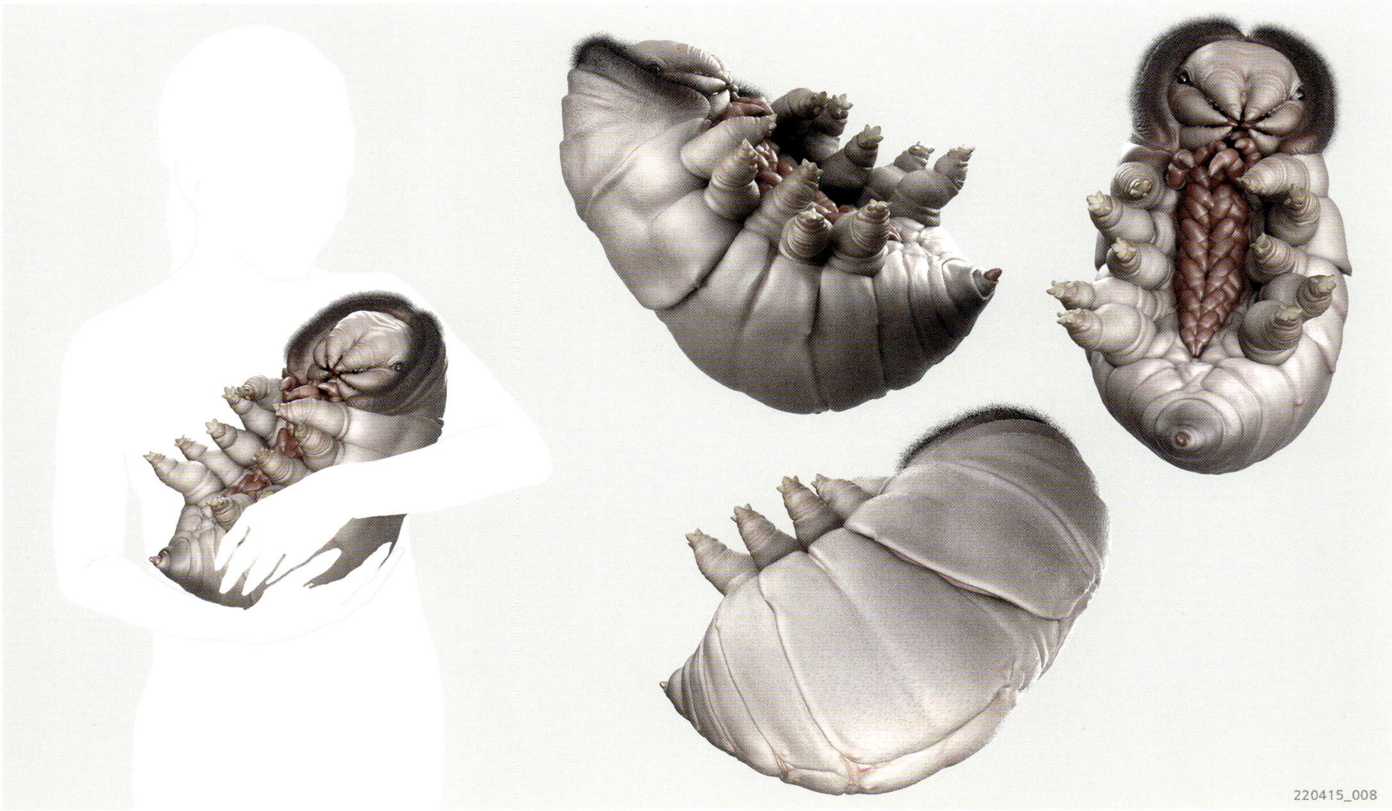

DAN GLASS

I've always been interested in cinema and love working with directors who are a little bit on the fringe, doing things differently—it's a rare treat for me. So when the opportunity to work on *Snowpiercer* came up, I was instantly drawn to it. My team at Method Studios, where I was a creative director at the time, created the visual effects for the interior of the train, including its incredible aquarium carriage. Director Bong reached out to thank me for that scene in particular, and we've continued working together, most recently on *Mickey 17*.

I often talk to others in my field about a dilemma of our own making: VFX has shown itself capable of near impossible ideas on near impossible timelines all too often. In some ways, this encourages a lack of planning in the sense that decisions can be delayed up until the very end. Working with a director like Bong, you'll never have that experience. His films are visually captivating because he builds their worlds and stories with such deep consideration. He takes time out between films to reflect and think and write so that when he comes to the table, he's got a very clear idea of what he wants. For each project we've worked on together, he'll show me concepts and designs, and already I'll see an incredible amount of insight put into how a creature will look and behave. This is something I deeply admire and appreciate about his process.

Bong and Jang Hee Chul, his longtime collaborator on character design, shared fantastic concept images, 3D models, and mood boards for *Mickey 17*. They had already been through an in-depth process of thinking through the evolution of the creepers and the form they would take on this snowbound planet. I would almost equate it to the writings of Tolkien, where you can feel the richness of the histories and backstories even though they aren't on the page. Some people might come on to a project like this and think, "Where's the interest if it's already been figured out?" But for me, there's still so much exciting work that happens to bring characters like this to life. Once you introduce motion, you realize how essential movement is for character design.

What especially drew me in was the complexity of these creatures that start out as terrifying, repulsive even, but you form an emotional connection with them by the end of the movie. The babies needed to feel cute, like you'd want to hold and cuddle them. It was a fascinating animation problem to solve. The idea for the creepers was that they would be big and furry but also insect-like, capable of flattening out or folding over. Director Bong initially imagined them as lightweight, essentially hollow inside to make them more agile, but we realized we had to give them some bulk and weight to be credible. We examined how various mammals and multi-legged invertebrates like centipedes moved at different speeds, and then we animated little vignettes. For the baby creeper, we looked at puppies; for the adolescents, Bong envisioned them as playful and a little bit naughty, so we thought of bear cubs that go out exploring and turning over trash cans. We could immediately see the creepers' personality and spirit, even in these crude studies.

With Director Bong, I always work fluidly, knowing there is an intention, a rationale, behind every choice he makes. He comes with many ideas formed but takes ours in as well, and he puts trust in his team. I'm very proud of my VFX artists and their work on *Mickey 17*. But I also think, aside from their fantastic talent and effort, a lot of the credit goes to Bong for having figured out what he wanted early on and sticking with it.

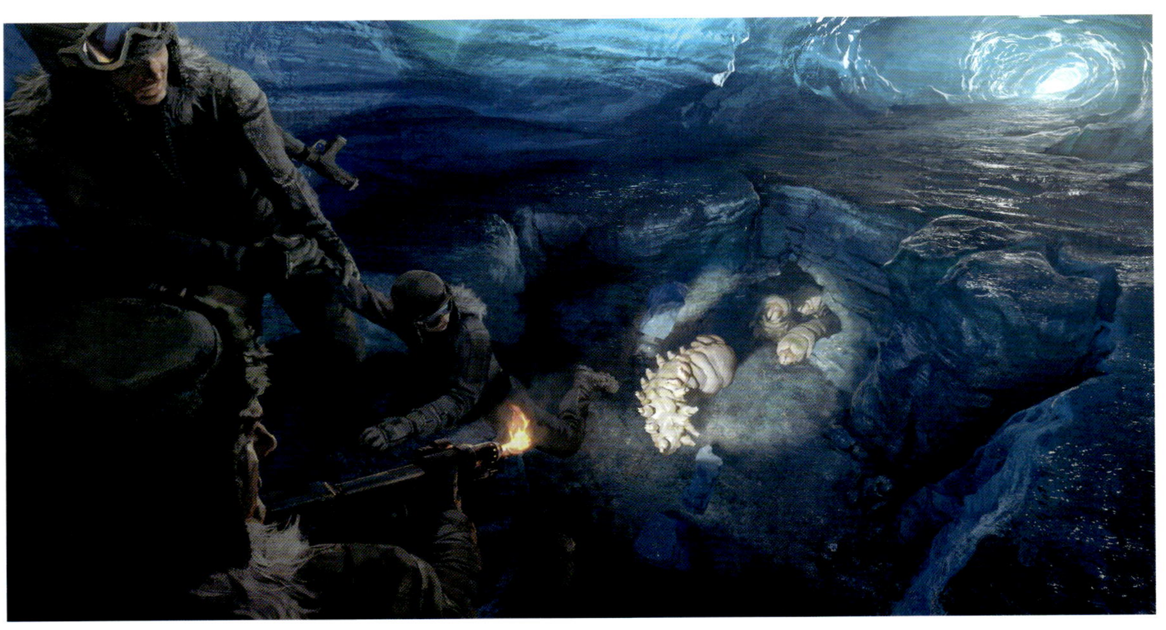

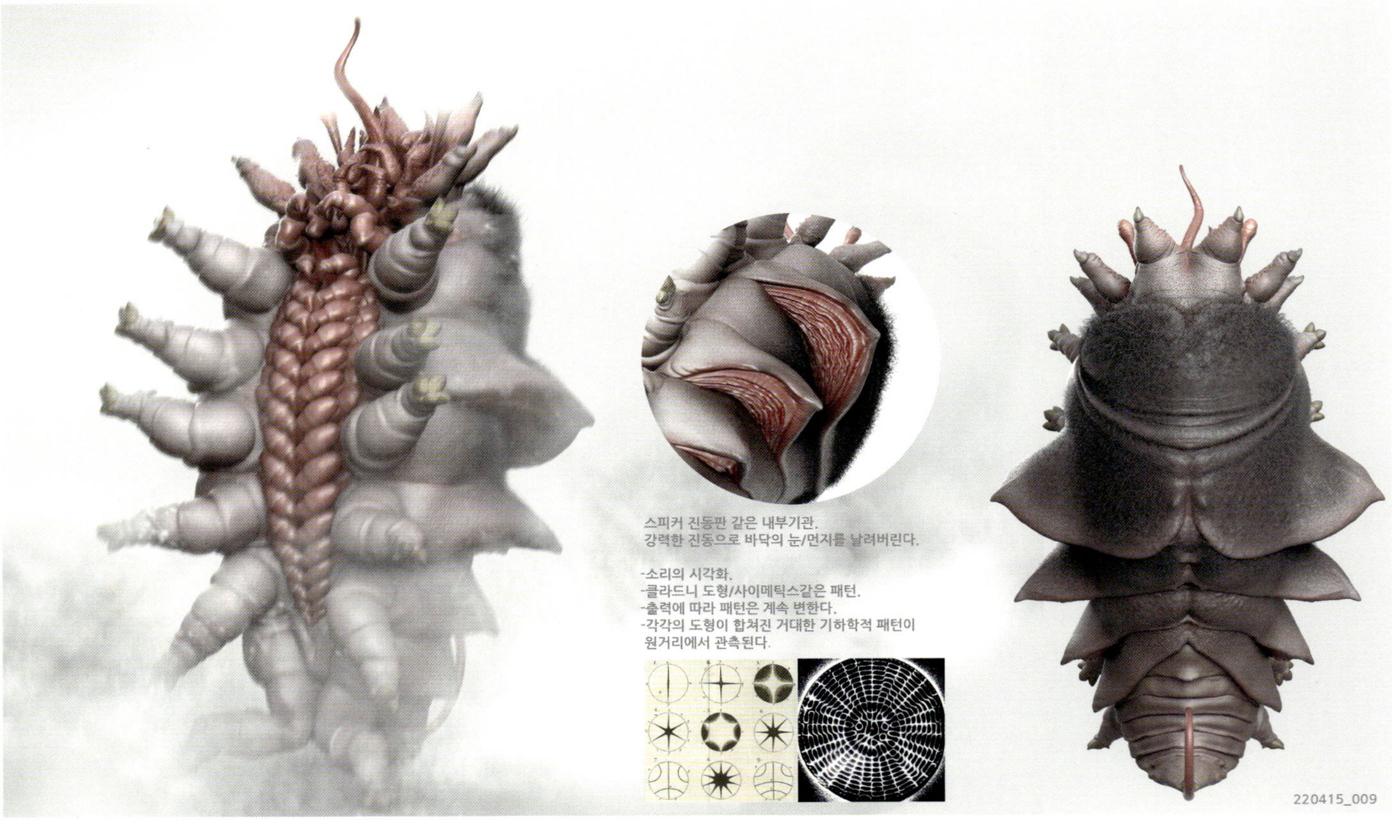

스피커 진동판 같은 내부기관.
강력한 진동으로 바닥의 눈/먼지를 날려버린다.

-소리의 시각화.
-클라드니 도형/사이메틱스같은 패턴.
-출력에 따라 패턴은 계속 변한다.
-각각의 도형이 합쳐진 거대한 기하학적 패턴이
원거리에서 관측된다.

220415_009

In the opening, I make it feel like the creeper is scary and disgusting. But gradually, we discover how they're intellectual and some of their other characteristics.

Opposite, top: Concept art for the ice cave

Opposite, bottom: Concept art for creeper

Right: Bong's storyboard for *Mickey 17*

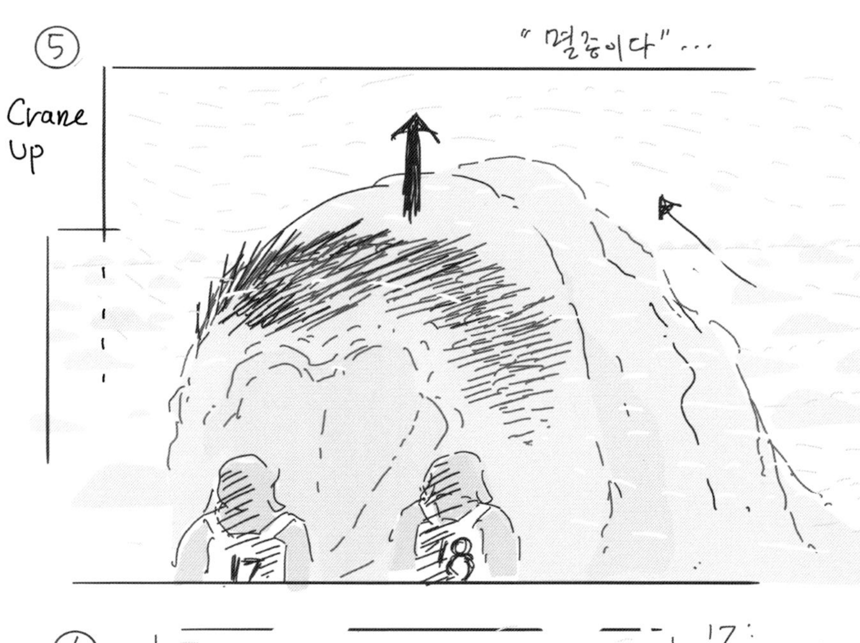

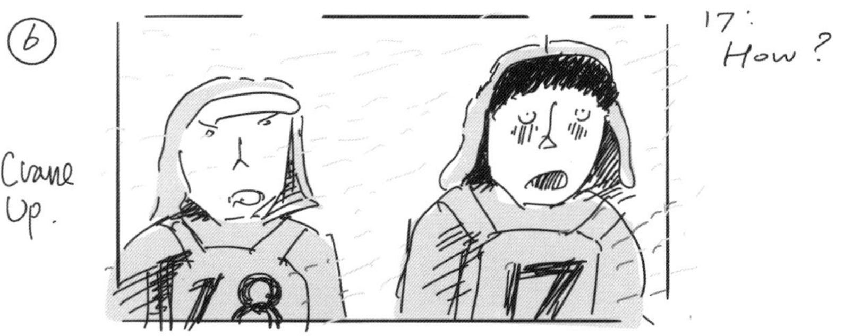

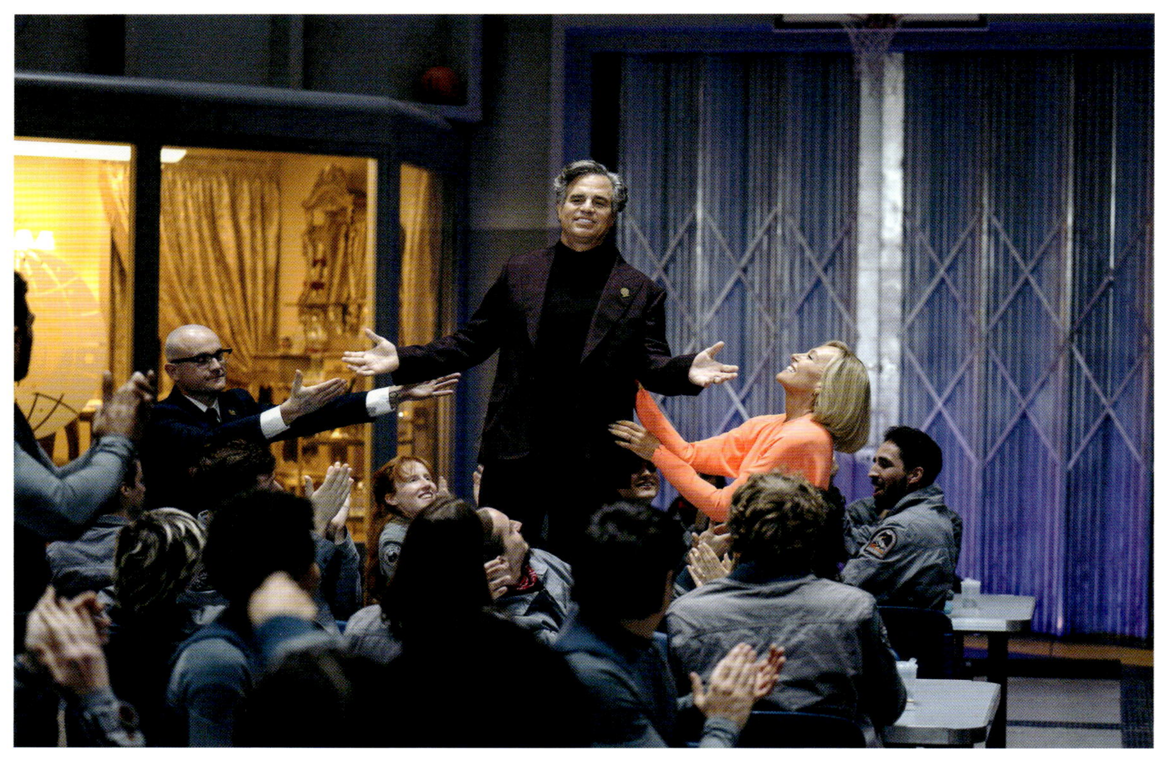

Mark [Ruffalo] showed me photos of a particular American governor, and I showed Mark photos of a particular Korean politician. What we mostly talked about was that dictators can be incredibly horrible and annoying, but they have this endearing quality that they use to charm the masses.

Mark Ruffalo plays the charismatic authoritarian Kenneth Marshall, the expedition's leader. "I grew up witnessing the military dictatorship," Bong says. "I saw the Gwangju massacre on TV. It's a layer I carry with me. It's always in the undercurrents of my creative process."

Above and opposite: Mark Ruffalo and Toni Collette in *Mickey 17*

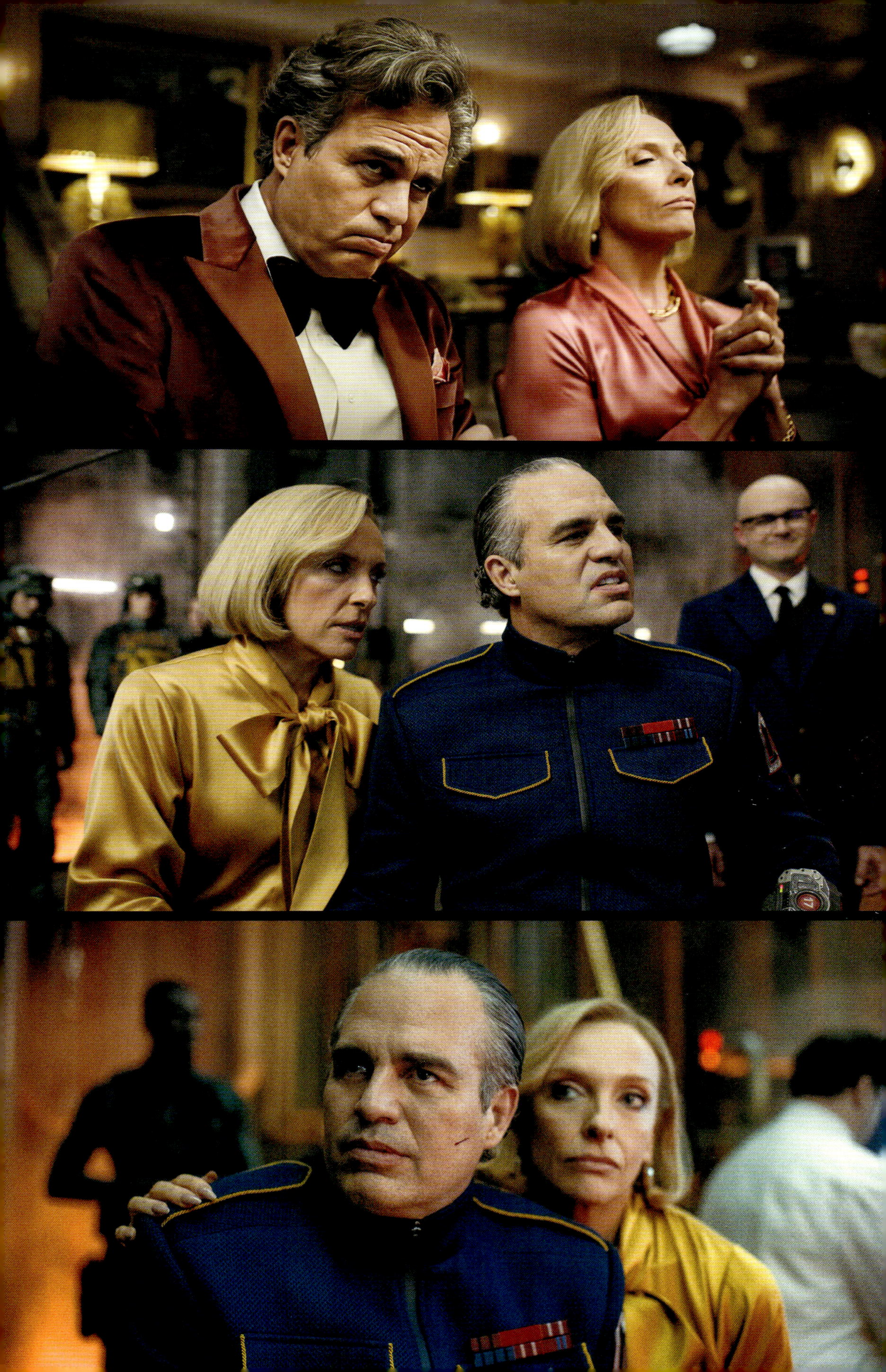

TONI COLLETTE

I'd seen and loved a couple of Bong's films, including his incredible award-winning hit, *Parasite*. I desperately wanted to work with him because his films are so original and authentic, which is actually very rare in our industry. Bong makes subtle statements, both political and social, while allowing his audiences to float in worlds of surprise and fun. Those worlds always feel new yet grounded and familiar; whether it's a character's perspective or an actual place, we buy into it with pleasure and know we're in for a rip-roaring time. And he makes these films with heart. Always with heart. As you can probably tell, Bong's work inspires me. I am a true fan.

In 2021, I heard he was going to be the head of the jury at the Venice Film Festival. I sent an inquiry to see if I could somehow join his jury, but all the positions were filled. When I got a call from my agent later that year telling me that Bong wanted to meet with me about a new film, I freaked out with excitement. The project was under wraps. There was nothing I could read or do to prepare. I was nervous. The day drew closer, and finally the morning of our meeting came. Suddenly there we were, blinking back at each other through our computer screens: Bong in Seoul, me in Sydney. The time difference was only slight. My heart was pounding. I needn't have felt nervous, though. Bong is the sweetest, coolest, most wonderful person.

He launched straight in, saying that we've both been doing this for so long, so let's just cut to the chase: he really wanted me to be in his next movie, *Mickey 17*. I cried a bit and probably screamed; I don't think I've ever felt so high on a work-related call. My witchy manifesting actually worked! Or maybe it was just meant to be. He went on to say the English translation of the script was forthcoming, and he would send it to me to see if I liked it. But honestly, there was no way I wasn't going to love it.

Everything about Bong is delightful and surprising. There is nobody like him. He's deep and endlessly creative. He communicates his wild vision with clarity and an infectious passion, giggling with glee at his own audacity and outrageous ideas. He is also humble and expresses gratitude and compassion for his actors and crew every single day. He is always interested in what others have to offer, and he is incredibly generous and kind, which allows those around him to feel emboldened and brave in their choices. And even though his ideas are crystal clear, he is completely collaborative and always open to the best idea, no matter where it comes from.

For my character's penultimate scene in *Mickey 17*, Bong asked me to convey an emotional state that would make the audience believe and understand what had happened to her in her final scene. There was no dialogue, just a reaction. It was an intense moment for my character, Ylfa. He had me do a first take without any direction, allowing me to just follow my intuition, and then he asked me to do about five more takes. Those subsequent takes felt cathartic in the moment, but later, upon reflection, I felt they were too much—too showy and derivative of some of my past work. I worried about that scene for two years after we finished filming.

When I finally saw *Mickey 17* cut together, I was enormously relieved to find that Bong used that first take. The trust and respect he creates on set, for everyone both in front of and behind the camera, is quiet and joyous. I love Bong. I admired him before I worked with him, and now I love him even more. Sometimes meeting a hero works out just fine.

Opposite: Toni Collette as
Ylfa Marshall in *Mickey 17*

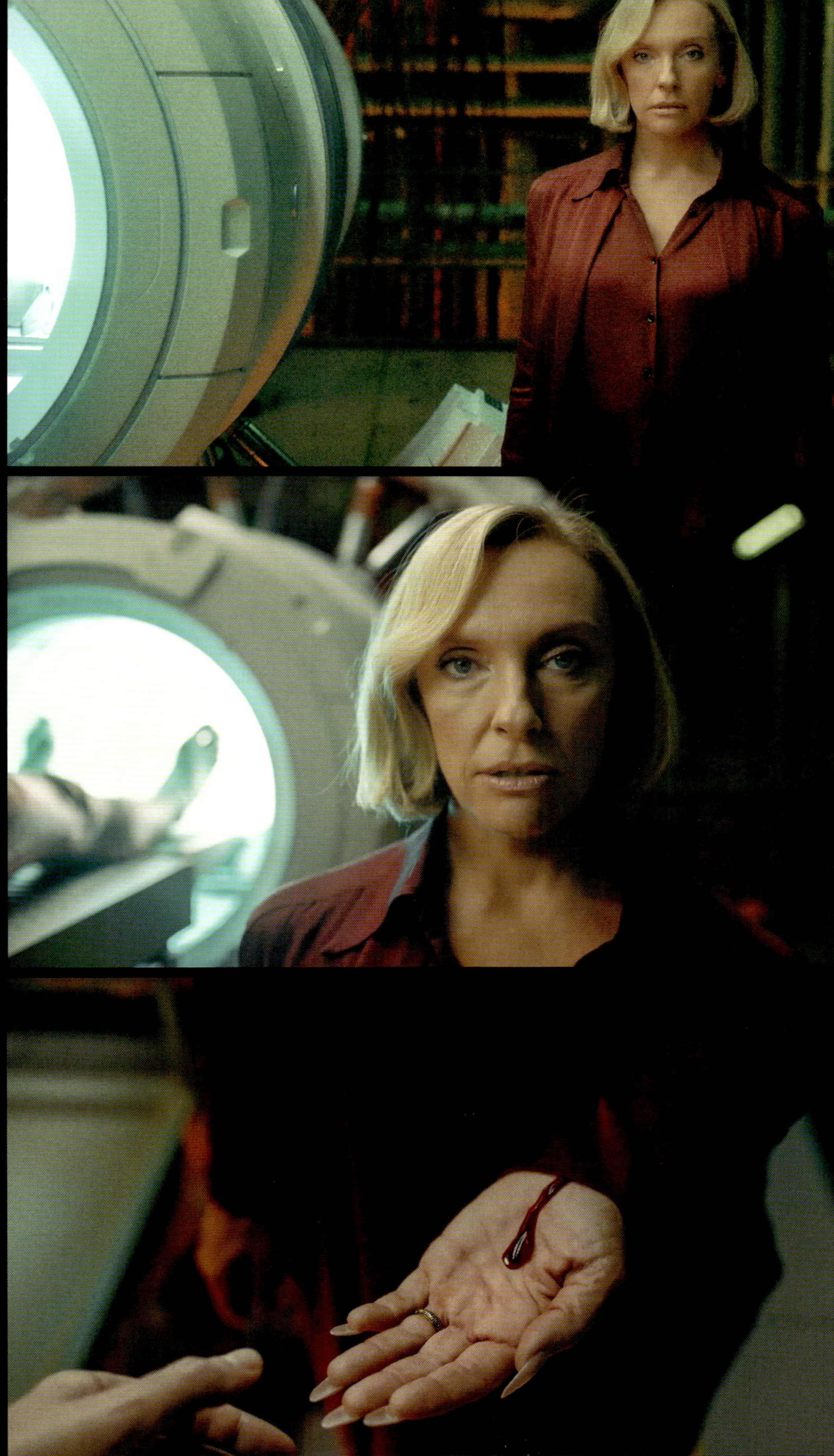

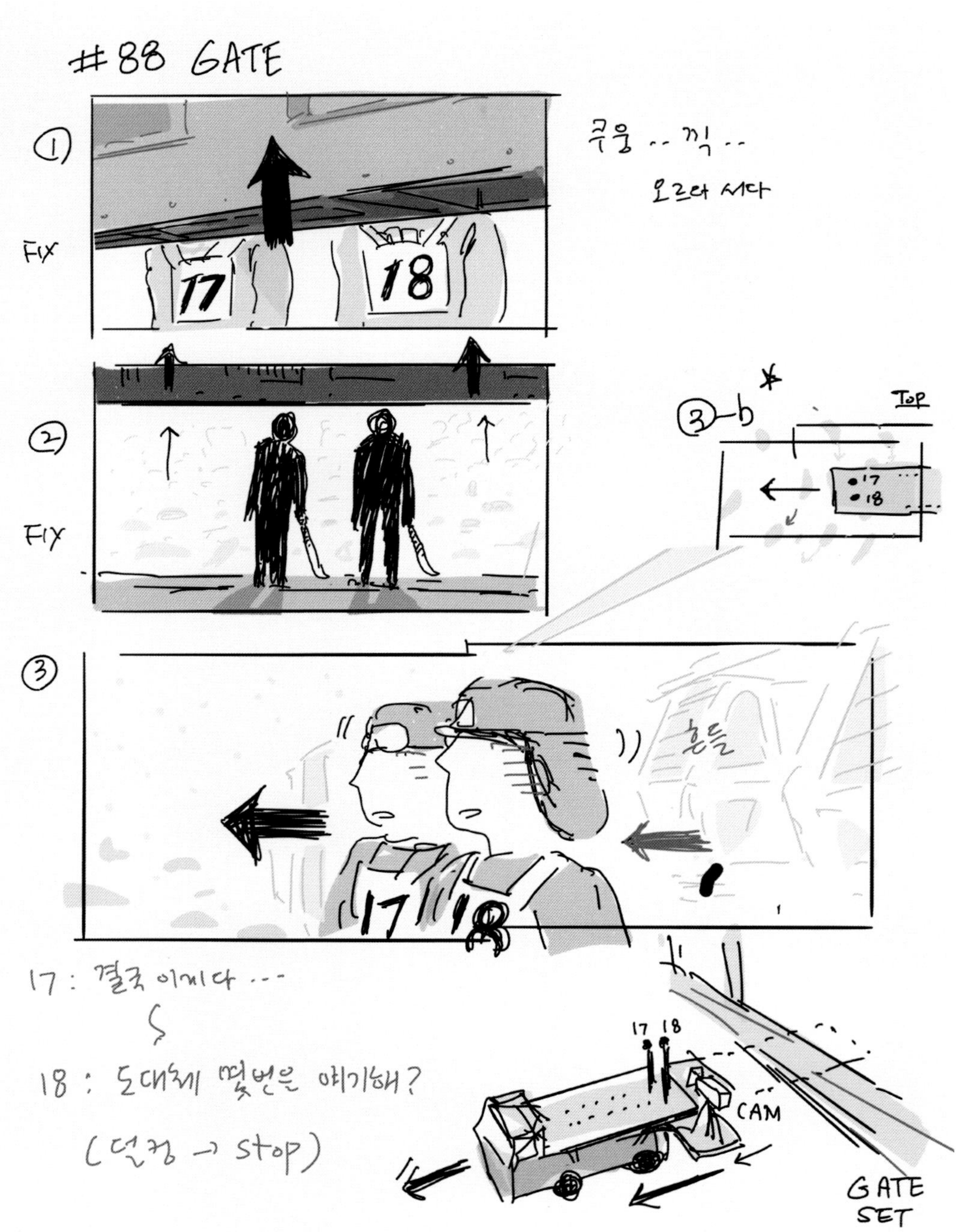

"I think sci-fi is more appealing when it deals with human characters that are weak and... kind of idiotic and repeat the same mistakes. I find those stories more interesting than superhero ones."

Left: Bong's storyboard for *Mickey 17*

Opposite: Robert Pattinson in *Mickey 17*

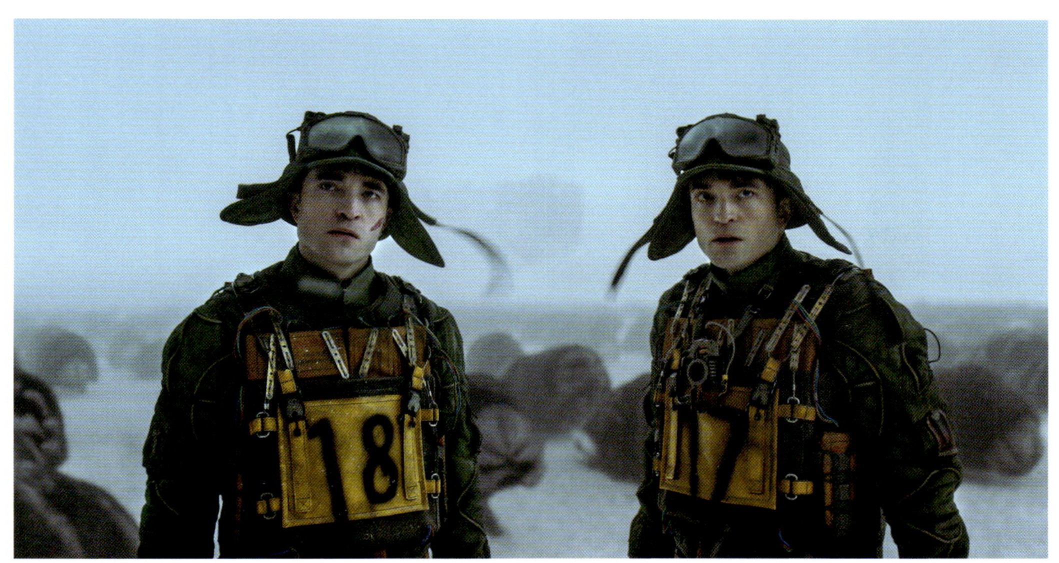

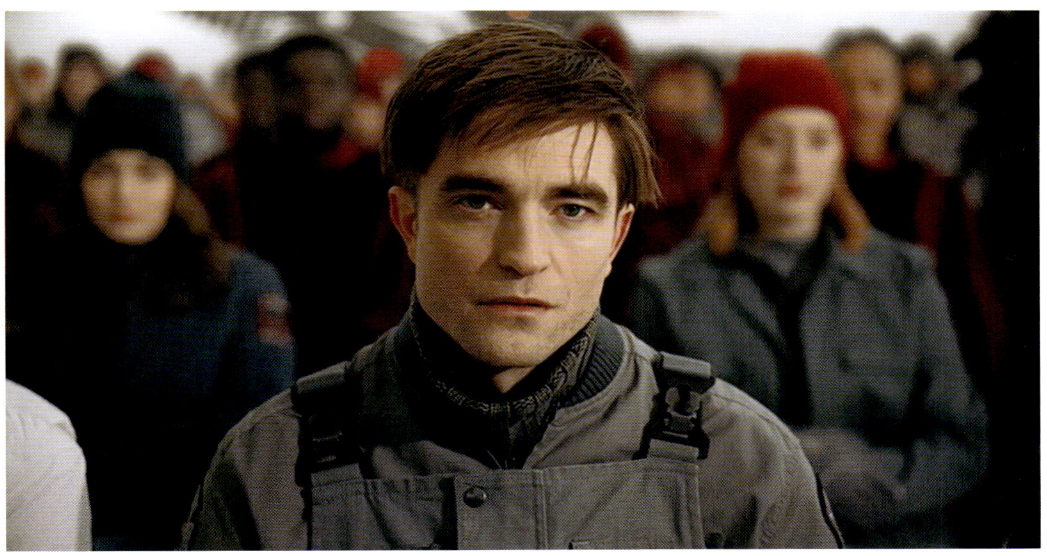

Mickey faces harsh conditions
and contempt, but at the end
of the film, he remains
unbroken. That's the message
I wanted to convey.

INTERVIEW: BONG JOON HO
Nam Lee

This conversation is an edited and condensed version of an interview conducted for this volume on January 9, 2025, in Seoul. It has been translated into English from the original Korean.

Nam Lee: Let's go back to your early childhood memories first. What is your earliest memory of watching a movie?

Bong Joon Ho: I remember when I was very young, my parents took me to see a nature documentary in a movie theater. The scene that stuck with me was of an African monkey in a tree eating fruit that contained alcohol. The monkey would stagger around as if drunk, then tumble down from the tree. I remember the kids clapping because it looked so funny, which stayed with me. Then, around the first or second grade, when I lived in Daegu, my older sister took me to see a rerelease of *The Sound of Music* [1965]. It was the early 1970s. What I remember more than the movie itself is that it was daytime when I went into the theater and dark when I came out, because the movie was three and a half hours long. I remember that felt very strange to me as a child.

NL: Do you think that these memories have influenced your filmmaking in any way?

BJH: I'm not sure. Anyway, we're talking about the theater experience. But in our family, everyone watched television all the time, so I ended up watching a lot of movies on TV that were not really appropriate for my age. They were often heavily censored or edited in Korea, but I was still deeply influenced by them. I devoured everything I could, and that gradually led me to want to be a movie director.

NL: Among the movies you watched on TV as a child, were there any that particularly captured your imagination or a particular genre that did so?

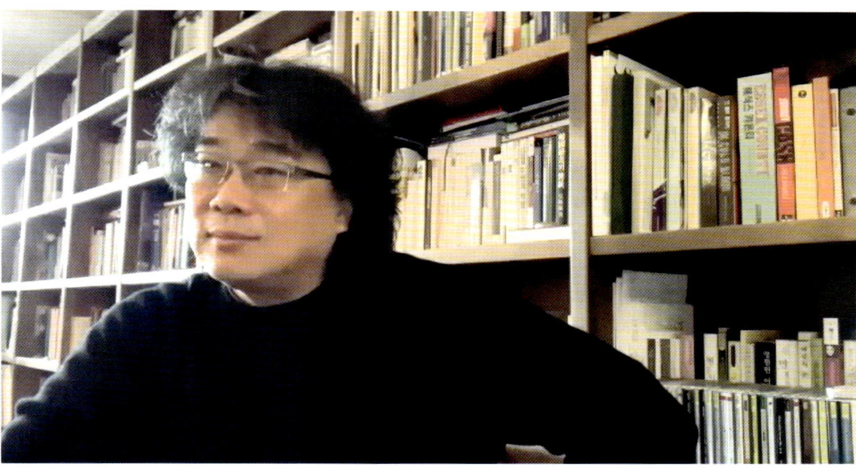

Director Bong Joon Ho, January 9, 2025

BJH: A movie that left me wholly breathless and deeply shocked was Henri-Georges Clouzot's *The Wages of Fear* [1953]. It's a real nail-biter, an incredible thriller. Even seeing it as a kid on a tiny TV, I was overwhelmed by the setting, the dark atmosphere, and the sheer pessimism of it all. I was so caught up in the tension that I didn't even want to go to the bathroom; I almost burst my bladder watching it through to the end. I saw Alfred Hitchcock's *Psycho* [USA, 1960] in the second or third grade. I remember being completely shocked by the plot, how the story unfolded, and the imagery. Those two movies were really intense for me. Then there was Vittorio De Sica's *Bicycle Thieves* [1948], which was often shown on TV. That was probably the first time that I really felt empathy or sadness through a movie, at least on an emotional level. It wasn't an edge-of-your-seat thriller or action movie but one where you get personally involved and emotionally submerged. *Bicycle Thieves* was the first movie that made me feel that kind of cinematic power.

NL: Listening to what you just said, the combination of genre films and the emotional influence of Italian neorealism somewhat represents your cinematic world today.

BJH: Yes. Back then, TV stations used to do their own film programming. MBC [Munhwa Broadcasting Corporation] aired a Sam Peckinpah series when I was in middle school, and since they were Peckinpah movies, you can imagine how much had to be cut. They showed *Straw Dogs* [1971], *The Getaway* [1972], and *Cross of Iron* [1977]. I really liked the idiosyncratic actor James Coburn when I was a kid, and *Cross of Iron* was a World War II movie starring him. They even showed *The Wild Bunch* [1969] on KBS [Korean Broadcasting Service] when I was in high school. I remember being absolutely shocked; they didn't censor a lot of the horrific violence in the climactic explosion. It's a famous sequence in film history, often discussed in the context of editing, and they aired it almost uncut. That had a huge impact on me. I realized, even at a young age, that there are particular thrills and excitements in the technical aspects of filmmaking and film editing.

NL: When you were growing up in the '70s and '80s, Korea's film culture wasn't exactly flourishing, was it?

BJH: This period is often referred to as the dark age of Korean cinema. After the golden era in the 1960s, the '70s and '80s were pretty bleak, and access to foreign films was limited. Under the military dictatorship, the government effectively controlled film imports and distribution. The number of foreign films released each year was limited, and apart from a small number of outstanding auteur directors, Korean cinema at that time was full of low-quality productions. I basically used television as my cinematheque and watched different foreign movies on TV, often dubbed, to overcome this hunger.

NL: You also watched a lot of movies on the American Forces Korea Network [AFKN].

BJH: Yes, AFKN was one of the few channels where we could access foreign films. You heard the voices of American or English-speaking actors—no dubbing—and there was virtually no censorship. At midnight on Fridays, they'd show these adult-oriented movies. Some of them were sophisticated thrillers by Brian De Palma or intense B movies by John Carpenter, but I only realized that much later. Watching movies on the sly on AFKN was a lot of fun. Later, when I got older and joined a university film club, I started watching Taiwanese New Wave films like those of Hou Hsiao-Hsien and Edward Yang. Or I'd seek out classic Japanese films by Akira Kurosawa and Shohei Imamura. That was a conscious effort to study the history of cinema. I also started watching Korean classics, like the incredible works of Kim Ki-young and Kim Soo-yong. But all of that had a deliberate element of learning. The Hitchcock movies I mentioned, or the Peckinpah movies I saw as a kid, that was much more primal. I was just absorbing the movies themselves, which were a total shock to my system. I think that early influence stayed with me.

NL: I also heard that you liked to draw comics when you were young.

Bong Joon Ho, 1974, photographed by his father, Bong Sang Kyung

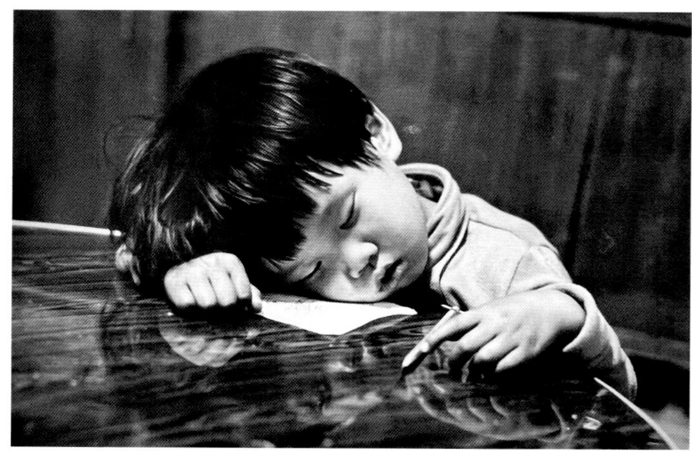

BJH: Yes. [*laughs*]

NL: What kind of comics did you draw?

BJH: There was a time when I seriously considered becoming a cartoonist. In fact, I drew cartoons all through college. Our university had a newspaper, the *Yonsei Chunchu*, and I actually got paid to do cartoons for it. As kids, we had easy access to Japanese manga, and manga like *Doraemon* were popular in Korea. I tried to draw pieces that imitated those famous Japanese comics. When I became a filmmaker, I drew my own storyboards, which reminded me of those days. After all, comics are also about arranging shots and how the frames go together. With storyboarding, I feel like I'm fulfilling my childhood dream of being a cartoonist; it's kind of a pleasant delusion.

NL: Watching movies and drawing comics served as training for filmmaking?

BJH: I never intended it that way, but I grew up loving comics. My father worked in graphic and industrial design, so our house was always full of art books and photo books. He also watched an incredible amount of TV. He was a huge TV drama addict, so the TV was always on, and he never made rules about how much we could watch.

NL: What about the rest of your family? Did your family strongly encourage your creative interests, or did you just pursue them on your own?

BJH: My eldest sister majored in fine arts, my eldest brother majored in English literature, and my mother was a teacher until she married and became a full-time housewife. Her father, Park Tae-won, was a novelist during the Japanese occupation. So, my mother and brother were more into literature, while my father and sister were

Bong's "Chunchu Manpyong" comic, published in the *Yonsei Chunchu*, ca. 1993

more into art. Maybe I, the youngest, became a filmmaker because those two influences merged. Who knows? I decided to be a filmmaker in middle school but rarely mentioned it to anyone, even at home.

NL: Did you actually act on the desire to make films then?

BJH: No. In middle and high school, it was purely theoretical—I read about it in books. At that time, younger scholars like Lee Yong-kwan, Kang Han-sup, Jeon Yang-joon, and Jung Sung-il were publishing articles in film magazines. There were some that were quite in-depth and not always easy to read. In college, I found Professor Kim Yeong-jin on the editorial board of such a magazine, and I also liked Professor Joo Jin-sook's writings. That was my period of deep study and contemplation of film. Then, in the early '90s, I started getting hands-on experience. That's when I really got into it.

NL: When did you get your first camera?

BJH: In terms of still cameras, my father had a very old Minolta at home. Since cameras were so rare and expensive back then, I couldn't just do whatever I wanted with it. When I grew up and went to college, I started using the 120mm camera he used to photograph his artwork—one of those older, big square film types that you look down into from above. It was a Mamiya RB67, an excellent model producing extremely high-resolution images. I started taking pictures with it in college, when I was a member of the Yellow Door film club. My first real experience was with the 8mm camera. There was a time in the '70s and '80s, not only in Korea but worldwide, when 8mm home movie cameras were all the rage. Many of our club members used them because everyone had one at home, like an antique covered in dust. In the early 1990s, only one place in Seoul still developed 8mm film. I later saved up and bought a Hitachi video camera made in Japan, which was considered quite high resolution then. With this big piece of gear over my shoulder, I would animate puppets, film people, record events, everything. Then I went to the film academy and finally got access to the equipment the professionals used. Film is a technology, so becoming familiar with the mechanical process is crucial.

NL: I heard you did a lot of scene and text analysis in the film club. Were there any particularly memorable themes among those you organized and studied in depth?

BJH: Looking back, it was all very amateurish [*laughs*], but I think it helped in its own way. We would question, "Why was the camera placed there? Why was this shot framed at this size? Why was shot B necessary between shots A and C?" Overanalyzing movies isn't always good, but we had this raw, explosive passion for it. We would choose a theme—like murder scenes, kissing scenes, car chases—and study these clips, then spend our evenings drinking and passionately discussing movies. It was an incredibly energetic time in our lives. And we didn't just watch the movies, we also held workshops and made movies ourselves. Nothing was structured for us in the early '90s, so we had to figure everything out on our own.

NL: How did studying at the Korean Academy of Film Arts [KAFA] for a year help you?

BJH: That's where I really mastered the technical side of filmmaking. There were a lot of great film schools in Korea, but KAFA's biggest strength was that the students could use the same equipment that professional filmmakers were using at the time. It was entirely hands-on and the actual mechanics, equipment, and technology of filmmaking became like an extension of my body. We were shooting all the time, loading film, and setting up the lighting ourselves—not only directing but also doing the cinematography and lighting for each other's projects. That's when I really understood how movies are made physically. It felt like rolling around in the mud of film production. Before, it was all about reading and analyzing. Suddenly, I was

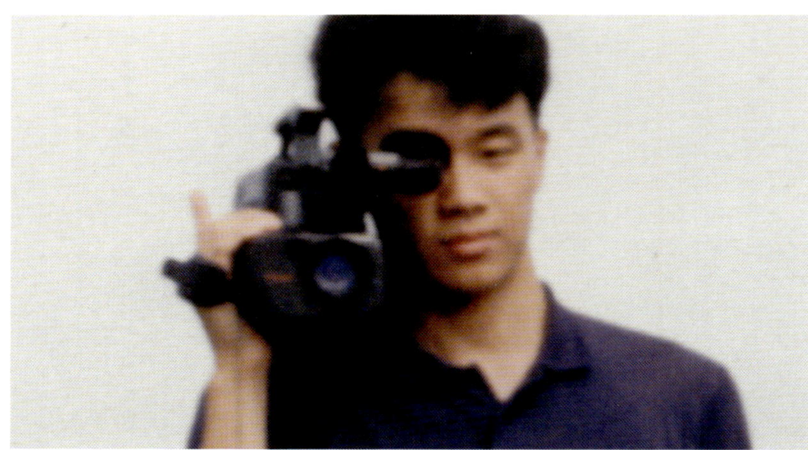

Bong holding his Hitachi 8200 Super VHS camera, ca. 1992

learning how heavy a 24-volt battery can be when I lug it up a mountain, what it feels like to hoist a huge HMI light on my shoulder and race against the setting sun. We experienced physical limitations and had to overcome them to get the images we wanted. We also got a glimpse of what it's like to be on the crew, which is important because we would only be working as directors after that. It was an incredibly intense year but also the happiest time of my life. It was great fun to meet colleagues who were all equally crazy about movies. We weren't tied to any investors or studios; we were blessed just to go out and make movies under the protective umbrella of the school.

NL: Your graduation film, *Incoherence*, received much attention. Can you take us through the process from releasing *Incoherence* to making your first commercial movie?

BJH: That was roughly from 1995 to 2000— four or five years of feeling frustrated, struggling, and going through hardships. [*laughs*]

NL: I heard you also wrote scripts for other directors then.

BJH: That's right. I had to make a living. I got married early and had a child early. Neither my wife nor I had a steady income, so we survived by doing all kinds of freelance work. Nowadays, when you work as an assistant director [AD] in Korea, there are proper salaries and labor standards. But the system was a mess when I was an AD in the late '90s. Frankly, how little we were paid for our work would shock people today. It was a transitional period before we moved from an apprenticeship system to a more professional film industry structure. Life was hard. I wanted to direct my own movie, but the opportunity seemed distant.

NL: How did your first opportunity to direct a movie come about?

BJH: It was through Uno Film, headed by producer Cha Seoung Jae, one of the most prominent producers then. Jang Joon-hwan and I were both part of the directing team for *Motel Cactus*, so we were on their radar. They said, "We've got a submarine action blockbuster called *Phantom*, why don't you guys try to write the script?" At production companies like Uno Film, when they see an assistant or second director who they think shows promise, they watch their short films and give them a script to develop. There's a belief in Korea that to become a director, you have to be able to write or work on a feature-length script first. So, that's how I eventually made *Barking Dogs Never Bite*, and how Jang Joon-hwan made *Save the Green Planet!* [2003]. It was a hard time, but

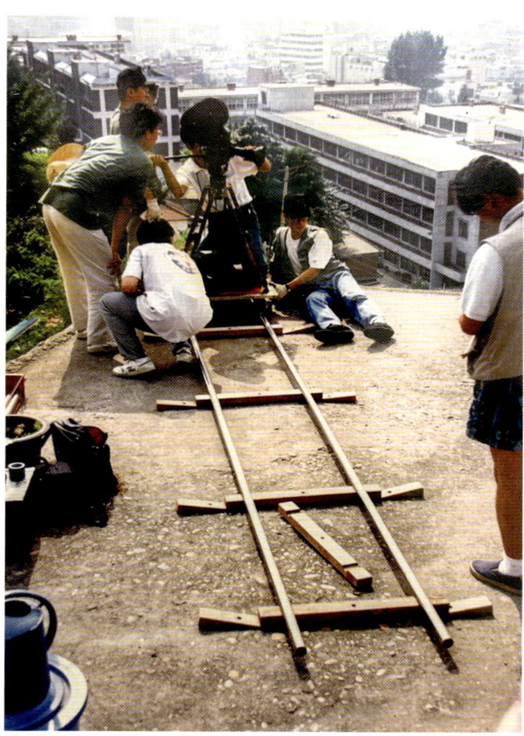

Bong (left) and crew filming *Barking Dogs Never Bite* (2000)

I got through it quickly. Some people spend 10, 15, or even 20 years as assistant directors or second directors. Making my debut feature film just five years out of film school was relatively quick.

NL: You wrote the screenplays for all your movies, including *Barking Dogs Never Bite*, right?

BJH: Yes.

NL: Have you always enjoyed writing?

BJH: I never wanted to be a literary writer, but I wanted to be a comic artist, and comics have dialogue. With screenplays, I have images and sounds in my head that I need to share with the actors and crew, so I write as effectively as possible and describe things vividly so they can understand what I see. I enjoy writing, refining expressions, and choosing the right words. Even when I work with co-writers, I select their best ideas but always write the screenplay myself. I'm the one at the keyboard. Every word comes from me, from the dialogue to the action, so I always do the final typing myself. There's a certain charm and pain in that process. It's the most isolating and agonizing phase, the one I want to avoid the most. But towards the end, when refining the language and polishing the script, there's also a deep sense of satisfaction and exhilaration. And once filming begins, I work with the actors, the cinematographer, and many other experts, which leads to discoveries and ideas I hadn't even considered. The process quickly expands and becomes a collective effort that brings a unique sense of joy.

NL: You mentioned that your movies begin with images and sounds that you carry inside. Could you give a concrete example from one of your films?

BJH: Before I finish a script, I often sketch ideas and share them with conceptual artists. For *The Host*, I had an image [in mind] of a strange creature hanging upside down with its tail wrapped around a bridge over the Han River, like a bat or a cocoon. I'd draw a picture in my notebook of the creature curling up in a weird way, like a rolled cake. Those visual ideas are usually my starting points. It's not just a process of completing the script and then visualizing it. Everything happens simultaneously. For *Mother*, for example, there's a scene of women dancing frantically on a moving bus. That image came first. I knew instinctively that this was how the movie had to end. The whole two-hour story builds to that moment. The narrative is built around getting to that shot.

NL: Was it the same for *Okja*?

BJH: With *Okja*, I'm unsure if it was a hallucination or just my imagination. One rainy day, I was driving near the Isu intersection in Seoul, where the film begins, and I imagined a huge pig under the overpass, sheltering from the rain and looking really sad. I thought, "Why does this pig look so sad?" Then, "Why is it so big?" A big pig suggests so many things. It implies a lot of meat, meaning it has a high market value, but from its own perspective, it's heavy and sad. That's where the whole story idea came from. Similarly, *The Host* started when I thought I saw something strange under the Jamsil Bridge in high school, probably because I was in a bad state from studying for college entrance exams. I never imagined it would become a real movie because it was just too absurd. But as a kid, I loved the Loch Ness Monster and collected articles about it from children's magazines.

NL: Your debut film, *Barking Dogs Never Bite*, is a unique black comedy that satirizes a society where no one follows any rules.

Where did the inspiration for this movie come from?

BJH: As I mentioned before, I had a short but difficult period around 1995. Looking back, I realize that the movie reflects my state of mind at that time. I was anxious and financially unstable and wondered if I could ever become a commercial filmmaker. I wanted to, but I was also afraid. I kept thinking, "Should I stay in independent films to keep the spirit and tone I want?" I had these very naive, binary dilemmas. "I'm making a feature film in Chungmuro, but I have to keep the sensibility I had when making shorts. I can't lose that." No one told me to feel that way, but I was worried and caught in a strange transitional phase. That's why the movie is so weird. It has a semi-amateur feel to it in places. People who like it find that fresh and innocent, but others say, "Isn't this basically a student movie?" I understand why some critics felt that way. It was a time when I didn't know how to define myself, so I flailed around.

What ultimately ended that phase was *Memories of Murder*. At that point, for better or worse, I was a full-fledged director. Instead of focusing on my personal struggles, I had to deal with this huge, real-life serial murder case. So, I took a radically different approach, asking myself, "What is my perspective on this crime event that traumatized so many people? How will I portray it?" That was me growing up. Looking back, *Memories of Murder* was a clean break from *Barking Dogs Never Bite*.

NL: In that sense, it was a break, but in another sense, a recurring motif in all your films is the idea of false assumptions. In *Barking Dogs Never Bite*, the story begins when a dog that has had vocal cord surgery— one that can't bark—is mistaken for a loud barking dog. In *Memories of Murder*, there is a similar misidentification. When you're

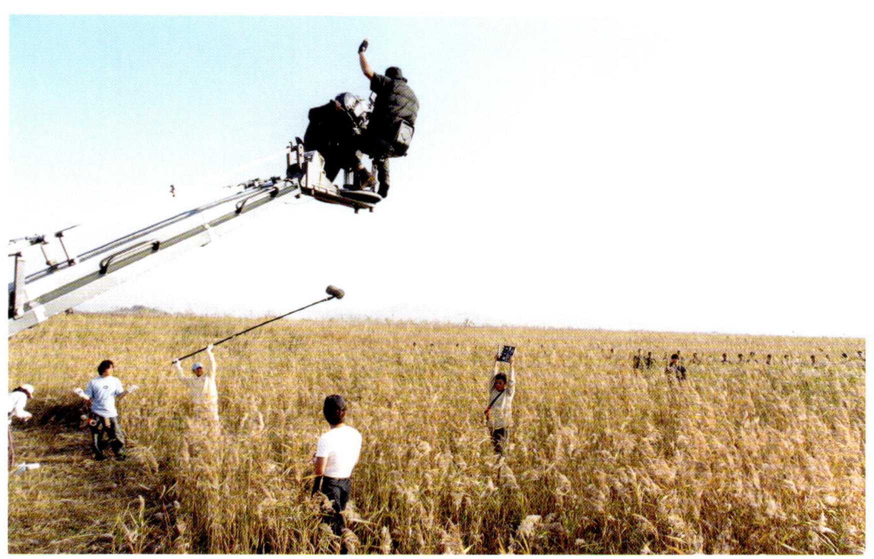

Cast and crew during production of *Memories of Murder* (2003)

writing a screenplay, do you consciously use these devices—false assumptions, reversals, twists—as narrative techniques?

BJH: I think it comes from my personality. I'm not very good at communicating with people. In my movies, you never see the characters achieving honest communication, fundamental understanding, and finally coming together. They keep missing each other's signals and misunderstanding each other, and the misunderstandings double or triple up until, even without a real villain, something tragic happens. *Parasite* works like that, right? It's not that there's a clear villain or evil force, yet it builds to a miserable conclusion. That's why I've always been drawn to the Coen brothers. Their movies are full of misunderstandings and misinterpretations, like in *The Big Lebowski* [1998] or *Burn After Reading* [2008], which revel in that playful confusion with mix-ups and crossed signals. I don't go to that extreme, but my characters still struggle to connect with each other. Strangely enough, I feel a certain reassurance watching them fail to communicate. As the narrative gets more tangled, I get excited by that cinematic tension.

NL: At the same time, as you mentioned, your films often expand into broader social themes. There's always this strong awareness of society.

BJH: Being misunderstood can be very painful. It isolates us and takes away our protection. In *The Host*, the family is mistaken for infected carriers. That is socially isolating. The fear of being isolated and unprotected has always been present in my work. I'm very comfortable portraying anxiety and fear in movies, but I can't do grand, heroic narratives. Some younger directors even tease me about it, like, "You don't really do those sweeping, epic emotions, do you?" And they are right. I tend to feel small, timid, and afraid. Maybe that's why I'm drawn to thrillers and horror movies. Hitchcock films, for example, are full of falsely accused protagonists on the run. That kind of injustice—being falsely accused and having to flee—is something I naturally gravitate towards. In *The Host*, even though the protagonists are kind of clueless, they're good people on the run. The very system that's supposed to help them ends up persecuting them. It's structurally similar to Hitchcock's films but with a stronger social and political dimension.

NL: In Hitchcock's films, misunderstandings are usually resolved in the end, but in your films, they often aren't.

BJH: [*laughs*] Not only unresolved—look at the end of *Parasite*. You can't even explain the incident itself. If you look at the news reports in the movie, there's no way to make sense of it. Why is this man dead on the lawn of a wealthy family, impaled by a strange thing? What happened to the former chauffeur? Why did this seemingly normal man suddenly snap and do what he did? As viewers, we have the whole picture, but no *60 Minutes* investigative report could ever really explain what happened in the world of the movie. There's a horror and despair in it. I made it, but sometimes I think, "This movie is pretty cruel." Maybe I should make a happy movie once in a while.

NL: You recently made the sci-fi movie *Mickey 17*. When you set your films in Korea, they can feel inevitably bleak, frustrating, and dark. I'm curious if sci-fi allows you to explore hope in a way that you can't in other genres and settings. *Snowpiercer* is also bleak, but there's a glimmer of hope at the end. Same with *Okja*.

BJH: I've loved sci-fi since I was a kid. So many cartoons and manga from my childhood were science-fiction themed, robots and space. *Okja* has a bit of a sci-fi feel to it, but with *Snowpiercer* and *Mickey 17*, I got to dive into full-fledged sci-fi. It's been really fulfilling for me. *Snowpiercer* is brutal, as you mentioned. It has violent energy and destruction on the train, but I've always insisted that it has a happy ending—there's hope at the very end. *Mickey 17* is similar. It portrays a cruel world, but it's very hopeful. That's the charm of

Robert Pattinson in
Mickey 17 (2025)

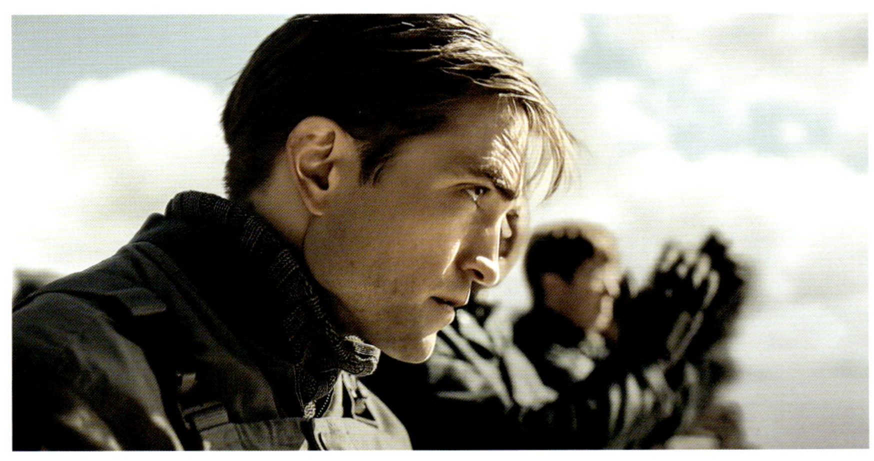

science fiction. It allows me to depict dystopias, worlds even more brutally bleak than ours. At the same time, there is room for abstraction and philosophy. Sci-fi characters can say things that would feel unnatural in other genres. They can express big, conceptual ideas. That's why sci-fi can sometimes explore the essence of human nature more deeply than realism. It also allows me, somewhat shamelessly, to introduce hope into the narrative.

NL: Would you say *Memories of Murder* was your biggest breakthrough movie? It was based on an unsolved serial murder case, as you mentioned. But from a genre point of view, a detective movie where the cops don't catch the killer—that's a massive risk in commercial cinema. When you were writing the script and going through the funding process, did anyone ever ask you to change the ending, or did you ever think of changing it yourself?

BJH: I wrote the script, did the casting, and went out looking for financiers around 2000 or 2001. At that time, gangster or romantic comedies were booming in the Korean film industry and getting all the attention. The thriller genre was basically considered impossible. Previous attempts at Korean thrillers had all failed at the box office. Looking back, it's amazing how much has changed. Today, Korean cinema boasts many thrillers and dark, intense stories. They're popular worldwide, and Korea has practically become a thriller powerhouse, but it was the complete opposite back then. On top of that, when people heard that my movie ended with the killer never being caught, some producers flat-out told me not to make it. Others insisted that since it was a movie, we needed a cathartic ending where justice is served. But producer Cha Seoung Jae, who was in charge, seemed to have real foresight. He told me not to worry about any of that.

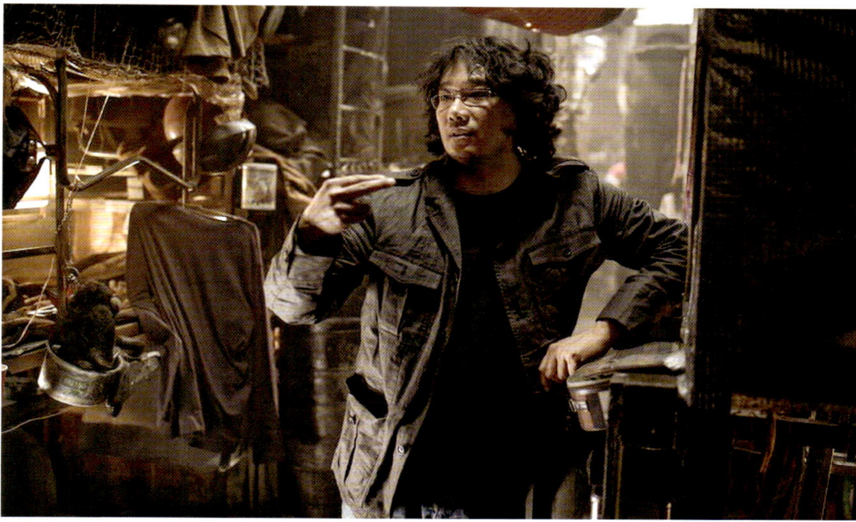

Bong during production of *Snowpiercer* (2013)

He said, "This is a dark story. It's a story of failure. There's no way to make it a happy story." He even encouraged me to let go of my own fear of failure. "Clear your mind, and if you're going to fail, fail spectacularly." It put me completely at ease. That is what a great producer does: They give the director the confidence to move forward.

As for the financing, Song Kang-ho's star power played a significant role. There was a lot of buzz about the script at the time. Our production company was also influential. So, we rode that momentum and got the investment we needed. It was only my second movie, and my debut had been a box-office disaster. But thanks to the production company, the cast, and the reputation of the script, I was able to make it happen. We shot it under really favorable conditions, with extensive support from the company. Our line producer, Kim Moo Ryoung, was incredibly dedicated. We had legendary craftsmen on the set: Our cinematographer, Kim Hyeong-gu, and our lighting director, Lee Kang-san, were already masters in their fields. I was young then and full of passion and energy. It starred Song Kang-ho, Kim Sang-kyung, Kim Roi-ha, and Byun Hee-bong; we also had the late Song Jae-ho and the late Jeon Mi-seon, who have since passed away. All the energy came together in a powerful way. We shot it as if everyone's collective spirit was converging into a single point, without a single misstep, like a molten energy furnace.

NL: The ending was already set, so the focus became "Why couldn't the detectives catch the killer?"

BJH: Why did we all fail? It feels like we had no choice but to find the answer in the context of the 1980s. That era was even darker than the murders themselves.

NL: When you started writing the script, did you plan to set it in the 1980s, or did that evolve along the way?

BJH: The movie is based on a hugely successful and brilliant play by Kim Kwang-rim, but the play doesn't focus on the sociopolitical landscape of the time. It's more about confronting the nature of true evil, how difficult it is to reach the truth, and how powerless humans become in the face of that challenge. The play conveys that with overwhelming intensity. It's an incredible piece of theater. But as a filmmaker, I wanted to capture the atmosphere of the 1980s. The darkness of the era overshadowed the crime and blurred the two. That's why I created sequences like the blackout drill. It took me a long time to come up with that idea. I spent six months researching the actual case, going to the National Assembly Library to read old newspapers. And when you do that, of course, you end up reading about more than just the case. There would be news about the 1986 Asian Games, and below that would be posters of movies coming out at the time. I really got a sense of the whole era, different than just typing keywords into an internet search as we do

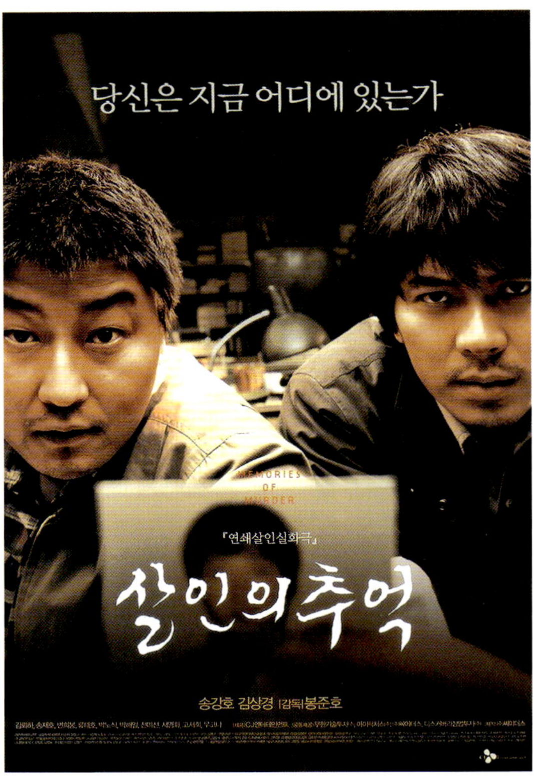

Korean poster for
Memories of Murder

today. That method of research influenced me a lot.

I also had a friend, the British film critic Tony Rayns, who knew I loved comic books and gave me the graphic novel *From Hell* by Alan Moore. It's about Jack the Ripper, one of history's most infamous serial killers. It's also an unresolved case. Five women who were sex workers were brutally murdered in Whitechapel, London, in the 1800s. There are countless theories about it, and in the graphic novel you see a stark depiction of how dark English society was in the Victorian era. It isn't just about the murders but expands into a story about the entire society of the time. Around that time, *Barking Dogs Never Bite* was invited to the London Film Festival, so I went and visited Whitechapel when I was already deep in research for *Memories of*

Murder. As I walked through the dark streets of London, I think that was the moment the idea took hold: Why did we fail? Why couldn't we catch the killer? The answer had to be found in the darkness of the 1980s military dictatorship. That's when the script really started to take shape.

NL: In your early films—*Barking Dogs Never Bite*, *Memories of Murder*, and *The Host*—the shadow of the 1980s looms large. Of course, *Memories of Murder* is explicitly set in the 1980s, but even *Barking Dogs Never Bite* has that bit with the story of Mr. Kim, the boiler repairman in the basement. And even in *The Host*, we can see many iconic images from the 1980s woven throughout. You entered the university in 1988. Does the 1980s have a special meaning for you? Do you consider yourself part of the so-called 386 generation, or do you see yourself as born a little later, with a slightly different cultural perspective?

BJH: I'm technically at the end of the 386 generation, but I always had a strong otaku streak—I was really into Japanese manga and anime and read many Korean fringe comics— and I was pretty isolated in my otaku-like world. Still, I couldn't escape the social and political turmoil around me. I was there during the June Democratic Struggle in 1987. I was a high school senior, but I had a deep dislike for the military dictatorship, probably more than most. My father had some of that feeling too. He worked at what was then called the Korea Design & Packaging Center, a government agency in the field of design. An army general with no background in the field was appointed by a crony to head the design center. You can imagine how stressed my father must have been, working directly under someone like that. He'd sit down to dinner with us and start complaining about this guy. I realized, even as a kid, that we were living under a military dictatorship and some

strange ex-soldier who knew nothing about design was bothering my father every day. When I got to high school, they appointed a Korea Military Academy graduate as our principal—a soldier with no educational background. He'd make us do army drills after class, out in the dusty schoolyard under the blazing sun, wearing training uniforms and shouting "Salute!" while carrying plastic rifles; that sort of thing. It's so absurd when I think about it now. Of course, antipathy built up. Our lived experience under that oppressive regime drove me and my high school classmates to take to the streets during the June Democratic Struggle in '87. We went to Euljiro and mingled with the college protesters, pretending to be university students. Some shopkeepers gave us strawberry milk or little moon-shaped pastries. Everyone across the country was united in support. At six p.m. on June 10, 1987, every car in Seoul honked in protest at the same time, and this massive sound of horns just washed over the city. It was absolutely electrifying. How can I even describe this moment?

NL: You remember it so vividly.

BJH: Yes, it was the thrill of revolution. Even though I was an otaku who stayed home and read comics all day, I went out in the streets to experience it. When I went to the university, I wasn't really interested in sociology but somehow ended up studying it. Being in that department allowed me to meet many fascinating people who were attuned to political and social issues, and hanging out with them meant I always had one foot in that political context. I had one foot in the otaku world and one foot in this sociopolitical world.

NL: This social awareness really comes through in your work. For example, *Snowpiercer* and *Parasite* both put class issues front and center. In *Snowpiercer*, it's sci-fi, so the people at the top talk about banding together. But when we get to *Parasite*, there's no solidarity at all—poor people are fighting each other just to survive. You have this way of capturing the essence of our times with sharp precision, like a cinematic sociologist.

BJH: Still, I want all that to come through individual characters. I don't like to start a movie with a political slogan or banner already raised. I want it to begin with a unique person in a specific situation, which is how *The Host* was. *Snowpiercer* is more conceptual. It started as a French graphic novel [*Le Transperceneige*, 1982] with a very distinctive premise: a train is divided into classes, with the rich in the front and the poor in the back. Because it starts with this kind of almost comic-book setup, there's something more blunt about it.

NL: We haven't even gotten to *The Host* yet. It broke box office records in Korea and was popular in the United States. But even though it's a monster movie, it avoids the typical formula and subverts the genre. Did you decide from the beginning to reveal the monster right away instead of hiding it?

BJH: How can I put this? I love genre movies, but at the same time I always feel the urge to rebel against them. I like to break conventions—it's almost a mischievous instinct. In most monster movies, you barely see the creature for the first 40 to 50 minutes. The buildup is so slow, and the movie is practically over by the time you finally get a full reveal. I hated that. So I had this bold idea: Within the first 15 minutes, I'm going to show the whole monster in broad daylight. It wasn't just a bravado choice; it perfectly fits the story's structure. There's an initial shock when the monster appears, but the real protagonists are the family. They get bizarrely sucked into this mess and get no protection from society or the system. It takes on a

political dimension, including US involvement with Agent Yellow as the origin of the monster itself—this was inspired by the McFarland incident of 2000, when the US military polluted the Han River with formaldehyde. So, the focus expands from the monster to the family to the society that harasses them both, and then to the larger political forces behind it all. That expanding narrative structure dovetailed with my determination to reveal the monster right up front. It fits both the story and the genre elements.

NL: Compared to something like Godzilla, the monster in *The Host* feels smaller, like it is waddling around.

BJH: Right. When I described it to people then, I said it was about the size of a city bus, maybe a little bigger. If a creature of that size is running around, it's still threatening, but it's only a little bigger than an elephant. It's dangerous but still feels grounded in reality. Creatures like Godzilla go around smashing buildings, but once we get to that scale, it moves into a completely different cinematic territory. *The Host* takes place in an everyday

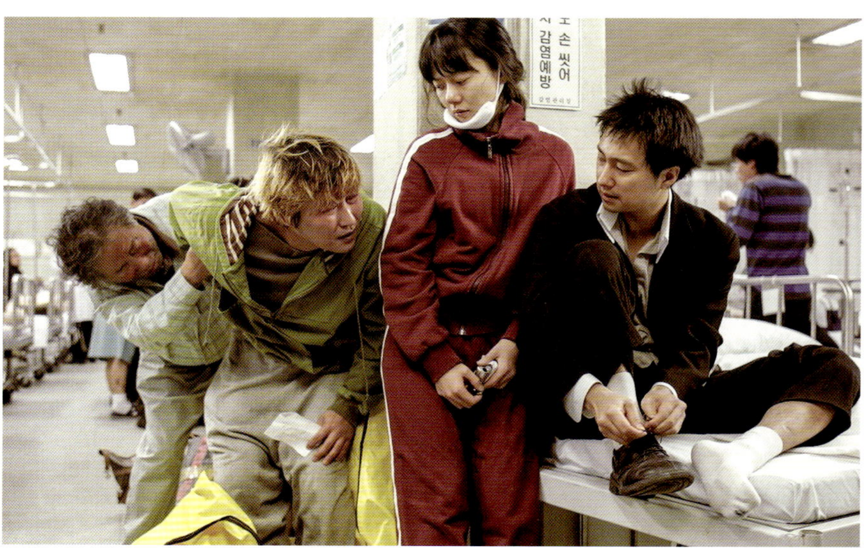

From left: Byun Hee-bong, Song Kang-ho, Bae Doona, and Park Hae-il in *The Host* (2006)

setting, the Han River, a space we all recognize. That contrast—something bizarre appearing in a familiar, everyday place—was central to the movie's tone. The unique aspect was that instead of killing its victims, the creature carries them away like a bird storing food for its nest or to feed its young. It turned the movie into a kidnapping story. It becomes a story about these families trying to rescue the kidnapped child.

NL: In most monster movies, the experts gather for a strategy meeting as soon as a creature appears—

BJH: The military shows up, the scientists, intelligence agencies—

NL: But not in this movie.

BJH: It's just a clueless snack shop owner. That's where I really wanted to break away from the usual monster movie formula.

NL: *Mother* also shows that when no help is available, ordinary people have to do the investigation themselves. That kind of narrative appears in a lot of your films. Your stories often focus on marginalized people who can't rely on the authorities, so they take on these overwhelming tasks and stumble through them.

BJH: In *Memories of Murder*, these rural detectives are doing haphazard police work at a time when no one even knew what profiling was. DNA testing was just being introduced, and they are saddled with a case that is beyond their abilities. Similarly, in *Mother*, the mother herself must investigate the crime like a detective. These powerless or underresourced characters are forced by circumstance to struggle along with little support from the system. I think that's where the real drama comes from. Isn't that the situation most audiences find themselves in?

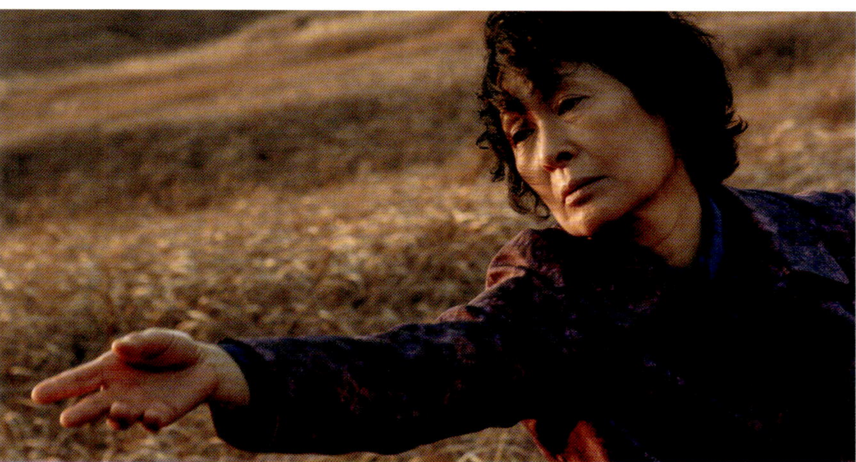

Kim Hye-ja in *Mother* (2009)

Isn't that the more natural reality? People with superhero-level powers, or those at the center of the system who wield their authority, are so rare in reality.

NL: We've talked about so many things that we haven't really touched on your technical style. In *Memories of Murder*, you start with these golden rice fields and a bright blue sky, and then gradually the color fades out, and you end up practically in monochrome, right?

BJH: Yes, exactly.

NL: In *Mother*, you used 2.35:1 CinemaScope for the first time, even though it's not a very dynamic movie. What was behind that decision?

BJH: When we were shooting *The Host*, some of the crew, like cinematographer Kim Hyeong-gu, would ask, "Shouldn't we go widescreen, 2.35:1?" After all, the Han River is so vast. Maybe it's my contrarian streak, but since it wasn't a typical monster blockbuster— rather a sad, somewhat unhappy family drama—I wanted a format that emphasized the characters more. Besides, the main location is the drainage pit where Hyun-seo, played by Ko Asung, is imprisoned. How will she escape, and how will her family try to rescue her? The monster's lair is the key location of the movie, where all the tension and pressure starts, and it's a very vertical space. It wasn't the horizontal expanse of the Han River that was important but the vertical feel of the monster's lair, along with the complicated structures like the storm drains and bridge piers. I felt that the vertical dimension was more important, so we went with 1.85:1.

On the other hand, *Mother* is not spectacular in the sense of huge set pieces; it focuses on the psychology of the character. The neighborhood we shot in was very small and cramped. Maybe it was my contrarian side again, but I wanted the powerful effect of doing close-ups in 2.35:1 where someone's chin or forehead might be cut off—something intense, especially since Kim Hye-ja's eyes are so expressive. There's an incredible depth of emotion, energy, and nuance in her gaze, and that's how I wanted to capture it. When we shoot that way, 2.35:1 leaves these weird blank spaces on either side. This out-of-focus background can create a sense of unease. I shared this idea with the crew, and our cinematographer, Hong Kyung Pyo, went so far as to bring back special lenses from Germany; I think they were Hawk lenses. They are made by a company of German masters and were used in Steven Spielberg's *Munich* [2005] and some other movies. They're quite large, and from the moment Hong Kyung Pyo chose these lenses, you could tell that *Mother* would have a very distinctive visual texture.

NL: You put so much effort into finding locations for *Memories of Murder*, *Mother*, and *Barking Dogs Never Bite*. But for *Parasite* you seem to have done a lot of shooting on sets. I'd love to hear how that came about.

BJH: About 90% of *Parasite* was shot on sets. When I hold Q&A sessions in Korea or other countries, people are always shocked to learn that all the sets were built. It's not like [director] Lee Myung-se's very stylized, beautiful sets that deliberately present themselves as sets. The rich family's house and the poor family's house—even the street in front of it, and the whole neighborhood, was a set, which surprises people even more. Of course, when they realize that it has to flood in the rain sequence, they think, "Ah, of course," but visually, no one can tell. They would never imagine that we would go so far as to build all that. It shows how high the quality of Korean production design has become. It's a blend of sets and CG [computer graphics], and the audience barely noticed. When I went to Cannes, I spoke with Alejandro González Iñárritu and the other jury members, and later with filmmakers in the US, and none of the experts even picked up on it.

It's not that we were going for the aesthetics of a set, but I really wanted the perfect location. Since it was impossible to find—imagine getting permission to shoot in a rich family's house, and the exact layout

Crew on the set of *Parasite* (2019)

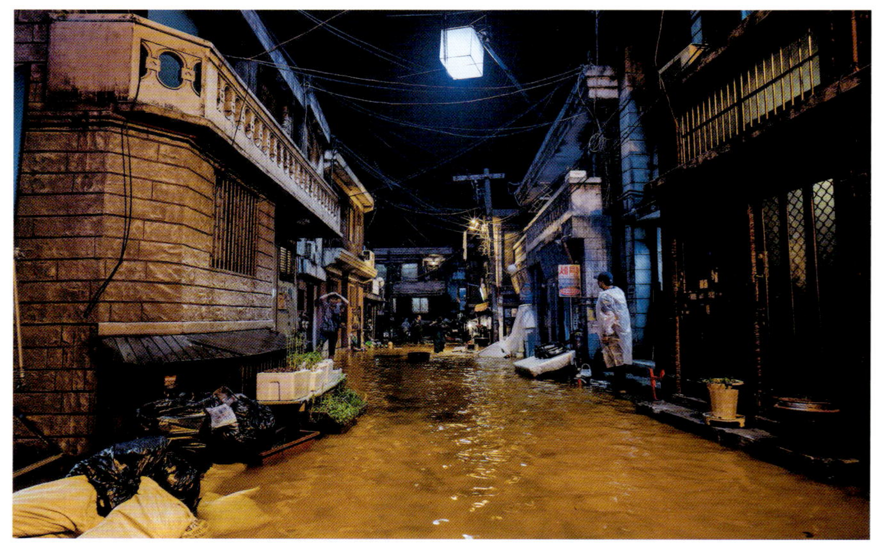

we needed didn't exist anyway—we had to build it. This wealthy house is about 60% of the movie. It's crucial that the characters' movements and blocking lines are laid out just right, otherwise the storytelling doesn't work. From the kitchen, if someone kicks something, that person has to be hidden from a certain angle. If the Kim family is hiding when the former housekeeper, Moon-gwang, comes through the front door, there has to be a place for them to hide. Without that precise spatial arrangement, we can't move the plot forward. The production designer created all the textures and details of the house, but the basic angles and movement of the characters had to come from me in the script. The Kims needed a way to slip out from under the table and exit through the garage, for example. All of the plot is tightly woven with physical constraints in mind. So, to make the story work, we had no choice but to build this particular set, and yet it had to look so natural on screen that no one would know it was fake. Sometimes, in foreign Q&As, I would even joke and lie about it. I'd say, "Oh, we shot in this really luxurious mansion. The owner was a huge cinephile, so he let us use the space. We were so lucky." [*laughs*] I don't know if I later clarified that it was a joke, I can't remember exactly, but I definitely said that somewhere.

Still, I love shooting on location. When we discover a location offering cinematic excitement, cinematographer Hong Kyung Pyo and I get this rush. I enjoy traveling to find those places, and I experienced that excitement a lot while working on *Okja* and *Mother*. *Parasite* even has some of that: During the rainstorm, the family walks from the rich house back to their own home in the downpour, which becomes a kind of short road-movie sequence, and those are all real locations put together. It's only about 10% of the movie, but we combined several very carefully chosen places. The villages are scattered in different parts of Seoul.

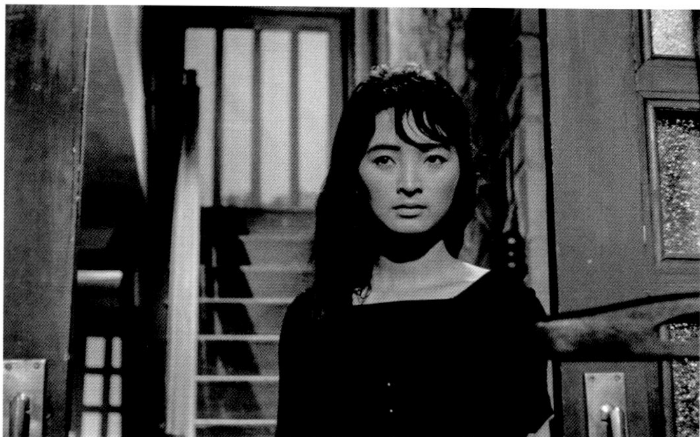

The Housemaid (1960), directed by Kim Ki-young

NL: You've mentioned that *Parasite* was inspired by Kim Ki-young's *The Housemaid* [1960]. When we compare the genre directors of the 1960s and '70s with Bong Joon Ho, the contemporary genre filmmaker, what similarities and differences do you see?

BJH: There was a time when I often met with director Lee Chang-ho. He once compared me to Lee Man-hee, and that was a great honor for me. Lee Man-hee didn't only make genre movies, but he had a strong mastery of genre. If you look at his *The Evil Stairs* [1964], it's incredibly fascinating and powerful. On *Parasite*, my assistant director and I kept saying, "This is a staircase movie. The stairs are paramount." The stairs are central to every important point in the movie. Stairs lead down to the hidden bunker. The stairs leading from the first floor to the second floor in the mansion, and the stairs in the neighborhood, are related to the idea of rising or falling in social status.

One of the movies that best used this concept was Kim Ki-young's *The Housemaid*. It was released around the same time as Joseph Losey's *The Servant* [1963], which also has crucial stairway imagery. And though the context is very different, Hitchcock's *Psycho* has some very memorable staircase scenes. But *The Housemaid*—the title alone suggests a story about class. I always recommend it to foreign directors, and I'm proud that it inspired me, because it's part of the tradition of Korean cinema. I discovered Kim Ki-young relatively late. Even during my days in the Yellow Door film club, I hadn't seen much of his work. The real turning point came around 1995, when Korea's first cable movie channel, CATCH ON, had a monthlong retrospective of Kim Ki-young's films. It was an incredible treasure trove of work: *Io Island* [1977], *Killer Butterfly* [1978], *Hunting of Fools* [1984], *Woman of Fire* 1971], *The Insect Woman* [1972], and so on. I recorded everything on VHS tapes and built up my own personal library. I was hooked and totally amazed to learn that someone was making movies like that in the '70s and '80s. I thought, "If he'd been born in Europe, he'd be on the same level as Luis Buñuel or Hitchcock." His bold, singular compositions, the energy in the way he arranged shots, the uninhibited use of color, these experimental images, this explosive palette, the uncontrolled and unpredictable progression of the narrative, the frank depiction of human desire—it all felt overwhelming.

NL: So, last question. *Mickey 17* is your first Hollywood studio movie, right? How was that experience?

BJH: Among the movies that excited me when I was young, I obviously watched a lot of Warner Bros. titles. They are really one of the old, classic studios like Paramount or Universal, part of that legendary studio system. Even though it's my first studio movie, a Warner Bros. movie, *Mickey 17* is a continuation of what I've always done. It's a very human sci-fi movie. The characters are absolutely pathetic; there's no other word for it. It's full of sad, stupid, and humorously pathetic people. How can I put it—a sci-fi movie with foot odor? [*laughs*] That's what

we used to joke about while making it. The protagonist is played by Robert Pattinson, who is essentially acting two roles. Or maybe it's one role? It's technically one person, but it's also two because he's playing Mickey 17 and Mickey 18, and their personalities are totally different. So, it's character-driven sci-fi, and there are creatures—after they migrate to another planet, these terrifying creatures show up and have their own story. As you'll see, it's still very much my own style of movie. The characters and their actions are familiar to my work. When you see it, you'll probably think, "There he goes, doing the same things he's always done." [*laughs*]

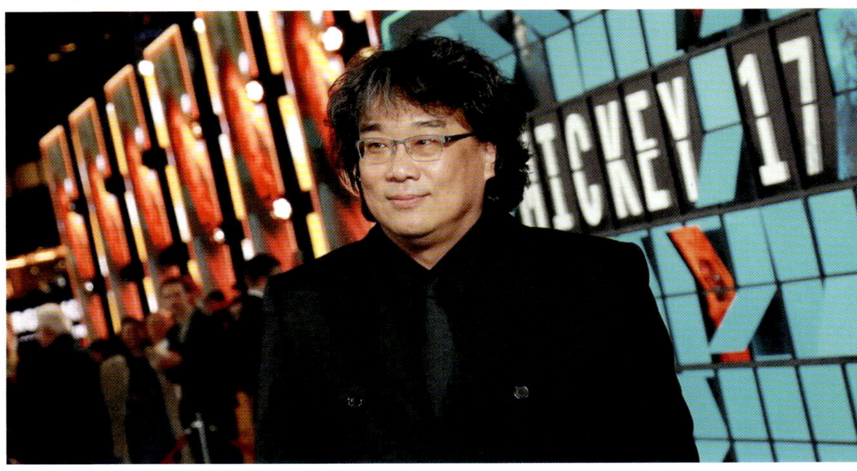

Bong Joon Ho at the world premiere of *Mickey 17*, February 13, 2025, in London

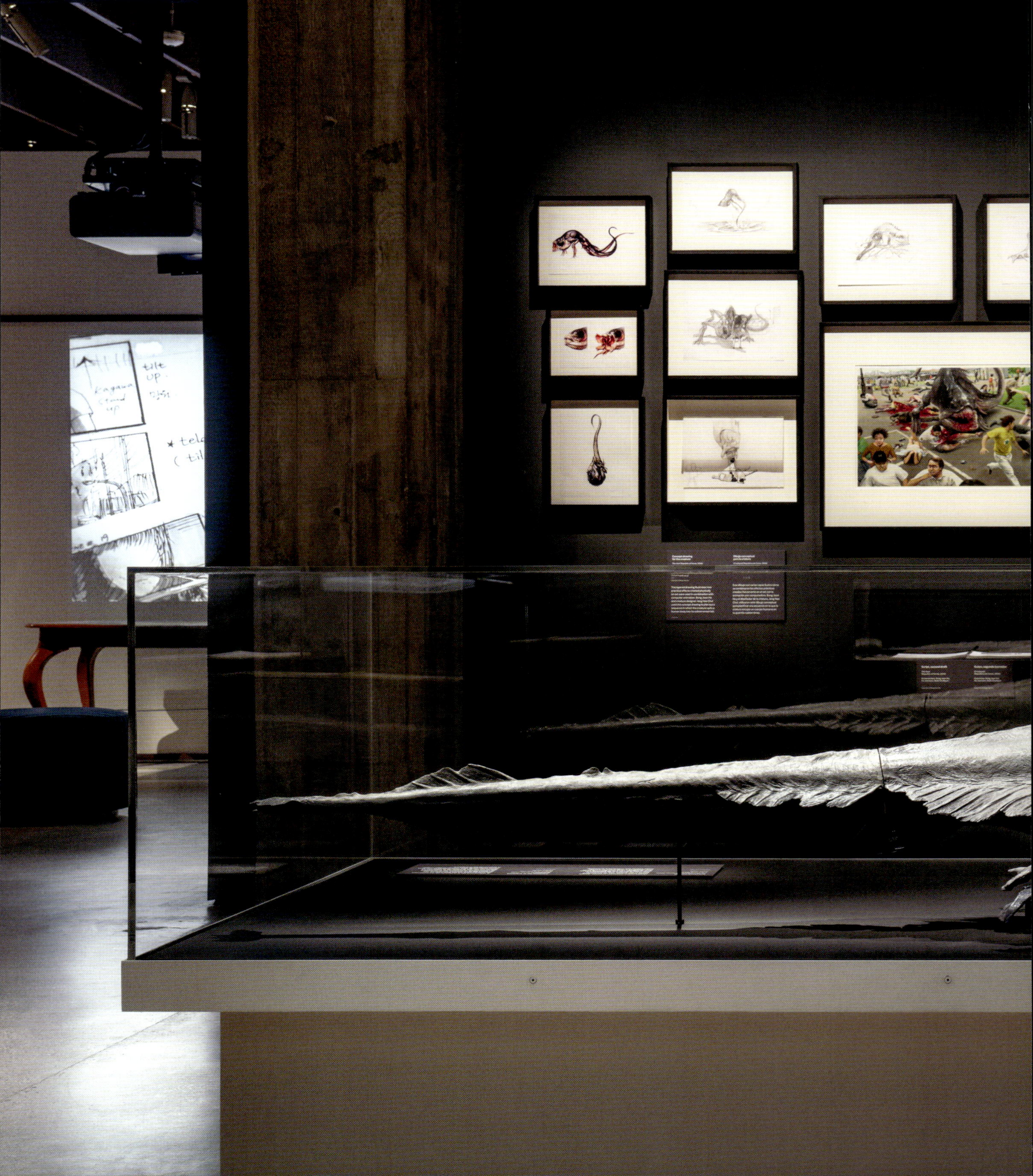

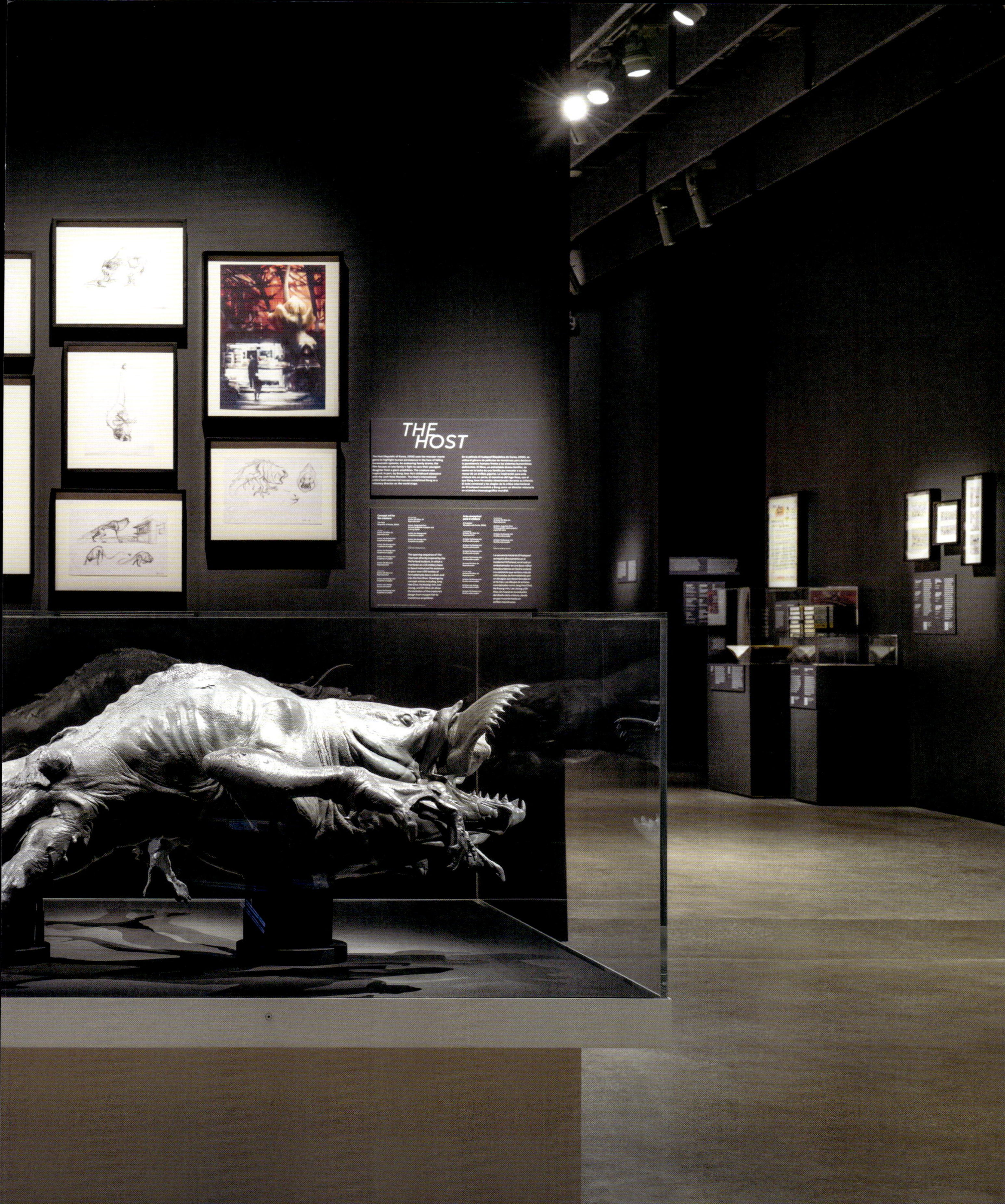

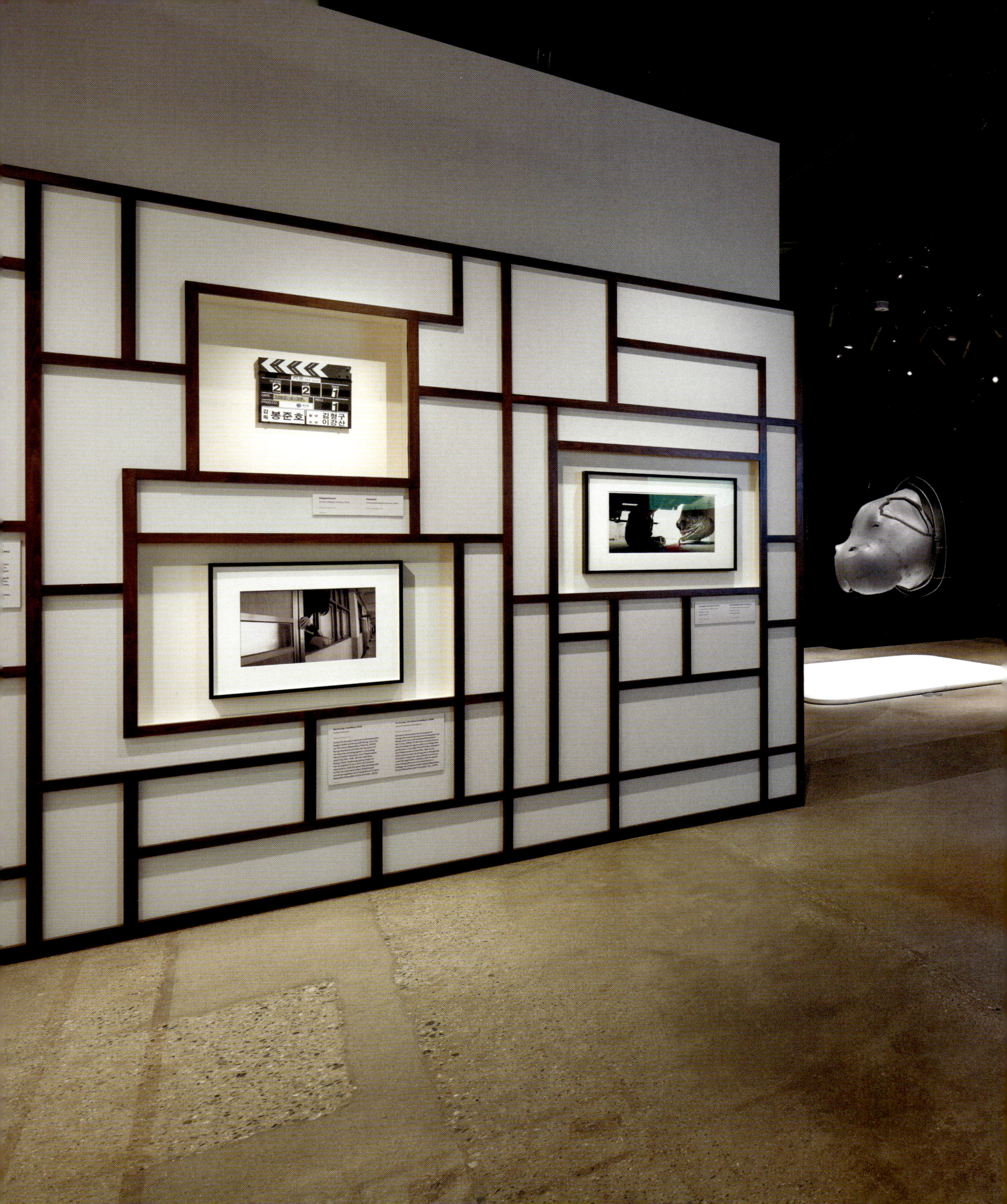
봉준호
김형구
이강산

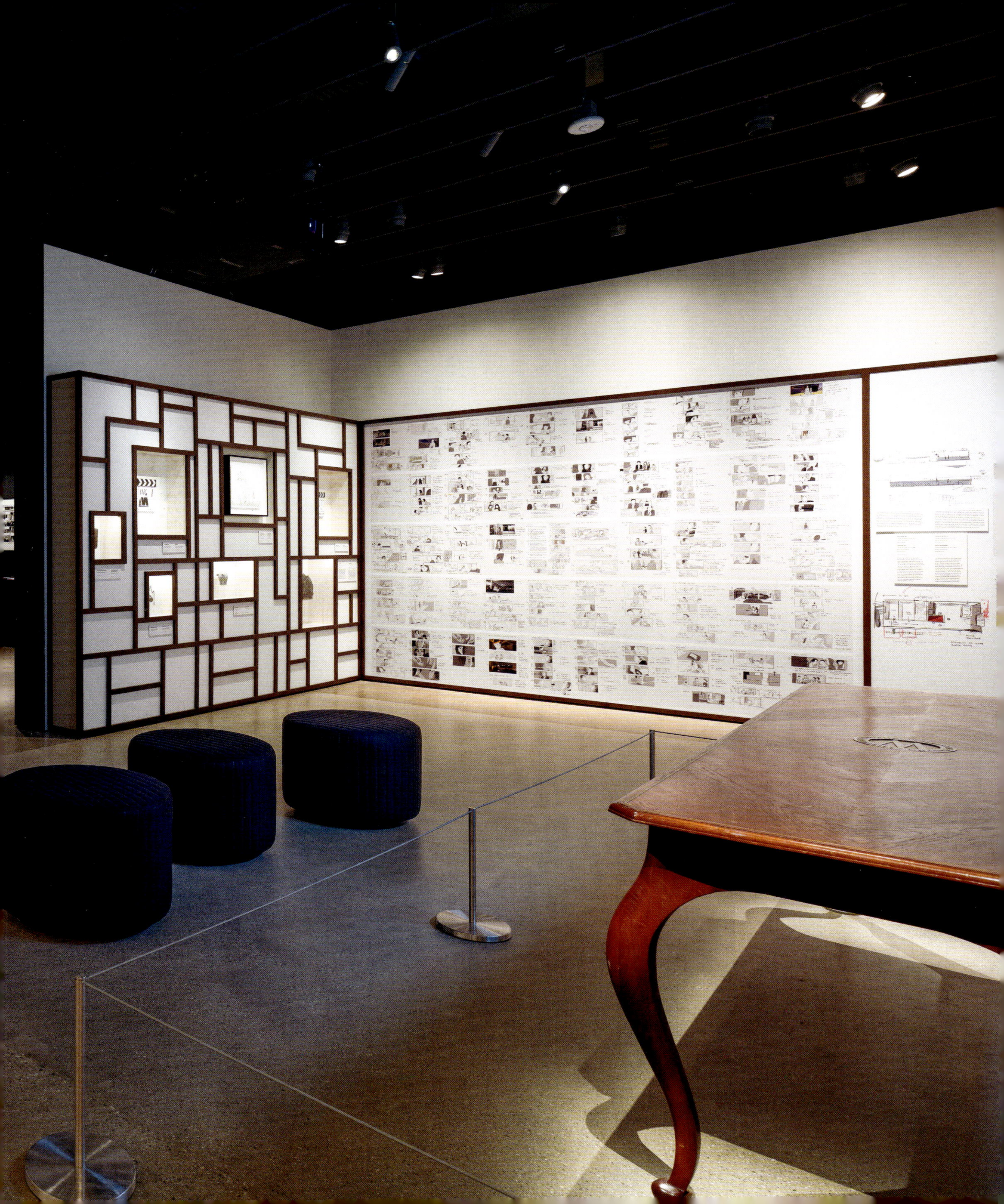

CONTRIBUTORS

Dooho Choi produced *Mickey 17* (2025), *Okja* (2017), and *Snowpiercer* (2013).

Choi Woo-shik (Edward Choi) was born in South Korea and emigrated to Canada at the age of 11. He returned to Korea in 2010 and, although not trained as an actor, started auditioning for film and television roles. In 2014, he won Actor of the Year at the Busan International Film Festival for his role in the independent film *Set Me Free* (2014). He subsequently appeared in films including *Train to Busan* (2016), *Okja* (2017), *The Witch: Part 1–The Subversion* (2018), *Parasite* (2019), and *Wonderland* (2024).

Lee Isaac Chung, the son of Korean immigrants, grew up on a farm in rural Arkansas. His acclaimed film *Minari* (2020) won Sundance's Grand Jury Prize and a Golden Globe and earned six Oscar nominations. His 2024 blockbuster *Twisters* achieved the highest opening weekend ever for a natural disaster film. Chung also directed the feature film *Munyurangabo*, which premiered at Cannes in 2007, and episodes of the Disney+ series *The Mandalorian* and *Star Wars: Skeleton Crew*. He currently resides in Los Angeles with his family.

Toni Collette made her breakout performance as the lead in P. J. Hogan's *Muriel's Wedding* (1994). She received an Academy Award nomination for her role in *The Sixth Sense* (1999) and had starring roles in *Velvet Goldmine* (1998), *About a Boy* (2002), *Little Miss Sunshine* (2006), and *Miss You Already* (2015). Additional film credits include *Hereditary* (2018), *Knives Out* (2019), *I'm Thinking of Ending Things* (2020), *Nightmare Alley* (2021), and *Mafia Mamma* (2023), which she also produced. Collette won an Emmy and a Golden Globe for her lead role in the Showtime series *United States of Tara* and earned a Golden Globe nomination for her lead role in the Netflix

miniseries *Unbelievable*. Her most recent films are *Juror #2* (2024) and *Mickey 17* (2025).

Guillermo del Toro is a Mexican filmmaker, actor, author, and artist whose work is characterized by elements of genre, sci-fi, fantasy, noir, and horror, and meticulously prepared, often operatic, audiovisual tableaux. His Oscar-winning films include *Pan's Labyrinth* (2006); *The Shape of Water* (2017), which earned him Oscars for Best Picture and Directing; and *Guillermo del Toro's Pinocchio* (2022), which won Best Animated Feature. His work has also garnered multiple Golden Globes and BAFTA Awards, as well as prizes at international festivals including Venice and Cannes. His upcoming film is an adaptation of Mary Shelley's *Frankenstein*, a passion project of his since childhood.

Dede Gardner and Jeremy Kleiner are two-time Academy Award–winning producers and co-presidents of Brad Pitt's Plan B Entertainment. Their body of work includes several Oscar-nominated and -winning films such as RaMell Ross's *Nickel Boys* (2024), Sarah Polley's *Women Talking* (2022), Andrew Dominik's *Blonde* (2022), Lee Isaac Chung's *Minari* (2020), and Barry Jenkins's *If Beale Street Could Talk* (2018) and *Moonlight* (2016). Recent features include Bong Joon Ho's *Mickey 17* (2025), Jon Watts's *Wolfs* (2024), and Tim Burton's *Beetlejuice Beetlejuice* (2024). Recent television projects include the Netflix series *Adolescence*.

Catherine George is a costume designer who was born in Belfast, Northern Ireland, and is now based in New York City. She has worked with Bong Joon Ho on *Snowpiercer* (2013), *Okja* (2017), and *Mickey 17* (2025). Previous credits include Lynne Ramsay's *We Need to Talk About Kevin* (2011) and *Die, My Love* (2025). She also designed the costumes for Jim Jarmusch's films *Paterson* (2016), *The Dead Don't Die* (2019), and the upcoming

Father, Mother, Sister, Brother. Her work in television includes the pilot episode of *Succession*, directed by Adam McKay, and the miniseries *The Night Of*, directed by Steven Zaillian.

Dan Glass has served as production visual effects supervisor on films ranging from *The Matrix: Reloaded* (2003) and *The Matrix: Revolutions* (2003) to *Batman Begins* (2005), *The Tree of Life* (2011), *Cloud Atlas* (2012), and *Mickey 17* (2025). He has worked with many esteemed film directors, including Bong Joon Ho, the Wachowskis, Christopher Nolan, Quentin Tarantino, George Miller, and Terrence Malick. Glass directed episodes for the Netflix series *Sense8*. He has also served as chief creative officer for Method Studios and global executive creative director for DNEG VFX.

Hong Kyung Pyo (Alex Hong) is a director of photography who has played a major role in the development of contemporary Korean cinema. He has shot over 30 features, including *The Foul King* (2000), *Il Mare* (2000), *Save the Green Planet!* (2003), *Tae Guk Gi: The Brotherhood of War* (2004), *M* (2007), *Mother* (2009), *Snowpiercer* (2013), *Sea Fog* (2014), *The Wailing* (2016), *Burning* (2018), *Parasite* (2019), *Broker* (2022), *Harbin* (2024), and the upcoming *Hope*.

Jung Jaeil began playing piano and guitar at a young age and joined the well-known alternative rock band GIGS as a teenager. A self-taught composer, he created his first solo album in 2004 and wrote his first original score for the film *Life Is Cool* (2008). He collaborated with Bong Joon Ho on *Okja* (2017), *Parasite* (2019), and *Mickey 17* (2025), and he received an Emmy nomination for his score for the Netflix series *Squid Game*. He has also worked with directors Kore-eda Hirokazu, on *Broker* (2022), and James Sweeney, on *Twinless* (2025).

Darius Khondji is a Paris-based cinematographer with a four-decade career collaborating with some of the world's most acclaimed filmmakers. Khondji's work has garnered two Academy Award nominations, three César Award nominations, and a BAFTA Award nomination. His credits include *Evita* (1996), which earned him his first Oscar nomination; *Se7en* (1995); *Panic Room* (2002); *Amour* (2012); *The Immigrant* (2014); and *The Lost City of Z* (2017). Other works include *Okja* (2017), *Uncut Gems* (2019), and *Bardo, False Chronicle of a Handful of Truths* (2022), the latter of which earned him an Oscar nomination, an ASC nomination, and a Silver Frog award at Camerimage. His recent work includes *Mickey 17* (2025) and the upcoming films *Marty Supreme* and *Eddington*.

Lee Hajun worked with Bong Joon Ho on the production design of *Okja* (2017) and *Parasite* (2019), designing spaces as an important axis of the story. A graduate of the Korea National University of Arts, he made his debut as a production designer with *Shadows in the Palace* (2007) and went on to work on films including *The Housemaid* (2010), *The Thieves* (2012), *The Face Reader* (2013), *Sea Fog* (2014), *The Beauty Inside* (2015), *Believer* (2018), *The Night Owl* (2022), *Alienoid: Return to the Future* (2024), and *My Name Is Loh Kiwan* (2024), among others.

Miky Lee is the vice chairwoman of CJ Group. As the founder of CJ's entertainment and media division and a founding investor in DreamWorks SKG, she has been instrumental in shaping the international cultural landscape. Her influence spans film, television, and music, from executive-producing the Oscar-winning *Parasite* (2019) to driving K-pop's global expansion through KCON and the MAMA Awards. Beyond entertainment, she has long supported the arts and education, serving on the boards of the Academy

Museum of Motion Pictures, Hammer Museum, Berklee College of Music, and Otis College.

Nam Lee is an associate professor of film and media studies at Chapman University. She is the author of *The Films of Bong Joon Ho* (2020) and also wrote the Bong Joon Ho entry for *Oxford Bibliographies*. In 2018, she conducted an interview with Lee Chang-dong for the Academy of Motion Picture Arts and Sciences Visual History Project. In 2024, she published a scholarly video essay, "Aging, Empathy, and Cinematic Metamorphosis: Through the Lens of Agnès Varda" in *[in]Transition*.

Robert Pattinson is known for his fearless choice of roles and his transformative performances. He recently appeared in *Mickey 17* (2025) and stars in the upcoming films *Die, My Love; The Drama; The Odyssey; The Batman Part II*; and *Dune 3*. Pattinson rose to fame with *The Twilight Saga* film series (2008–12) and continues to collaborate with top filmmakers across a wide variety of genres and platforms. As a producer, he's developing several projects under his banner, Icki Eneo Arlo.

Michelle Puetz is exhibitions curator at the Academy Museum of Motion Pictures, where she curated *Director's Inspiration: Bong Joon Ho* and *Barbie to Anna Karenina: The Cinematic Worlds of Sarah Greenwood and Katie Spencer* (both 2025). Previously, as the Pick-Laudati Curator of Media Arts at the Block Museum of Art, she co-curated the touring exhibition *A Feast of Astonishments: Charlotte Moorman and the Avant-Garde, 1960s–1980s* and *Salaam Cinema! 50 Years of Iranian Movie Posters* (both 2016). She also curated the group exhibition *Body Doubles* (2014) and solo exhibitions with the artists Lilli Carré (2013) and Phil Collins (2016) at the Museum of Contemporary Art, Chicago. She holds a PhD in cinema and media studies from the University of Chicago.

Seo Woo-Sik entered the industry as an assistant director before making his debut as a producer on Song Neung-han's acclaimed *No. 3* (1997). At Barunson Group, he served as producer or executive producer on a string of acclaimed films including *Hansel & Gretel* (2007), *The Good the Bad the Weird* (2008), *Mother* (2009), *The Servant* (2010), and *The Target* (2014). After producing *Okja* (2017) and the massively successful television series *Descendants of the Sun*, Seo founded the subsidiary Barunson C&C. He is currently collaborating with Bong Joon Ho on the production of the filmmaker's upcoming animated feature.

Amy Taubin writes and lives in New York City. She was a film and television critic at the *Village Voice* from 1987 to 2001 and a contributing editor for *Film Comment* and *Artforum* magazines for roughly 20 years. Her 2012 monograph on the film *Taxi Driver* is in the BFI's Film Classics series, and her writing has been anthologized in many collections. In an earlier life, she was an actor playing leading roles on and off Broadway, but her purchase on immortality is her appearance in Michael Snow's *Wavelength* (1967).

Steven Yeun is an Oscar-nominated, Golden Globe– and Emmy Award–winning actor and producer. He has captivated audiences with his performances across film and television. His upcoming films include Joe Carnahan's *RIP* and Ben Affleck's *Animals*. Past credits include the hit television series *The Walking Dead*, Bong Joon Ho's *Okja* (2017), Lee Chang-dong's *Burning* (2018), Boots Riley's *Sorry to Bother You* (2018), Lee Isaac Chung's *Minari* (2020), Jordan Peele's *Nope* (2022), the award-winning Netflix series *Beef*, and Bong Joon Ho's *Mickey 17* (2025).

CREDITS

Unless otherwise noted, images courtesy of Bong Joon Ho. Bong Joon Ho collection photography by Joshua White/JWPictures.com. Installation photography by Fredrik Nilsen.

The film images and production materials in this book are reproduced with permission. All efforts have been made to identify the copyright holders. Errors or omissions will be corrected in future editions.

The romanization and ordering of Korean names in this volume follow the individual preferences of contributors and public figures. Exceptions include spellings that appeared in previously published and copyrighted materials. Some quotations have been lightly modified for this publication.

Films

White Man © Bong Joon Ho, courtesy of the Korean Film Archive

Incoherence © Korean Film Council

Barking Dogs Never Bite, *Memories of Murder*, *Mother*, and *Parasite* © CJ ENM Co., Ltd.

The Host © Chungeorahm Film

Shaking Tokyo, from the feature film *Tokyo!* © Comme des Cinémas, Bitters End, Kansai Telecasting Corporation, Sponge Ent., and ARTEFrance Cinéma

Snowpiercer courtesy of Lions Gate Films Inc.

Okja courtesy of Netflix

Mickey 17 © Warner Bros. Entertainment, Inc. Images licensed by Warner Bros. Discovery

Images

Pages 9, 11, 24, 182–85: © Academy Museum Foundation

Page 17: © CJ ENM, courtesy of Mary Evans/Ronald Grant/Everett Collection

Page 19: Photo12/Chungeorahm Film

Pages 20, 80 (top), 177: © CJ ENM, photo: Hong Kyung Pyo

Pages 21, 125 (bottom), 127, 129, 131, 133, 139: © CJ ENM, photo: Jaehyuk Lee

Pages 29 (left), 179: Courtesy of Korean Film Archive

Pages 63, 64: © Magnolia Pictures, courtesy Everett Collection

Page 74: © Liberation Entertainment, courtesy Everett Collection

Pages 91, 92, 94, 98 (top), 173: Courtesy of Lions Gate Films, photo: Jaehyuk Lee

Pages 109, 110, 120: Courtesy of Netflix, photo: Jaehyuk Lee

Pages 130, 141, 178: © CJ ENM, photo: Lee Hajun

Page 134: © CJ ENM, photo: Bong Joon Ho

Page 180: Dave Benett/WireImage

Quotations

Pages 26, 27, 29, 126 (caption), 134 (caption): "Bong Joon-ho Discusses *Parasite*, Genre Filmmaking and the Greatness of *Zodiac*," interview by Evan Saathoff, Birth.Movies.Death., October 16, 2019, youtube.com/watch?v=dXuXfgquwkM.

Pages 26 (caption), 28, 51: "Bong Joon Ho: Beyond Boundaries," interview by Scott Foundas, Walker Art Center, Minneapolis, February 12, 2020, youtube.com/watch?v=mycWA6QFOaQ.

Pages 29 (caption), 57: Bong Joon Ho, "Kim Kiyoung," *Sight and Sound*, March 2020, 37.

Pages 30, 37: Joo Sung-chul, *Moment of Debut*, (Green Forest, 2014), 186.

Pages 31, 31 (caption), 46 (caption), 67 (caption), 74, 89 (caption), 103: Interview by Nam Lee, January 9, 2025, edited and translated for this volume.

Page 32: *Yellow Door: '90s Lo-fi Film Club*, directed by Lee Hyuk-rae (2023, Netflix).

Page 39: Jung Ji-youn, *Korean Film Directors: Bong Joon Ho* (Seoul Selection USA, 2009), 156.

Pages 41, 56: Giuseppe Sedia, "Interview with Bong Joon-ho," Korean Film, October 2007, koreanfilm.org/bongjh.html.

Page 41 (caption): "Screenwriters' Lecture Series: Bong Joon Ho," interview by Ian Haydn Smith, British Academy of Film and Television Arts, London, December 12, 2019, youtube.com/watch?v=fHegs8zgDdk.

Page 42: Interview by Bu Ji-young, Korean Academy of Film Arts, May 5, 2015, youtube.com/watch?v=Ayyl3FVoVaY.

Page 44: Jung, *Korean Film Directors*, 154.

Page 46: "Bong Joon-ho interview footage in 2004, 2009 by KBS Archive," interview, Korean Broadcasting System, June 27, 2009, youtube.com/watch?v=oRz8b3aDmxA.

Pages 49, 50 (caption), 94 (caption): Interview by Scott Feinberg, Santa Barbara International Film Festival, Santa Barbara, CA, January 23, 2020, youtube.com/watch?v=7YT73OORMHo.

Page 50: Tony Rayns, "Suspicious Minds," *Sight and Sound*, September 2004, 18.

Page 52: "Making of D'Époque," *Memories of Murder*, directed by Bong Joon Ho (2003; France: La Rabbia, 2018), DVD.

Page 57: Bong Joon Ho, "My Brain is Optimized for Cinema," *Sight and Sound*, March 2020, 34.

Pages 63, 65: Kevin B. Lee, "The Han River Horror Show: Interview with Bong Joon-ho," *Cineaste*, 2007, cineaste.com/spring2007/interview-with-bong-joon-ho.

Page 63 (caption): Jung, *Korean Film Directors*, 126.

Page 64 (caption): Jung, *Korean Film Directors*, 139.

Pages 68 (caption), 69, 71 (caption): Adam Nayman, "Fish Out of Water: An Interview with Bong Joon Ho," *Reverse Shot*, March 20, 2007, reverseshot.org/interviews/entry/370/bong-joon-ho.

Pages 74 (caption), 79: Rob Hunter, "Joon-ho Bong Talks *Tokyo!*, *Mother* and *Transperceneige*," *Film School Rejects*, March 27, 2009, filmschoolrejects.com/joon-ho-bong-talks-tokyo-mother-and-transperceneige.

Page 79 (caption): Karen Han, *Bong Joon Ho: Dissident Cinema* (Abrams, 2022), 178.

Page 80: Christina Radish, "Bong Joon Ho Looks Back on *The Host*, *Snowpiercer*, *Parasite* and More at SBIFF," Collider, January 28, 2020, collider.com/bong-joon-ho-interview-parasite-snowpiercer.

Page 81: Kee Chang, "The Lost Interview: Bong Joon-Ho," *Anthem*, April 13, 2017, anthemmagazine.com/the-lost-interview-bong-joon-ho.

Page 84 (caption): Christina Radish, "Bong Joon-ho Talks *Snowpiercer*, Casting Chris Evans, Being a 'Control Freak,' His Desire to Return to Smaller Budget Movies, and More," Collider, June 24, 2014, collider.com/bong-joon-ho-snowpiercer-interview.

Page 85: Virginie Selavy, "*Mother*: Interview with Bong Joon-Ho," *Electric Sheep*, August 1, 2010, electricsheepmagazine.co.uk/2010/08/01/mother-interview-with-bong-joon-ho-2.

Page 91: Bong Joon Ho, "Let's take a bizarre train ride with Bong Joon-Ho. And the train is called Snowpiercer. Ask Me Anything.," Reddit, June 2013, reddit.com/r/IAmA/comments/293cd9.

Page 92: David Chen, "Bong Joon-Ho Talks About Using Violence, Writing an English Script, and Getting Final Cut For *Snowpiercer*," /Film, June 27, 2014, slashfilm.com/532548/bong-joon-ho-snowpiercer-interview.

Page 92 (caption): David Gregory Lawson, "Interview: Bong Joon Ho," *Film Comment*, June 27, 2014, filmcomment.com/blog/interview-bong-joon-ho.

Page 94: Don Kaye, "*Snowpiercer* director Bong Joon-Ho Discusses the Film," Den of Geek, June 24, 2014, denofgeek.com/movies/snowpiercer-director-bong-joon-ho-discusses-the-film.

Page 98 (caption): Anne-Katrin Titze, "Piercing Vision: The Unpredictable Engines of Bong Joon Ho," Eye for Film, June 27, 2014, https://www.eyeforfilm.co.uk.

Page 103 (caption): Simon Abrams, "Director Bong Joon-ho Breaks Down *Snowpiercer*'s Ending," Vulture, June 29, 2014, vulture.com/2014/06/director-bong-joon-ho-talks-snowpiercers-ending.html.

Pages 105, 120, 121: David Jenkins, "Bong Joon-ho: '*Okja* is about what's happening to us in real life,'" *Little White Lies*, June 28, 2017, lwlies.com/interviews/bong-joon-ho-okja.

Page 106: Curtis Tsui, "The Evolution of a 'Superpig': Designing Okja, from Start to Finish," Criterion Collection, July 14, 2022, criterion.com/current/posts/7858.

Pages 106 (caption), 108: Brooke Heinz, "Interview: Director Bong Joon-Ho Talks *Okja*," Filmed in Ether, June 27, 2017, filmedinether.com/features/interview-director-bong-joon-ho-talks-okja.

Page 110: Jonathan Hatfull, "'We wanted to leap over boundaries': Bong Joon-ho Talks *Okja*," *SciFiNow*, June 26, 2017, scifinow.co.uk/interviews/we-wanted-to-leap-over-boundaries-bong-joon-ho-talks-okja.

Page 117: Diva Vélez, "Interview: Bong Joon-ho on *Okja*'s Inspirations and Controversies," *ScreenAnarchy*, July 2, 2017, screenanarchy.com/2017/07/interview-bong-joon-ho-on-okjas-inspirations-and-controversies.

Page 119: Simon Ward, *Okja: The Art and Making of the Film* (National Geographic Books, 2018), 126.

Page 125: Interview by Son Seok-hee, *JTBC News*, Joongang Tongyang Broadcasting Company, June 6, 2019, youtube .com/watch?v=ZxWbHtNYbUw.

Page 127: Tim Gray, "*Parasite* Director Bong Joon Ho on His Core Crew and Their 'Risky Choices,'" *Variety*, December 5, 2019, variety.com/2019/artisans /awards/parasite-bong-joon-ho -crew-1203422973.

Page 129: Li-Wei Chu, "Interview: Dissecting the Hidden Motifs of *Parasite* with Director Bong Joon-Ho," From the Intercom, October 3, 2019, fromtheintercom.com/interview -director-bong-joon-ho.

Pages 130, 141: Jack Moulton, "Brief Takes with…Bong Joon-ho," Letterboxd, October 11, 2019, letterboxd.com/journal/brief -takes-bong-joon-ho.

Pages 130 (caption), 134: Jean Noh, "Bong Joon Ho on His Painstaking Approach to *Parasite*, Oscar Hopes," *Screen Daily*, January 3, 2020, screendaily. com/5145625.article.

Page 131 (caption): Patrick Brzeski, "Bong Joon Ho Reveals the Significance of *Parasite*'s Scholar Stone," *Hollywood Reporter*, January 7, 2020, hollywoodreporter .com/news/general-news/bong -joon-ho-reveals-significance- parasites-scholar-stone-1265811.

Page 138: Sandi Tan, "The Name Is Bong," *Vanity Fair*, Awards Extra Oscars Edition, January 2020, archive.vanityfair.com /article/20200129020.

Page 139: E. Alex Jung, "Bong Joon-ho's Dystopia Is Already Here," Vulture, October 7, 2019, vulture.com/2019/10/bong-joon -ho-parasite.html.

Page 140 (caption): Yohana Desta, "Bong Joon-Ho Looked to Hitchcock When Making *Parasite*: 'He Always Gives Me Very Strange Inspiration,'" *Vanity Fair*, October 11, 2019, vanityfair. com/hollywood/2019/10 /bong-joon-ho-parasite-interview.

Page 145: "Bong Joon Ho Reveals a Multiplicity of Robert Pattinsons in First *Mickey 17* Trailer," The Credits, April 10, 2024, motionpictures. org/2024/04/bong-joon-ho -reveals-crackling-first-trailer-for -robert-pattinson-led-mickey-17.

Page 146: Jimin Choi, "Bong Joon Ho Talks *Mickey 17* Release Delays and Outsmarting AI," *Screen Daily*, January 20, 2025, screendaily.com/5200939.article.

Pages 149 (caption), 154 (caption), 157, 158 (caption): Jonah Weiner, "The *Parasite* Director Brings Class Warfare to Outer Space," *New York Times Magazine*, March 4, 2025.

Pages 151 (caption), 162 (caption): Karlie Rogers, "Bong Joon Ho Is Reborn in *Mickey 17*," *Exclaim!*, March 5, 2025, exclaim.ca/film/article/bong-joon -ho-interview-mickey-17.

Pages 153, 153 (caption): Kim Ji-ye, "Bong Joon-ho Keeps 'Weird' Edge but Breaks a Few Rules in *Mickey 17*," *Korea JoongAng Daily*, February 21, 2025, koreajoongangdaily.joins .com/news/2025-02-21 /entertainment/movies/2246160.

Page 158: Alison Willmore, "How Bong Joon Ho Crafted His First (Mostly) Happy Ending," Vulture, March 7, 2025, vulture.com /article/mickey-17s-optimistic -ending-explained-by-bong-joon -ho.html.

Page 163: Baek Byung-yeul, "Bong Joon-ho Explores Human Resilience with New Film *Mickey 17*," *Korea Times*, February 21, 2025, koreatimes.co.kr /entertainment/films/20250221 /interview-bong-joon-ho-explores -human-resilience-with-new-film -mickey-17.